Translation & Adaptation,
Retouch, Lettering and Design -
Kitty Media

YANNATCHAUKURAI AISHITERU Vol. 2
Original Japanese version © Row Takakura 2004.
Originally published in Japan in 2004
by BIBLOS Co., Ltd. English version in U.S.A.
and CANADA published by Kitty Media
under the license granted by BIBLOS Co., Ltd.

Kitty Press
Office of publication 519 8th Avenue, 14th floor
New York, NY 10018.

ISBN: 1-58655-889-7

Printed in Canada.

Second Printing

CONTENTS

"I can't stop loving you"

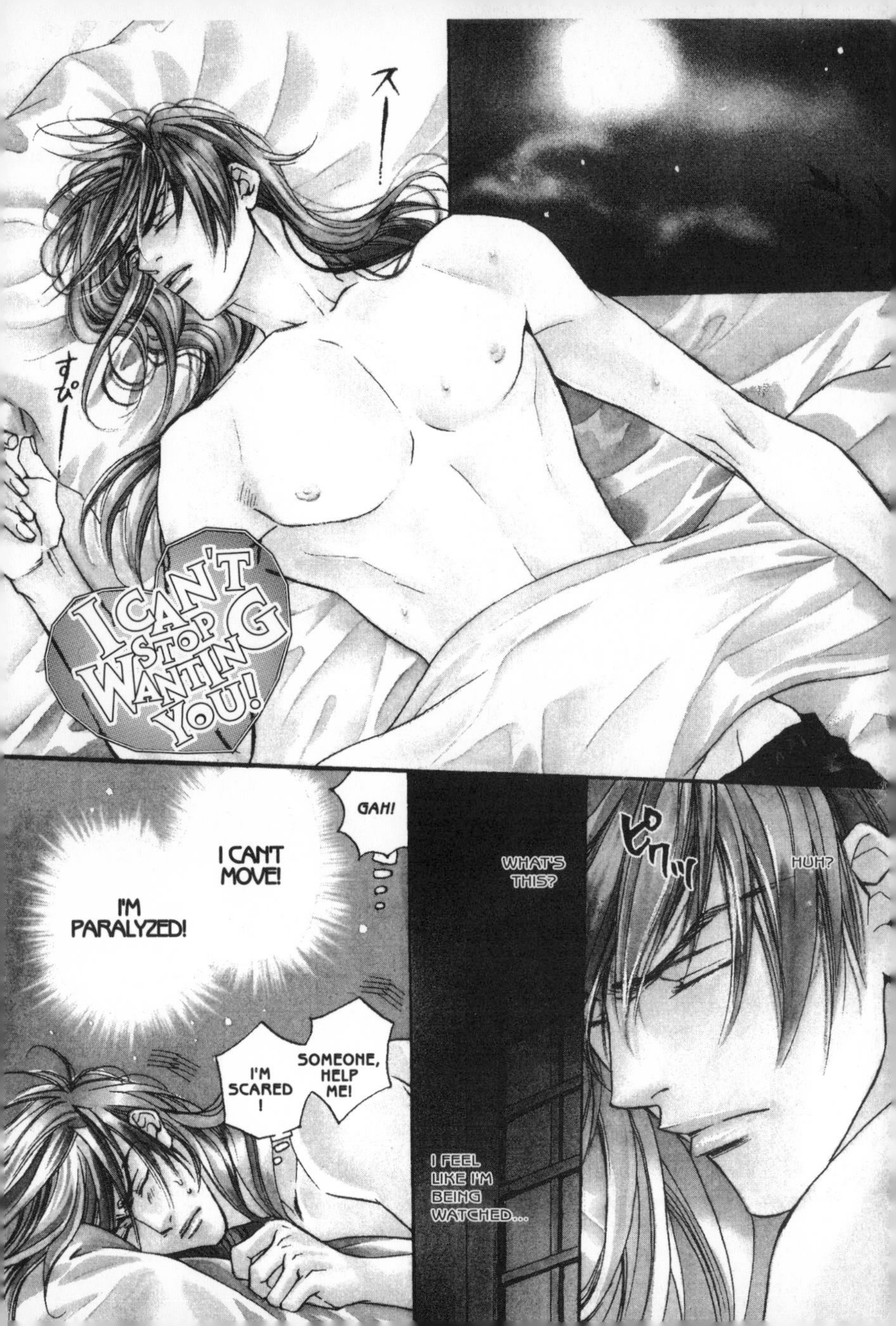
スーー…
すぴー…
I CAN'T STOP WANTING YOU!
ピクッ
HUH?
WHAT'S THIS?
I FEEL LIKE I'M BEING WATCHED...
GAH!
I CAN'T MOVE!
I'M PARALYZED!
SOMEONE, HELP ME!
I'M SCARED!

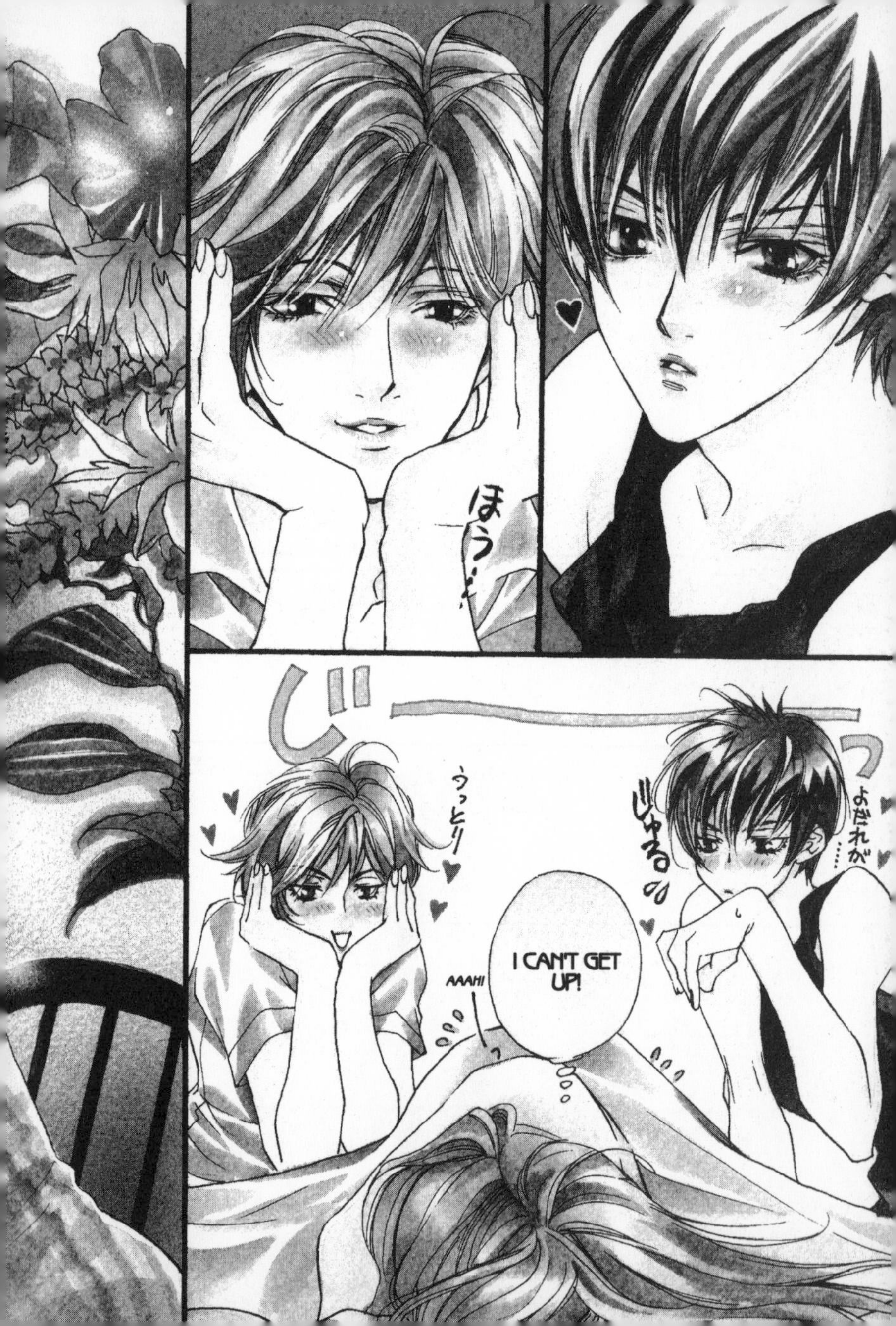
ほう……
じーっ
よだれが……
じゅる
うっとり!!
I CAN'T GET UP!
AAAH!

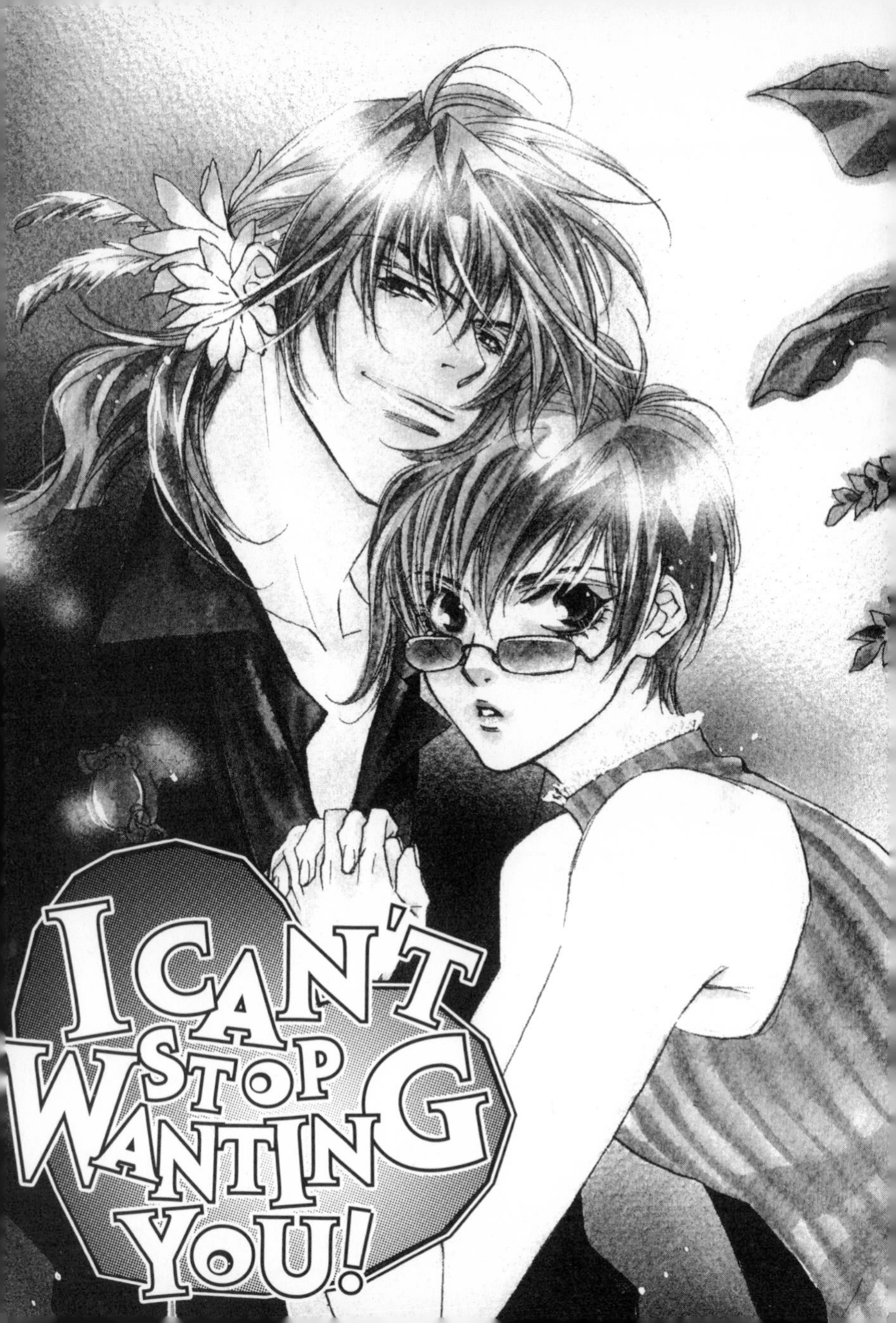
I CAN'T STOP WANTING YOU!

IF YOU
CAN'T HEAR
IT...

I can't stop loving you ■ ■ ■ ■

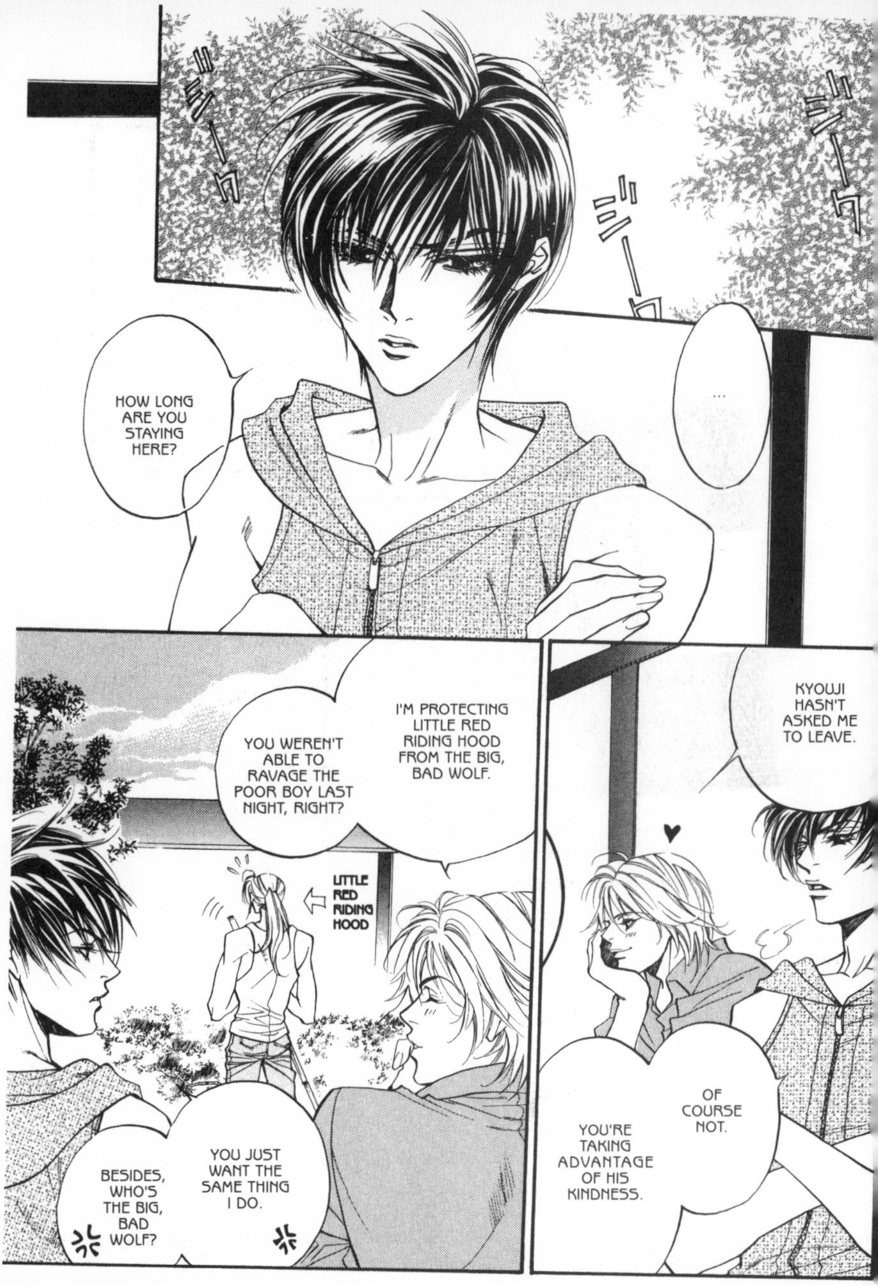
...
HOW LONG ARE YOU STAYING HERE?
KYOUJI HASN'T ASKED ME TO LEAVE.
OF COURSE NOT.
YOU'RE TAKING ADVANTAGE OF HIS KINDNESS.
I'M PROTECTING LITTLE RED RIDING HOOD FROM THE BIG, BAD WOLF.
YOU WEREN'T ABLE TO RAVAGE THE POOR BOY LAST NIGHT, RIGHT?
LITTLE RED RIDING HOOD
YOU JUST WANT THE SAME THING I DO.
BESIDES, WHO'S THE BIG, BAD WOLF?

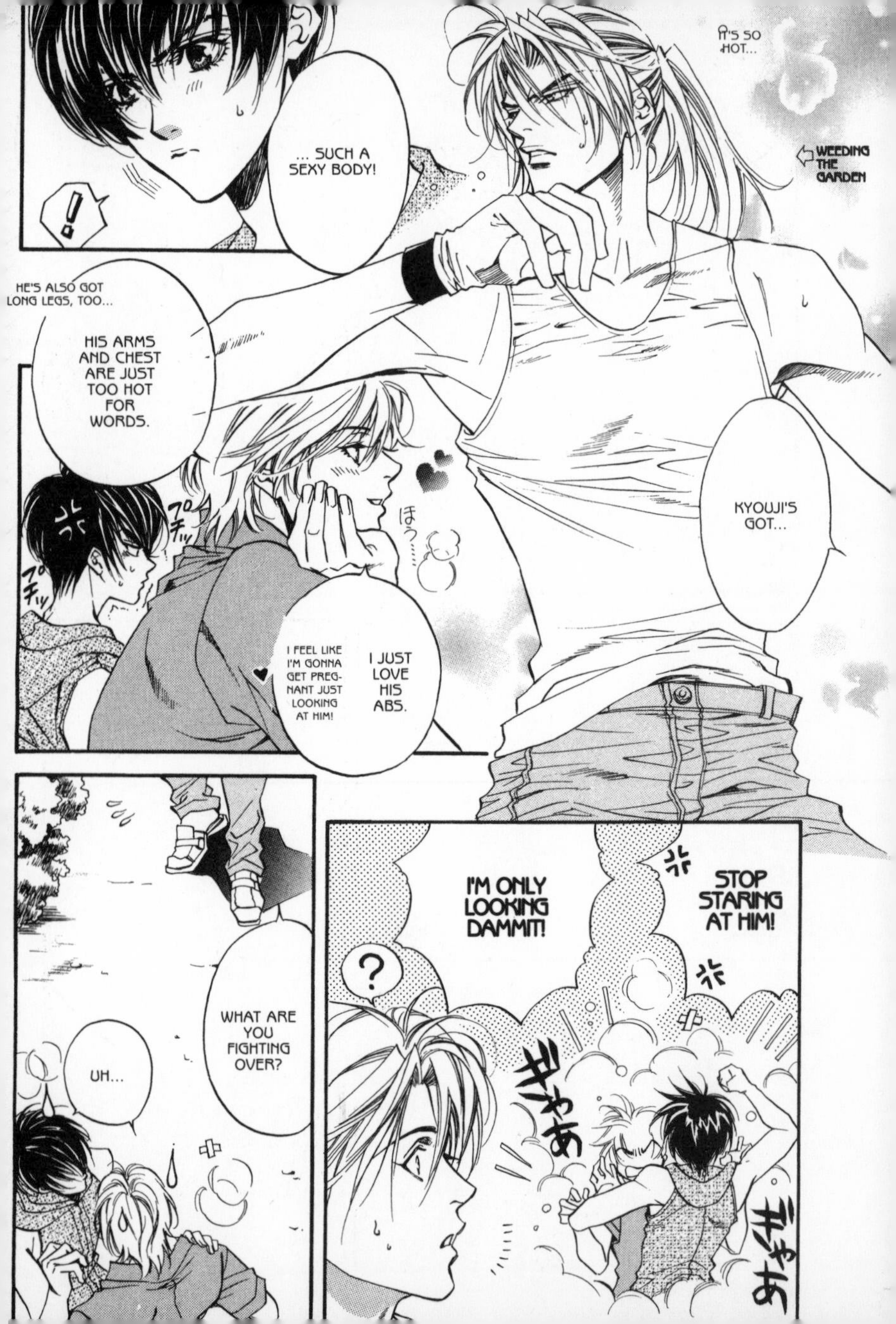

IT'S SO HOT...
WEEDING THE GARDEN
KYOUJI'S GOT...
... SUCH A SEXY BODY!
!
HIS ARMS AND CHEST ARE JUST TOO HOT FOR WORDS.
HE'S ALSO GOT LONG LEGS, TOO...
I JUST LOVE HIS ABS.
I FEEL LIKE I'M GONNA GET PREG-NANT JUST LOOKING AT HIM!
STOP STARING AT HIM!
I'M ONLY LOOKING DAMMIT!
?
WHAT ARE YOU FIGHTING OVER?
UH...

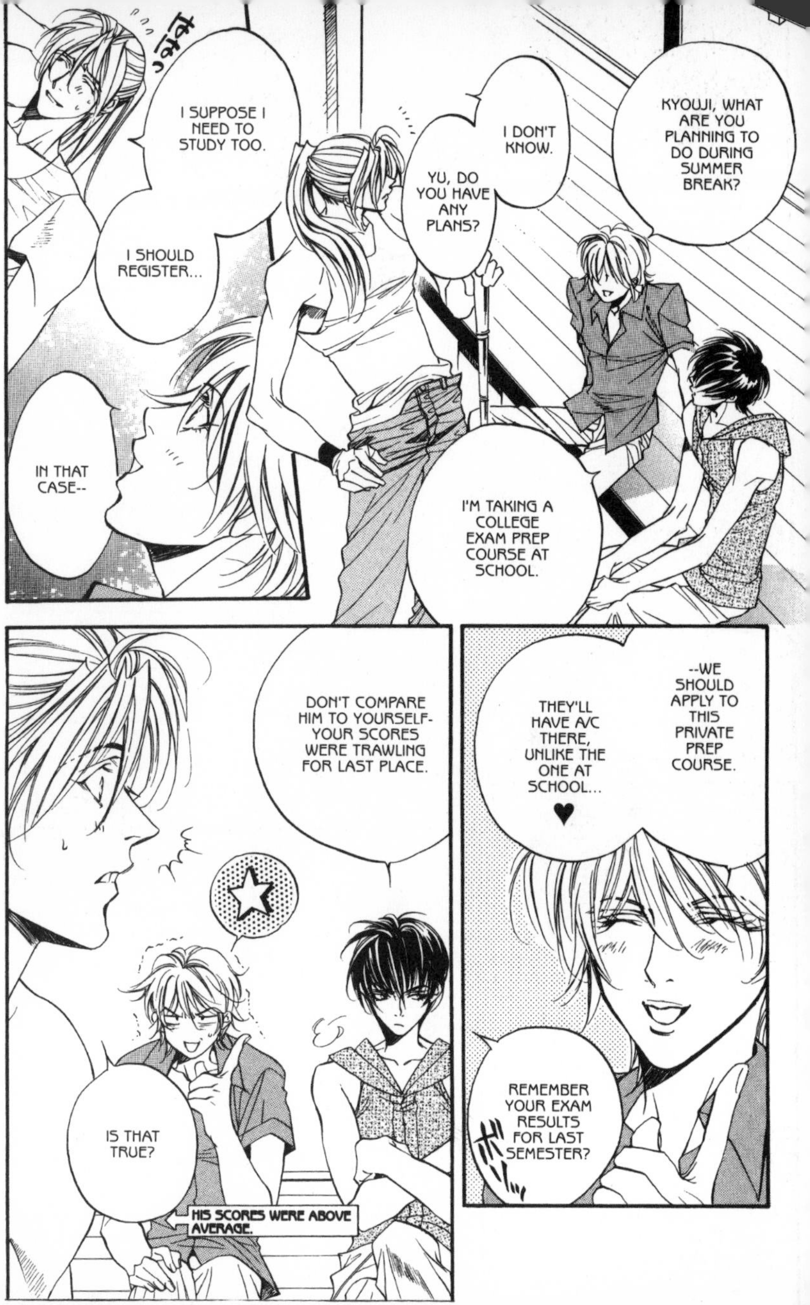
KYOUJI, WHAT ARE YOU PLANNING TO DO DURING SUMMER BREAK?
I DON'T KNOW.
YU, DO YOU HAVE ANY PLANS?
I'M TAKING A COLLEGE EXAM PREP COURSE AT SCHOOL.
I SUPPOSE I NEED TO STUDY TOO.
I SHOULD REGISTER...
IN THAT CASE--
--WE SHOULD APPLY TO THIS PRIVATE PREP COURSE.
THEY'LL HAVE A/C THERE, UNLIKE THE ONE AT SCHOOL... ♥
REMEMBER YOUR EXAM RESULTS FOR LAST SEMESTER?
DON'T COMPARE HIM TO YOURSELF- YOUR SCORES WERE TRAWLING FOR LAST PLACE.
IS THAT TRUE?
HIS SCORES WERE ABOVE AVERAGE.

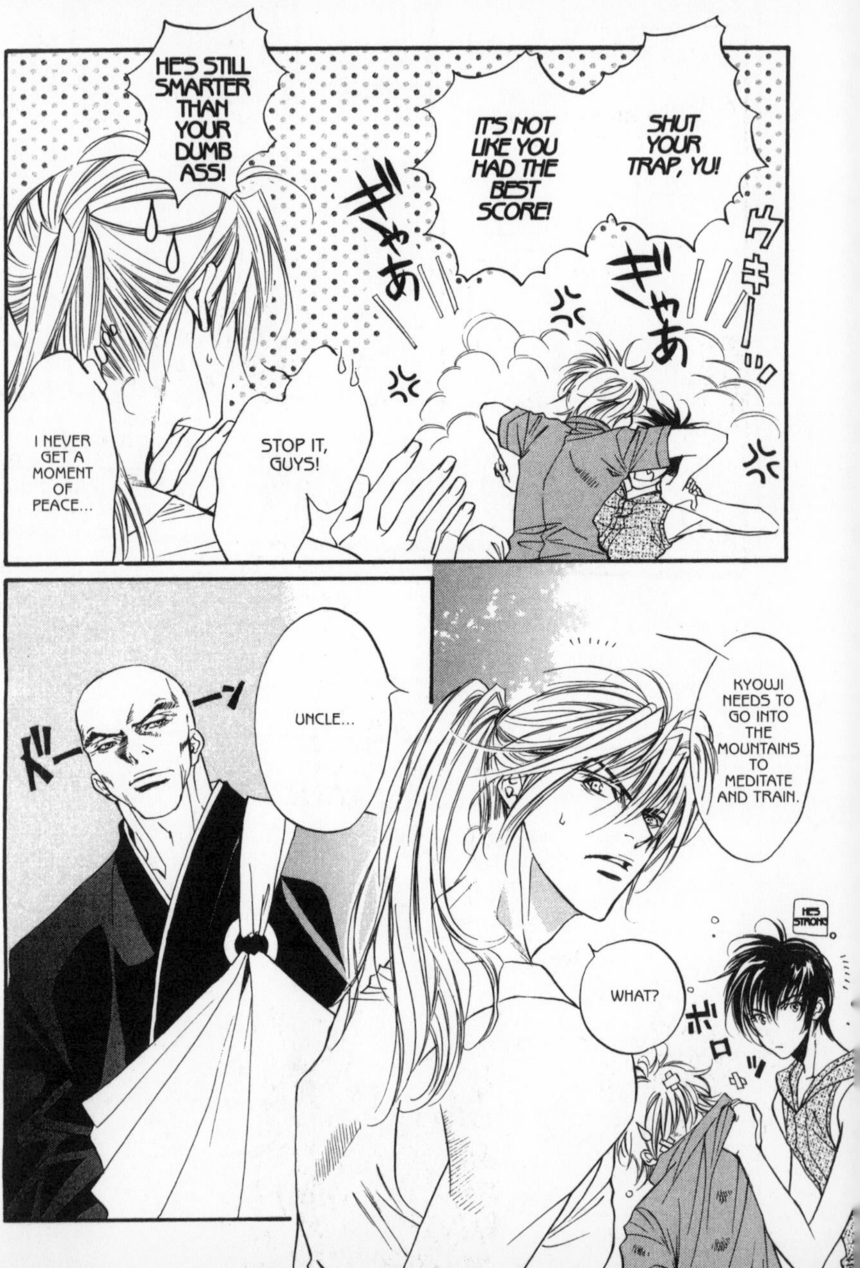
SHUT YOUR TRAP, YU!
IT'S NOT LIKE YOU HAD THE BEST SCORE!
HE'S STILL SMARTER THAN YOUR DUMB ASS!
STOP IT, GUYS!
I NEVER GET A MOMENT OF PEACE...
KYOUJI NEEDS TO GO INTO THE MOUNTAINS TO MEDITATE AND TRAIN.
HE'S STRONG
WHAT?
UNCLE...

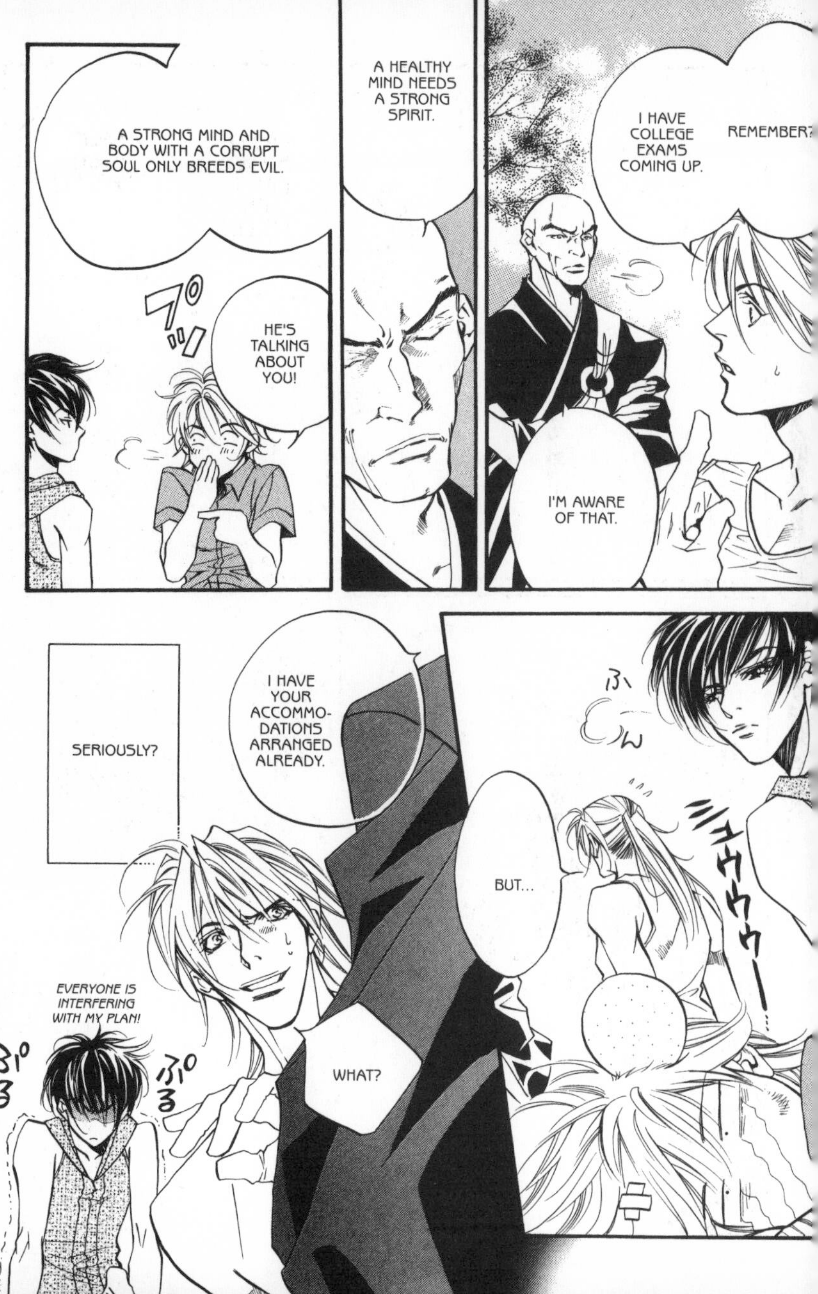
I HAVE COLLEGE EXAMS COMING UP.
REMEMBER?
I'M AWARE OF THAT.
A HEALTHY MIND NEEDS A STRONG SPIRIT.
A STRONG MIND AND BODY WITH A CORRUPT SOUL ONLY BREEDS EVIL.
プッ
HE'S TALKING ABOUT YOU!
ふん
シュウウウー…
BUT...
I HAVE YOUR ACCOMMODATIONS ARRANGED ALREADY.
WHAT?
SERIOUSLY?
EVERYONE IS INTERFERING WITH MY PLAN!
ぷる ぷる

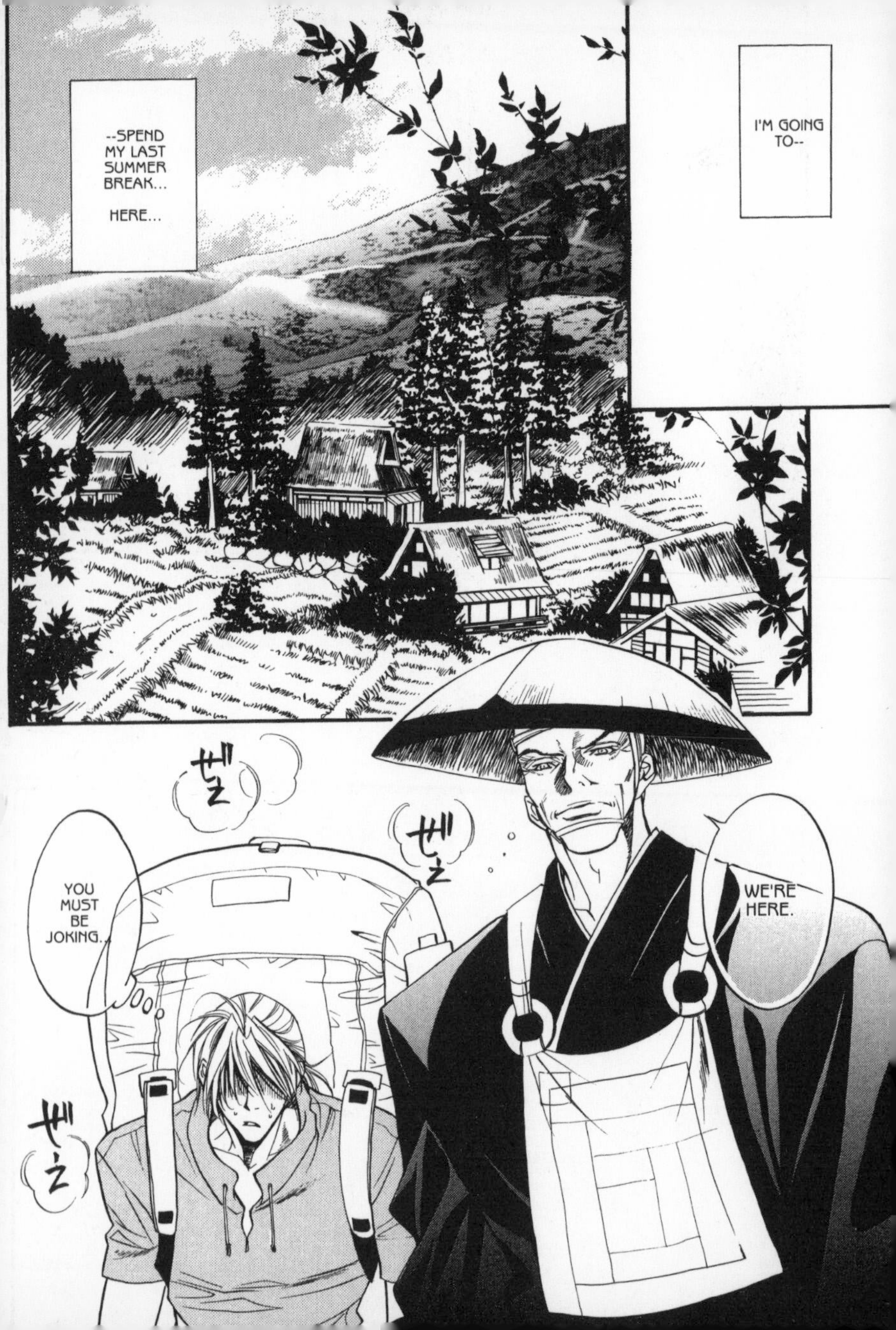

I'M GOING TO--
--SPEND MY LAST SUMMER BREAK... HERE...
ぜぇ
ぜぇ
WE'RE HERE.
YOU MUST BE JOKING...
ぜぇ

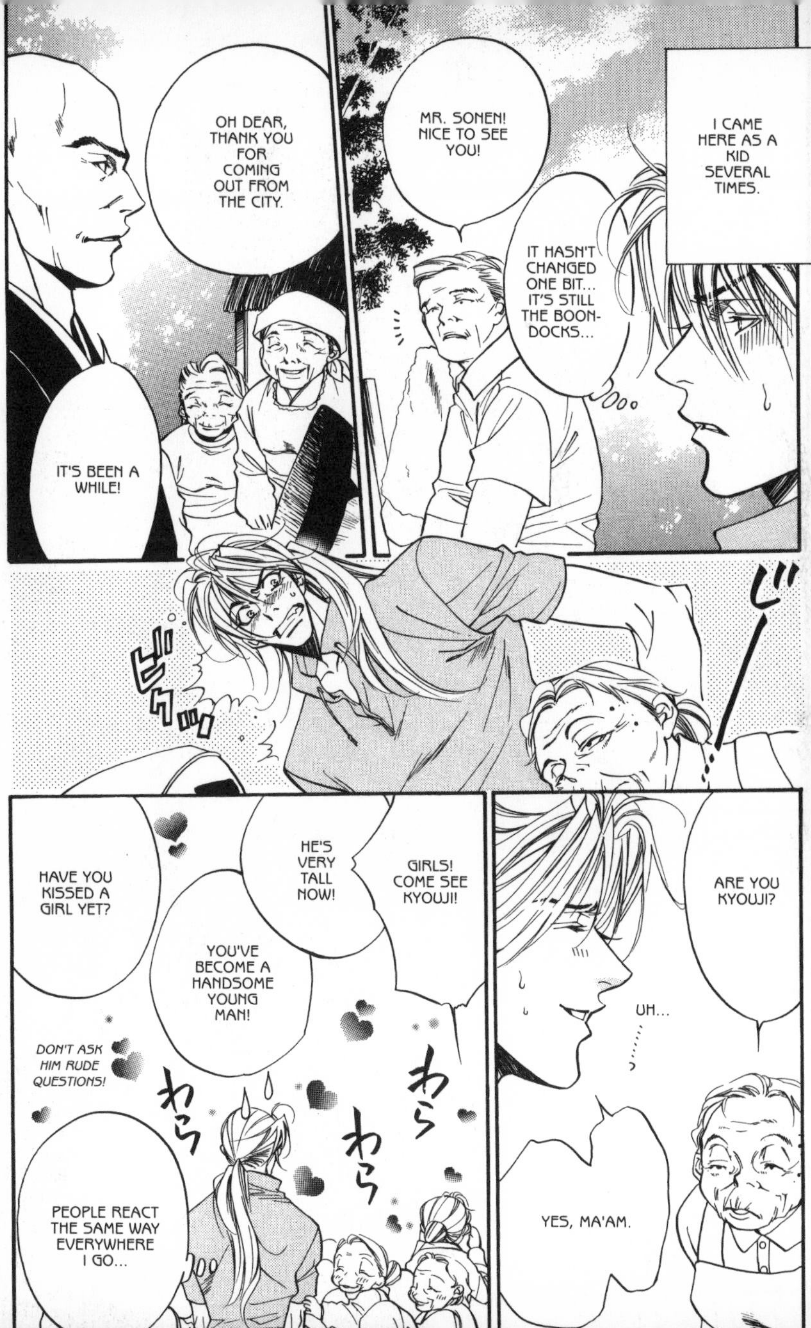
I CAME HERE AS A KID SEVERAL TIMES.
MR. SONEN! NICE TO SEE YOU!
IT HASN'T CHANGED ONE BIT... IT'S STILL THE BOONDOCKS...
OH DEAR, THANK YOU FOR COMING OUT FROM THE CITY.
IT'S BEEN A WHILE!
じー
ビクッ
ARE YOU KYOUJI?
UH...
YES, MA'AM.
GIRLS! COME SEE KYOUJI!
HE'S VERY TALL NOW!
YOU'VE BECOME A HANDSOME YOUNG MAN!
HAVE YOU KISSED A GIRL YET?
DON'T ASK HIM RUDE QUESTIONS!
わら
わら
わら
PEOPLE REACT THE SAME WAY EVERYWHERE I GO...

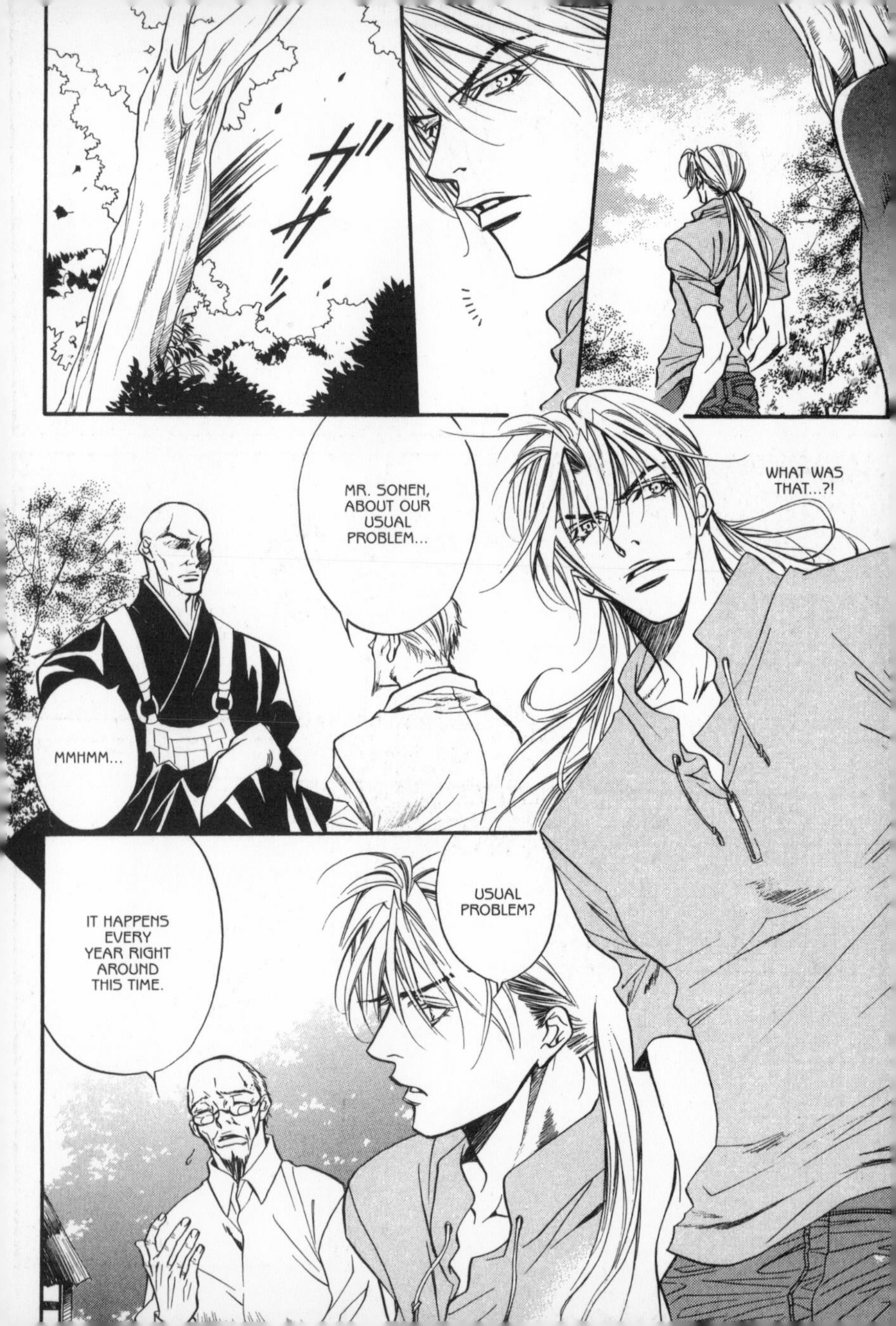
WHAT WAS THAT...?!
MR. SONEN, ABOUT OUR USUAL PROBLEM...
MMHMM...
USUAL PROBLEM?
IT HAPPENS EVERY YEAR RIGHT AROUND THIS TIME.

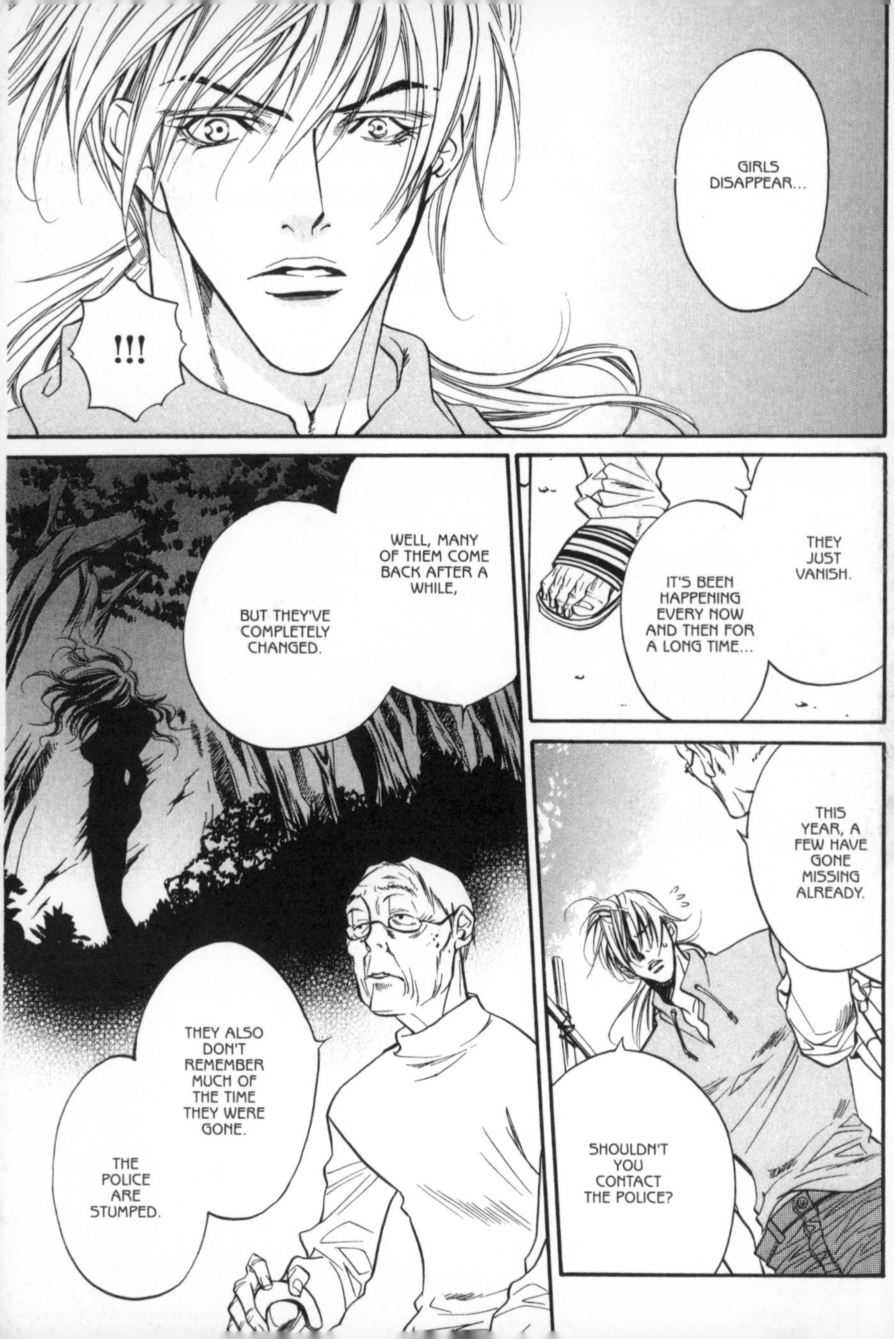
GIRLS DISAPPEAR...
!!!
THEY JUST VANISH.
IT'S BEEN HAPPENING EVERY NOW AND THEN FOR A LONG TIME...
THIS YEAR, A FEW HAVE GONE MISSING ALREADY.
SHOULDN'T YOU CONTACT THE POLICE?
WELL, MANY OF THEM COME BACK AFTER A WHILE,
BUT THEY'VE COMPLETELY CHANGED.
THEY ALSO DON'T REMEMBER MUCH OF THE TIME THEY WERE GONE.
THE POLICE ARE STUMPED.

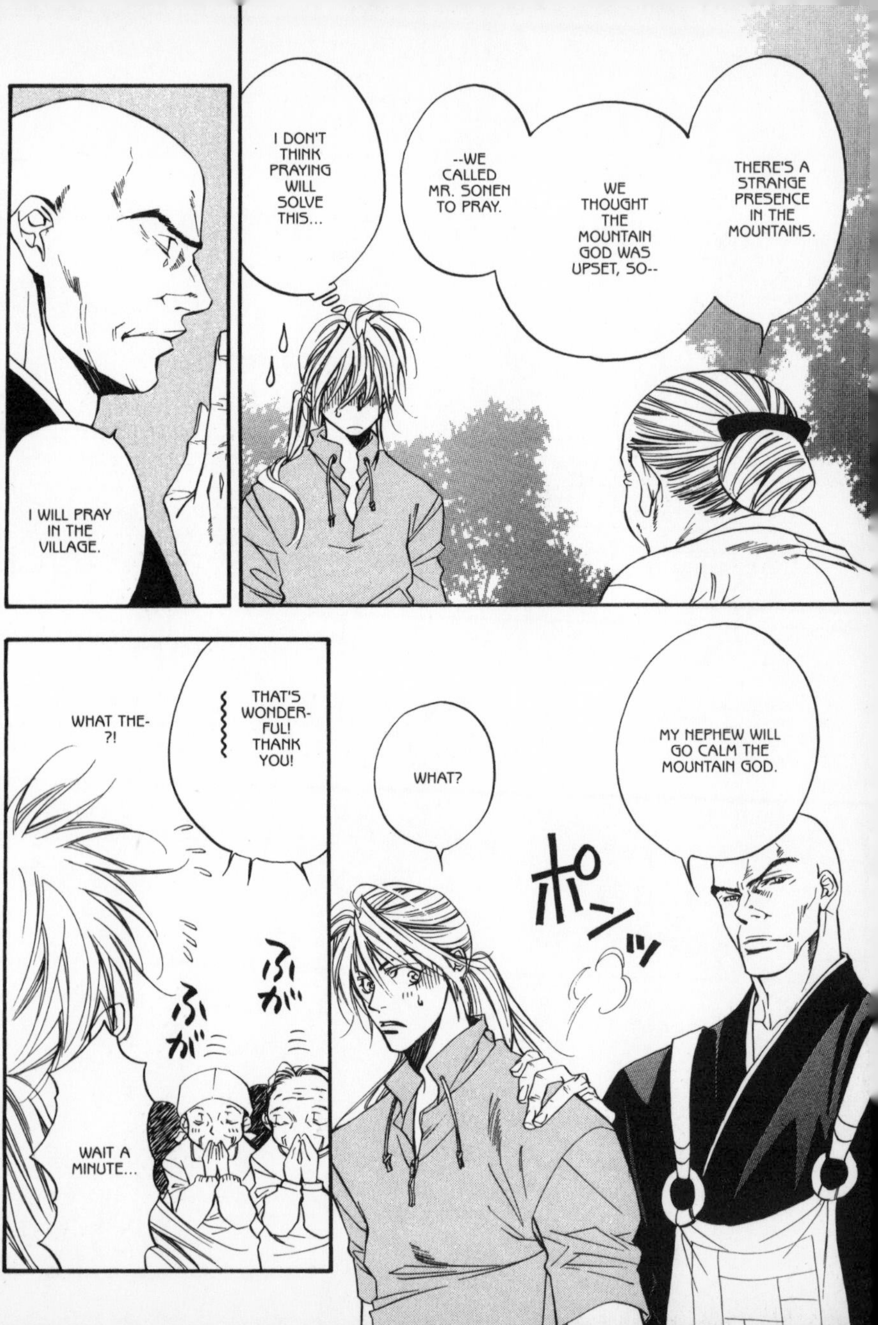
THERE'S A STRANGE PRESENCE IN THE MOUNTAINS.
WE THOUGHT THE MOUNTAIN GOD WAS UPSET, SO--
--WE CALLED MR. SONEN TO PRAY.
I DON'T THINK PRAYING WILL SOLVE THIS...
I WILL PRAY IN THE VILLAGE.
MY NEPHEW WILL GO CALM THE MOUNTAIN GOD.
ポンッ
WHAT?
THAT'S WONDERFUL! THANK YOU!
ふが
ふが
WHAT THE-?!
WAIT A MINUTE...

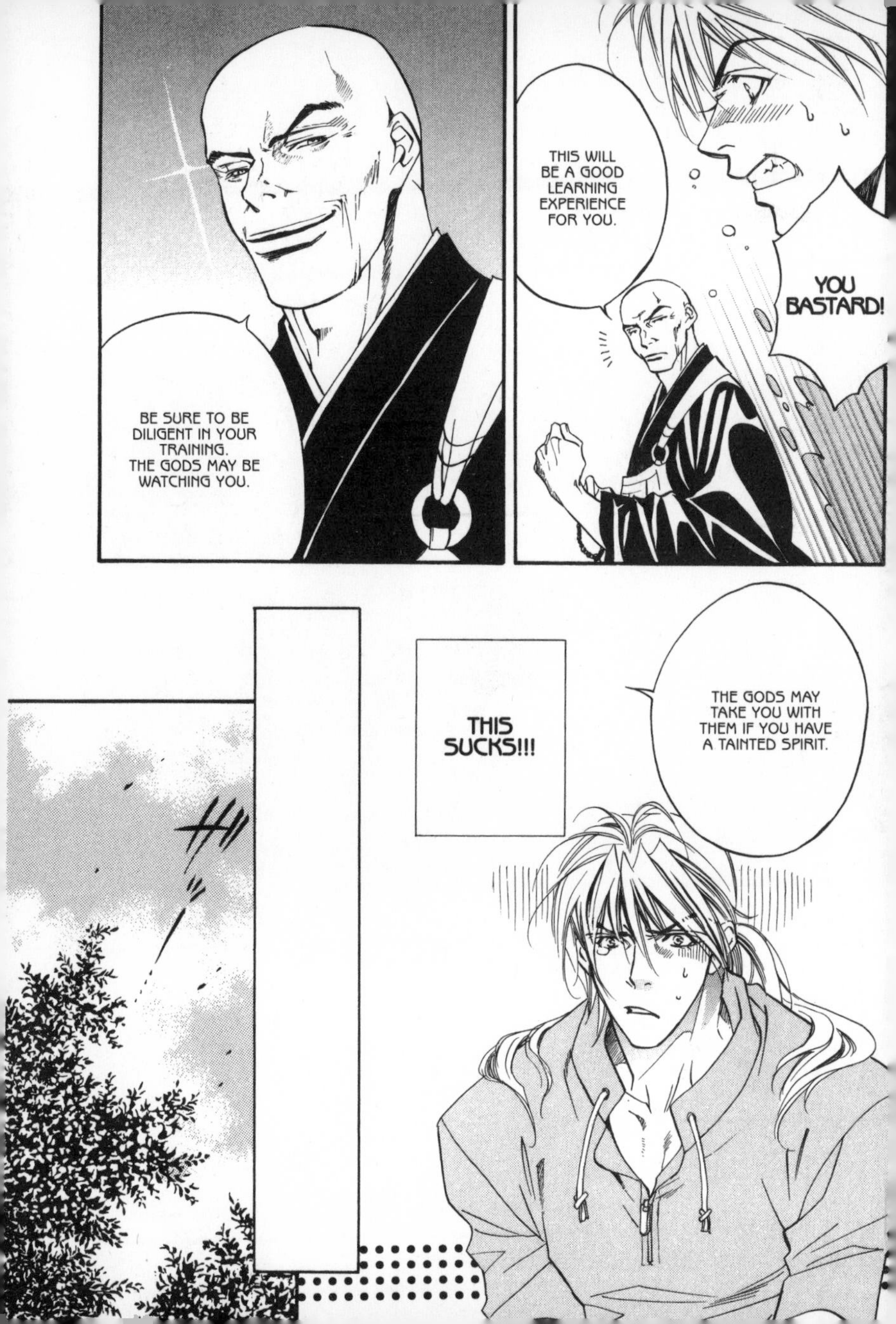
THIS WILL BE A GOOD LEARNING EXPERIENCE FOR YOU.
YOU BASTARD!
BE SURE TO BE DILIGENT IN YOUR TRAINING. THE GODS MAY BE WATCHING YOU.
THE GODS MAY TAKE YOU WITH THEM IF YOU HAVE A TAINTED SPIRIT.
THIS SUCKS!!!

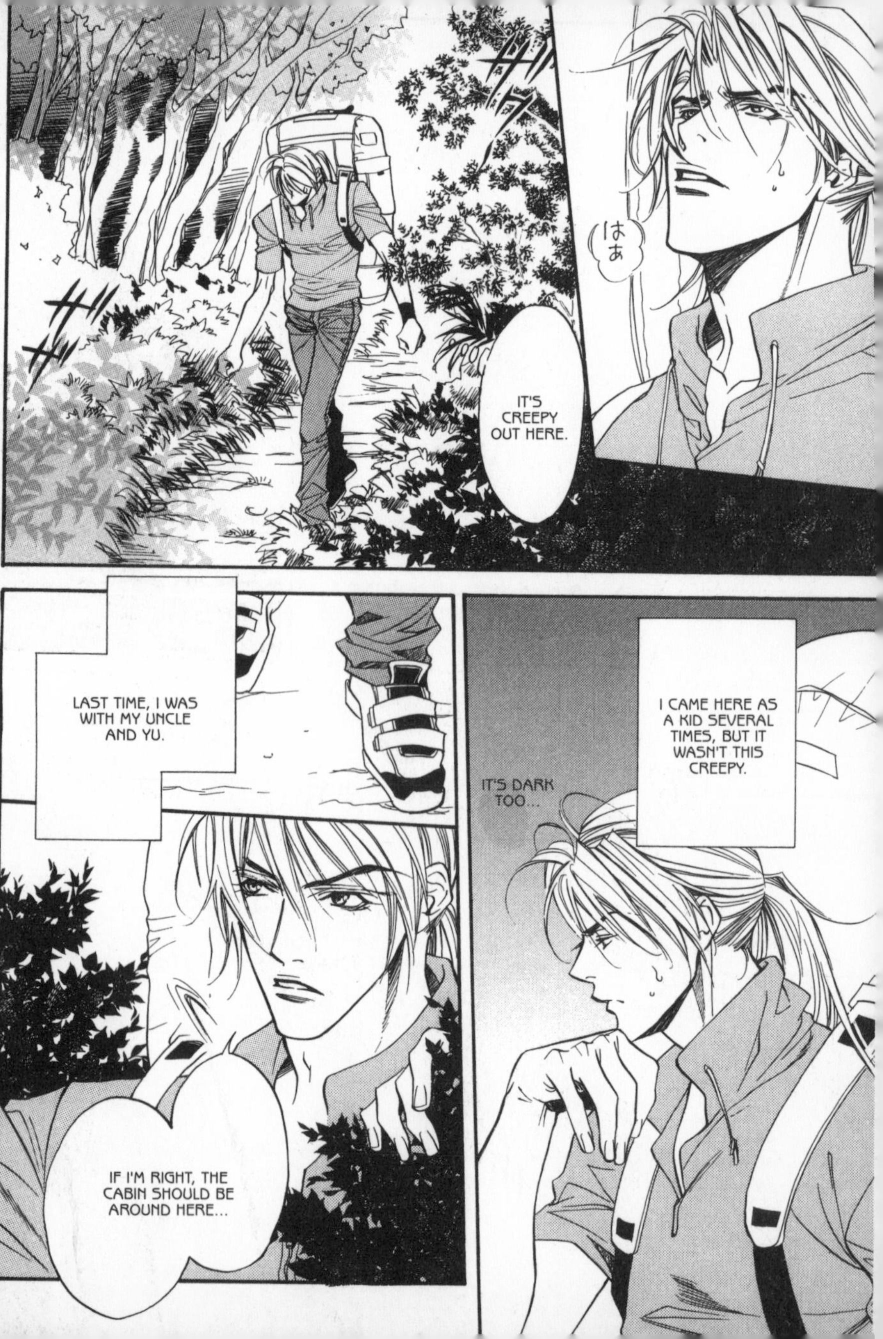
はぁ
IT'S CREEPY OUT HERE.
I CAME HERE AS A KID SEVERAL TIMES, BUT IT WASN'T THIS CREEPY.
IT'S DARK TOO...
LAST TIME, I WAS WITH MY UNCLE AND YU.
IF I'M RIGHT, THE CABIN SHOULD BE AROUND HERE...

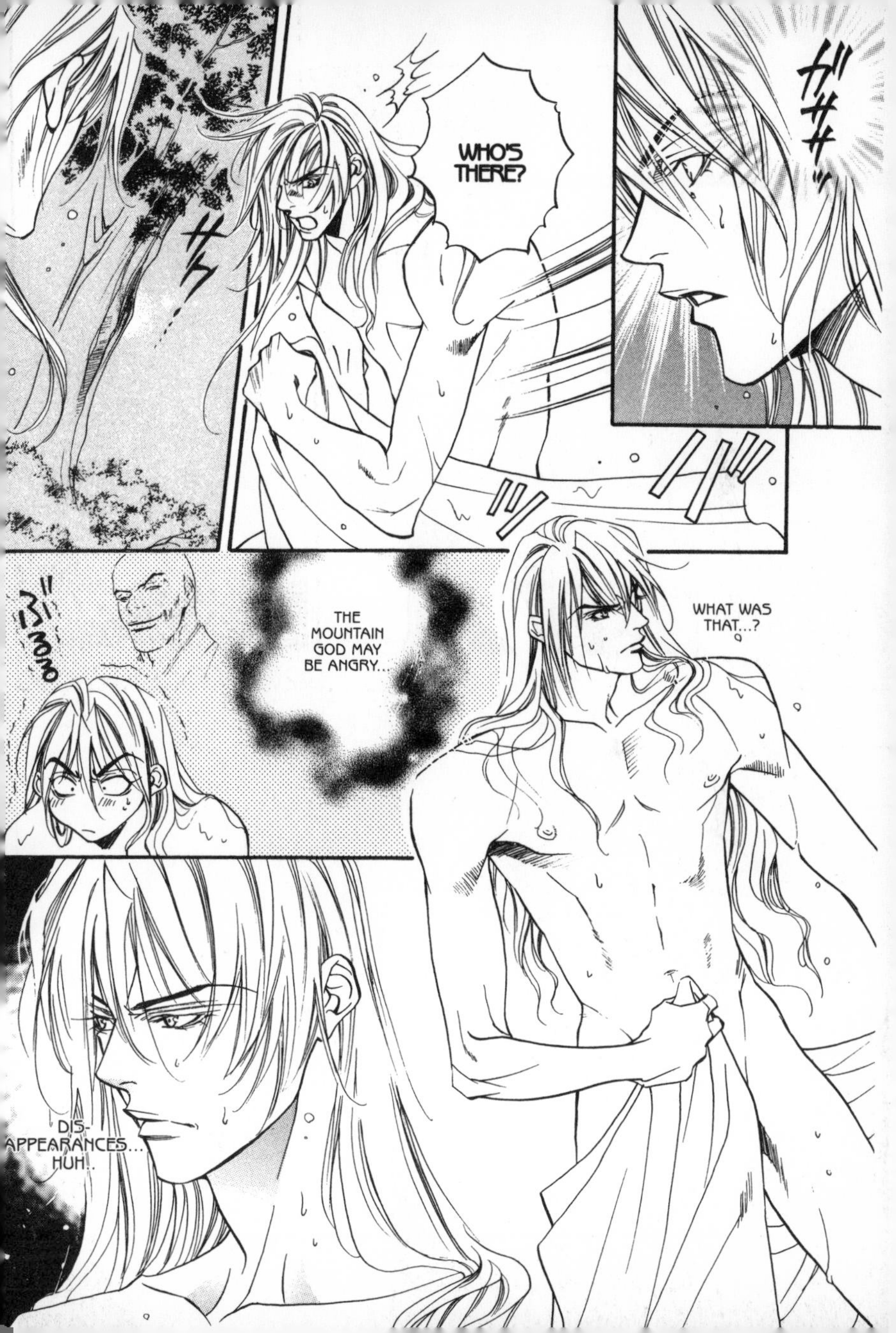
WHO'S THERE?
WHAT WAS THAT...?
THE MOUNTAIN GOD MAY BE ANGRY...
DIS-APPEARANCES... HUH..

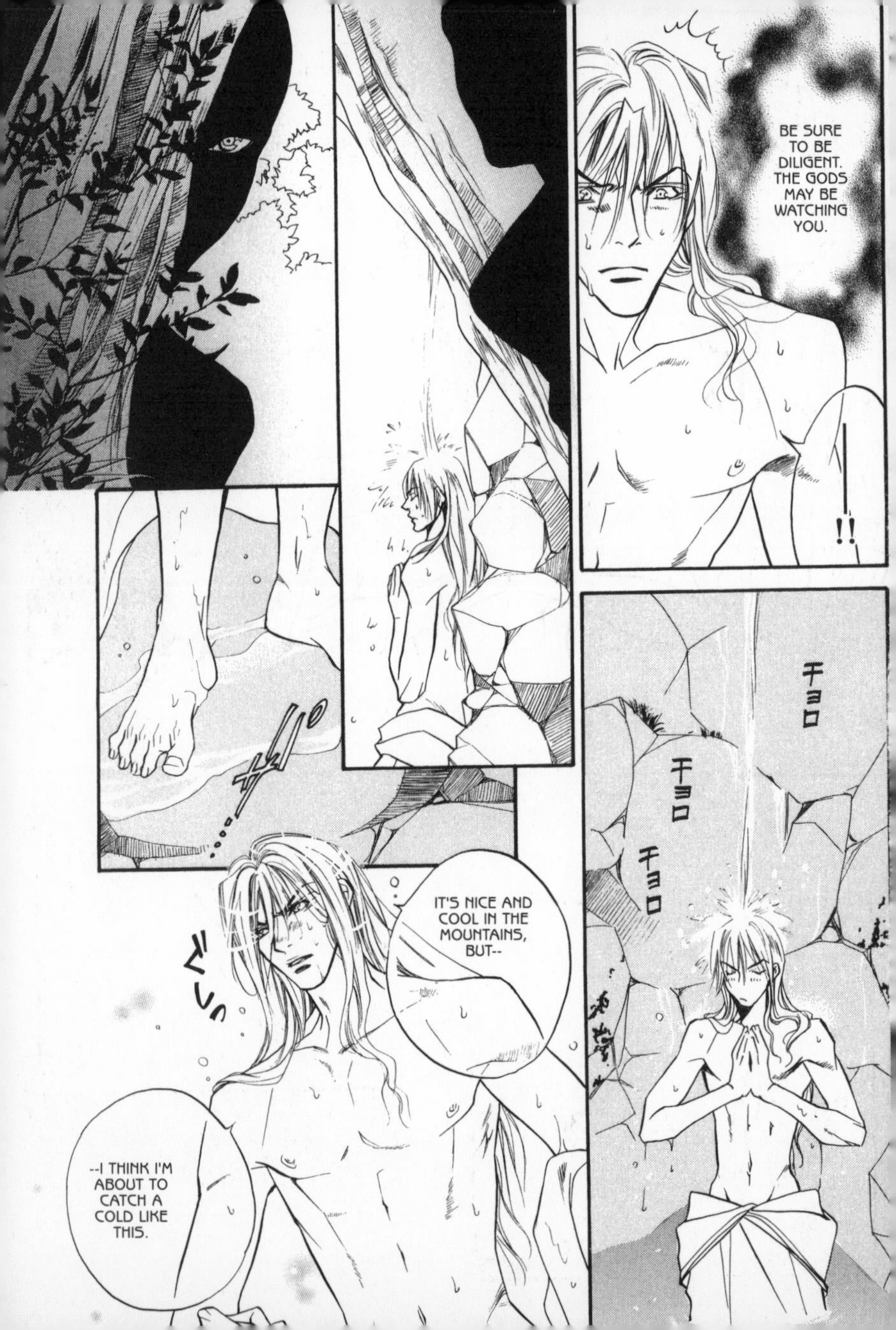
BE SURE TO BE DILIGENT. THE GODS MAY BE WATCHING YOU.
!!
チョロ
チョロ
チョロ
IT'S NICE AND COOL IN THE MOUNTAINS, BUT--
--I THINK I'M ABOUT TO CATCH A COLD LIKE THIS.

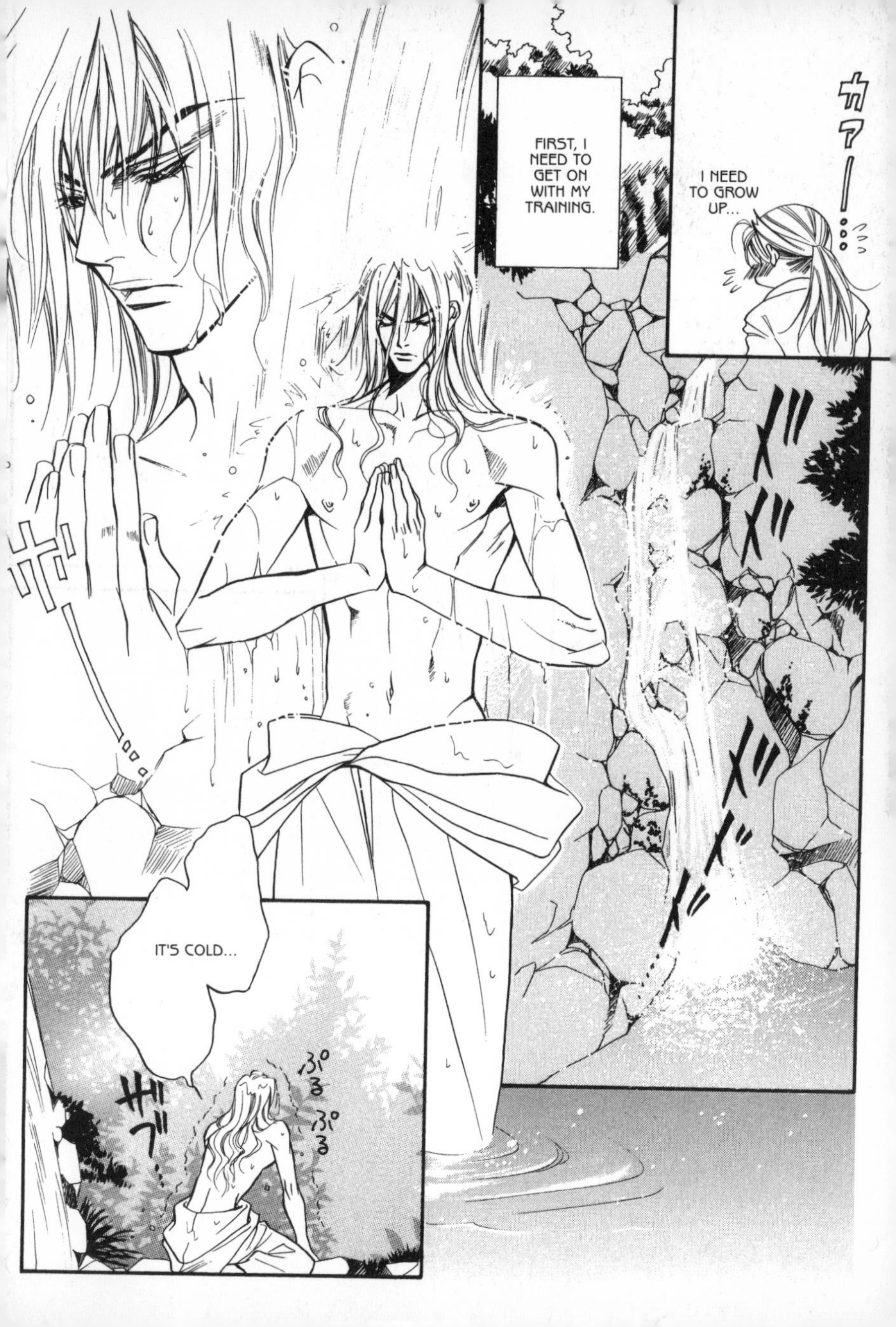
I NEED TO GROW UP...
FIRST, I NEED TO GET ON WITH MY TRAINING.
IT'S COLD...

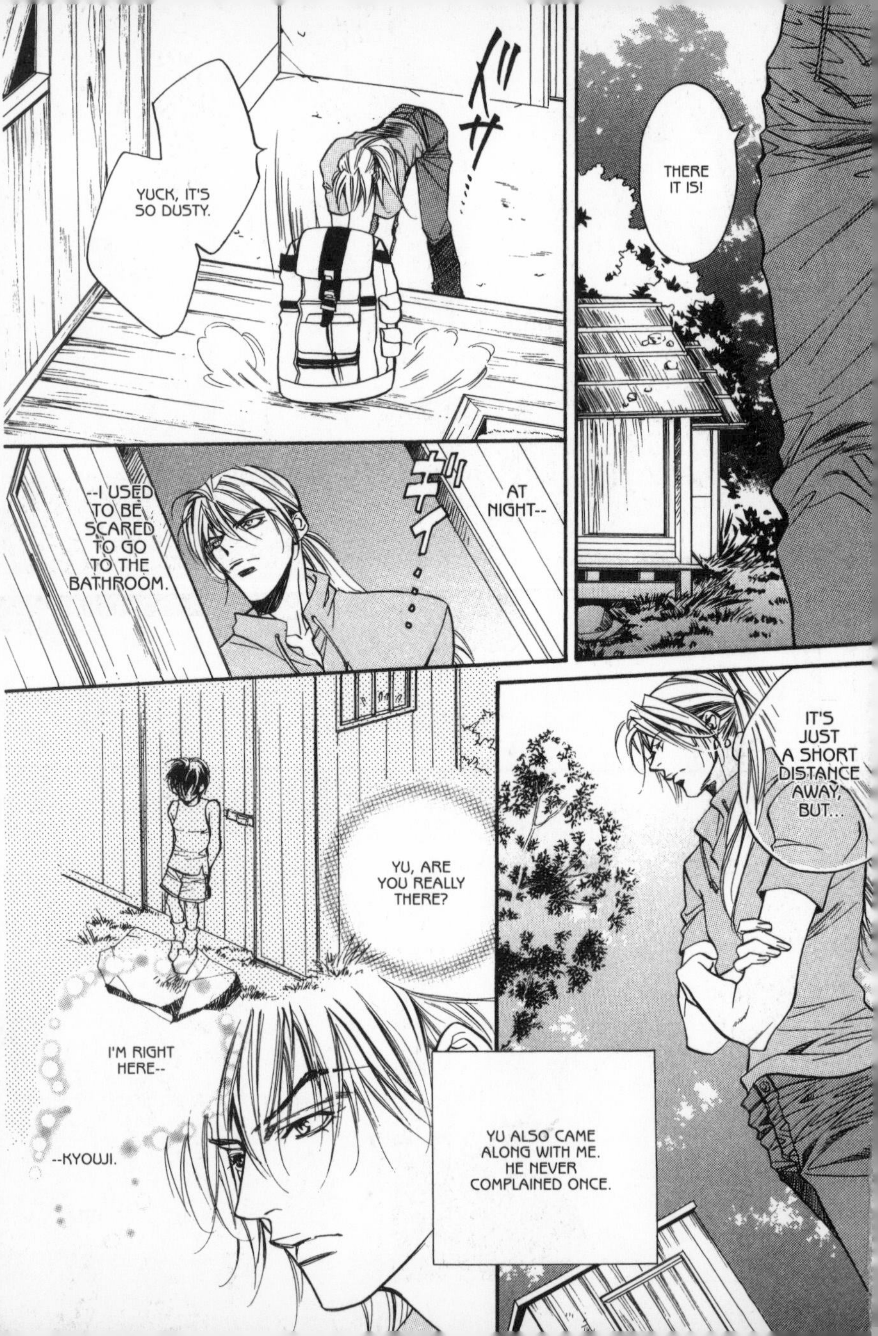
THERE IT IS!
YUCK, IT'S SO DUSTY.
AT NIGHT--
--I USED TO BE SCARED TO GO TO THE BATHROOM.
IT'S JUST A SHORT DISTANCE AWAY, BUT...
YU ALSO CAME ALONG WITH ME. HE NEVER COMPLAINED ONCE.
YU, ARE YOU REALLY THERE?
I'M RIGHT HERE--
--KYOUJI.

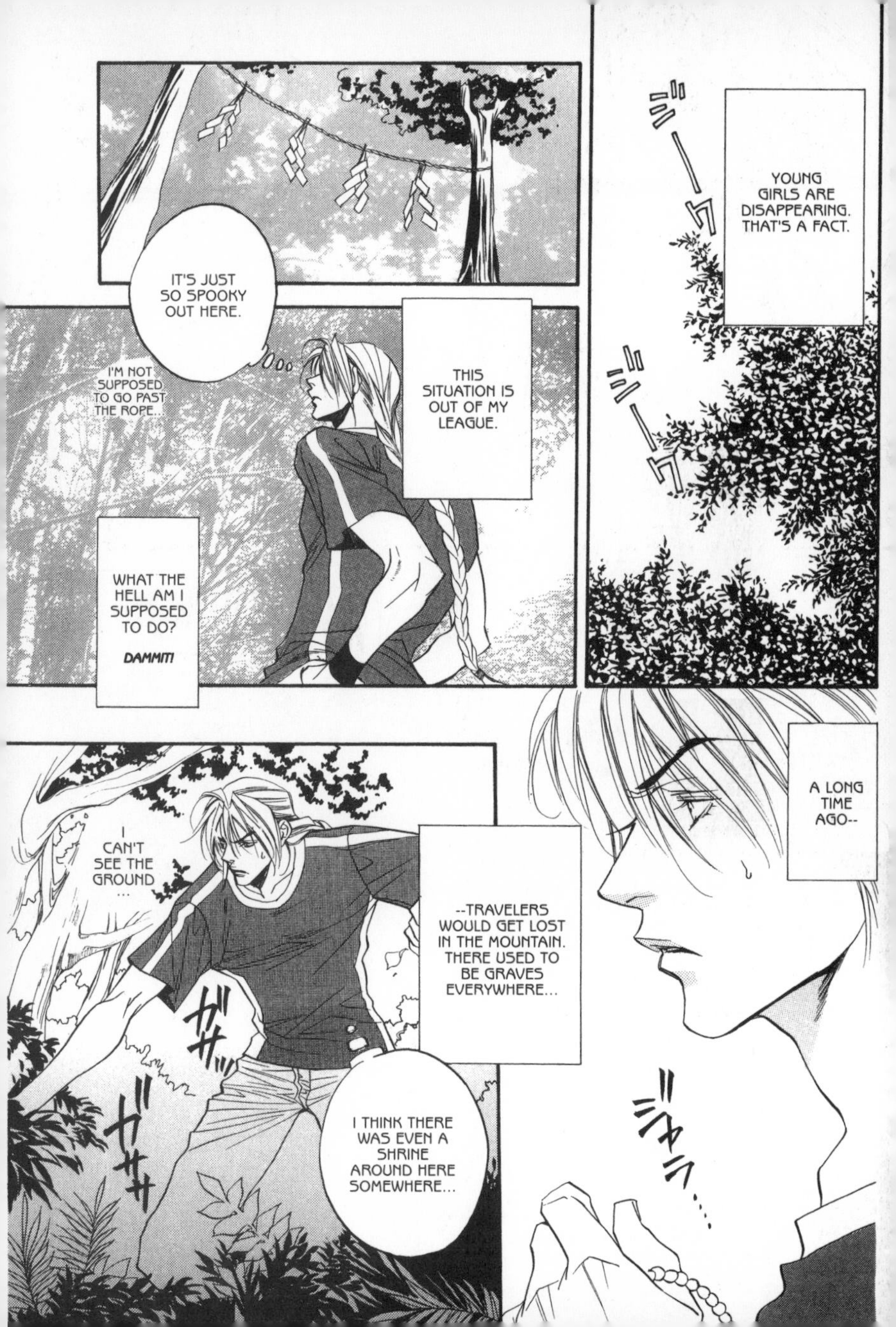
YOUNG GIRLS ARE DISAPPEARING. THAT'S A FACT.
IT'S JUST SO SPOOKY OUT HERE.
THIS SITUATION IS OUT OF MY LEAGUE.
I'M NOT SUPPOSED TO GO PAST THE ROPE...
WHAT THE HELL AM I SUPPOSED TO DO?
DAMMIT!
A LONG TIME AGO--
--TRAVELERS WOULD GET LOST IN THE MOUNTAIN. THERE USED TO BE GRAVES EVERYWHERE...
I CAN'T SEE THE GROUND ...
I THINK THERE WAS EVEN A SHRINE AROUND HERE SOMEWHERE...

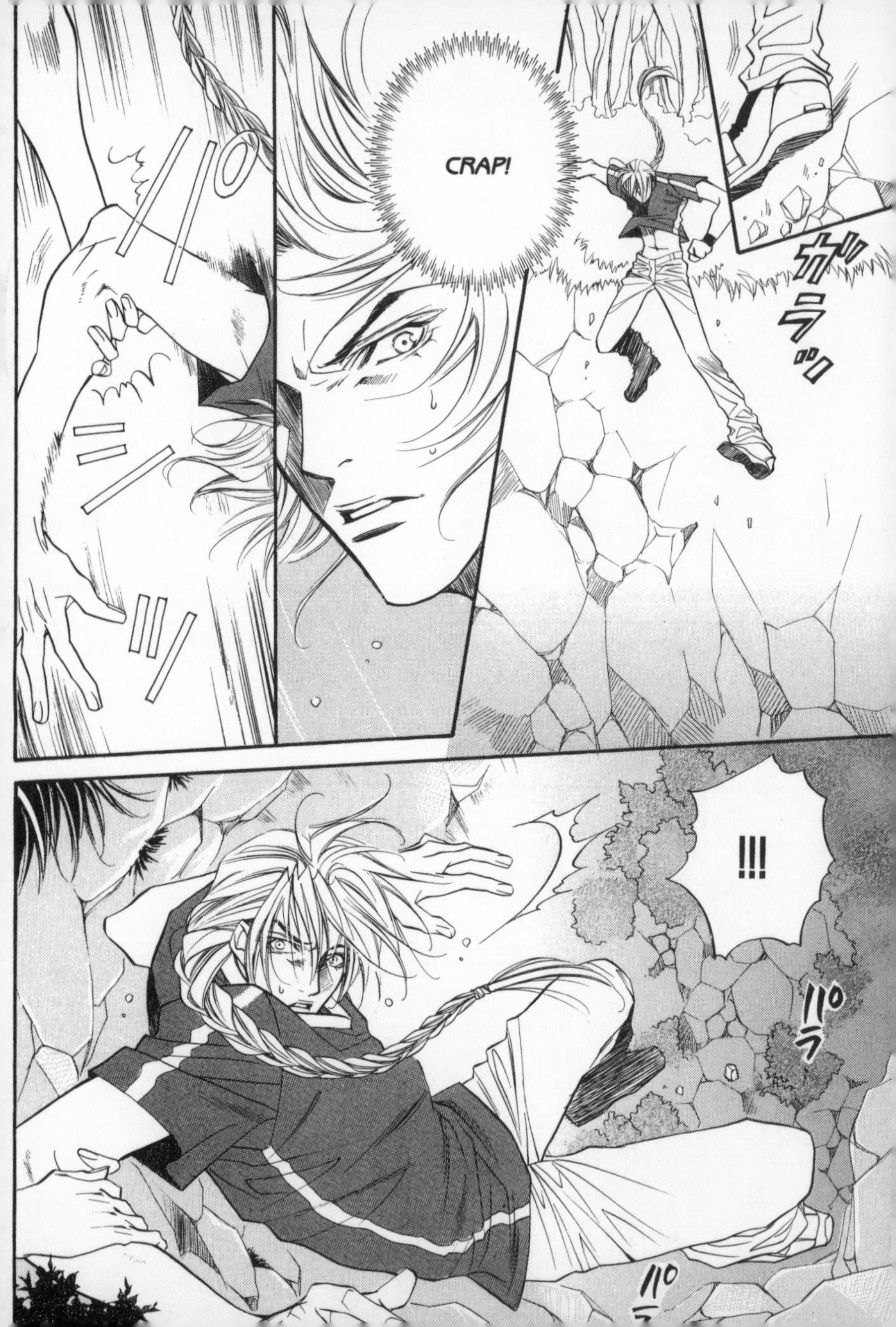
ガラッ
CRAP!
!!!
パラ

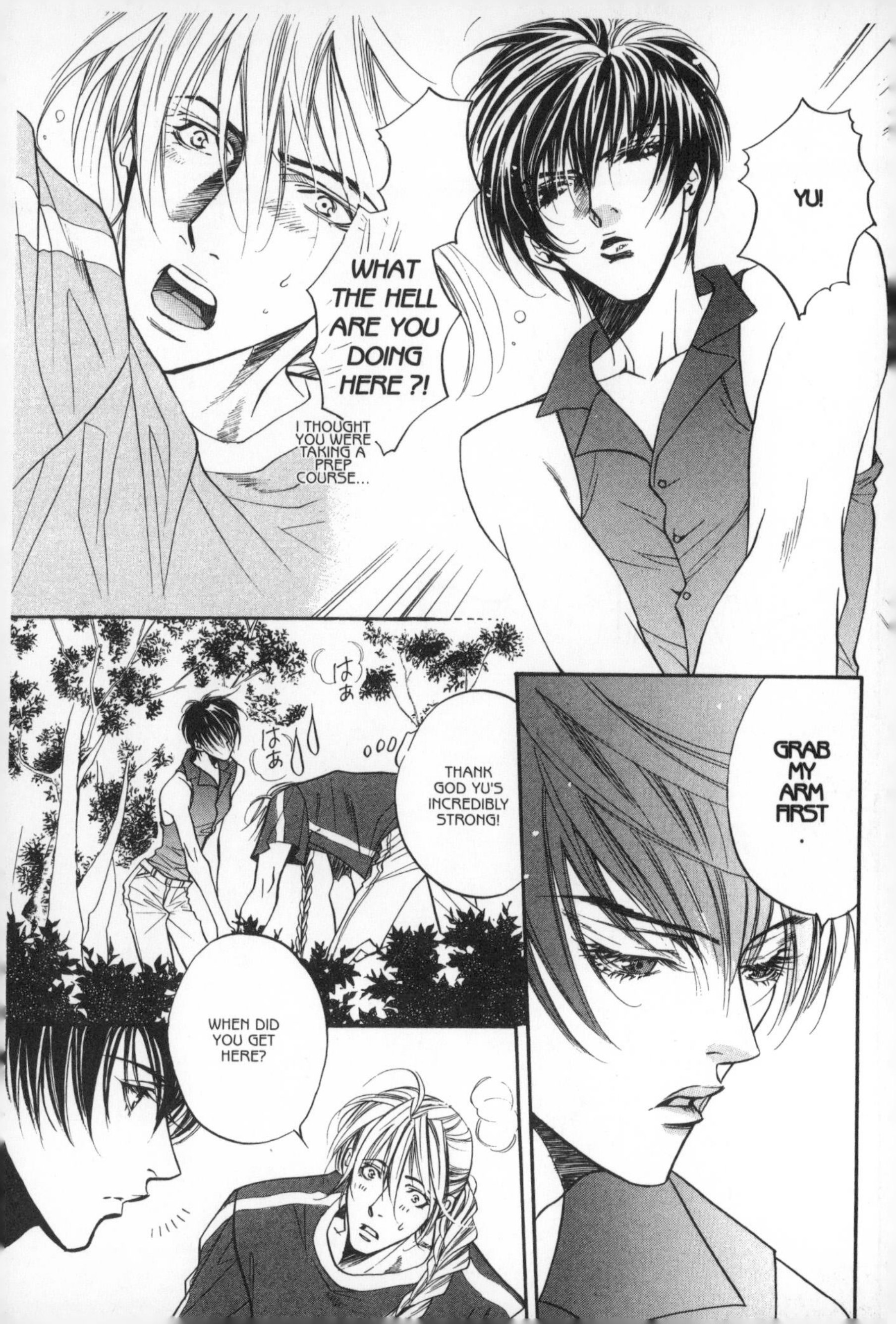
YU!
WHAT THE HELL ARE YOU DOING HERE ?!
I THOUGHT YOU WERE TAKING A PREP COURSE...
GRAB MY ARM FIRST.
はぁ
はぁ
THANK GOD YU'S INCREDIBLY STRONG!
WHEN DID YOU GET HERE?

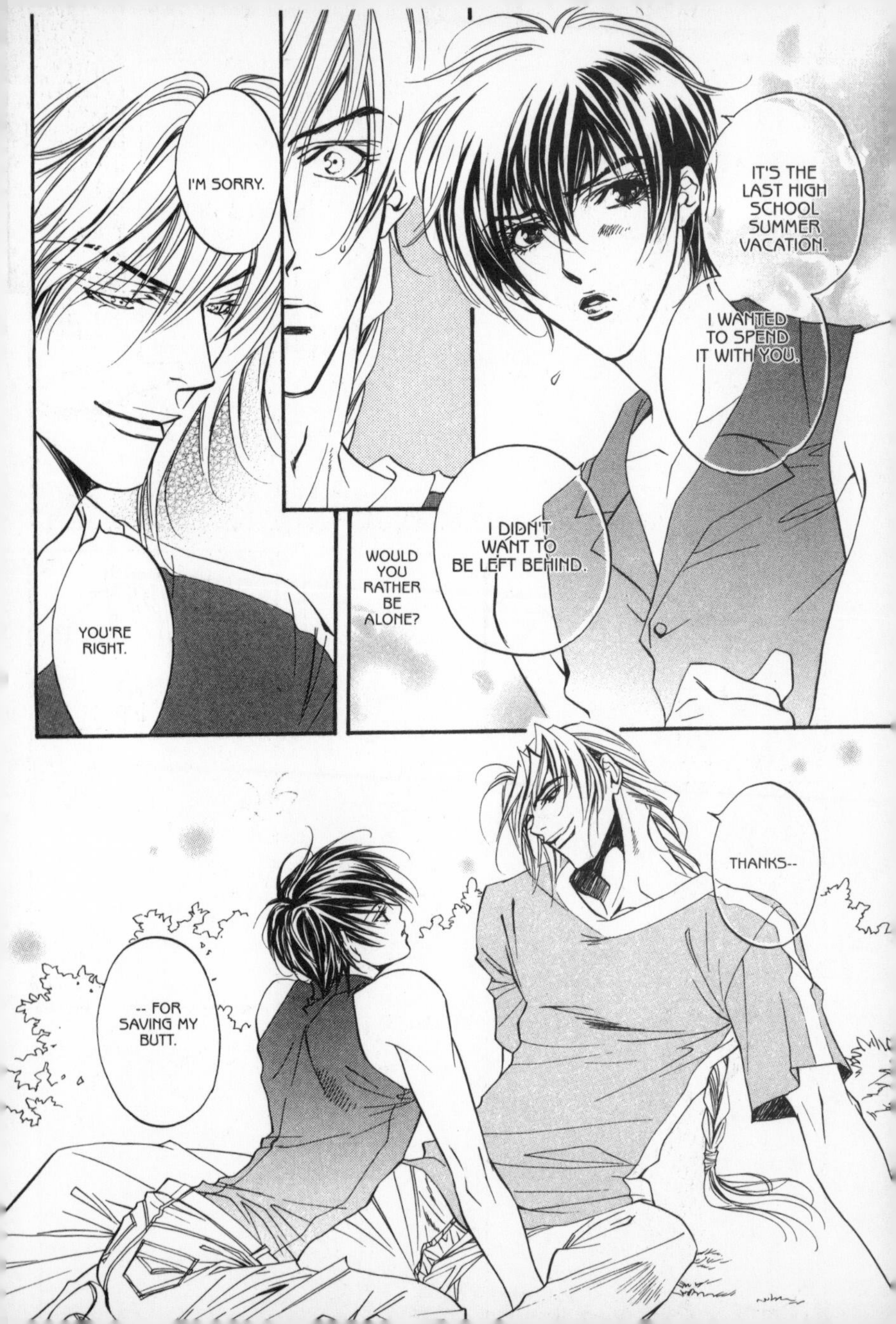
IT'S THE LAST HIGH SCHOOL SUMMER VACATION.
I WANTED TO SPEND IT WITH YOU.
I DIDN'T WANT TO BE LEFT BEHIND.
I'M SORRY.
WOULD YOU RATHER BE ALONE?
YOU'RE RIGHT.
THANKS--
-- FOR SAVING MY BUTT.

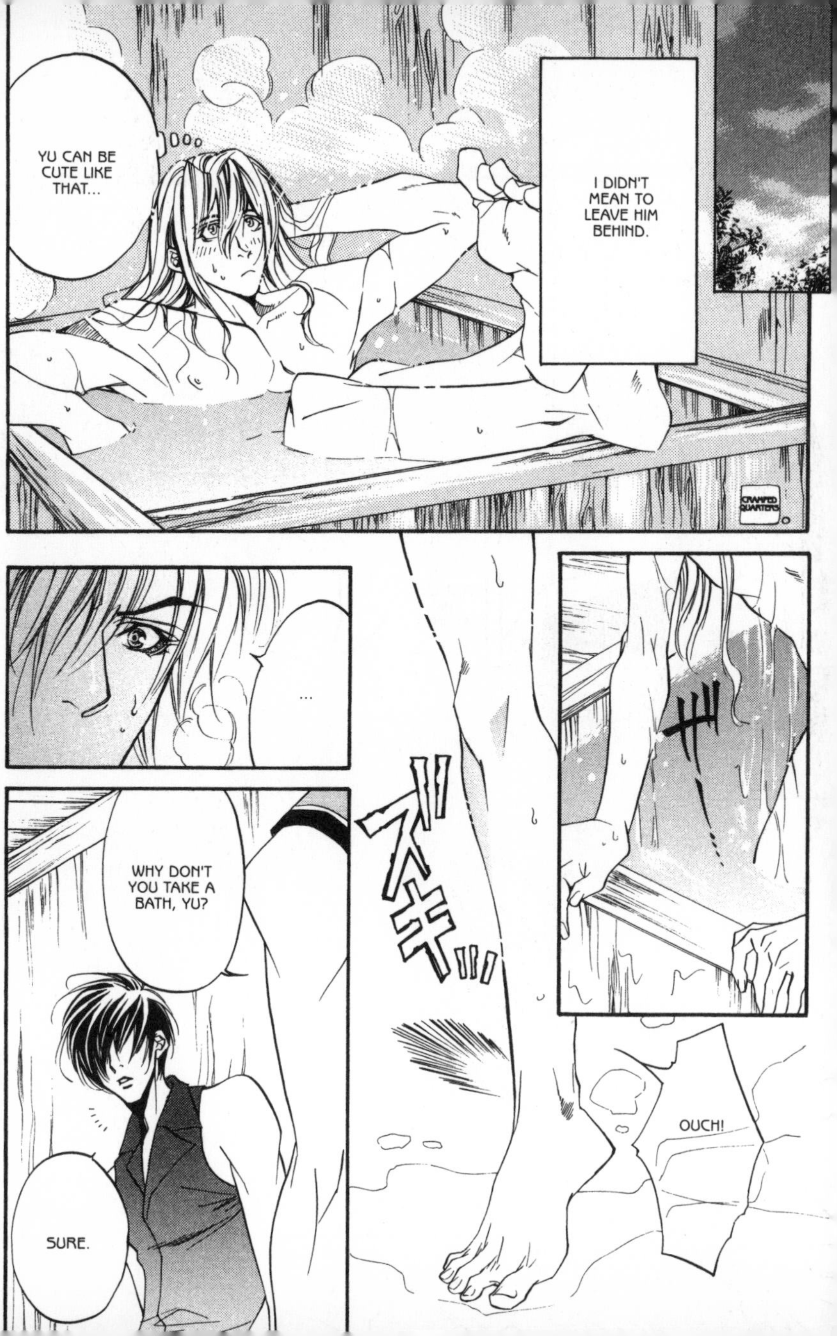

I DIDN'T MEAN TO LEAVE HIM BEHIND.
YU CAN BE CUTE LIKE THAT...
CRAMPED QUARTERS
ギ
...
ズキ
OUCH!
WHY DON'T YOU TAKE A BATH, YU?
SURE.

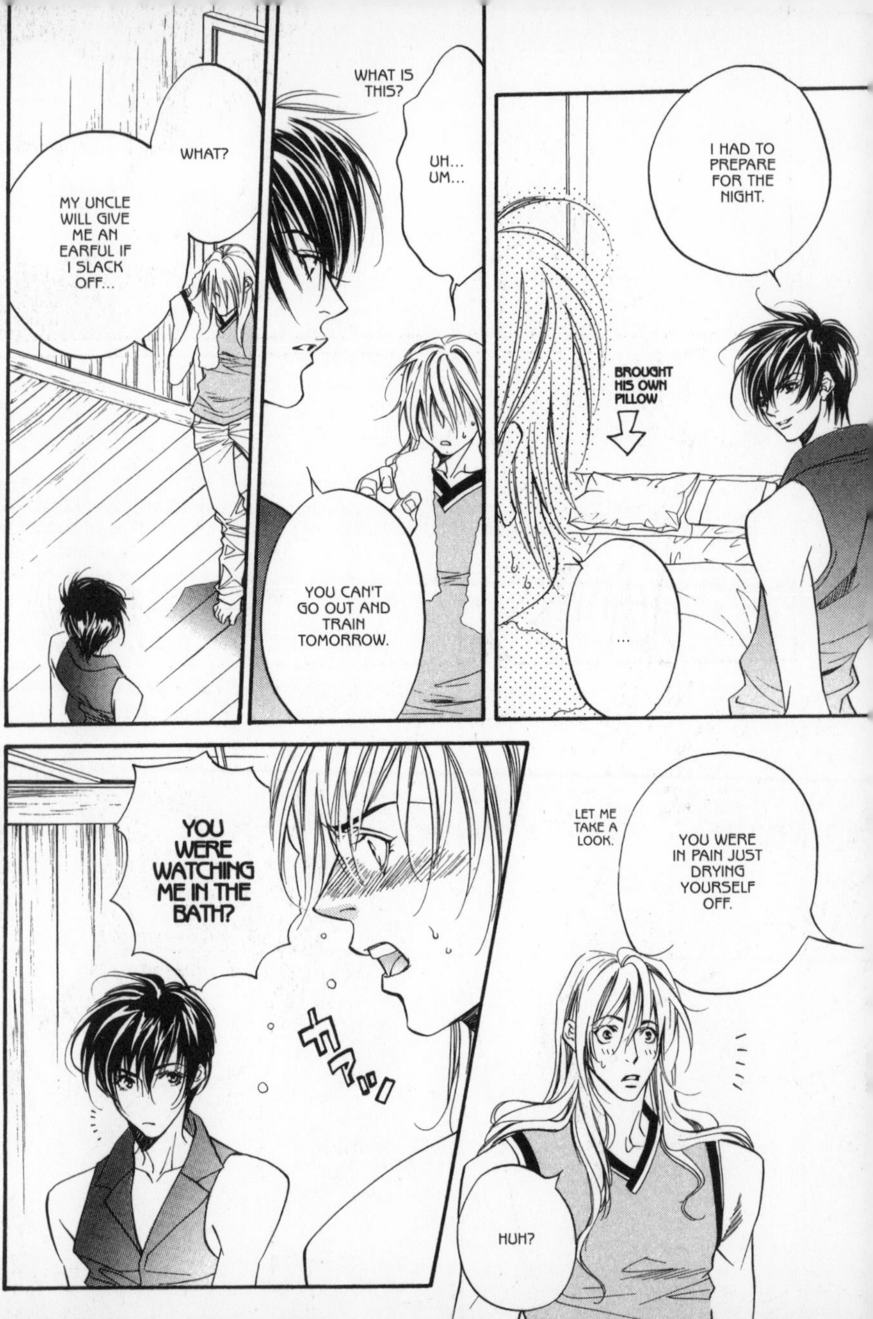
I HAD TO PREPARE FOR THE NIGHT.
BROUGHT HIS OWN PILLOW
...
WHAT IS THIS?
UH... UM...
YOU CAN'T GO OUT AND TRAIN TOMORROW.
WHAT?
MY UNCLE WILL GIVE ME AN EARFUL IF I SLACK OFF...
YOU WERE IN PAIN JUST DRYING YOURSELF OFF.
LET ME TAKE A LOOK.
HUH?
YOU WERE WATCHING ME IN THE BATH?

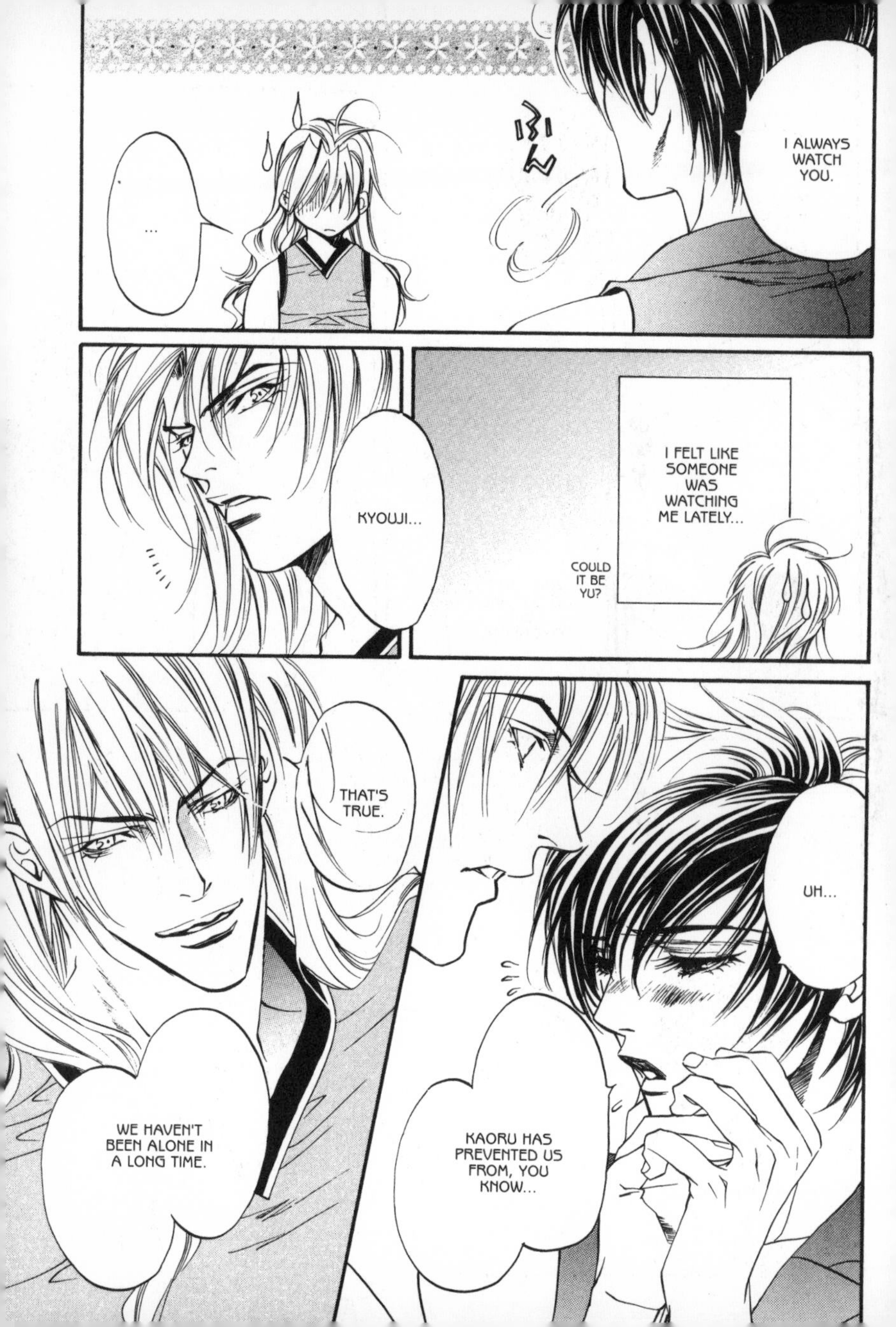
I ALWAYS WATCH YOU.
ふん
...
I FELT LIKE SOMEONE WAS WATCHING ME LATELY...
COULD IT BE YU?
KYOUJI...
UH...
KAORU HAS PREVENTED US FROM, YOU KNOW...
THAT'S TRUE.
WE HAVEN'T BEEN ALONE IN A LONG TIME.

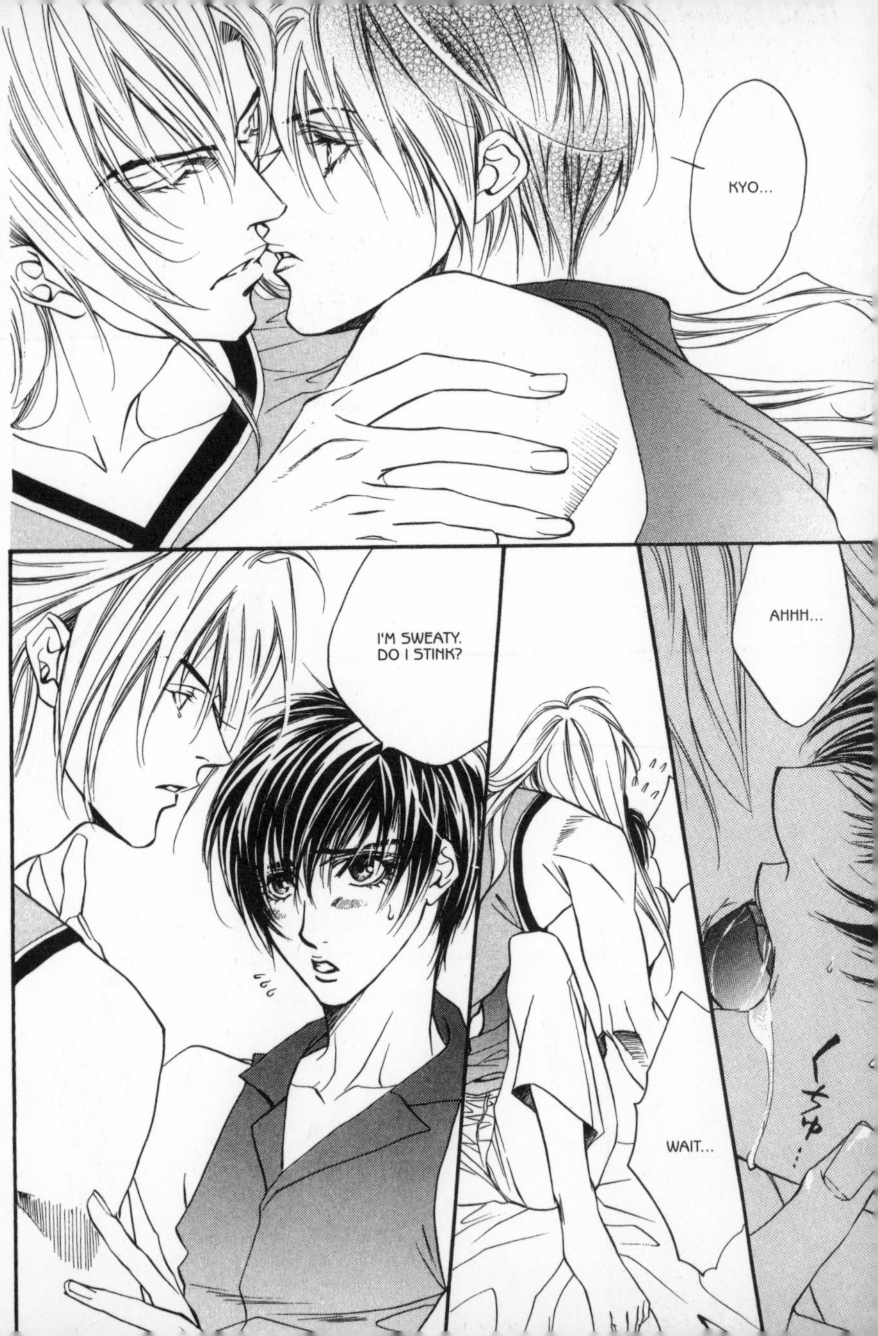
KYO...
AHHH...
WAIT...
I'M SWEATY. DO I STINK?

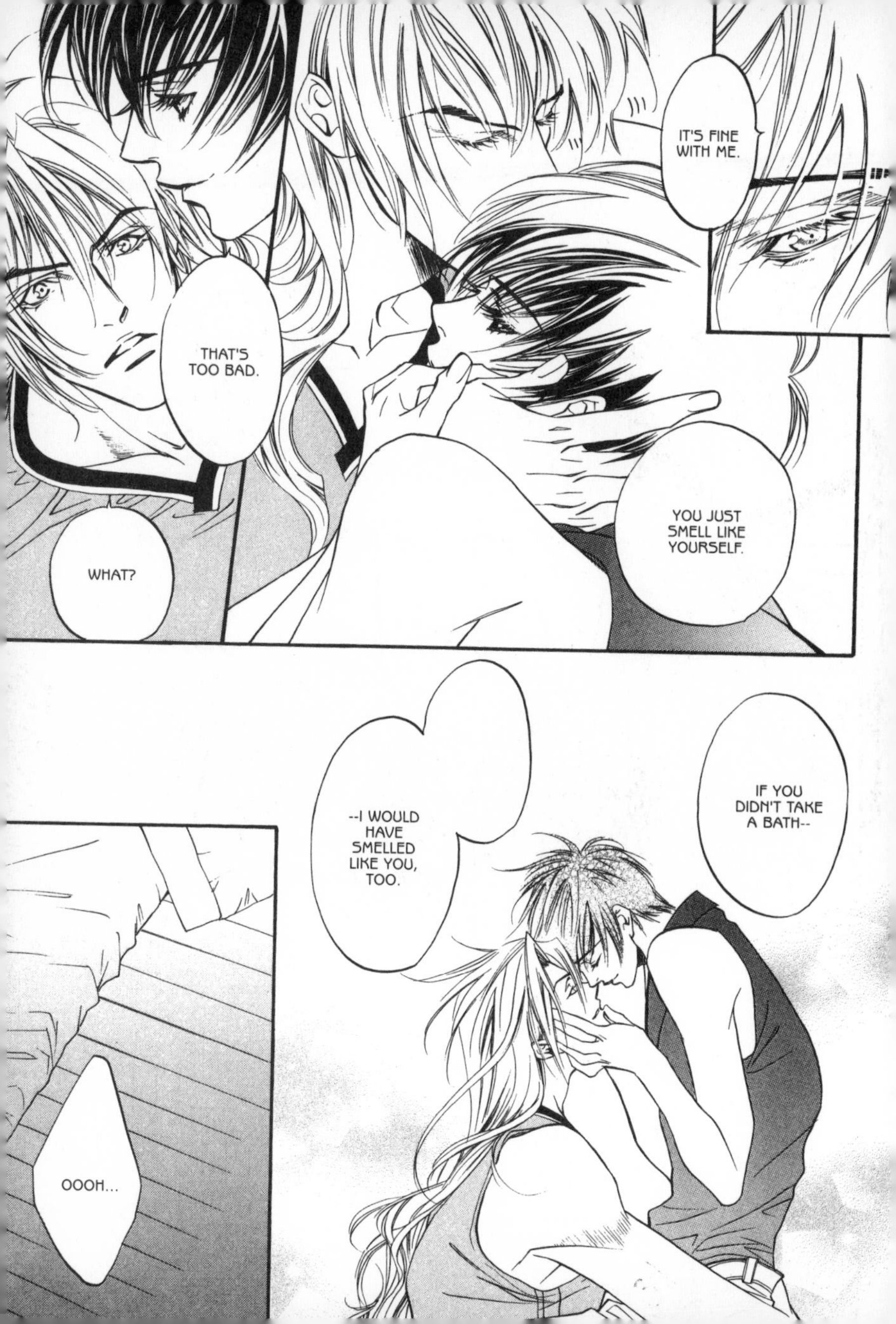
IT'S FINE WITH ME.
THAT'S TOO BAD.
YOU JUST SMELL LIKE YOURSELF.
WHAT?
IF YOU DIDN'T TAKE A BATH--
--I WOULD HAVE SMELLED LIKE YOU, TOO.
OOOH...

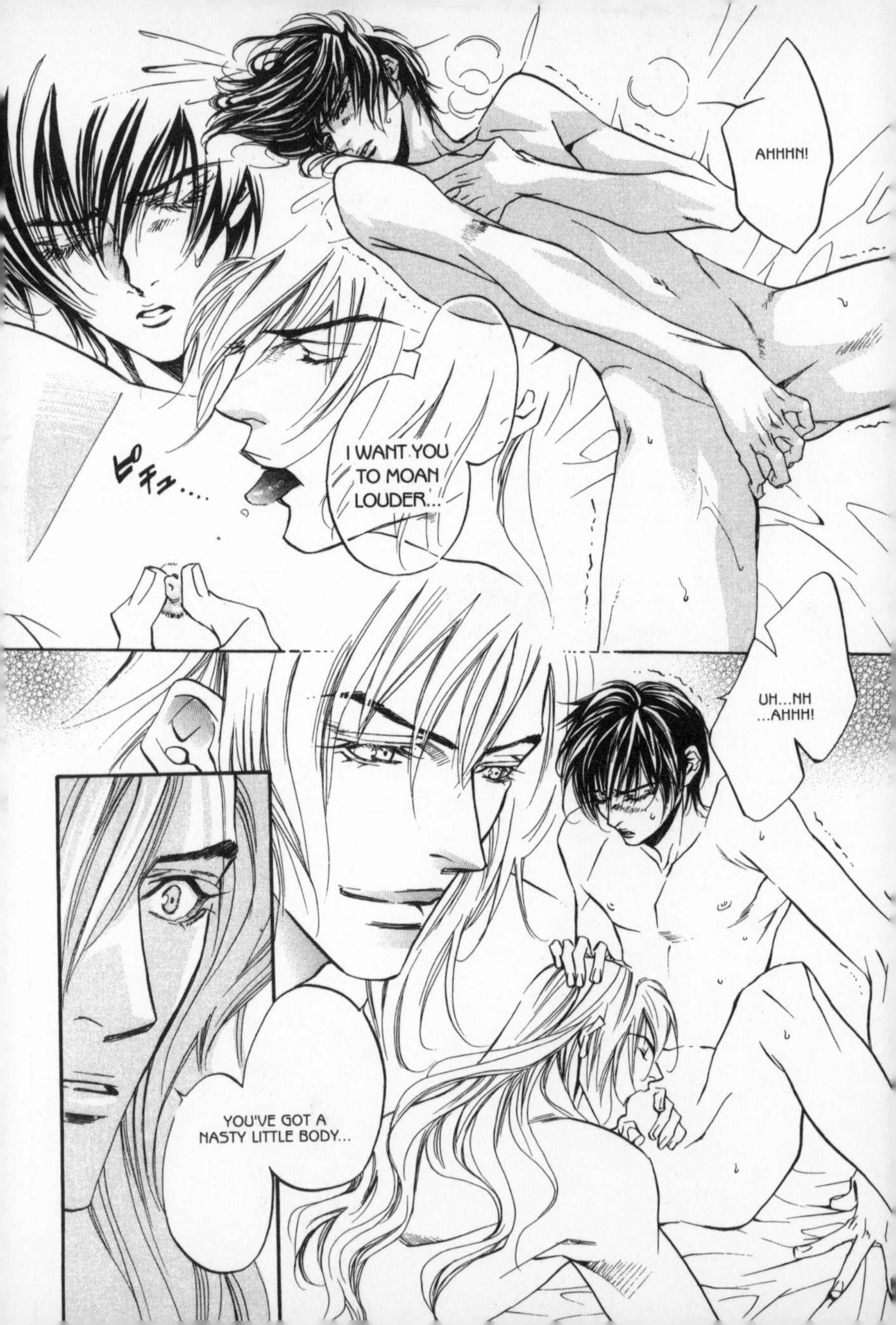
AHHHN!
I WANT YOU TO MOAN LOUDER...
ピチュ....
UH...NH ...AHHH!
YOU'VE GOT A NASTY LITTLE BODY...

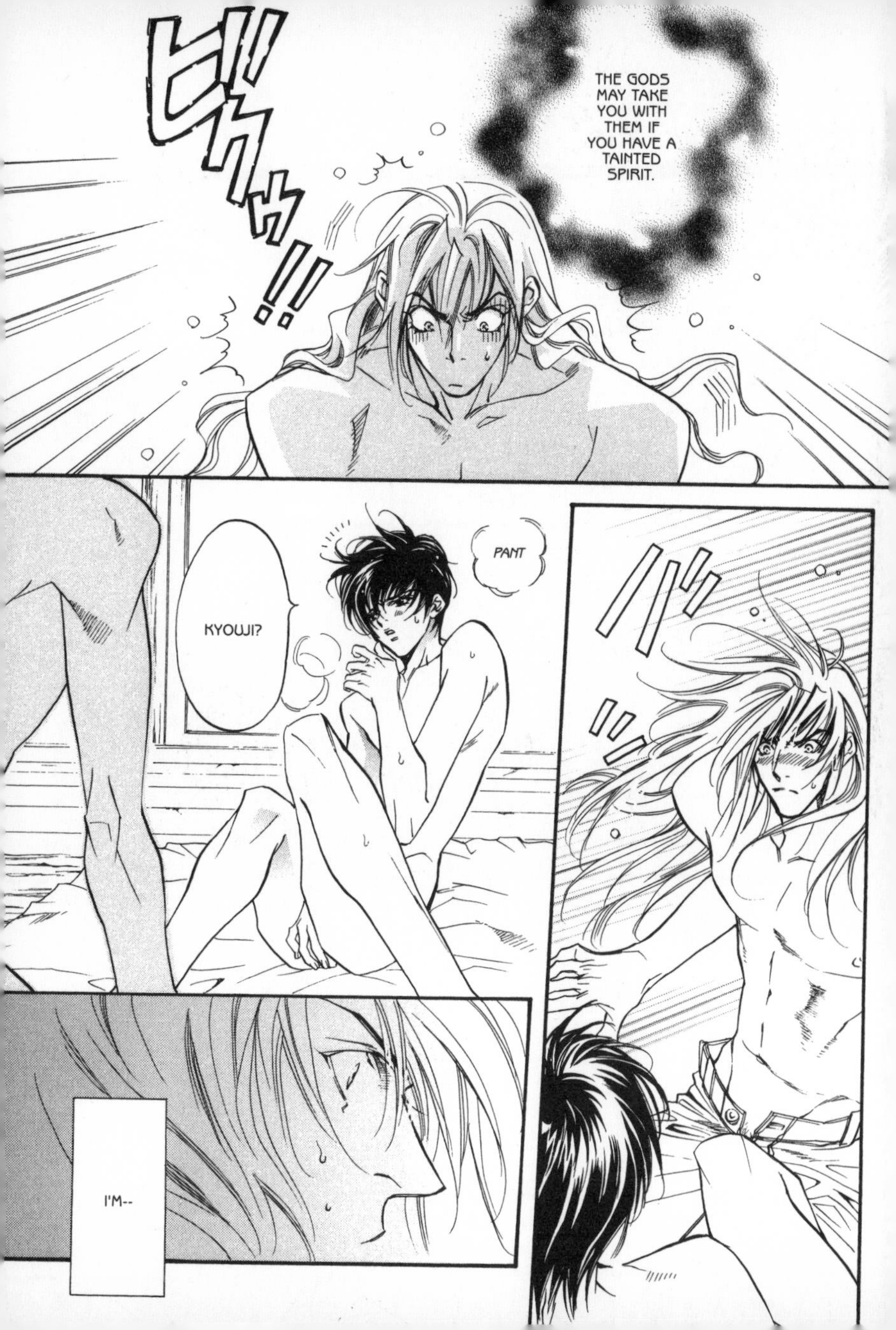
THE GODS MAY TAKE YOU WITH THEM IF YOU HAVE A TAINTED SPIRIT.
ビクゥ!!
PANT
KYOUJI?
バッ
I'M--

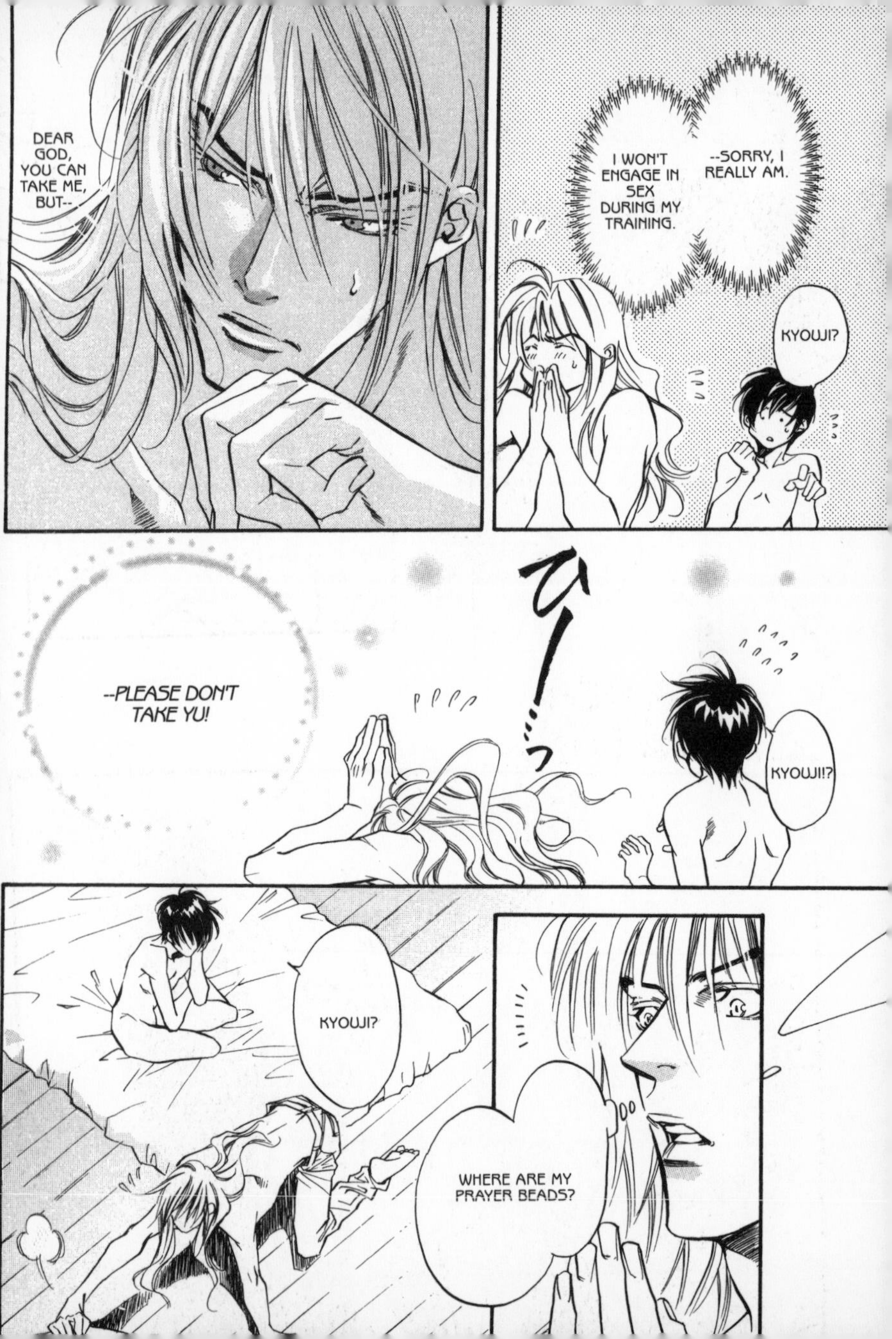
--SORRY, I REALLY AM.
I WON'T ENGAGE IN SEX DURING MY TRAINING.
KYOUJI?
DEAR GOD, YOU CAN TAKE ME, BUT--
KYOUJI!?
ひーっ
--PLEASE DON'T TAKE YU!
WHERE ARE MY PRAYER BEADS?
KYOUJI?

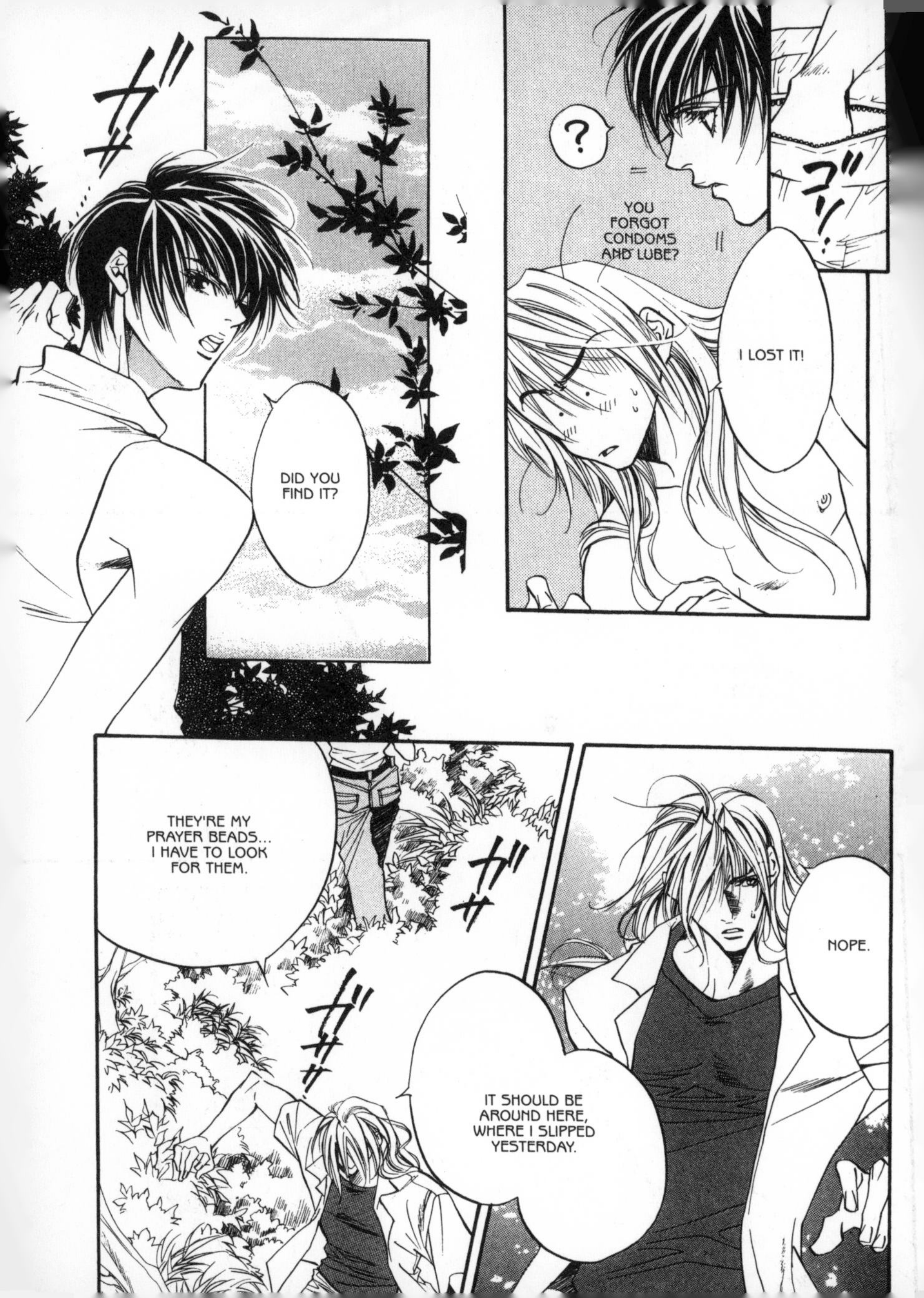

?
YOU FORGOT CONDOMS AND LUBE?
I LOST IT!
DID YOU FIND IT?
NOPE.
THEY'RE MY PRAYER BEADS... I HAVE TO LOOK FOR THEM.
IT SHOULD BE AROUND HERE, WHERE I SLIPPED YESTERDAY.

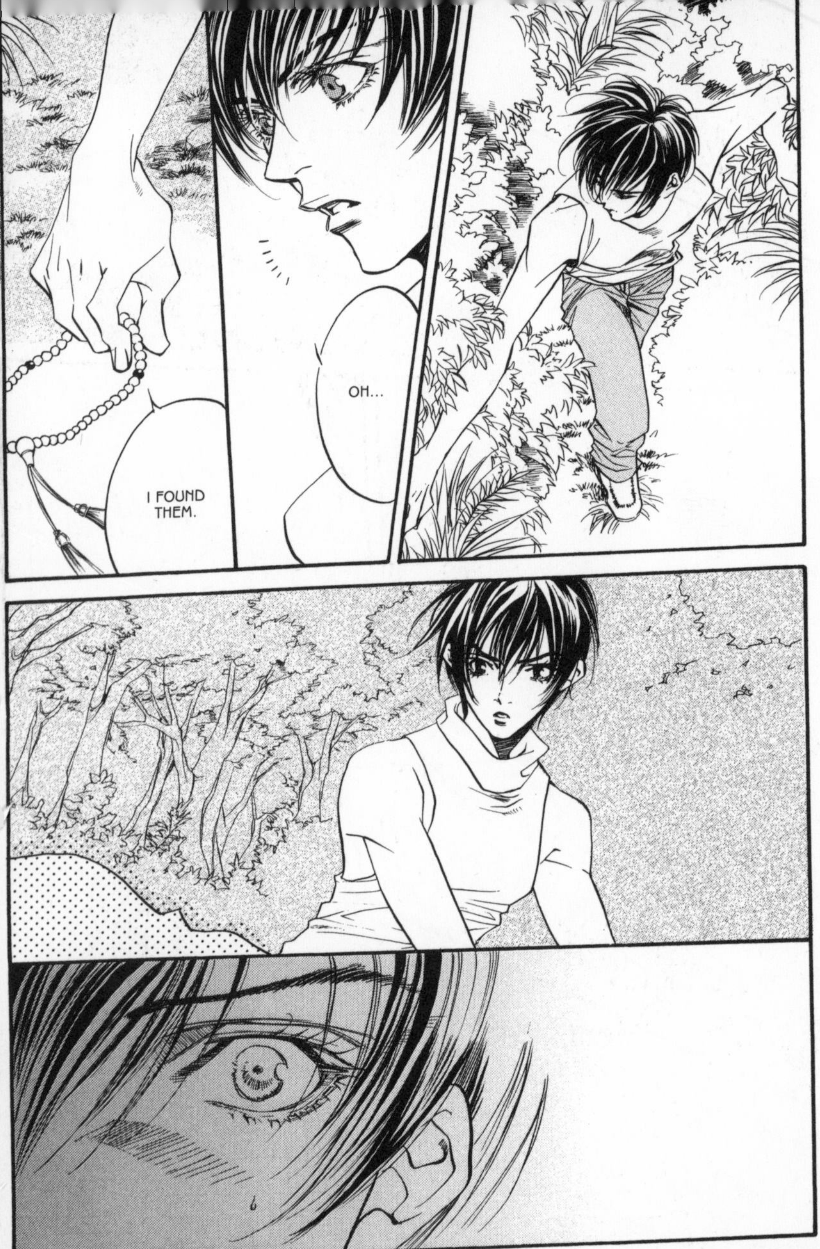
OH...
I FOUND THEM.

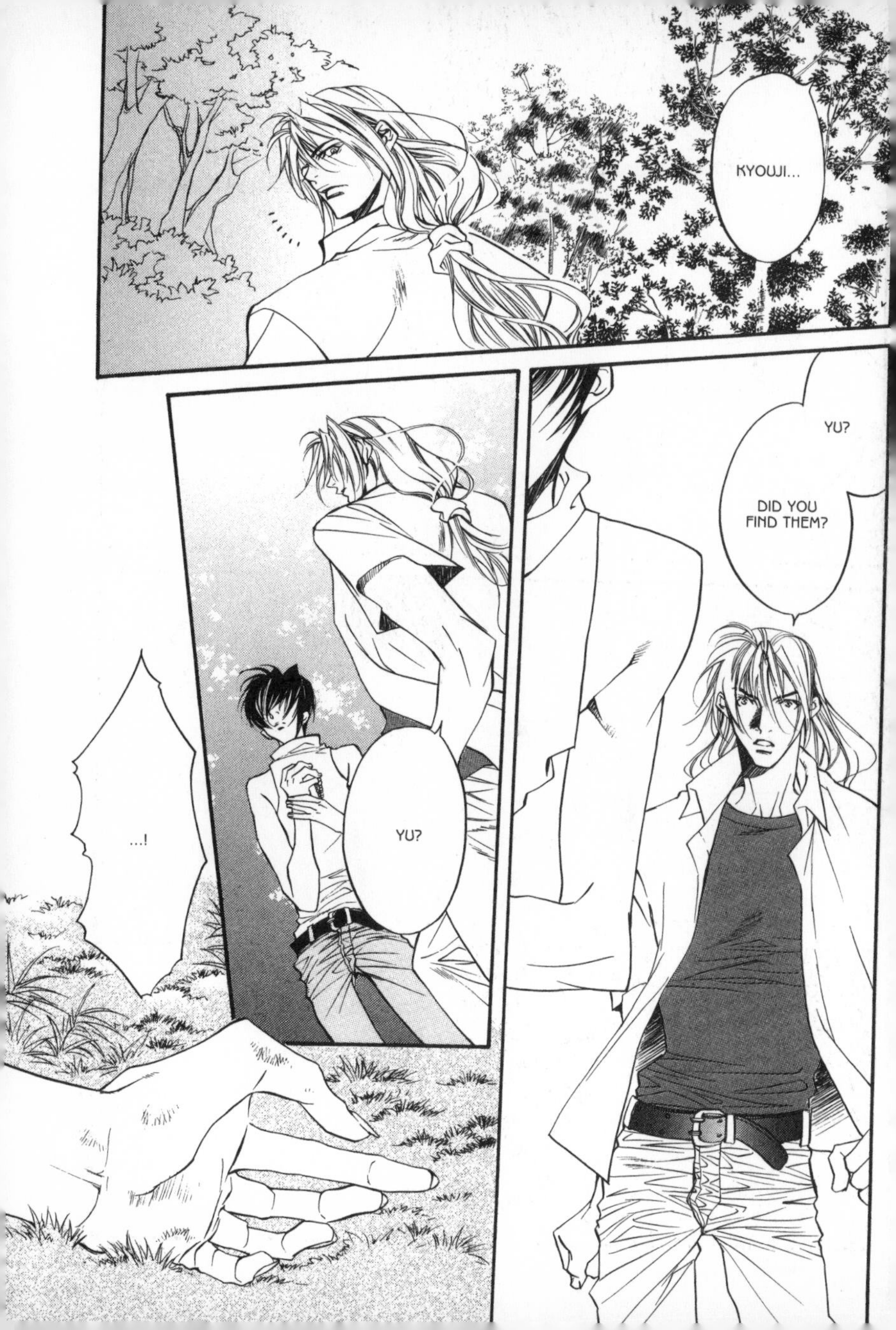
KYOUJI...
YU?
DID YOU FIND THEM?
YU?
...!

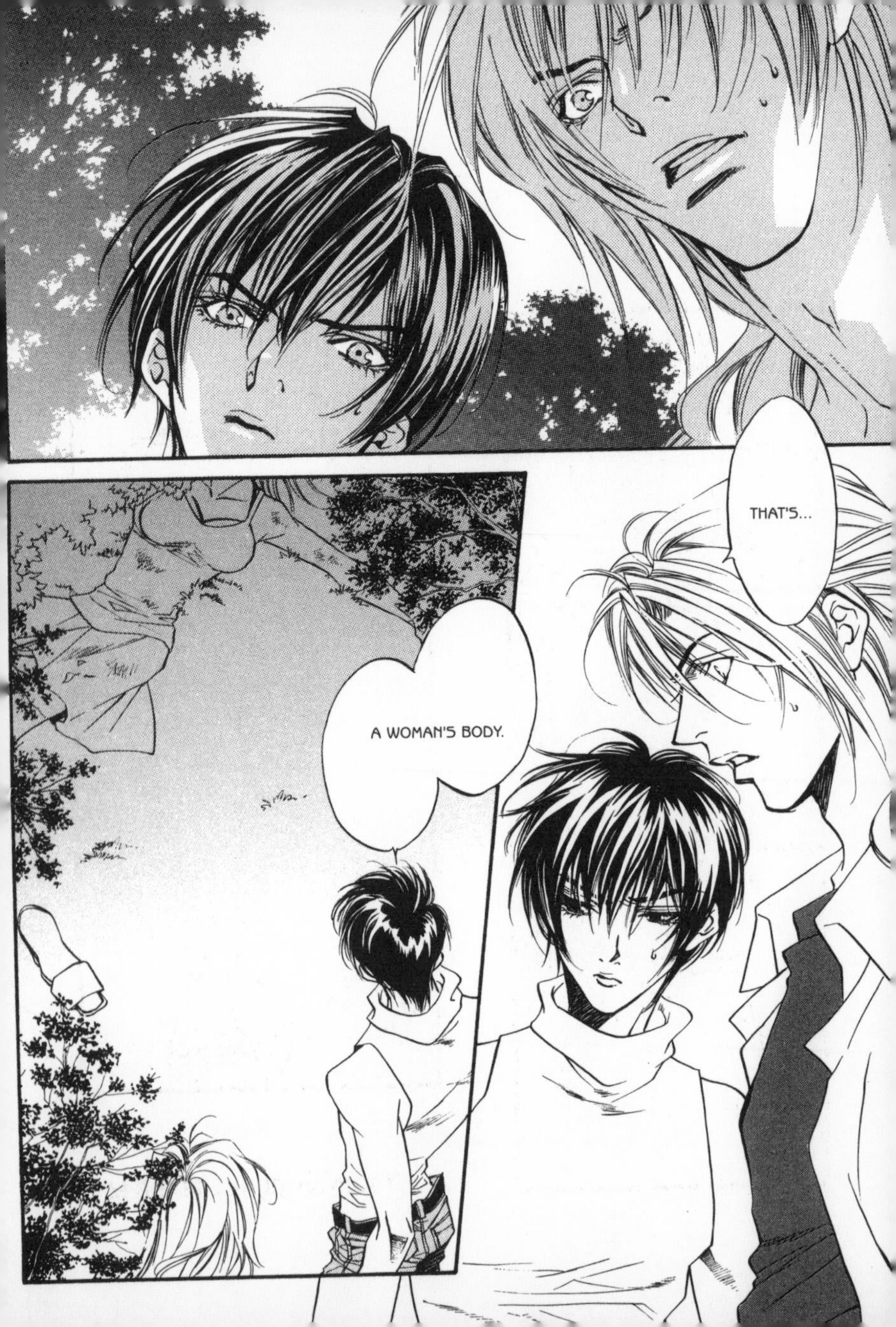
THAT'S...
A WOMAN'S BODY.

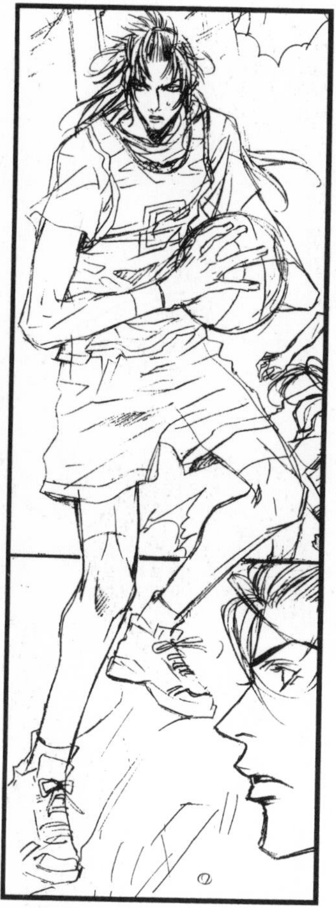

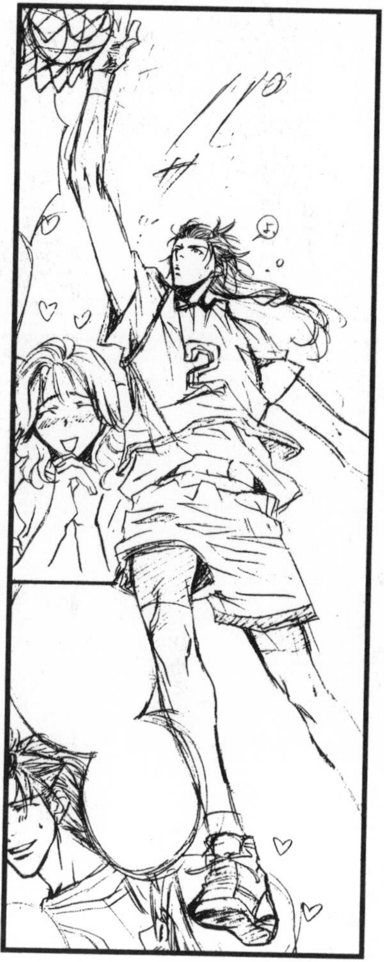

I can't stop loving you ■■■■

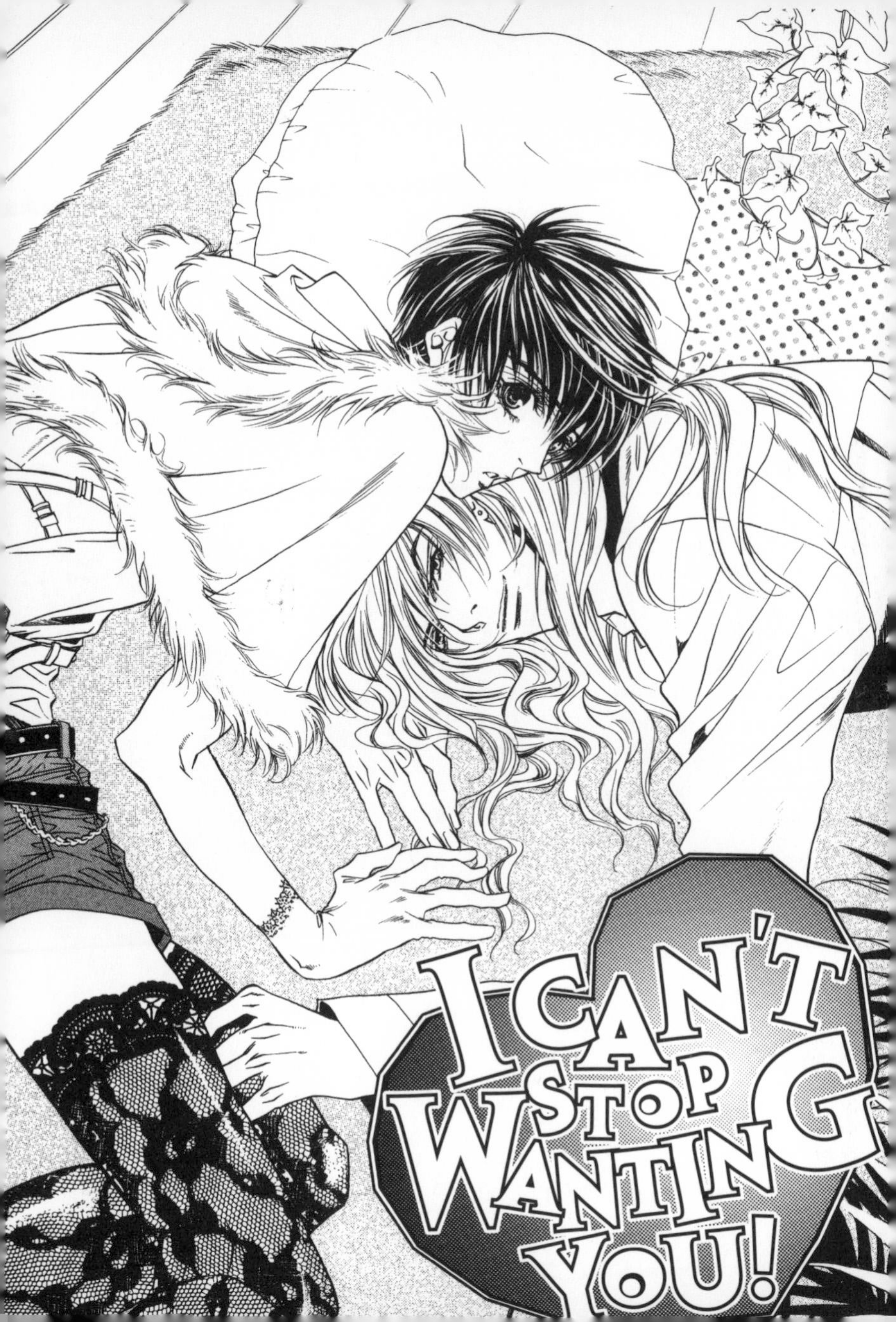
I CAN'T STOP WANTING YOU!

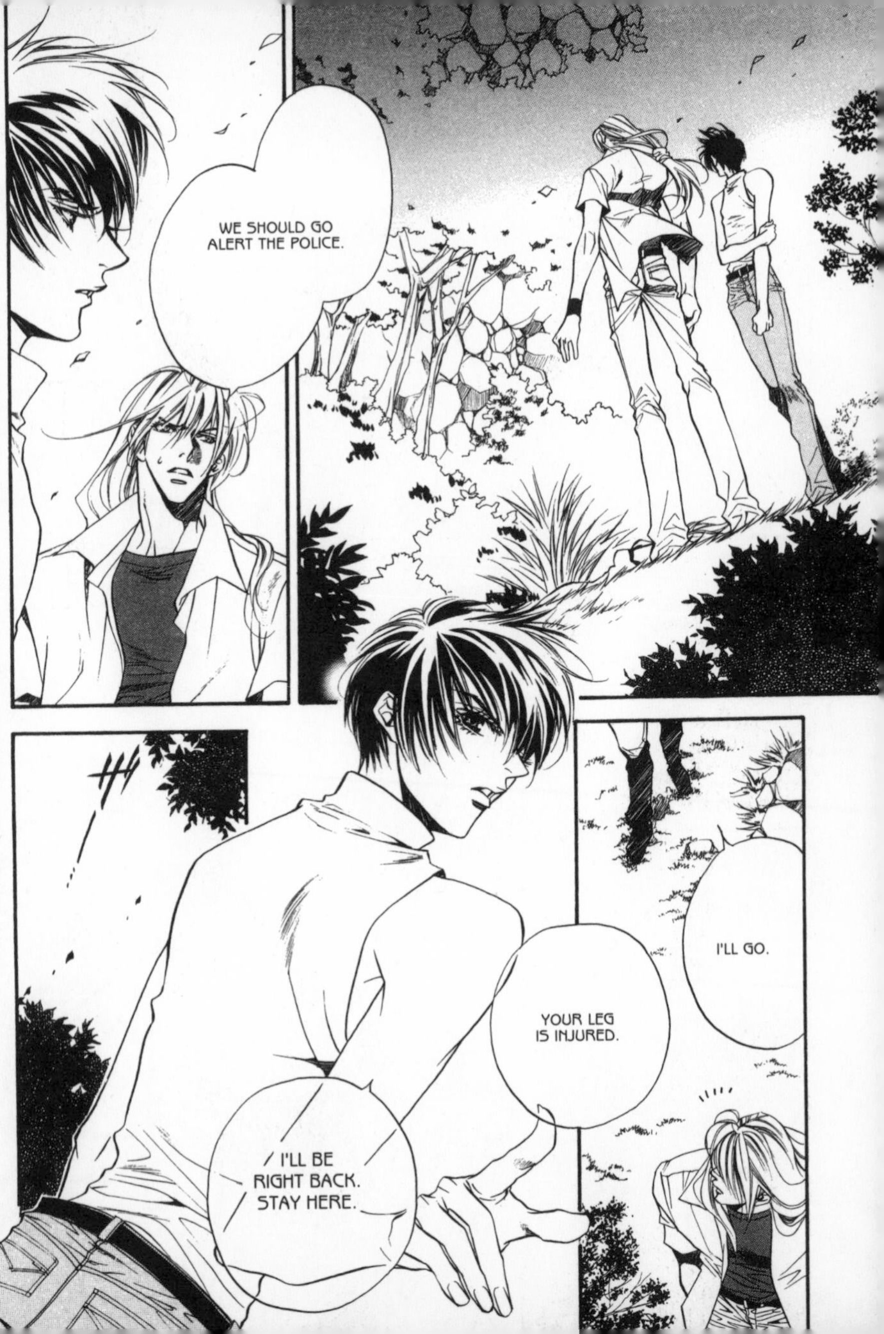
WE SHOULD GO ALERT THE POLICE.
I'LL GO.
YOUR LEG IS INJURED.
I'LL BE RIGHT BACK. STAY HERE.

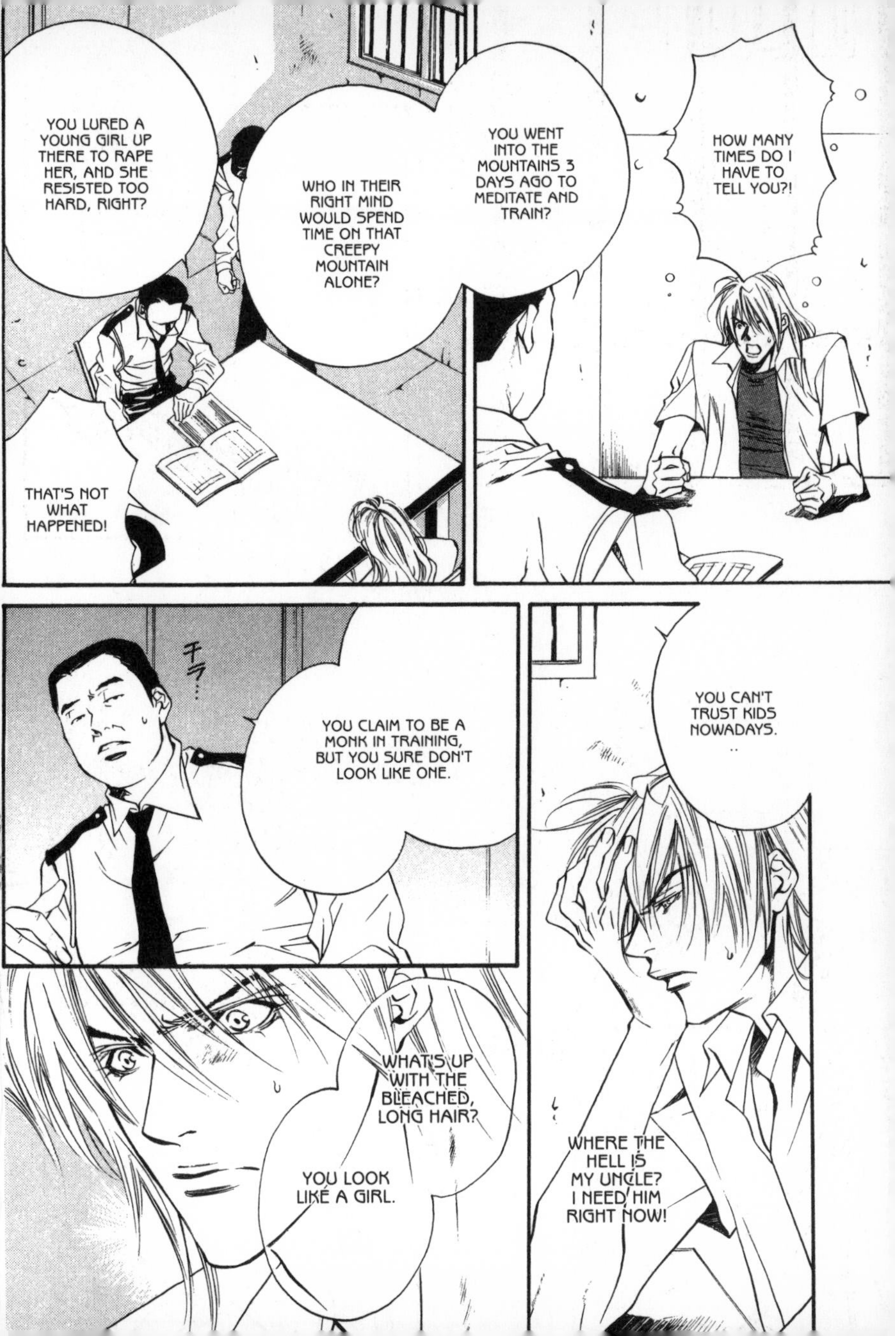
YOU WENT INTO THE MOUNTAINS 3 DAYS AGO TO MEDITATE AND TRAIN?
HOW MANY TIMES DO I HAVE TO TELL YOU?!
WHO IN THEIR RIGHT MIND WOULD SPEND TIME ON THAT CREEPY MOUNTAIN ALONE?
YOU LURED A YOUNG GIRL UP THERE TO RAPE HER, AND SHE RESISTED TOO HARD, RIGHT?
THAT'S NOT WHAT HAPPENED!
YOU CAN'T TRUST KIDS NOWADAYS.
チラ…
YOU CLAIM TO BE A MONK IN TRAINING, BUT YOU SURE DON'T LOOK LIKE ONE.
WHAT'S UP WITH THE BLEACHED, LONG HAIR?
YOU LOOK LIKE A GIRL.
WHERE THE HELL IS MY UNCLE? I NEED HIM RIGHT NOW!

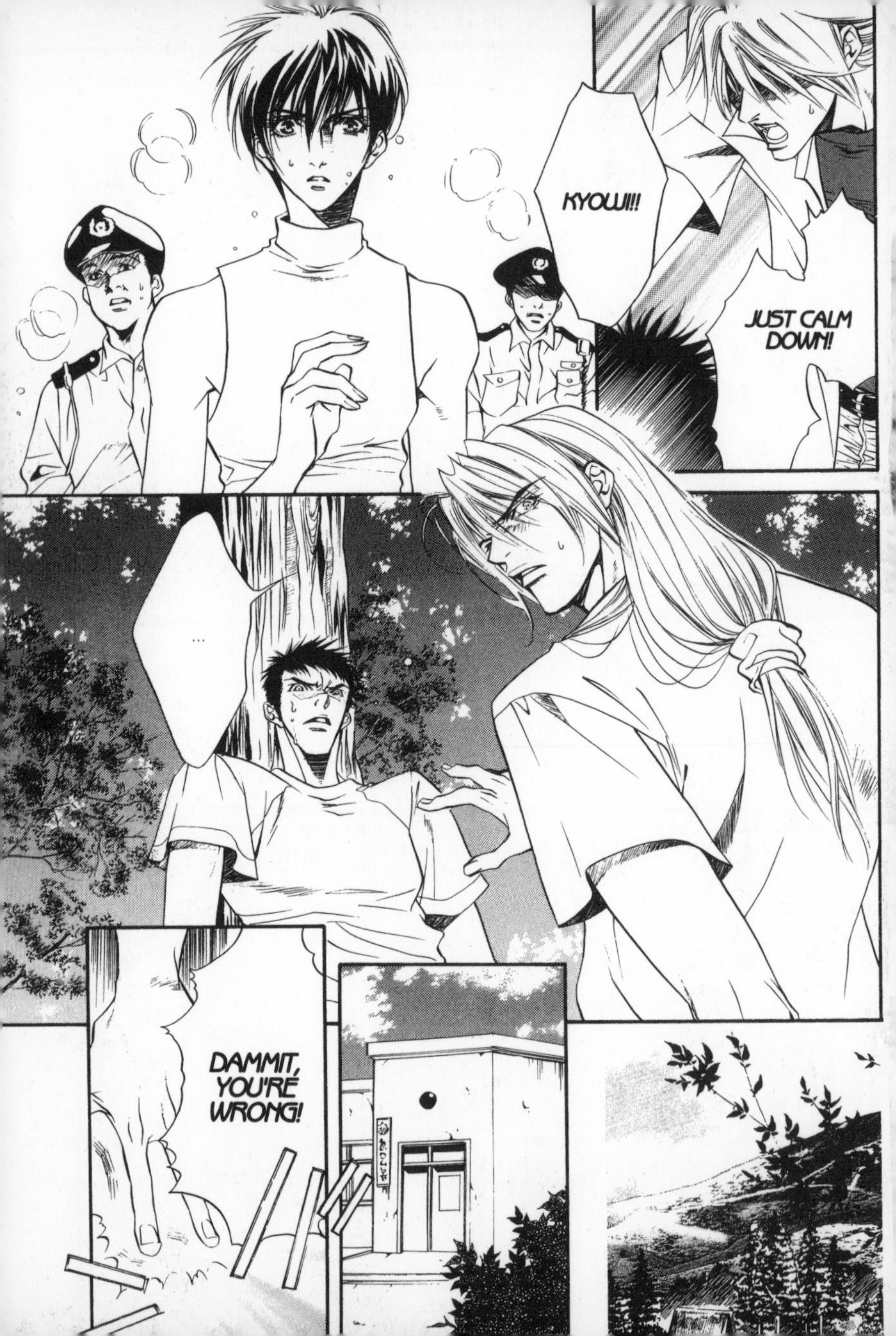
KYOUJI!!!
JUST CALM DOWN!
...
DAMMIT, YOU'RE WRONG!

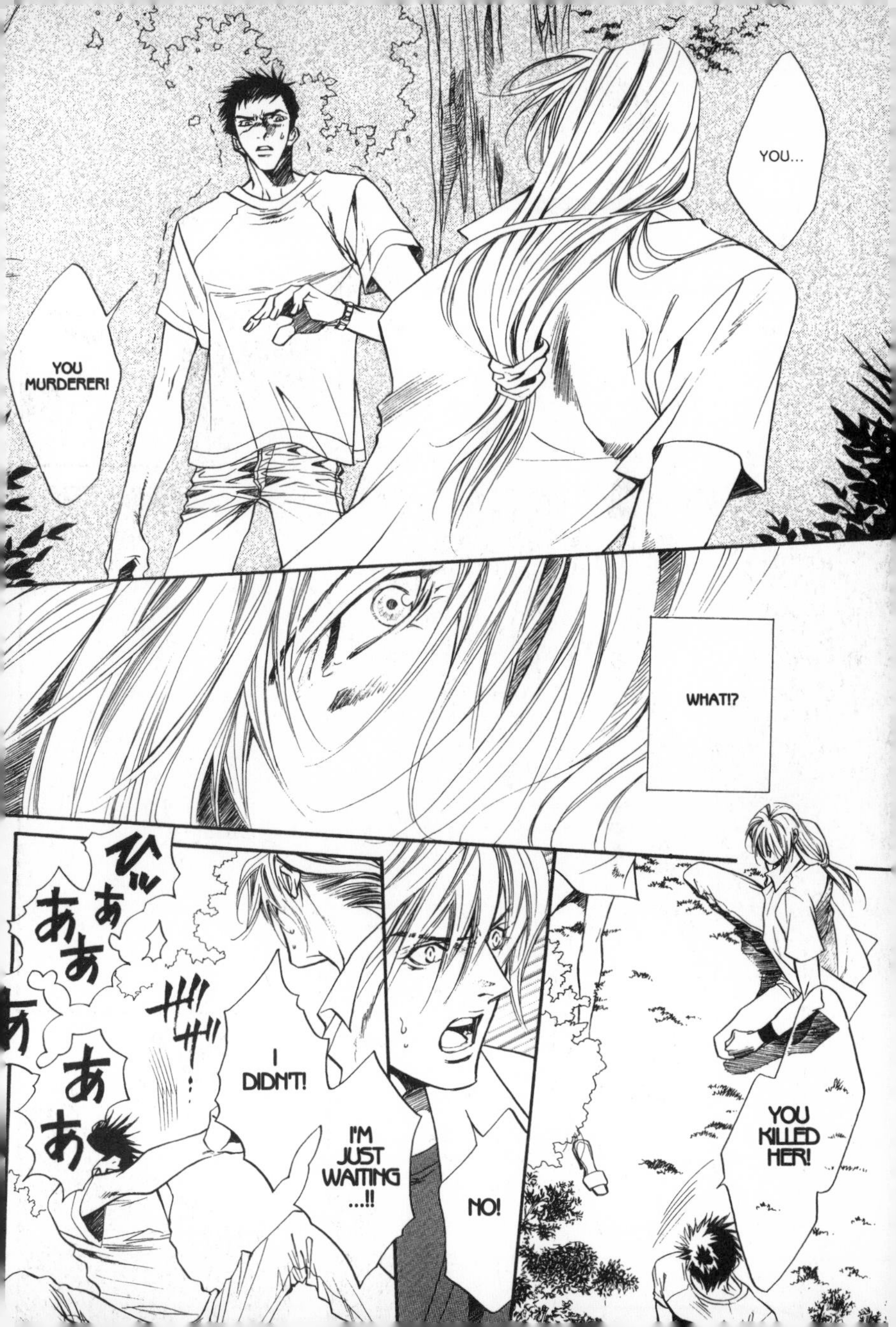
YOU...
YOU MURDERER!
WHAT!?
YOU KILLED HER!
NO!
I'M JUST WAITING ...!!
I DIDN'T!
ひッぁあああああ
ザザ…

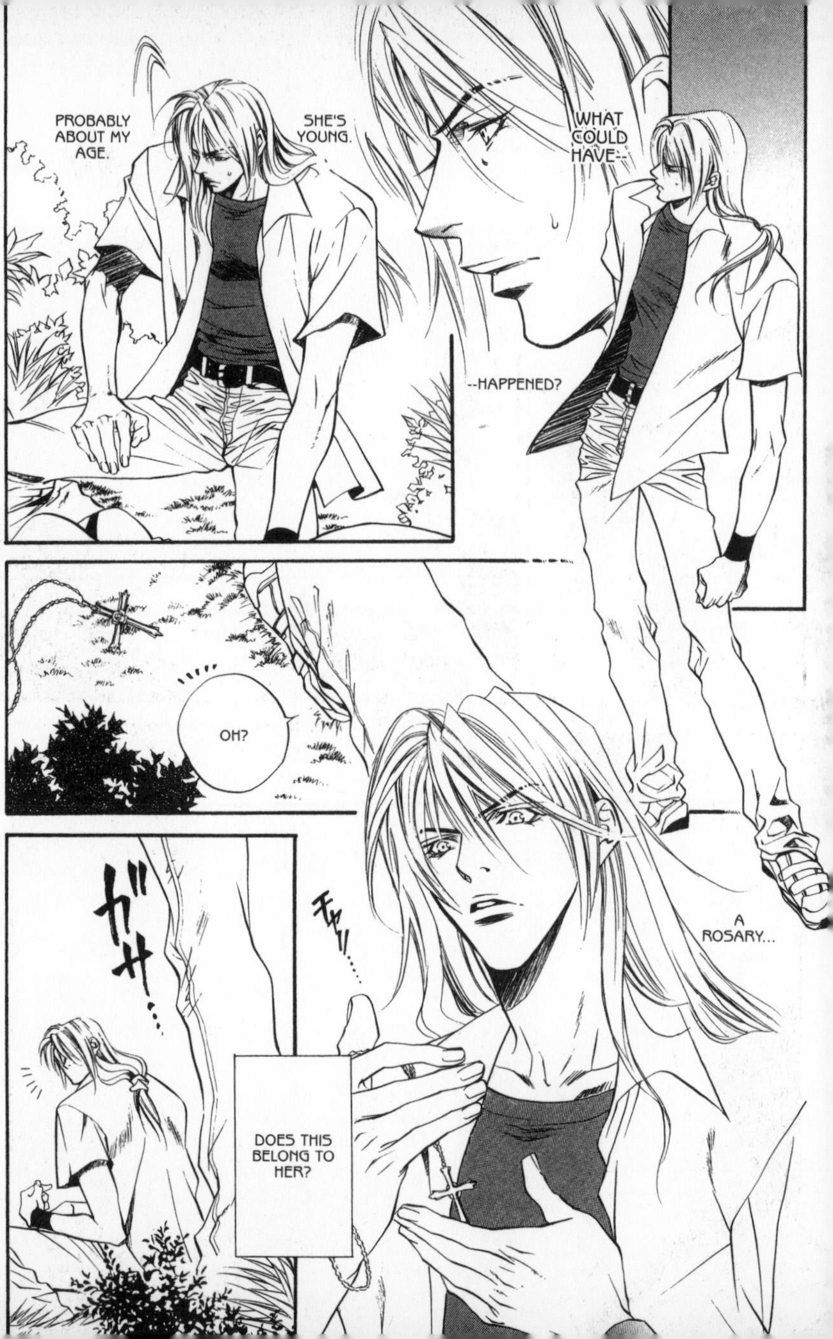
WHAT COULD HAVE--
--HAPPENED?
SHE'S YOUNG.
PROBABLY ABOUT MY AGE.
A ROSARY...
OH?
DOES THIS BELONG TO HER?

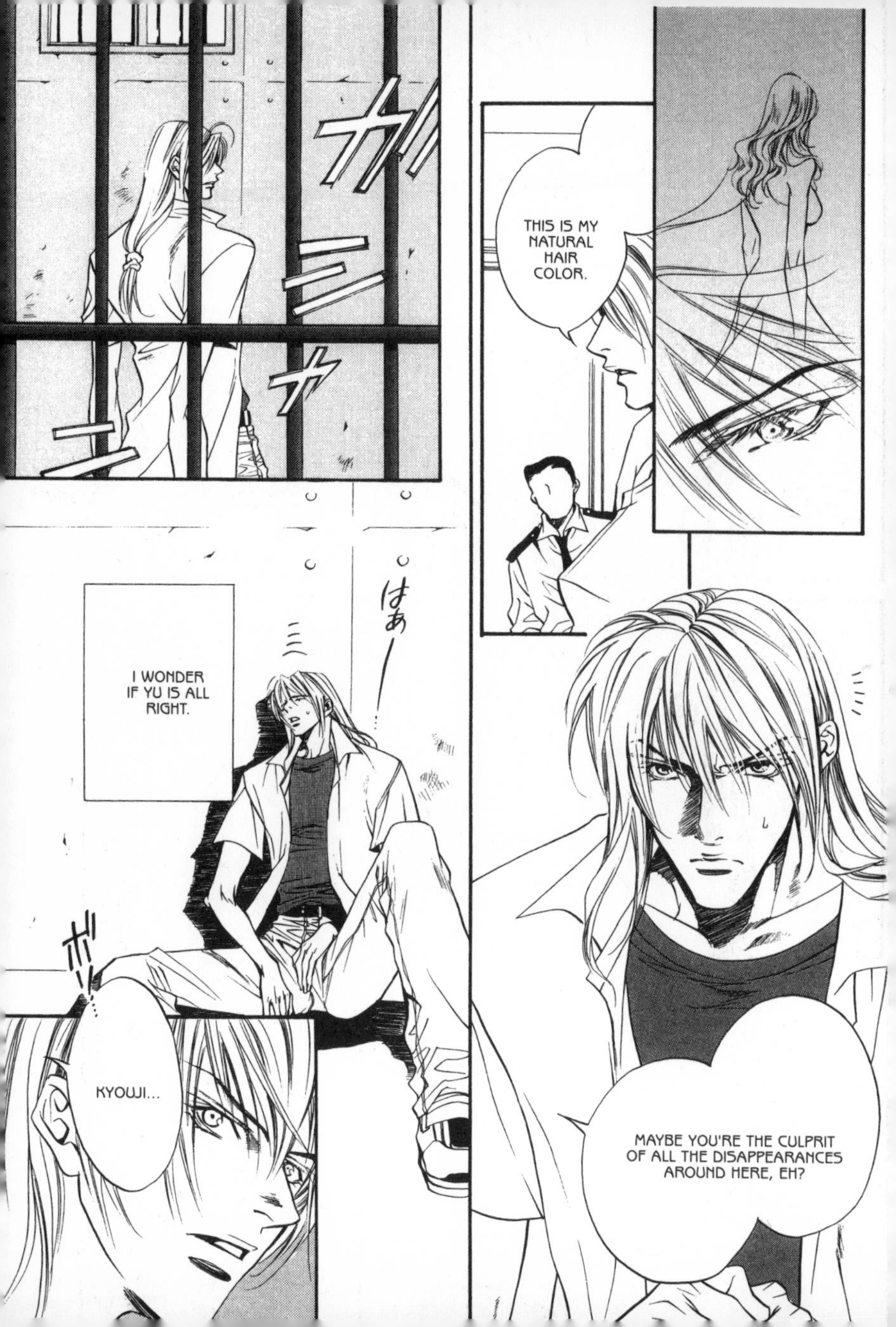

THIS IS MY NATURAL HAIR COLOR.
MAYBE YOU'RE THE CULPRIT OF ALL THE DISAPPEARANCES AROUND HERE, EH?
I WONDER IF YU IS ALL RIGHT.
はぁ
KYOUJI...

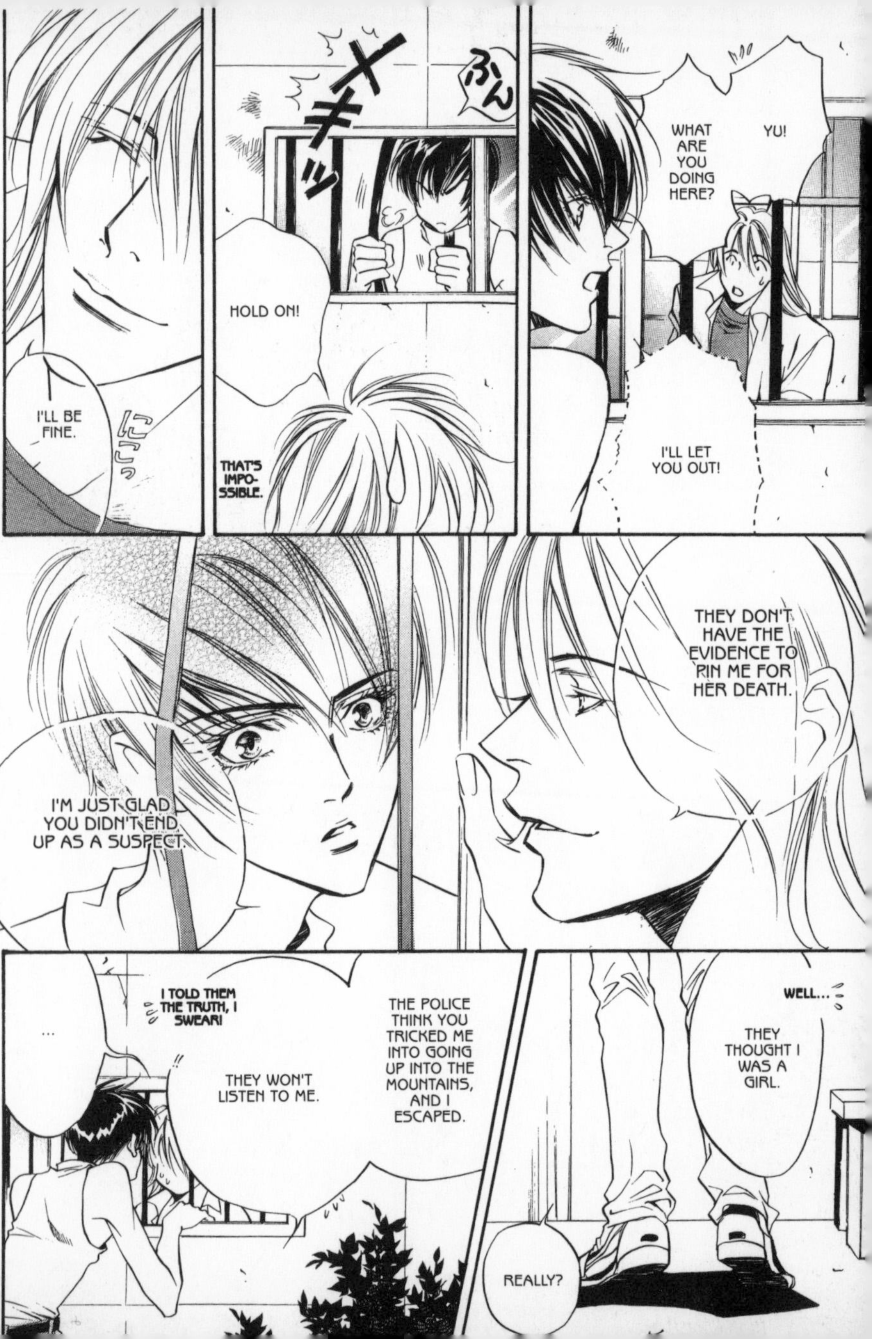
YU!
WHAT ARE YOU DOING HERE?
I'LL LET YOU OUT!
メキッ
ふん
HOLD ON!
THAT'S IMPOSSIBLE.
I'LL BE FINE.
にこっ
THEY DON'T HAVE THE EVIDENCE TO PIN ME FOR HER DEATH.
I'M JUST GLAD YOU DIDN'T END UP AS A SUSPECT.
WELL...
THEY THOUGHT I WAS A GIRL.
REALLY?
THE POLICE THINK YOU TRICKED ME INTO GOING UP INTO THE MOUNTAINS, AND I ESCAPED.
THEY WON'T LISTEN TO ME.
I TOLD THEM THE TRUTH, I SWEAR!
...

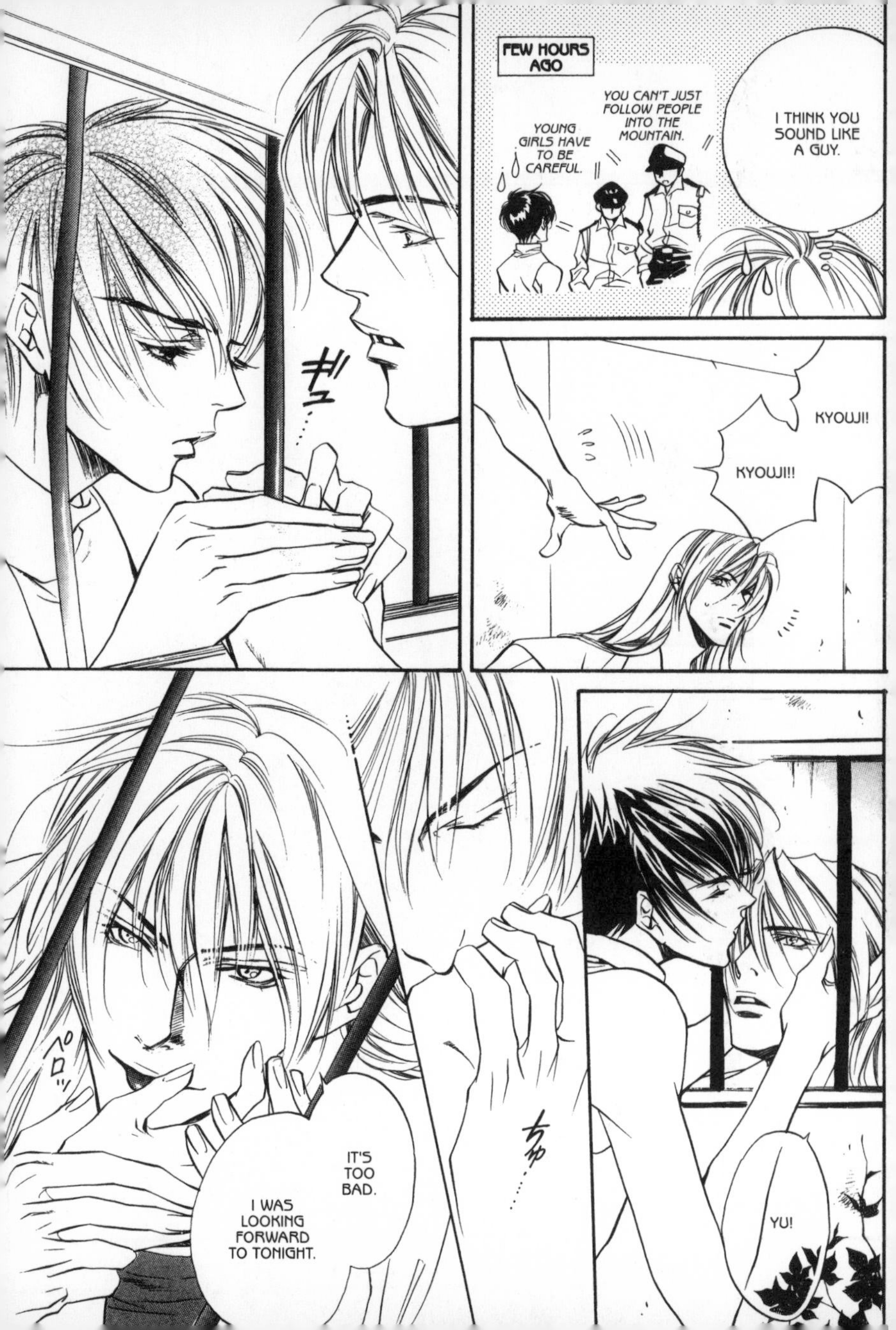
FEW HOURS AGO
I THINK YOU SOUND LIKE A GUY.
YOU CAN'T JUST FOLLOW PEOPLE INTO THE MOUNTAIN.
YOUNG GIRLS HAVE TO BE CAREFUL.
KYOUJI!
KYOUJI!!
YU!
IT'S TOO BAD.
I WAS LOOKING FORWARD TO TONIGHT.

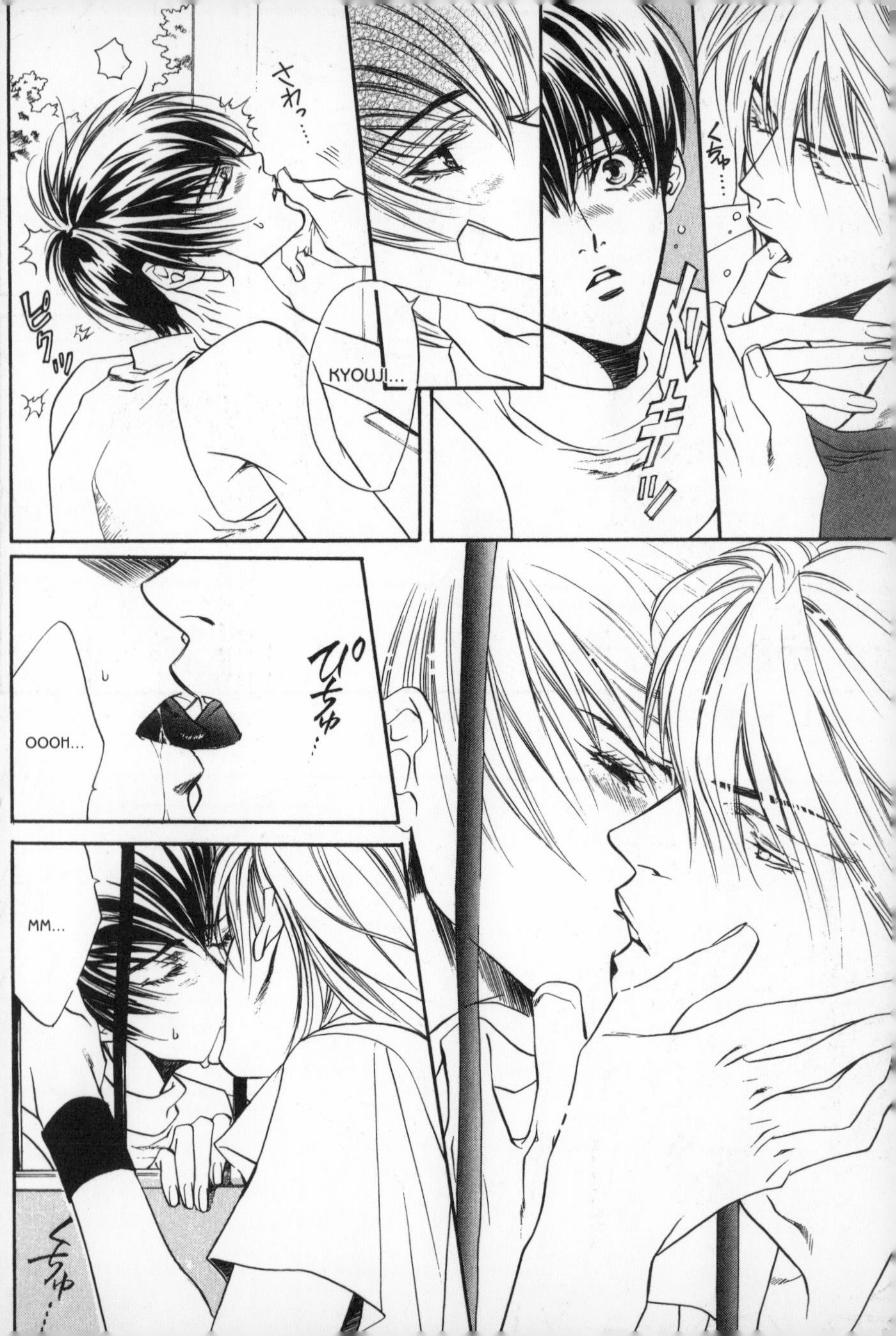

くちゅ…
ドキッ
KYOUJI...
さわっ…
ピクッ
ぴちゅ…
OOOH...
MM...
くちゅ…

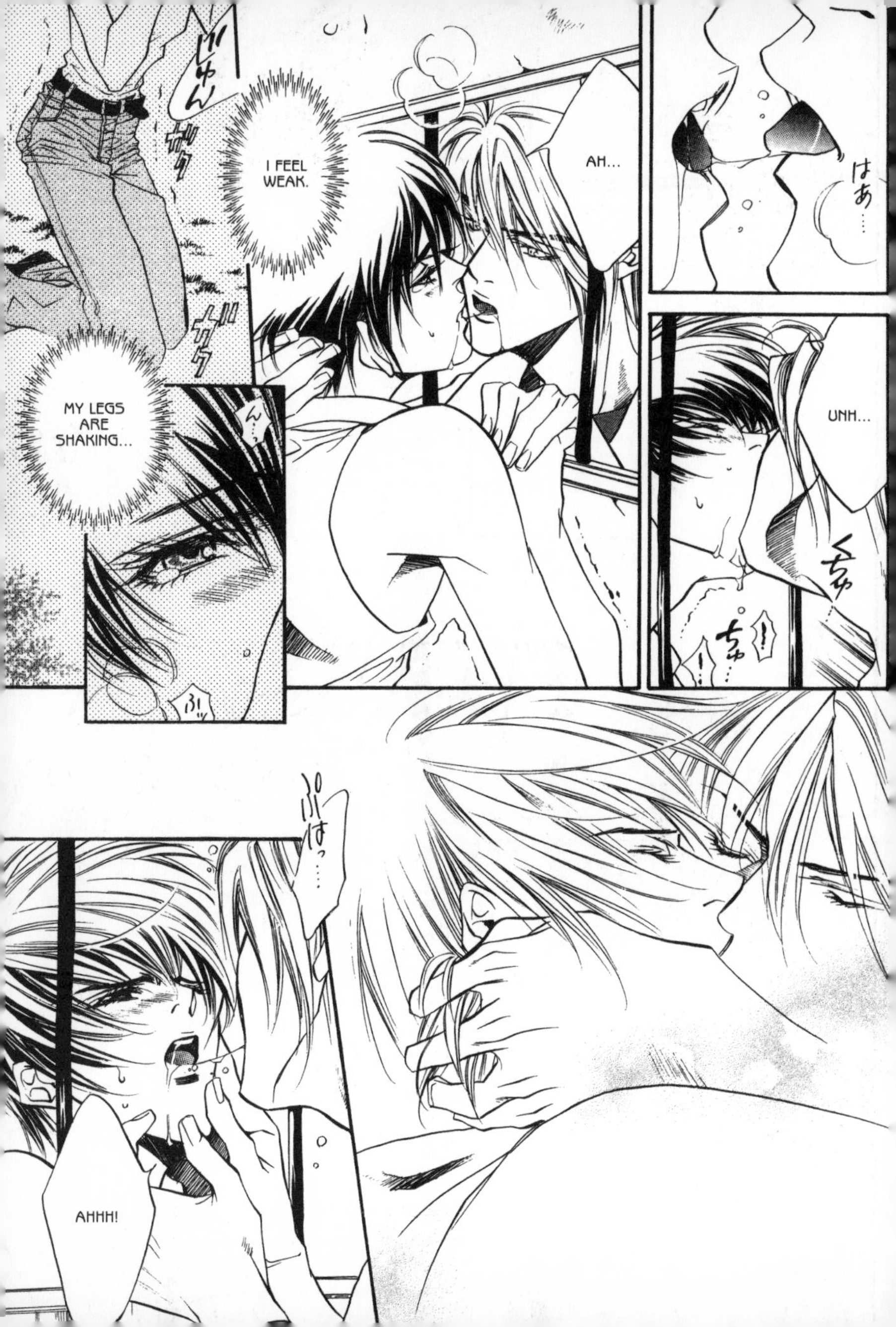

はあ…
AH...
UNH...
くちゅ
ちゅ…
!
I FEEL WEAK.
じゅん
ガク
ガクガク
MY LEGS ARE SHAKING...
ん…
ふっ
ぷはっ……
AHHH!

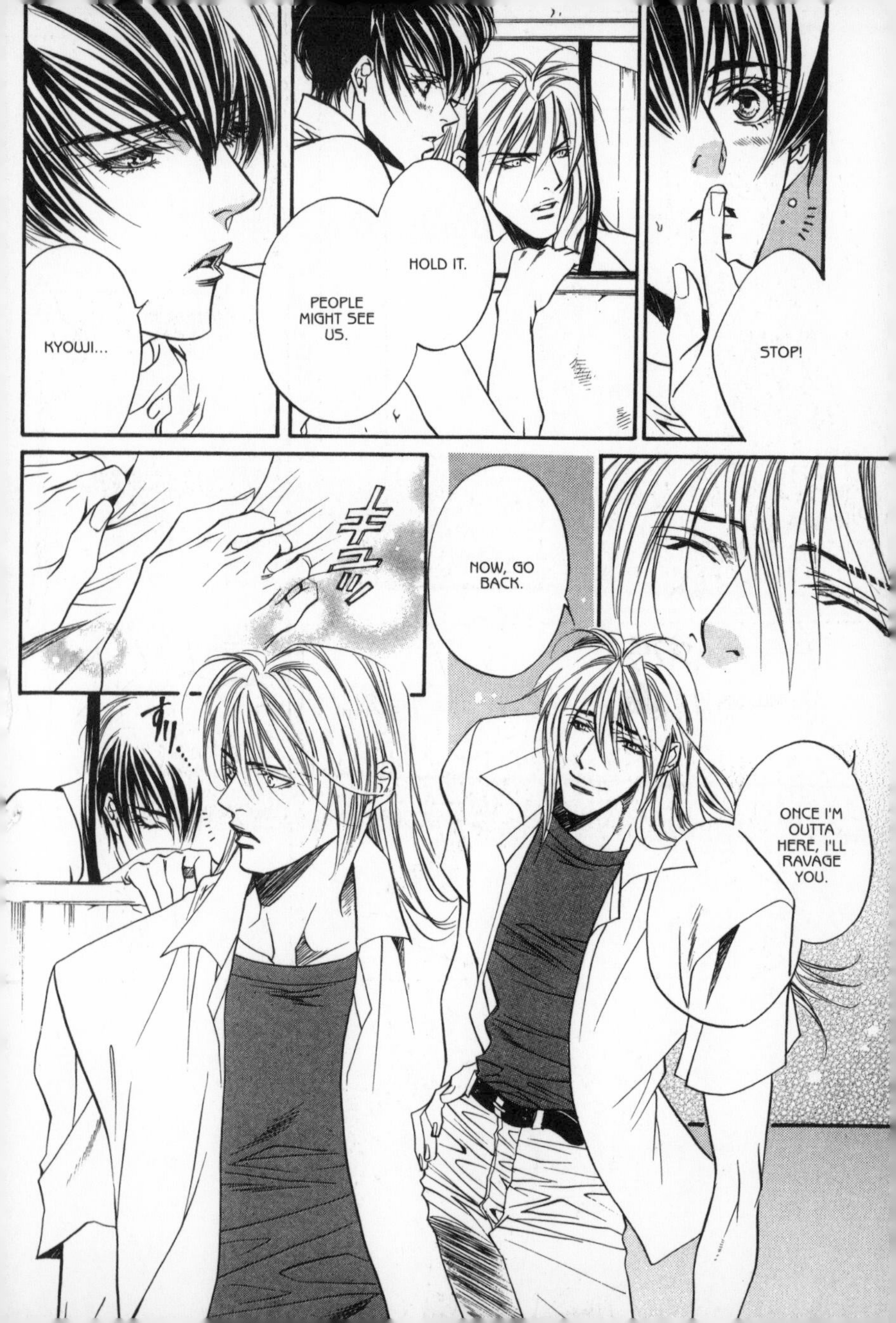
STOP!
HOLD IT.
PEOPLE MIGHT SEE US.
KYOUJI...
NOW, GO BACK.
キュッ
ONCE I'M OUTTA HERE, I'LL RAVAGE YOU.
すり…

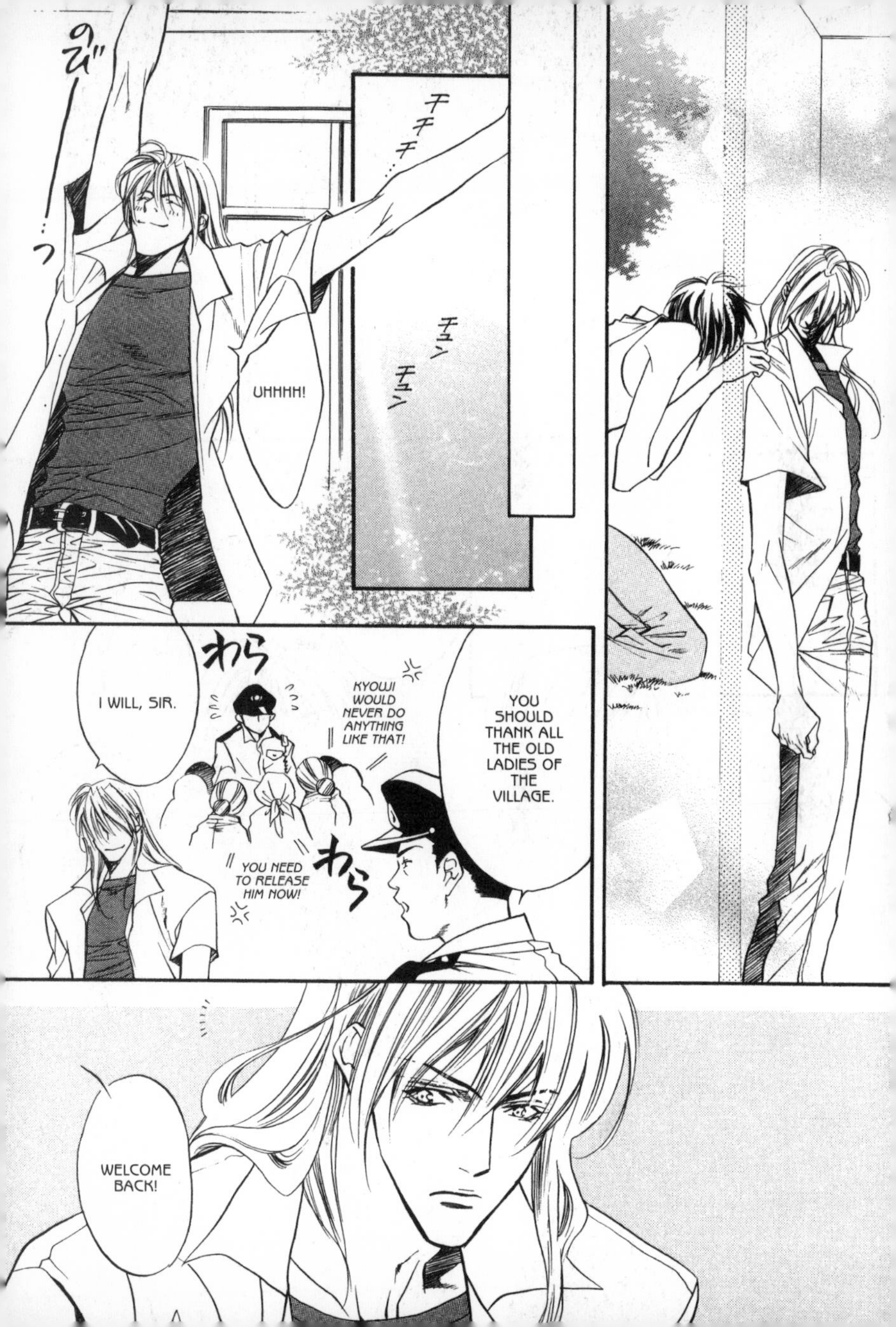
チチチ…
チュン
チュン
のび—…っ
UHHHH!
YOU SHOULD THANK ALL THE OLD LADIES OF THE VILLAGE.
KYOWJI WOULD NEVER DO ANYTHING LIKE THAT!
YOU NEED TO RELEASE HIM NOW!
わら
わら
I WILL, SIR.
WELCOME BACK!

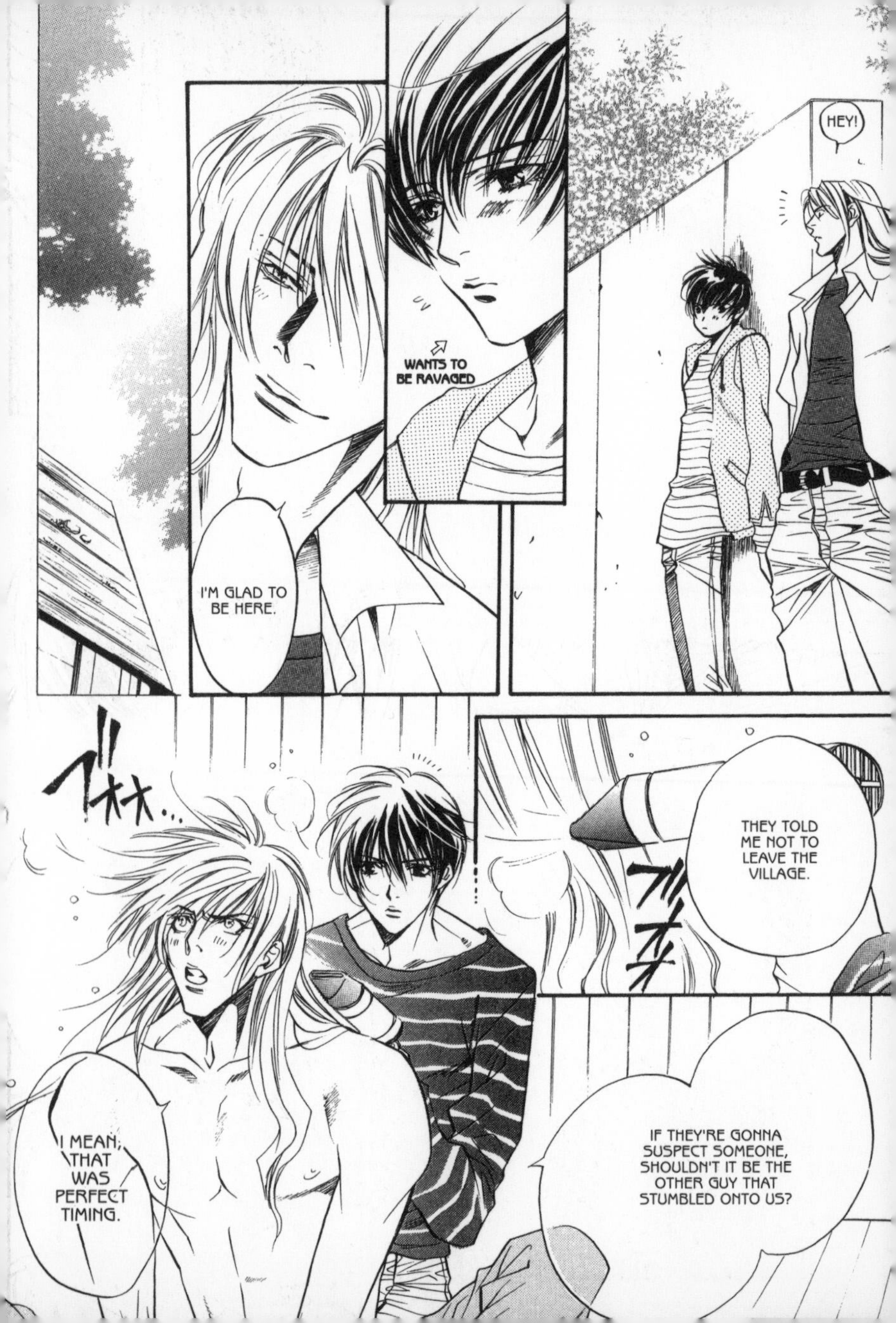
HEY!
WANTS TO BE RAVAGED
I'M GLAD TO BE HERE.
THEY TOLD ME NOT TO LEAVE THE VILLAGE.
IF THEY'RE GONNA SUSPECT SOMEONE, SHOULDN'T IT BE THE OTHER GUY THAT STUMBLED ONTO US?
I MEAN, THAT WAS PERFECT TIMING.

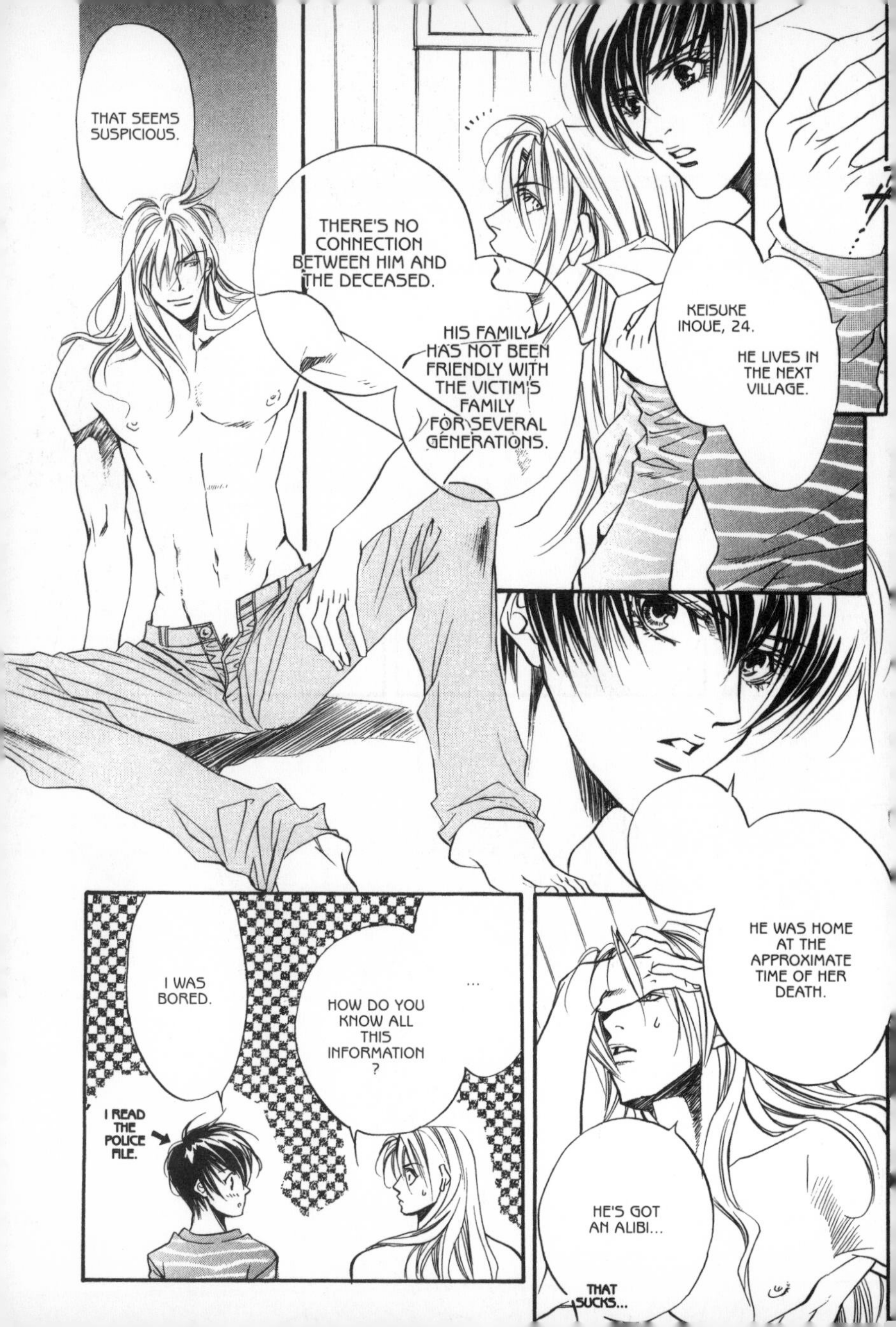
KEISUKE INOUE, 24.
HE LIVES IN THE NEXT VILLAGE.
THERE'S NO CONNECTION BETWEEN HIM AND THE DECEASED.
HIS FAMILY HAS NOT BEEN FRIENDLY WITH THE VICTIM'S FAMILY FOR SEVERAL GENERATIONS.
THAT SEEMS SUSPICIOUS.
HE WAS HOME AT THE APPROXIMATE TIME OF HER DEATH.
HE'S GOT AN ALIBI...
THAT SUCKS...
...
HOW DO YOU KNOW ALL THIS INFORMATION ?
I WAS BORED.
I READ THE POLICE FILE.

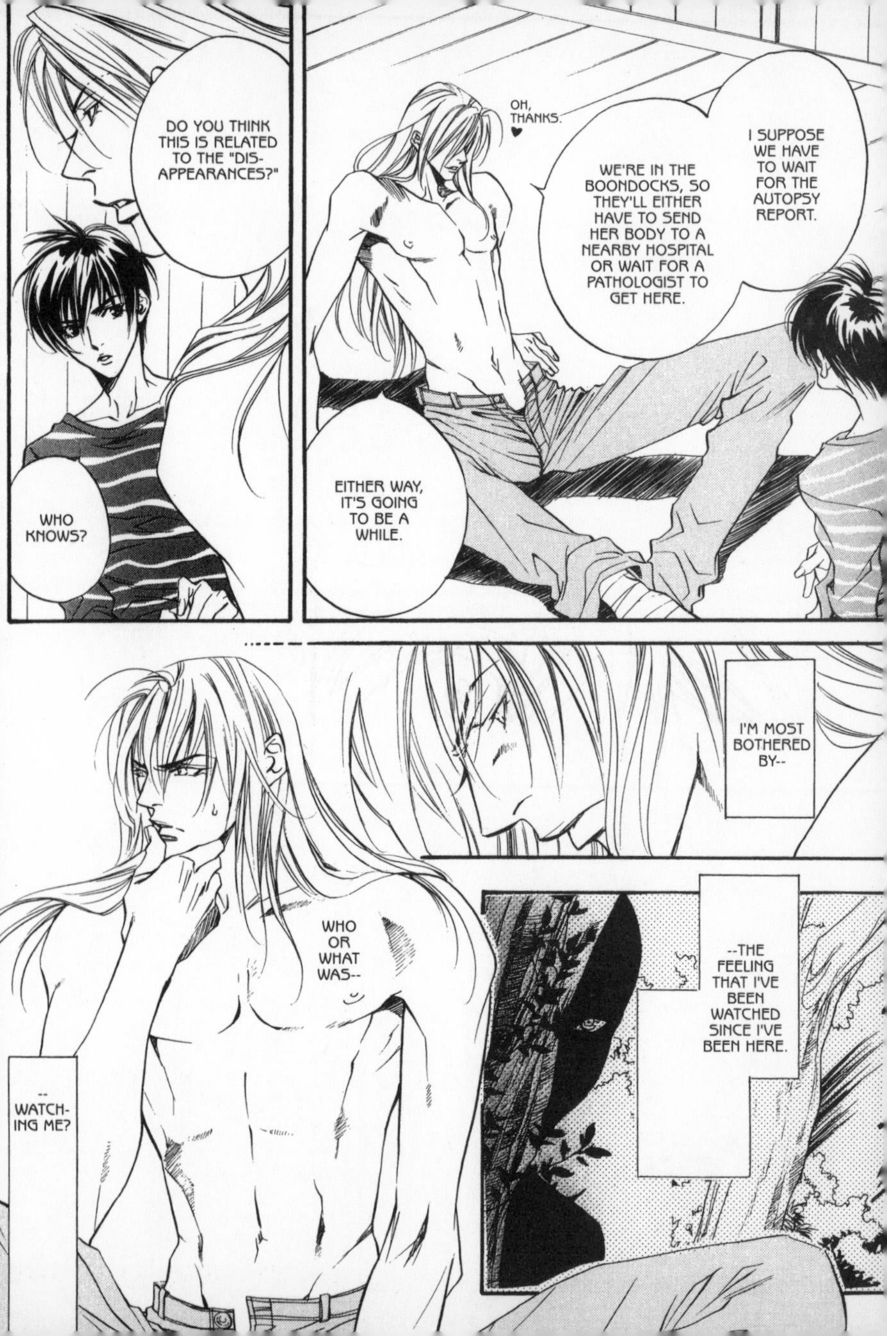

DO YOU THINK THIS IS RELATED TO THE "DIS-APPEARANCES?"
WHO KNOWS?
I SUPPOSE WE HAVE TO WAIT FOR THE AUTOPSY REPORT.
WE'RE IN THE BOONDOCKS, SO THEY'LL EITHER HAVE TO SEND HER BODY TO A NEARBY HOSPITAL OR WAIT FOR A PATHOLOGIST TO GET HERE.
OH, THANKS. ♥
EITHER WAY, IT'S GOING TO BE A WHILE.
I'M MOST BOTHERED BY--
--THE FEELING THAT I'VE BEEN WATCHED SINCE I'VE BEEN HERE.
WHO OR WHAT WAS--
--WATCHING ME?

I can't stop loving you ■■■■

I can't stop loving you ■ ■ ■ ■

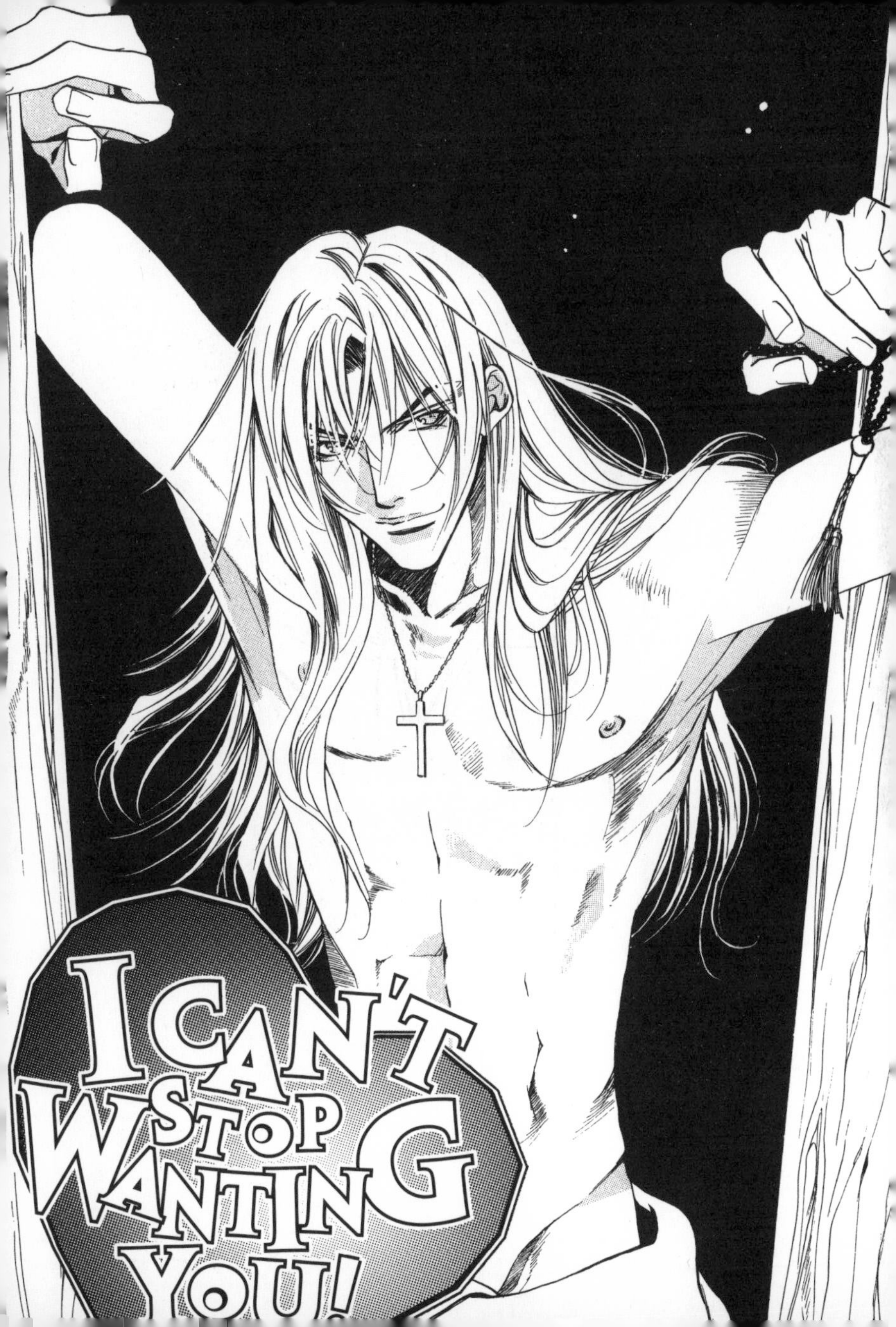
I CAN'T STOP WANTING YOU!

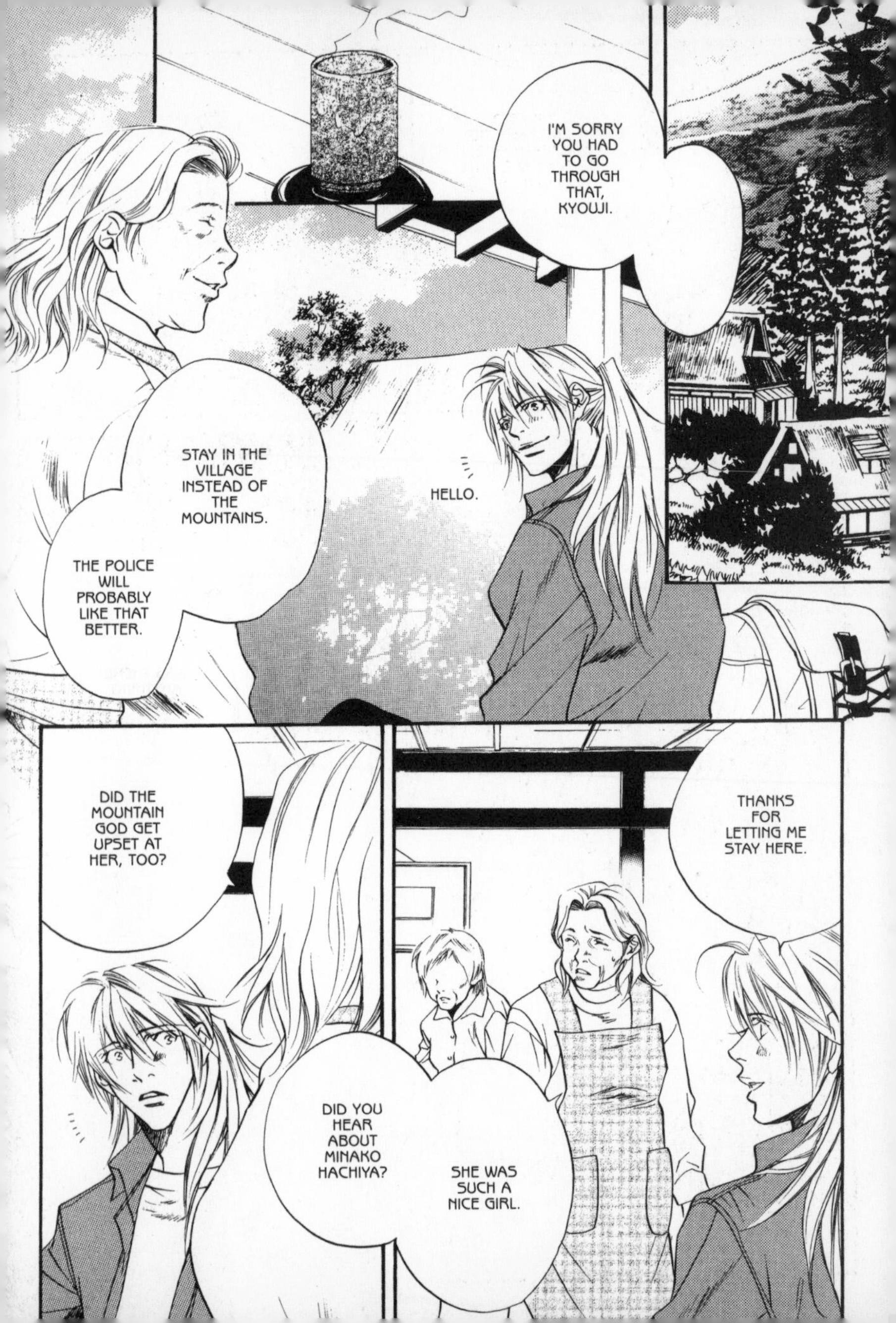
I'M SORRY YOU HAD TO GO THROUGH THAT, KYOUJI.
HELLO.
STAY IN THE VILLAGE INSTEAD OF THE MOUNTAINS.
THE POLICE WILL PROBABLY LIKE THAT BETTER.
THANKS FOR LETTING ME STAY HERE.
SHE WAS SUCH A NICE GIRL.
DID YOU HEAR ABOUT MINAKO HACHIYA?
DID THE MOUNTAIN GOD GET UPSET AT HER, TOO?

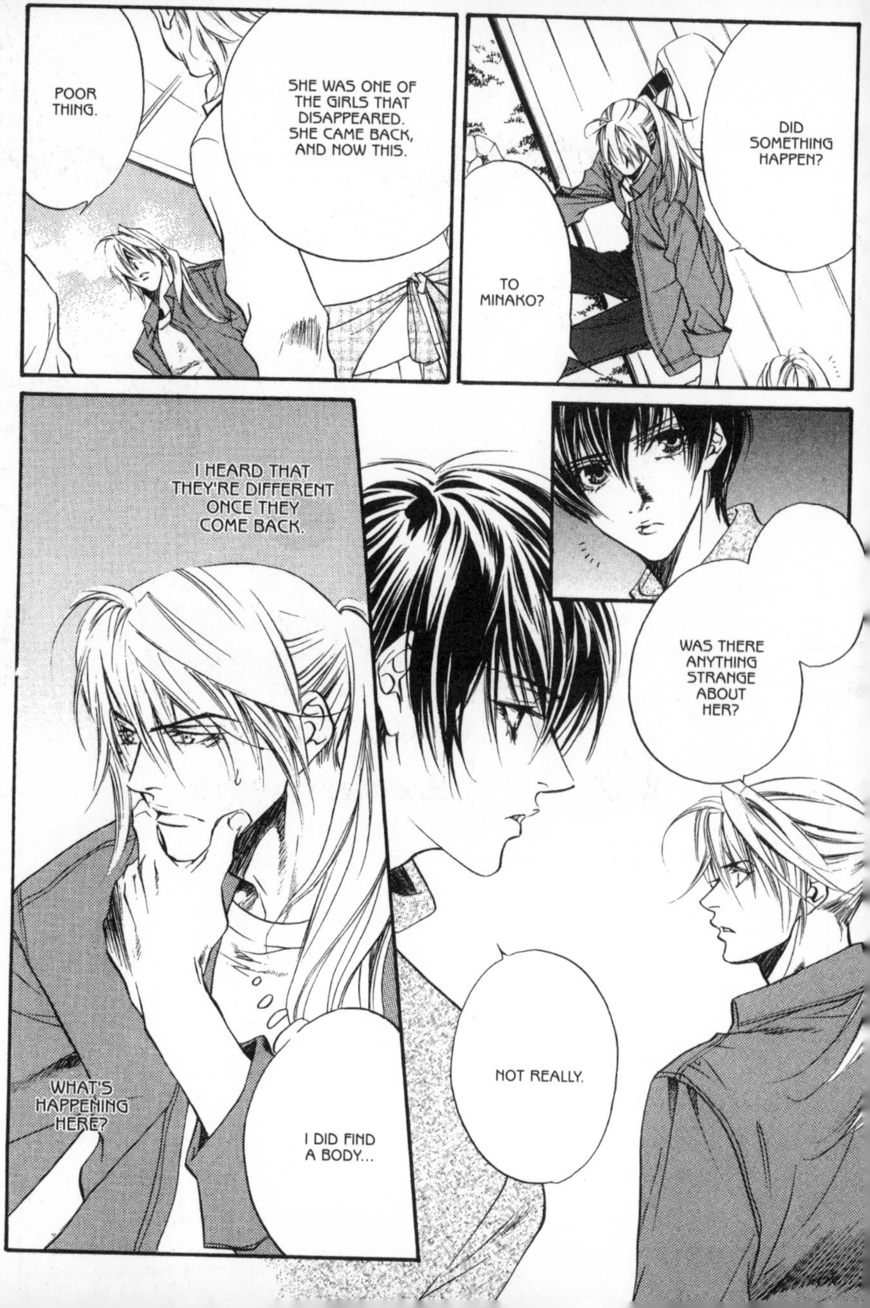
POOR THING.
SHE WAS ONE OF THE GIRLS THAT DISAPPEARED. SHE CAME BACK, AND NOW THIS.
DID SOMETHING HAPPEN?
TO MINAKO?
I HEARD THAT THEY'RE DIFFERENT ONCE THEY COME BACK.
WAS THERE ANYTHING STRANGE ABOUT HER?
NOT REALLY.
I DID FIND A BODY...
WHAT'S HAPPENING HERE?

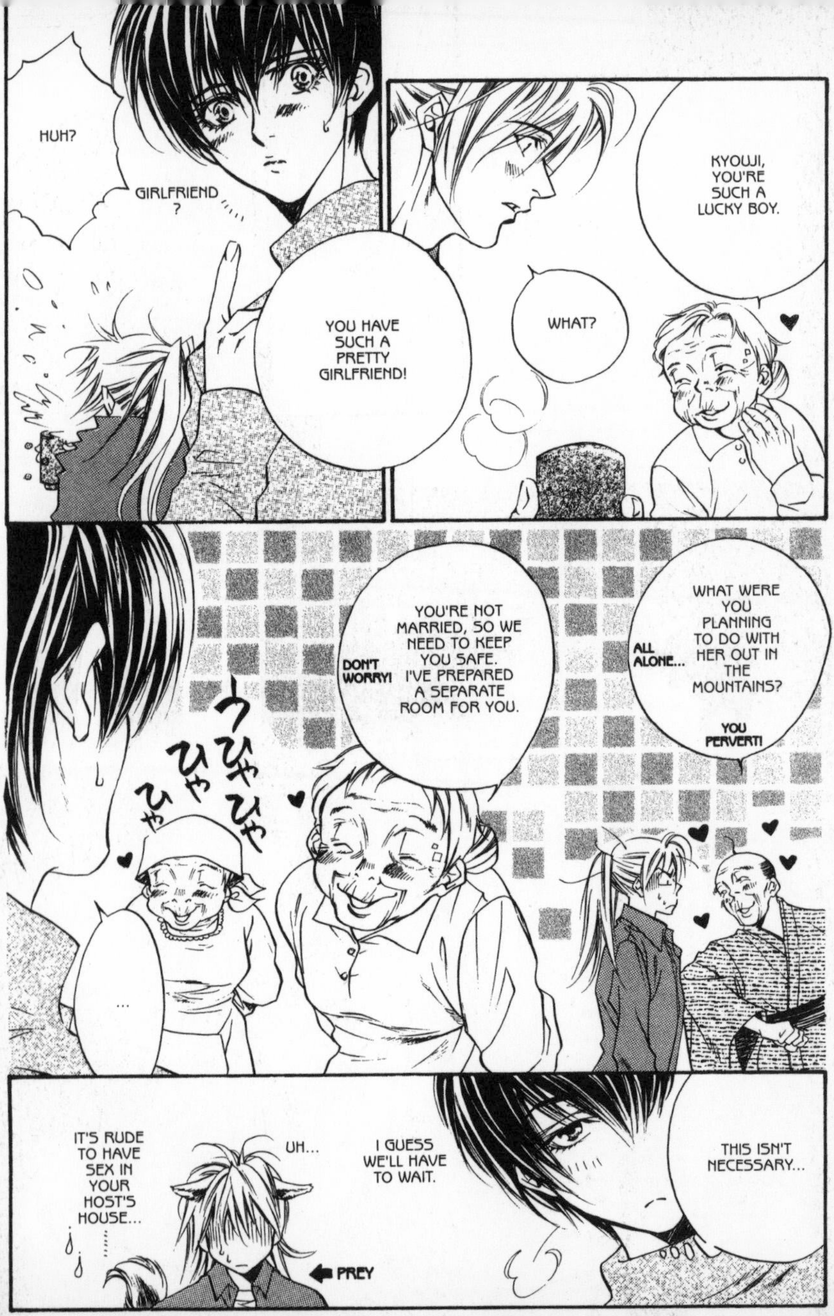
KYOUJI, YOU'RE SUCH A LUCKY BOY.
WHAT?
YOU HAVE SUCH A PRETTY GIRLFRIEND!
GIRLFRIEND?
HUH?
WHAT WERE YOU PLANNING TO DO WITH HER OUT IN THE MOUNTAINS?
ALL ALONE...
YOU PERVERT!
YOU'RE NOT MARRIED, SO WE NEED TO KEEP YOU SAFE.
DON'T WORRY! I'VE PREPARED A SEPARATE ROOM FOR YOU.
うひゃひゃひゃひゃ
...
THIS ISN'T NECESSARY...
I GUESS WE'LL HAVE TO WAIT.
UH...
IT'S RUDE TO HAVE SEX IN YOUR HOST'S HOUSE...
PREY

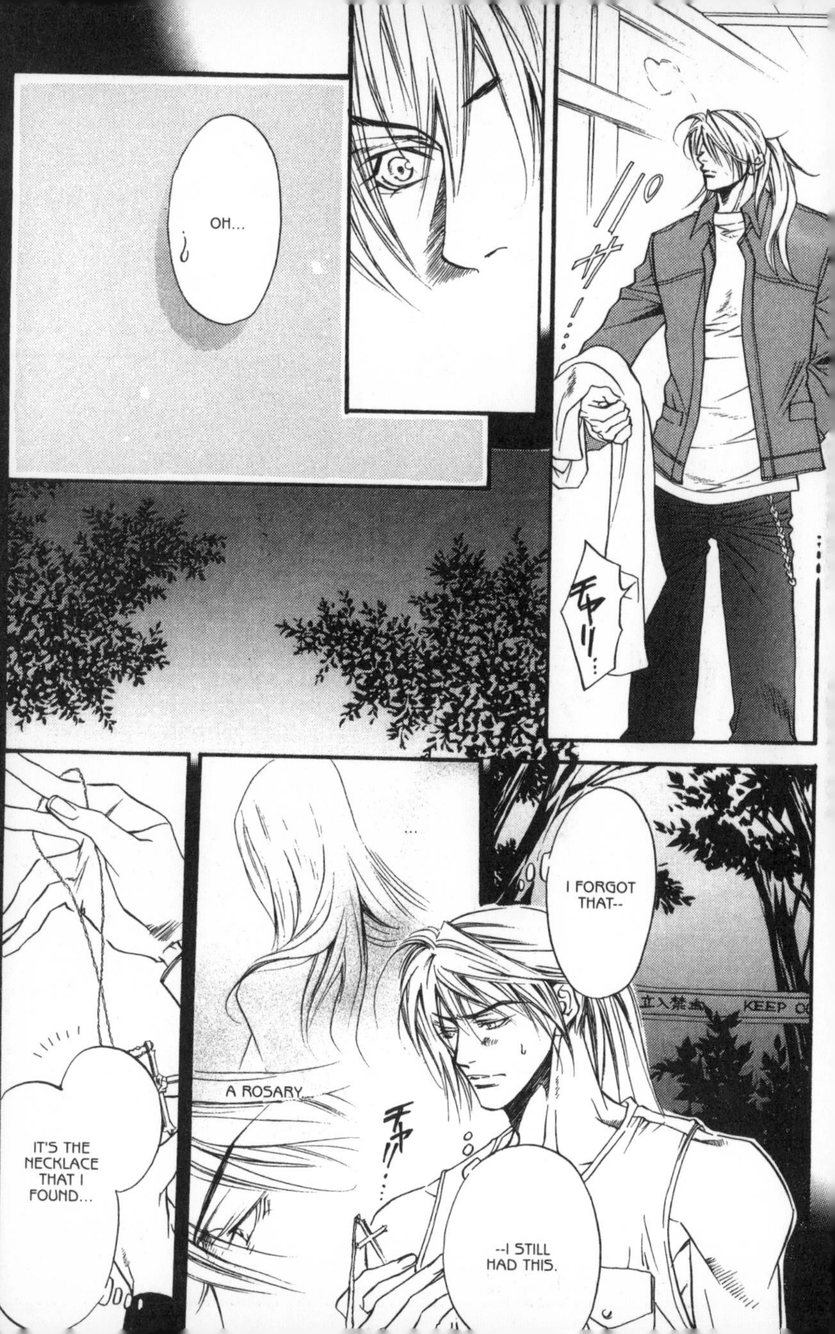

パサー…
チャリ…
OH...
I FORGOT THAT--
立入禁止
--I STILL HAD THIS.
...
A ROSARY
IT'S THE NECKLACE THAT I FOUND...

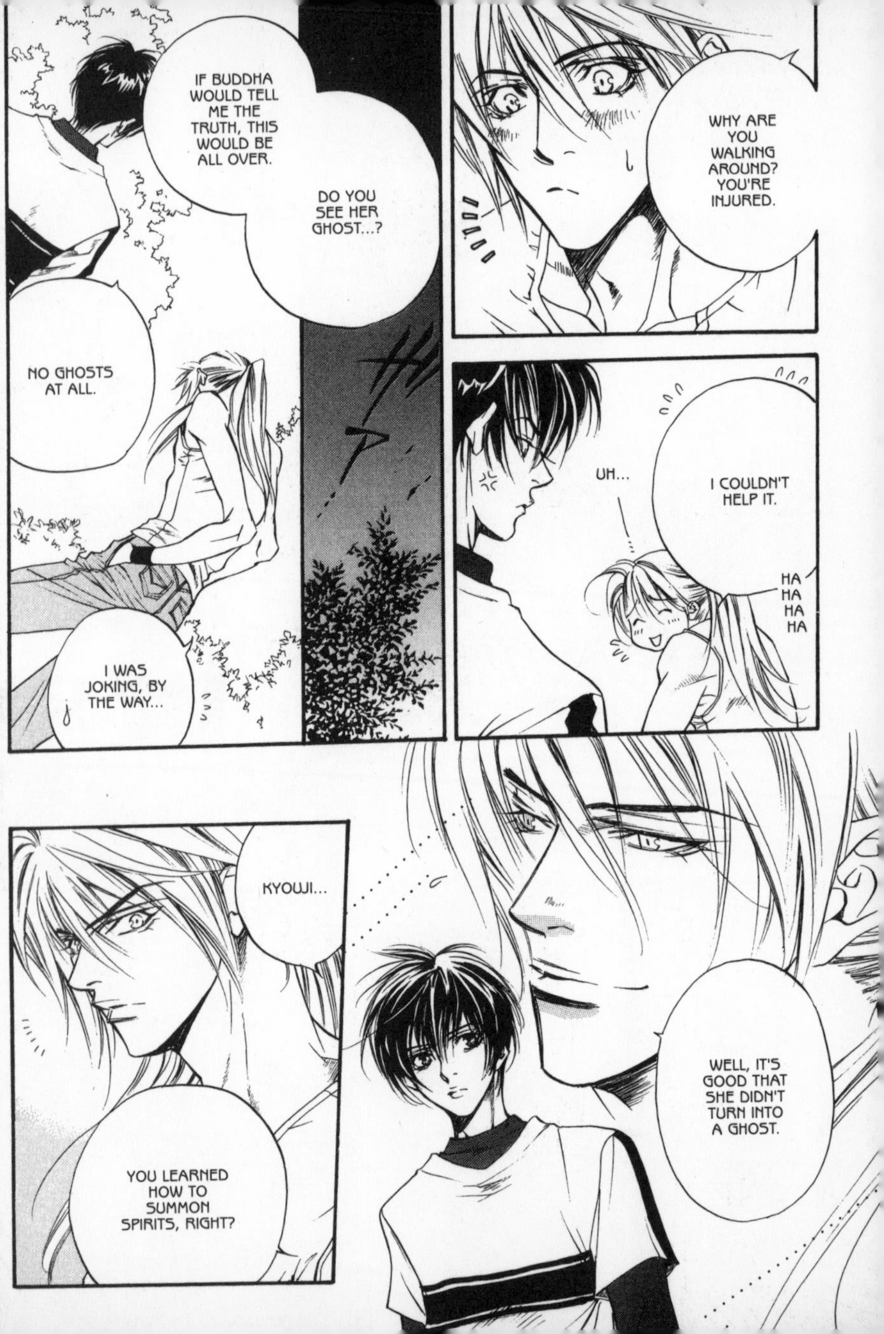
WHY ARE YOU WALKING AROUND? YOU'RE INJURED.
UH...
I COULDN'T HELP IT.
HA HA HA HA
IF BUDDHA WOULD TELL ME THE TRUTH, THIS WOULD BE ALL OVER.
DO YOU SEE HER GHOST...?
NO GHOSTS AT ALL.
I WAS JOKING, BY THE WAY...
WELL, IT'S GOOD THAT SHE DIDN'T TURN INTO A GHOST.
KYOUJI...
YOU LEARNED HOW TO SUMMON SPIRITS, RIGHT?

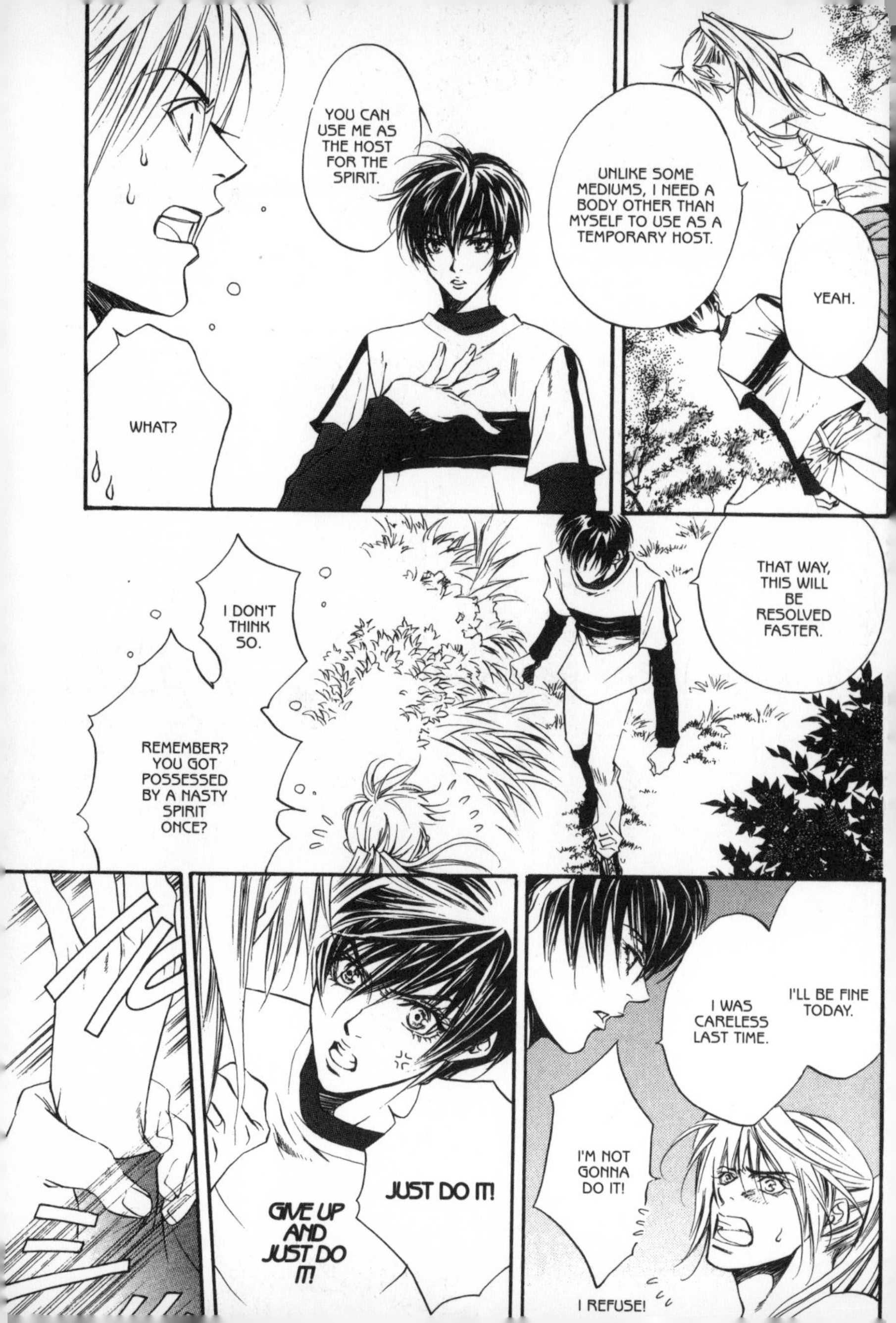

YOU CAN USE ME AS THE HOST FOR THE SPIRIT.
WHAT?
UNLIKE SOME MEDIUMS, I NEED A BODY OTHER THAN MYSELF TO USE AS A TEMPORARY HOST.
YEAH.
THAT WAY, THIS WILL BE RESOLVED FASTER.
I DON'T THINK SO.
REMEMBER? YOU GOT POSSESSED BY A NASTY SPIRIT ONCE?
I WAS CARELESS LAST TIME.
I'LL BE FINE TODAY.
I'M NOT GONNA DO IT!
I REFUSE!
JUST DO IT!
GIVE UP AND JUST DO IT!

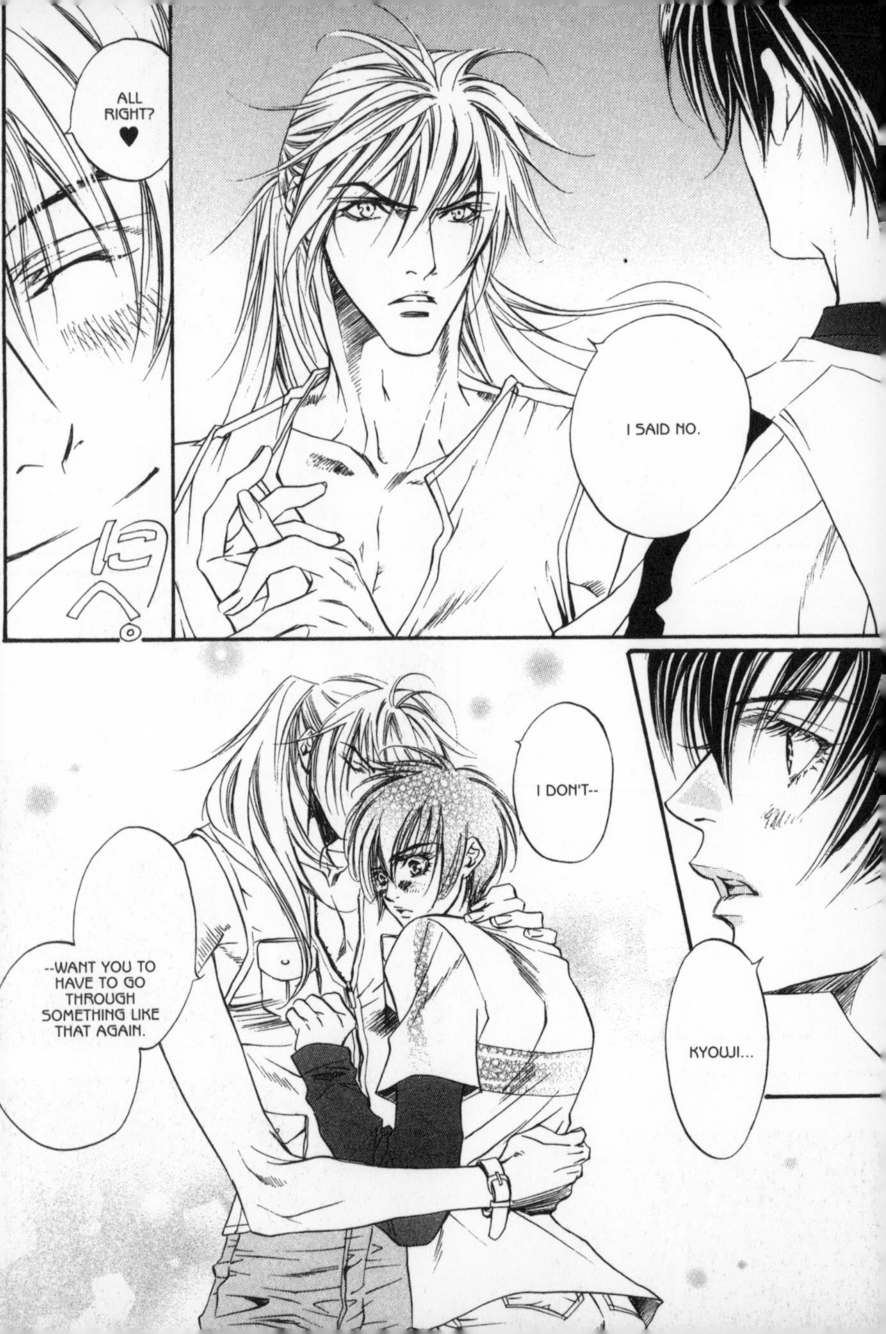
ALL RIGHT? ♥
にへ。
I SAID NO.
KYOUJI...
I DON'T--
--WANT YOU TO HAVE TO GO THROUGH SOMETHING LIKE THAT AGAIN.

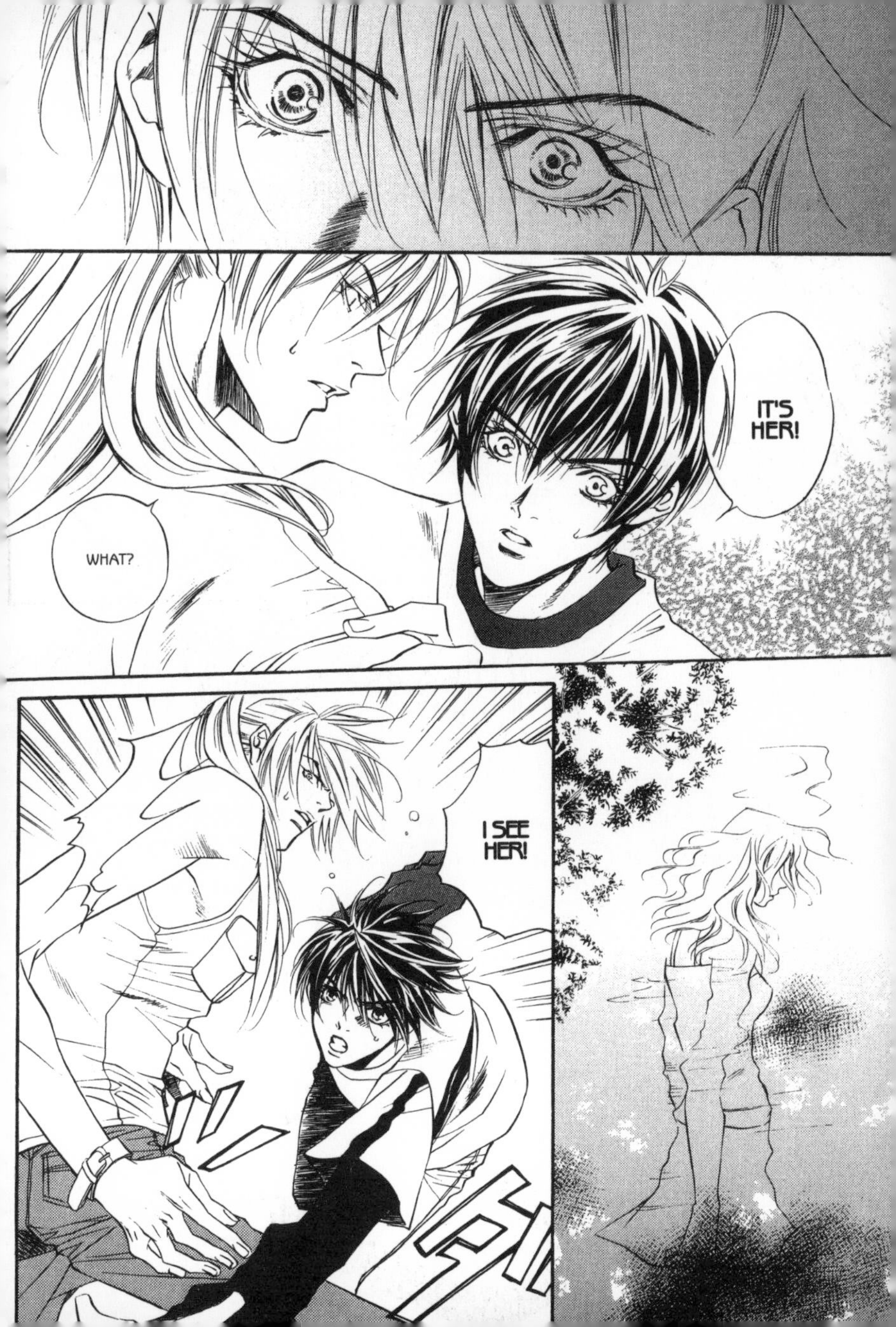
IT'S HER!
WHAT?
I SEE HER!

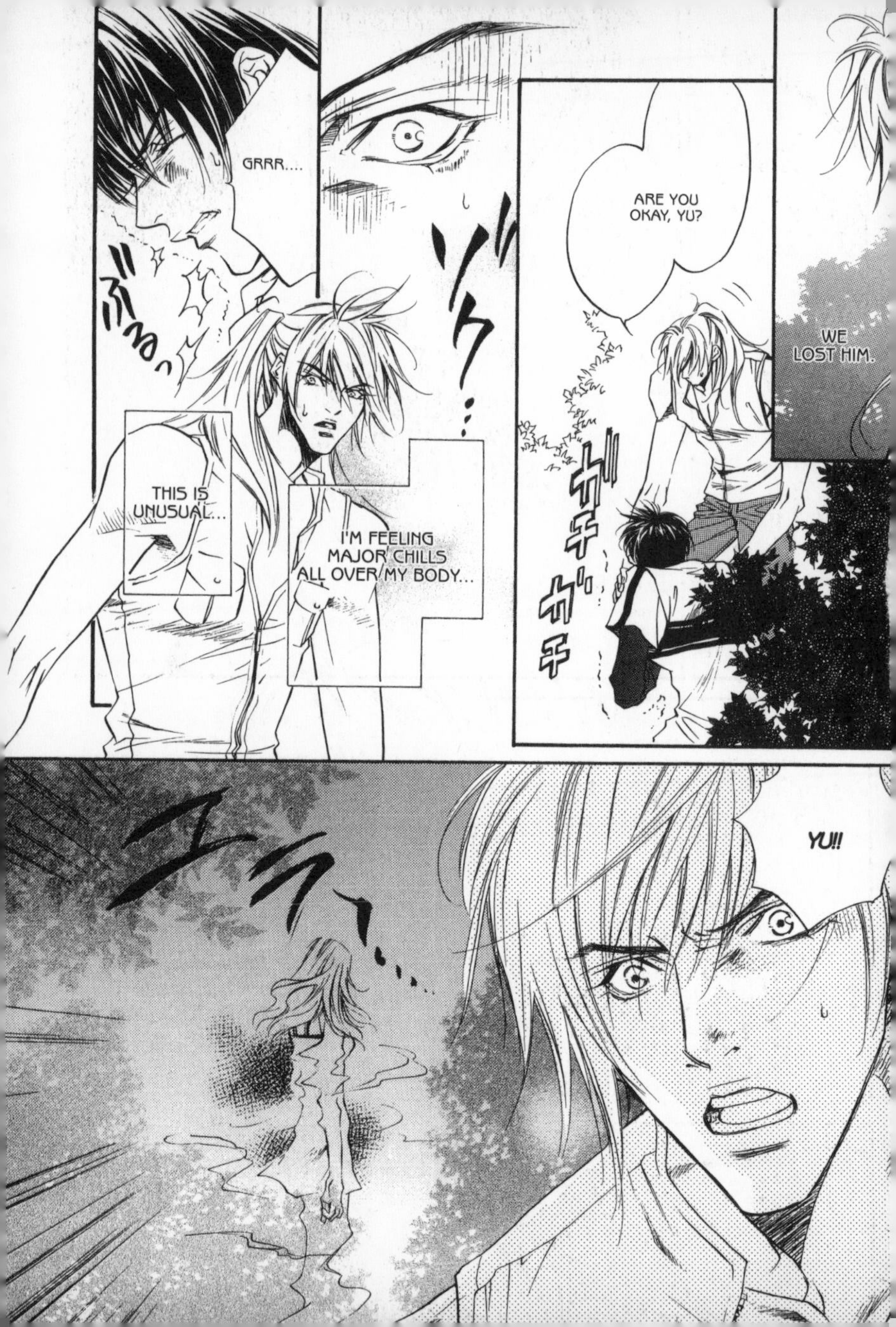
WE LOST HIM.
ARE YOU OKAY, YU?
GRRR....
THIS IS UNUSUAL...
I'M FEELING MAJOR CHILLS ALL OVER MY BODY...
YU!!

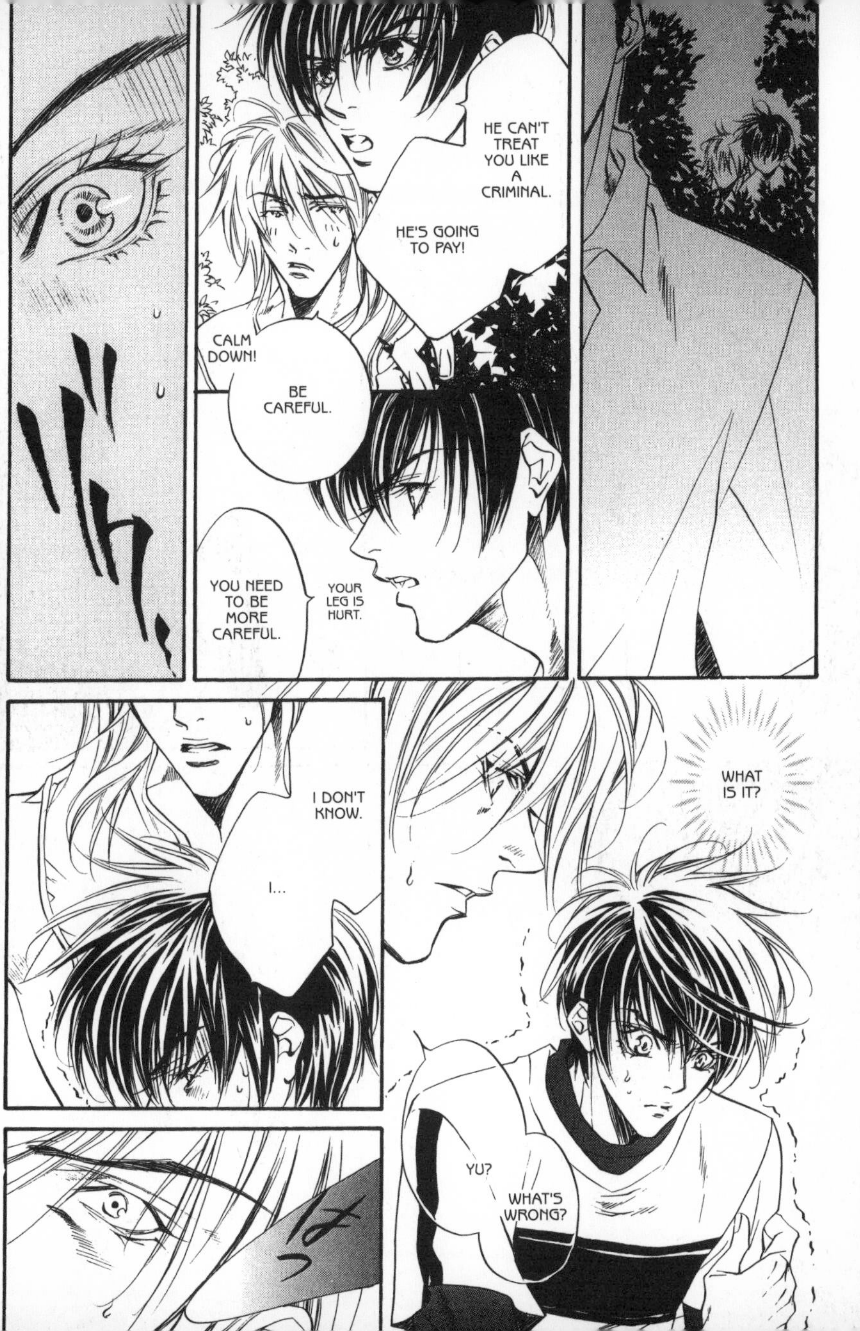
HE CAN'T TREAT YOU LIKE A CRIMINAL.
HE'S GOING TO PAY!
CALM DOWN!
BE CAREFUL.
YOUR LEG IS HURT.
YOU NEED TO BE MORE CAREFUL.
WHAT IS IT?
I DON'T KNOW.
I...
YU?
WHAT'S WRONG?

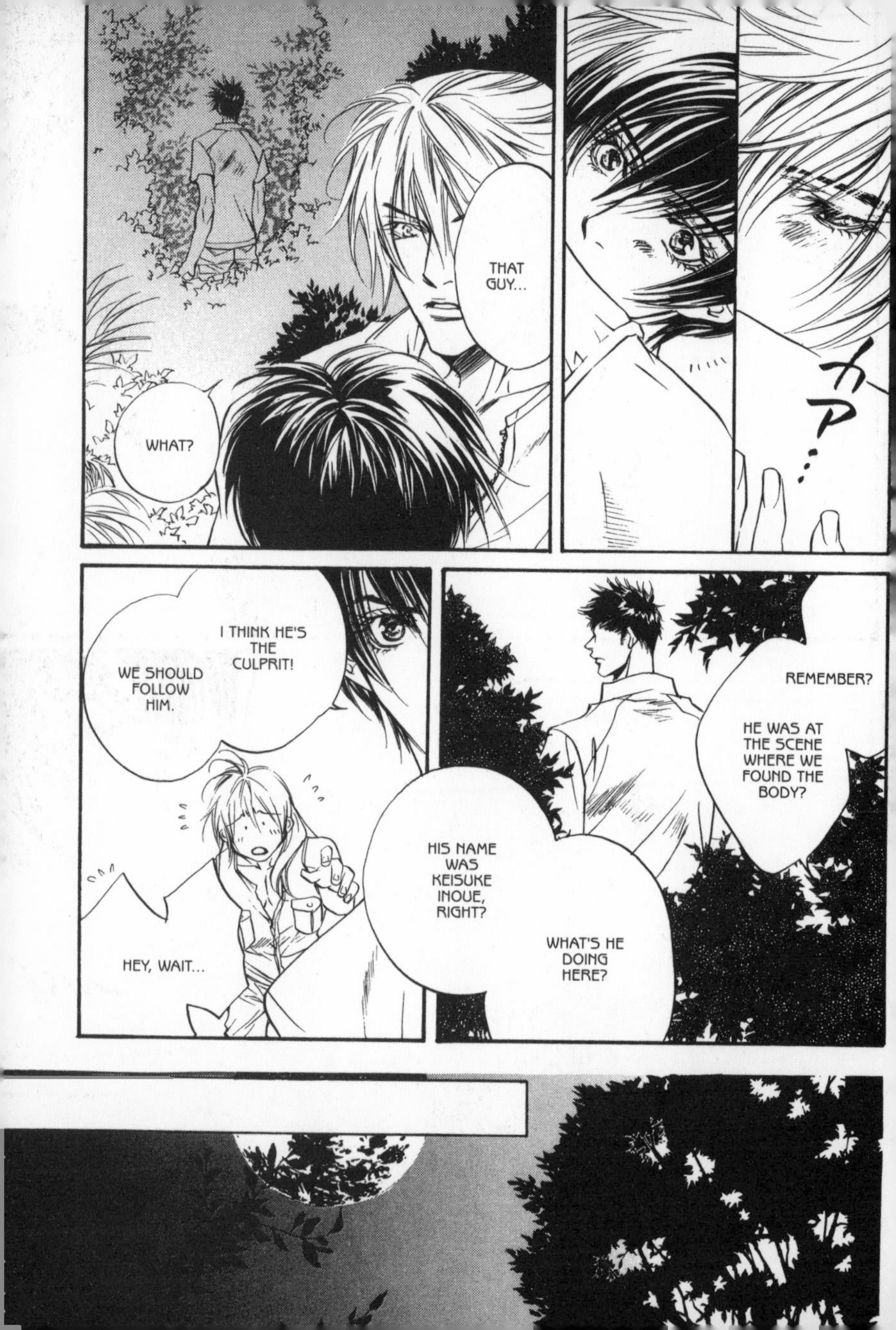
カア…
THAT GUY...
WHAT?
REMEMBER?
HE WAS AT THE SCENE WHERE WE FOUND THE BODY?
HIS NAME WAS KEISUKE INOUE, RIGHT?
WHAT'S HE DOING HERE?
I THINK HE'S THE CULPRIT!
WE SHOULD FOLLOW HIM.
HEY, WAIT...

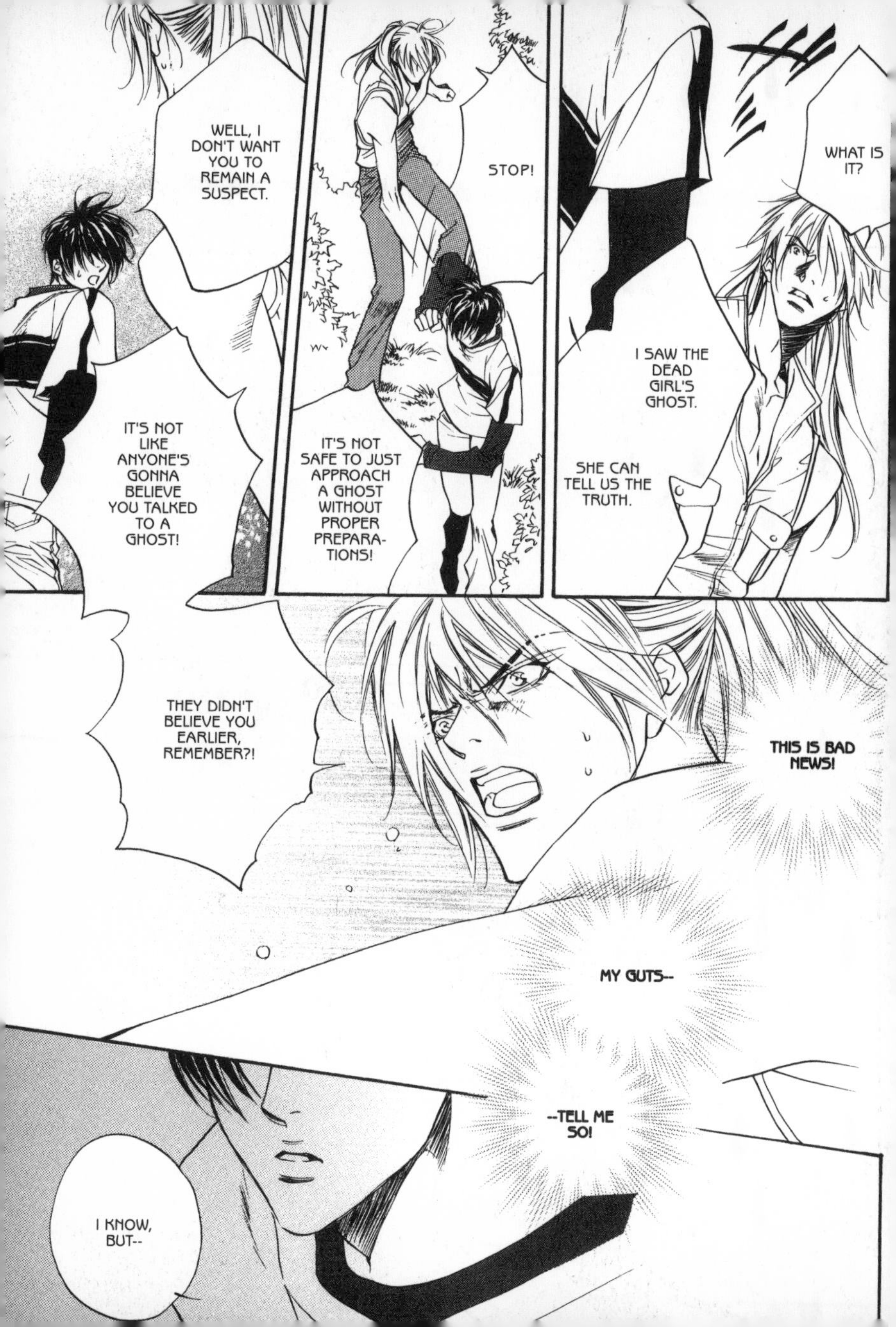
WHAT IS IT?
I SAW THE DEAD GIRL'S GHOST.
SHE CAN TELL US THE TRUTH.
STOP!
IT'S NOT SAFE TO JUST APPROACH A GHOST WITHOUT PROPER PREPARATIONS!
WELL, I DON'T WANT YOU TO REMAIN A SUSPECT.
IT'S NOT LIKE ANYONE'S GONNA BELIEVE YOU TALKED TO A GHOST!
THEY DIDN'T BELIEVE YOU EARLIER, REMEMBER?!
THIS IS BAD NEWS!
MY GUTS--
--TELL ME SO!
I KNOW, BUT--

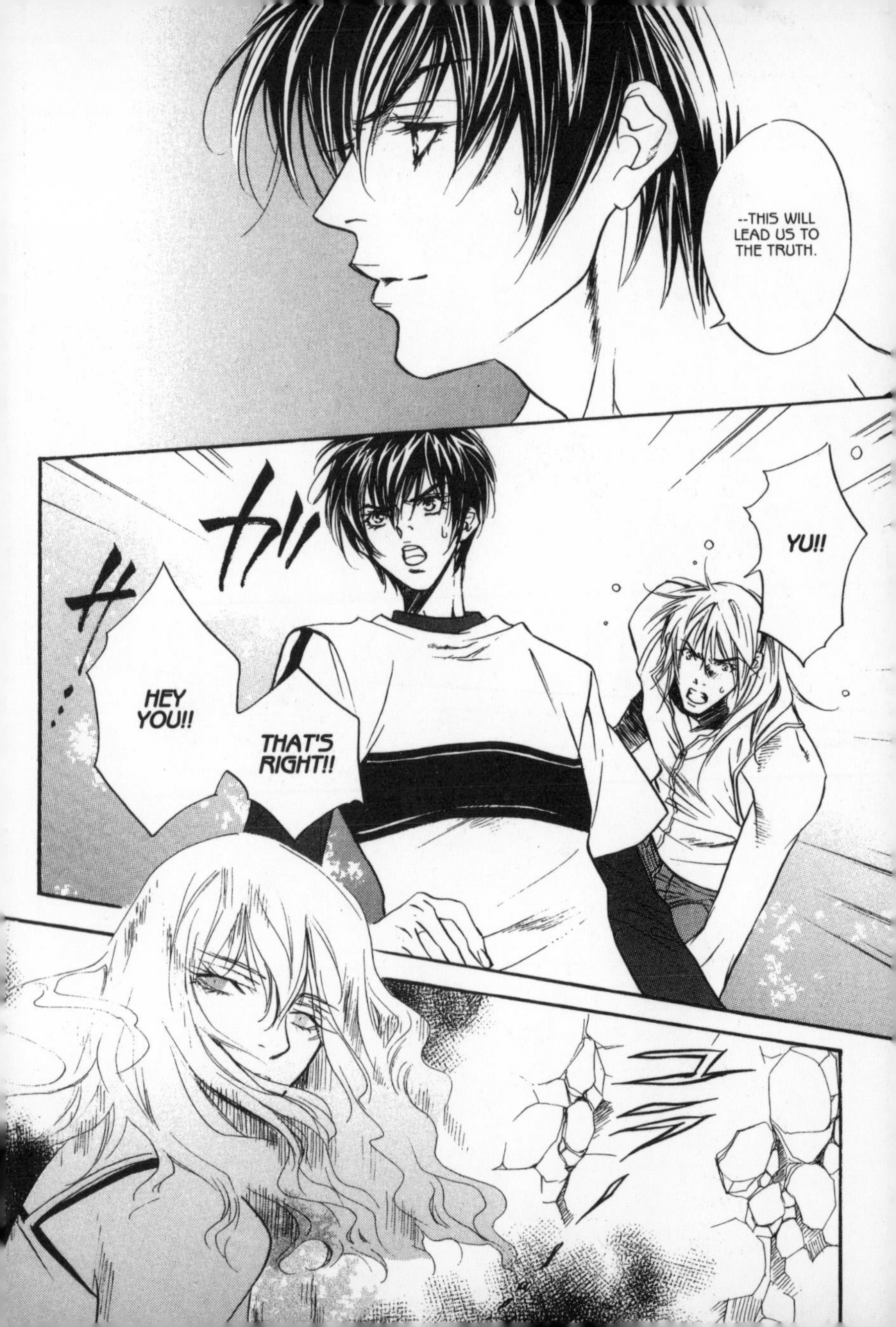
--THIS WILL LEAD US TO THE TRUTH.
YU!!
THAT'S RIGHT!!
HEY YOU!!

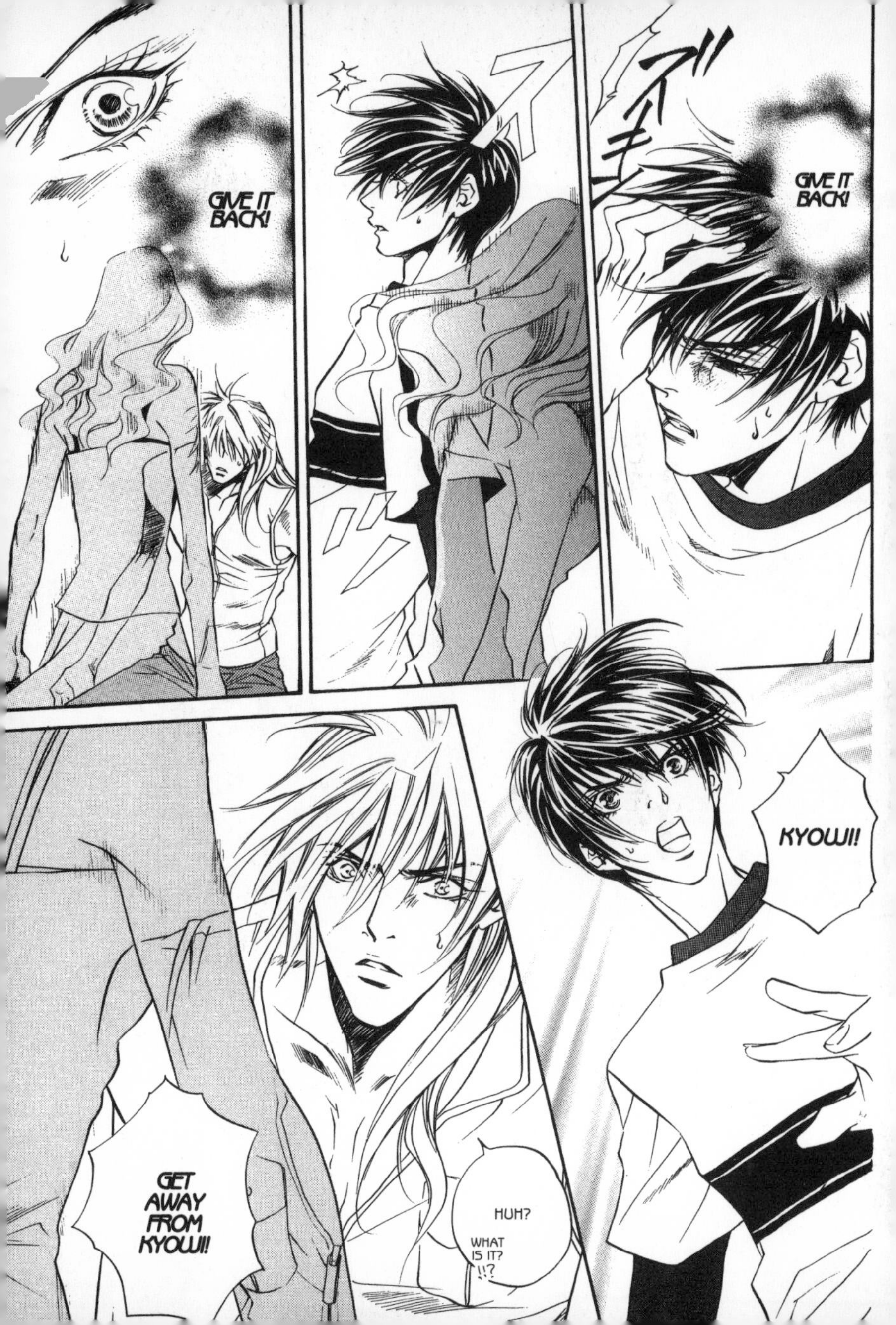
GIVE IT BACK!
GIVE IT BACK!
KYOJI!
HUH?
WHAT IS IT?
!!?
GET AWAY FROM KYOJI!

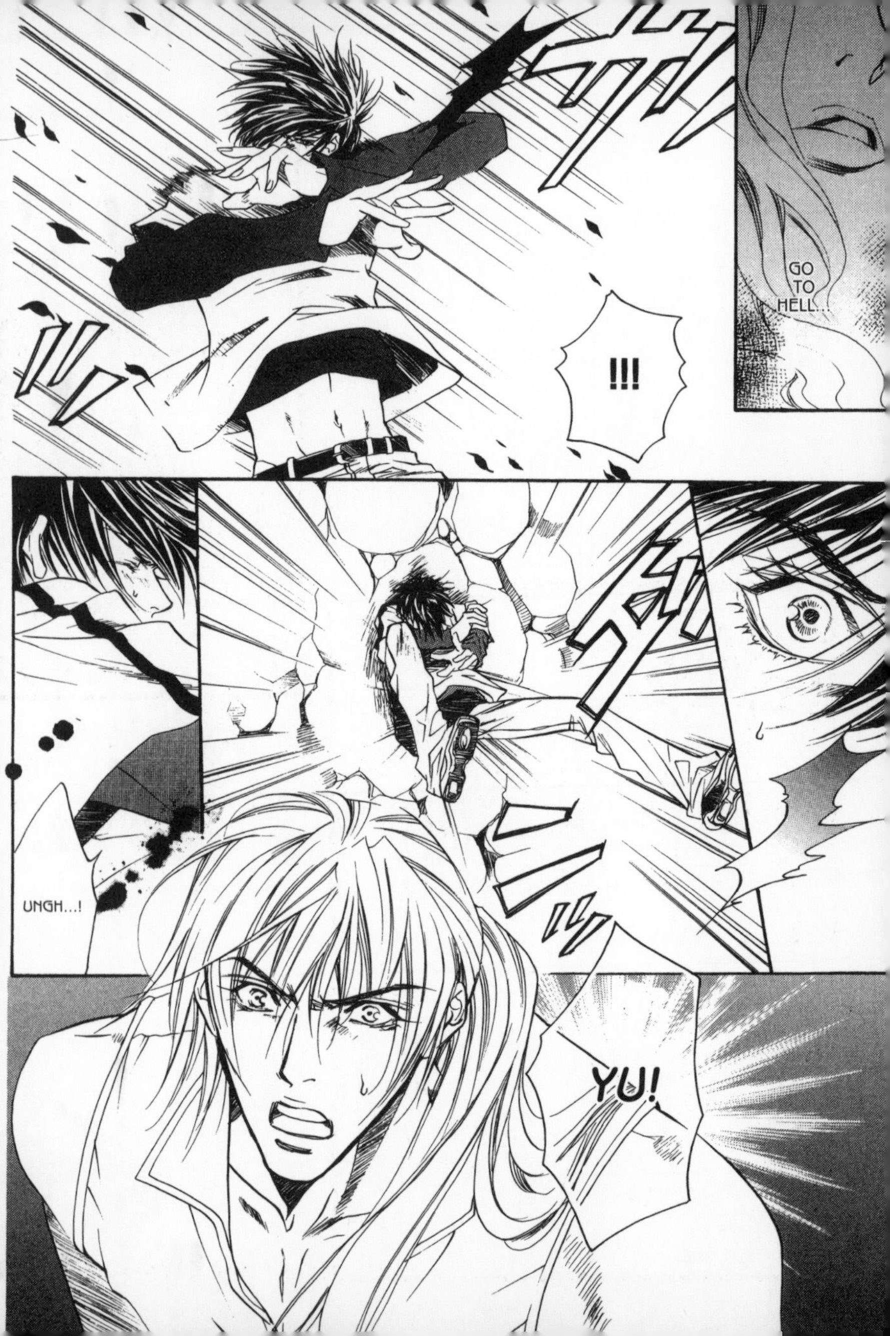
GO TO HELL...
!!!
UNGH...!
YU!

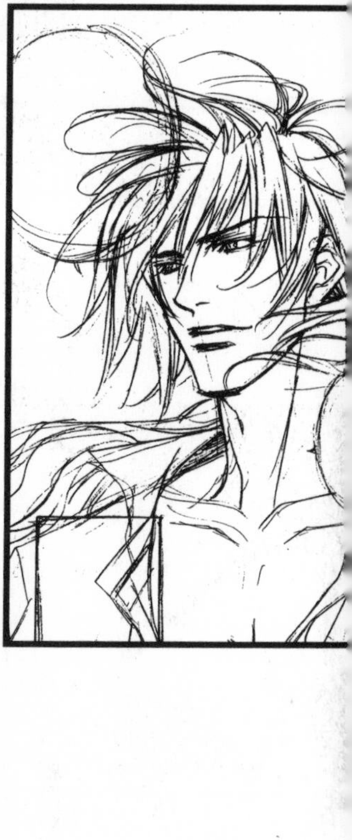

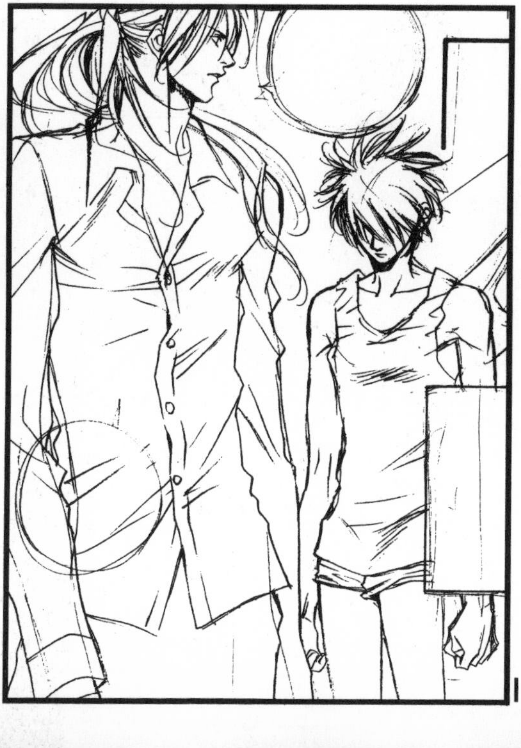

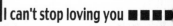

I can't stop loving you ■■■■

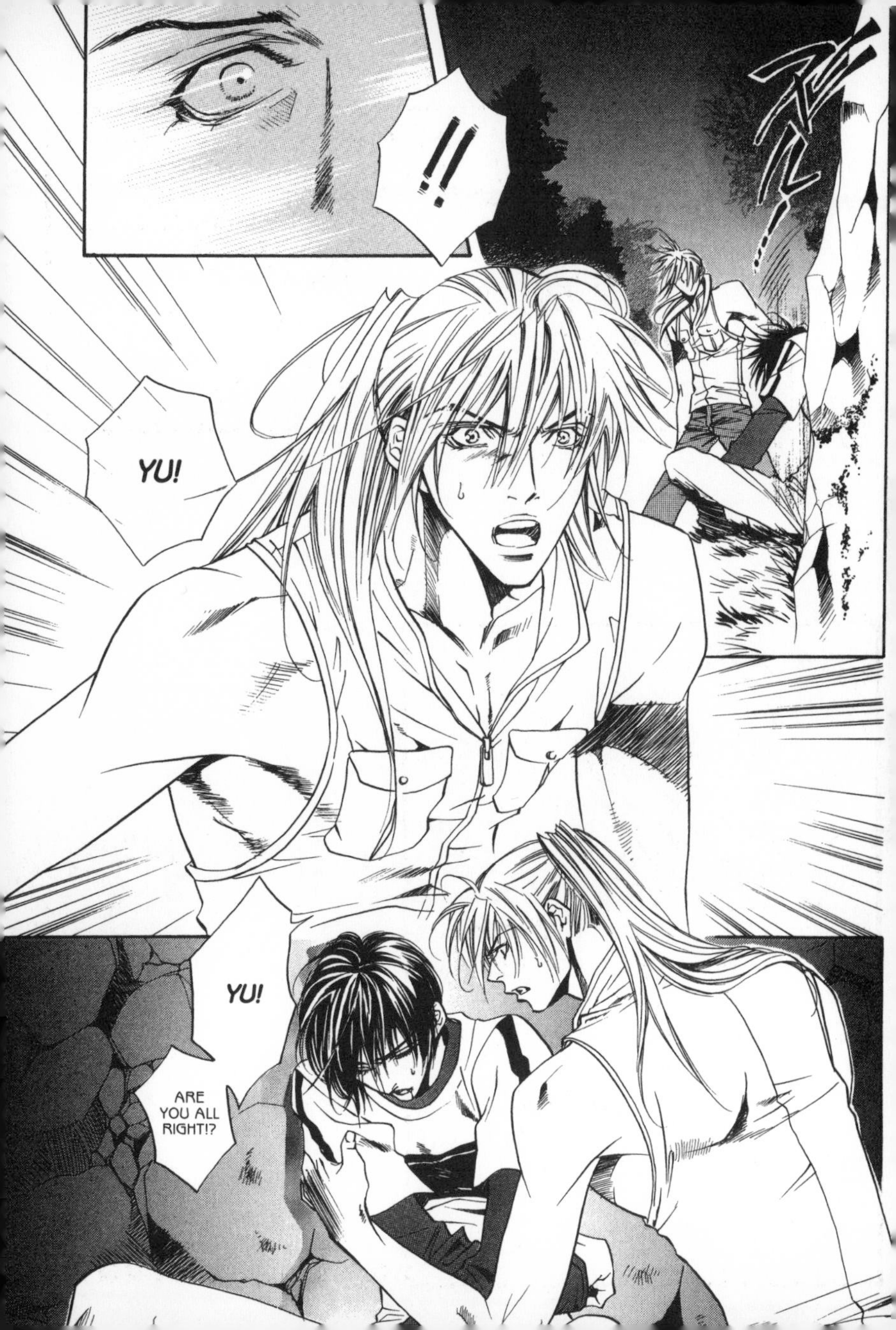
!!
YU!
YU!
ARE YOU ALL RIGHT!?

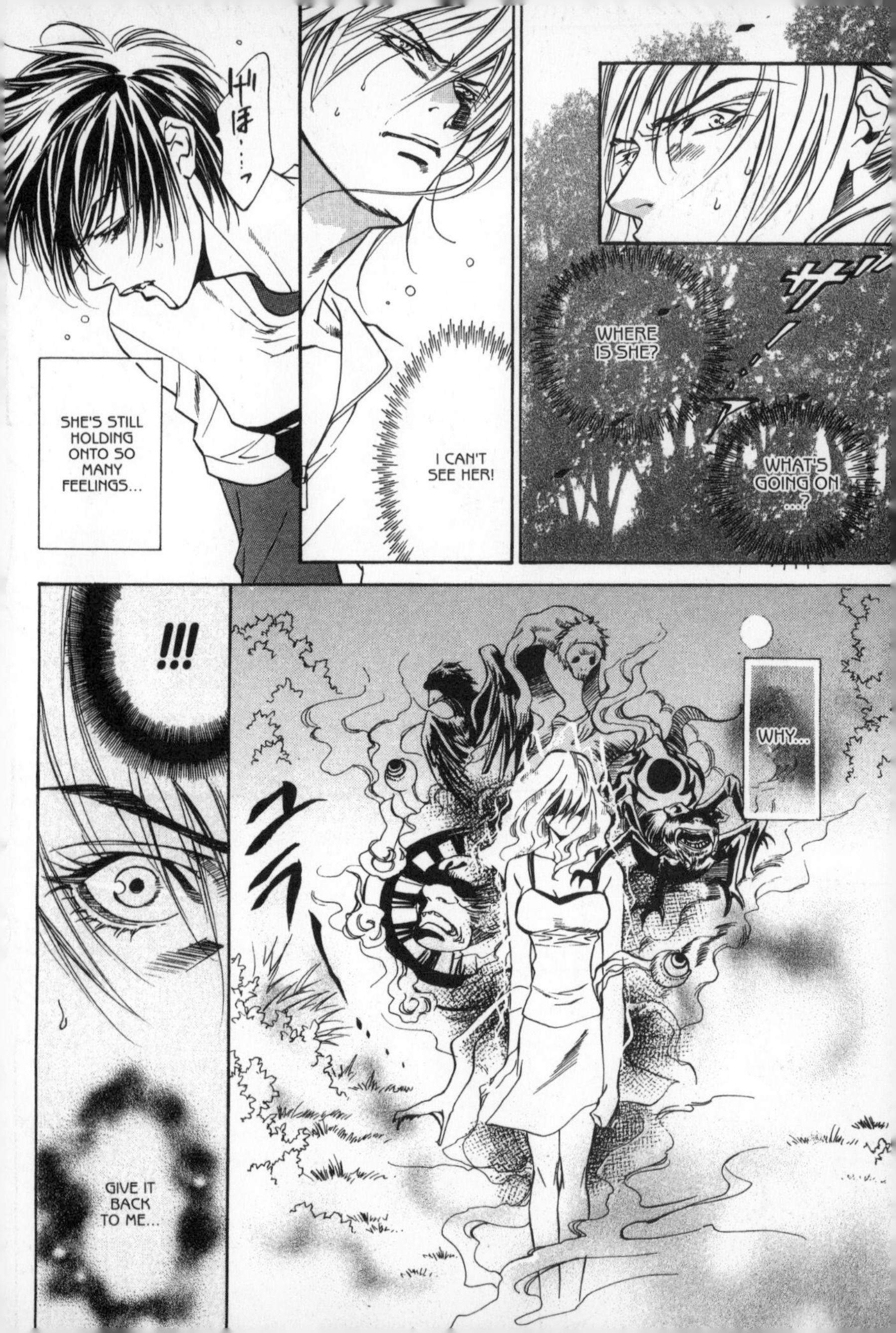
サー
WHERE IS SHE?
WHAT'S GOING ON ...?
I CAN'T SEE HER!
げほ…っ
SHE'S STILL HOLDING ONTO SO MANY FEELINGS...
WHY...
ユラ
!!!
GIVE IT BACK TO ME...

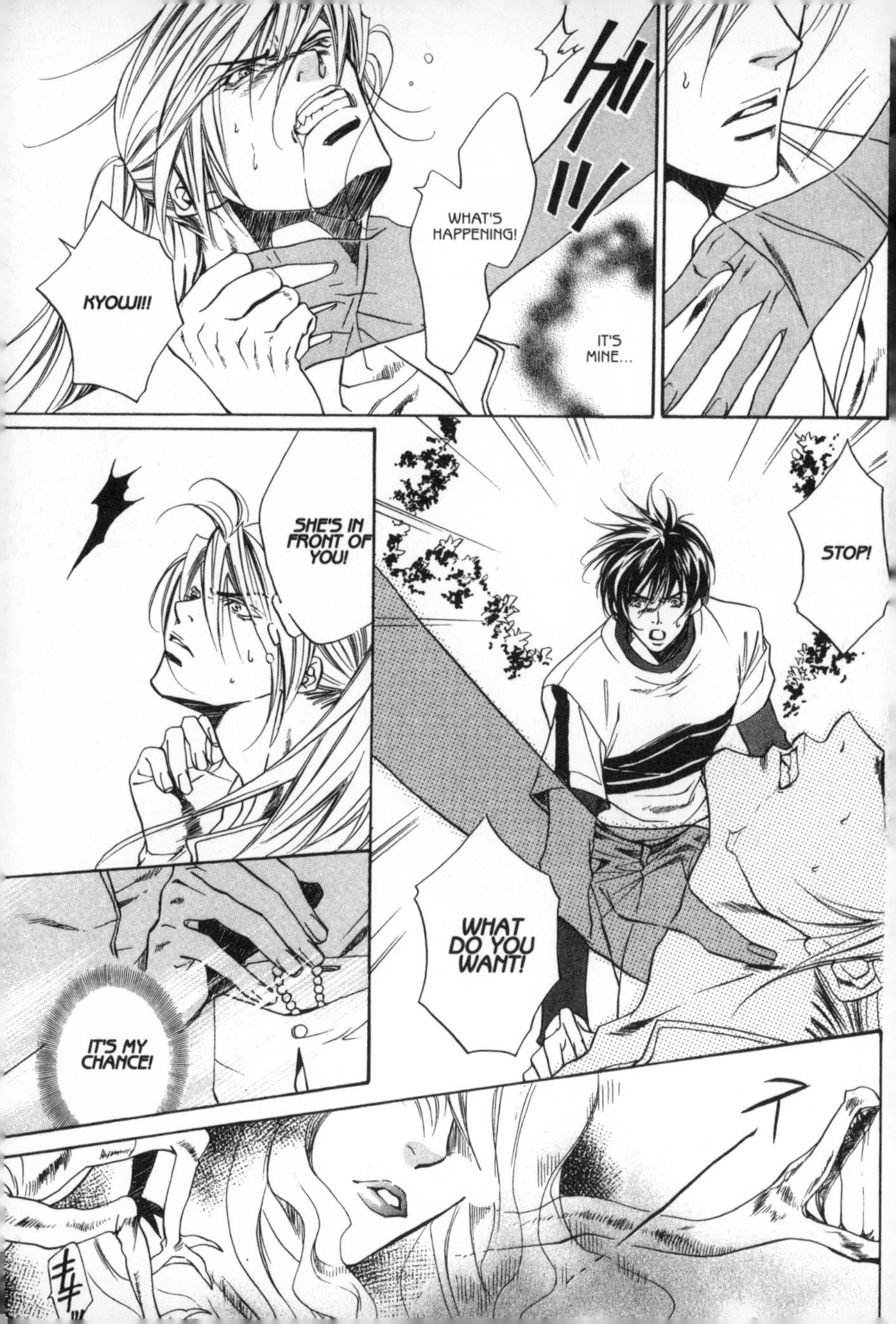
WHAT'S HAPPENING!
IT'S MINE...
KYOWII!!
STOP!
WHAT DO YOU WANT!
SHE'S IN FRONT OF YOU!
IT'S MY CHANCE!

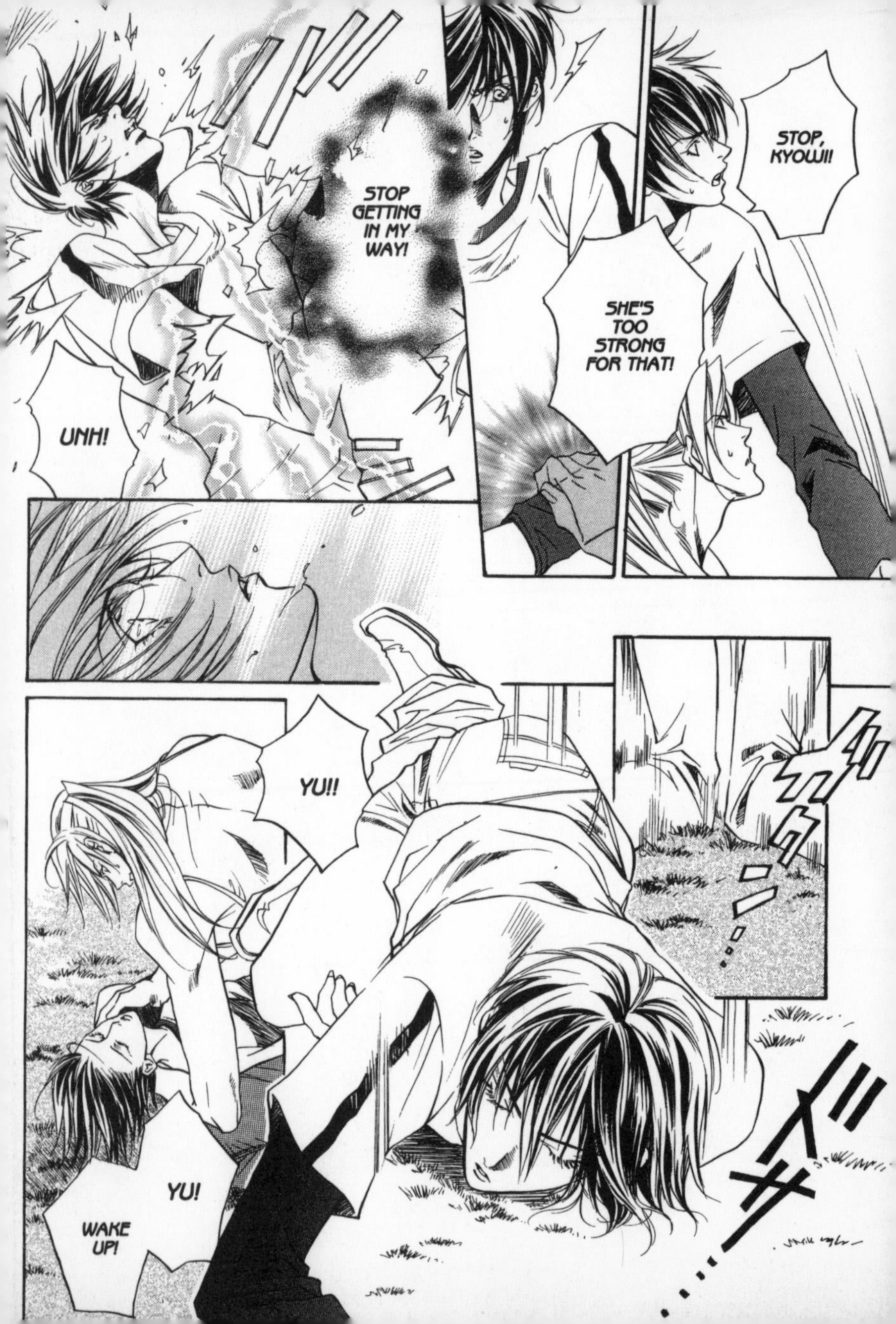
STOP, KYOUJI!
SHE'S TOO STRONG FOR THAT!
STOP GETTING IN MY WAY!
UNH!
YU!!
YU!
WAKE UP!

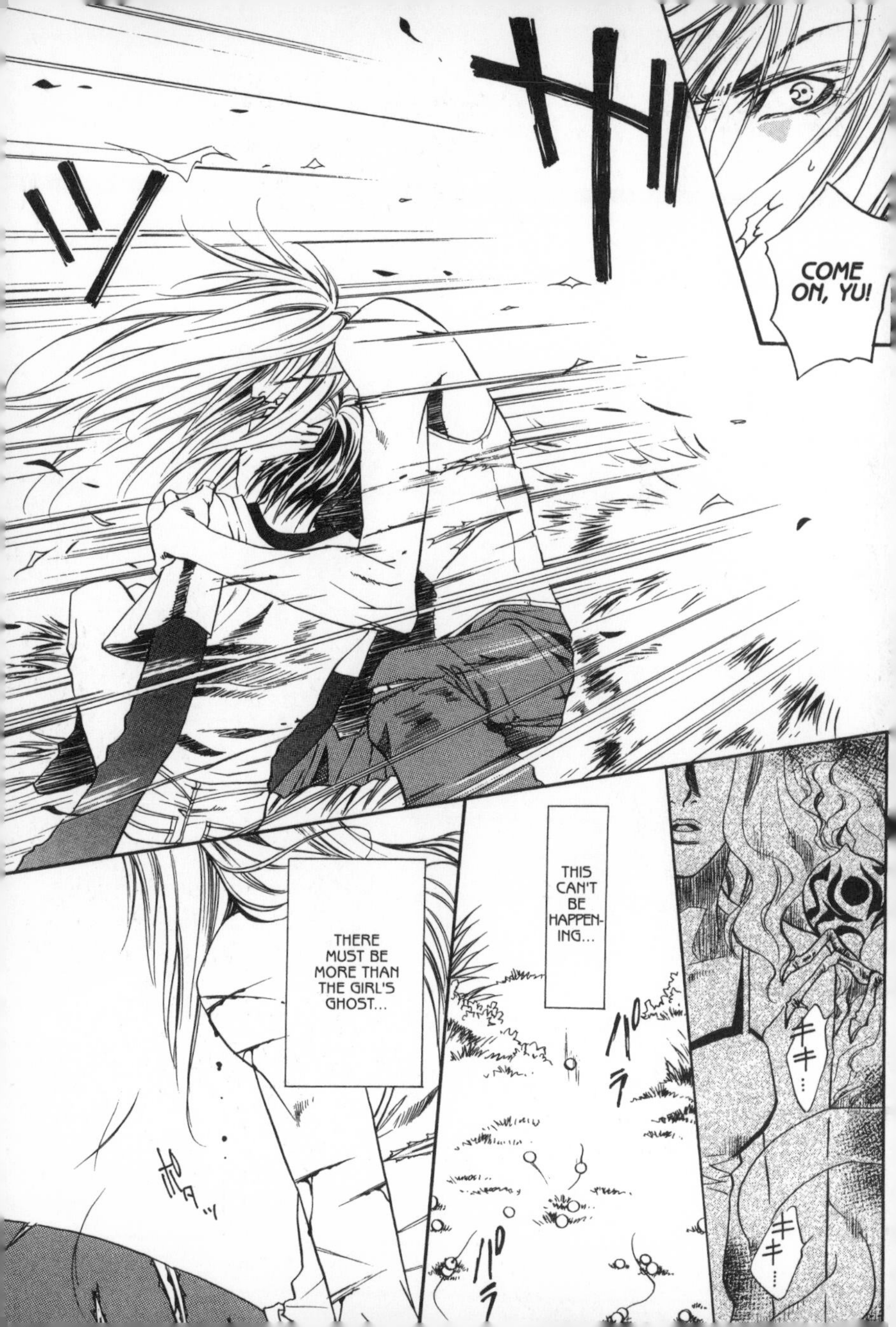
COME ON, YU!
THIS CAN'T BE HAPPEN- ING...
THERE MUST BE MORE THAN THE GIRL'S GHOST...

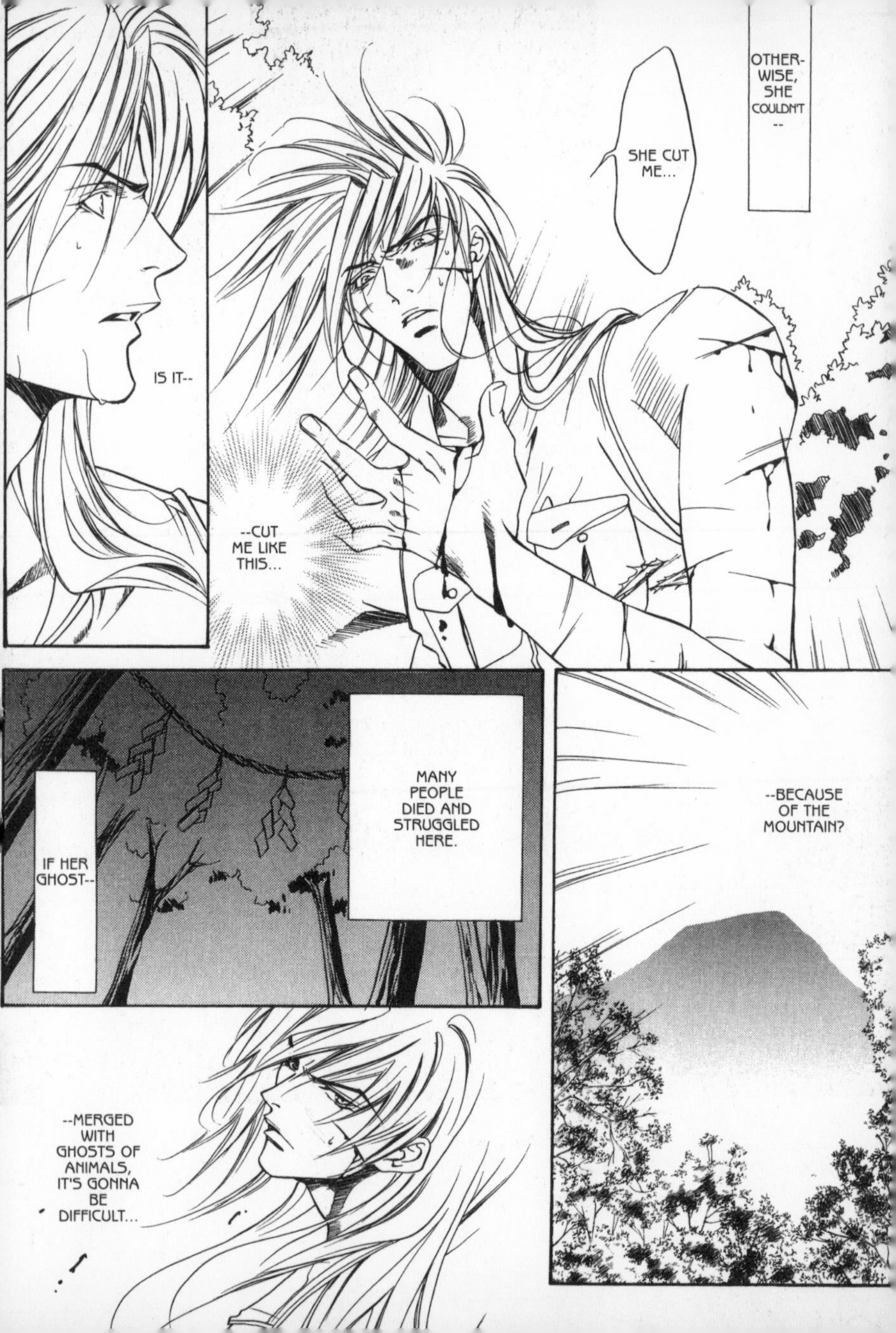
OTHER-WISE, SHE COULDN'T --
SHE CUT ME...
--CUT ME LIKE THIS...
IS IT--
--BECAUSE OF THE MOUNTAIN?
MANY PEOPLE DIED AND STRUGGLED HERE.
IF HER GHOST--
--MERGED WITH GHOSTS OF ANIMALS, IT'S GONNA BE DIFFICULT...

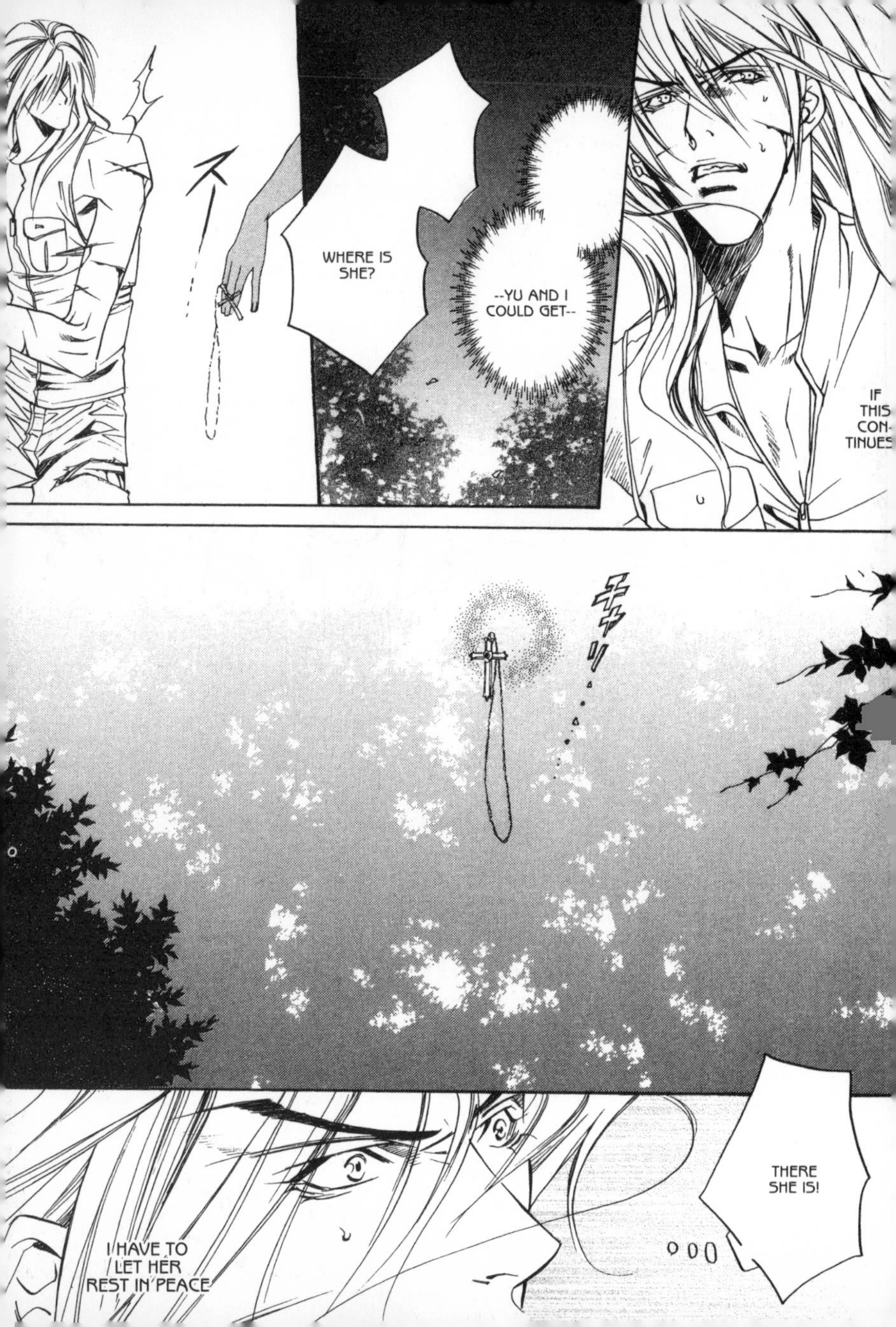
IF THIS CON-TINUES
--YU AND I COULD GET--
WHERE IS SHE?
THERE SHE IS!
I HAVE TO LET HER REST IN PEACE

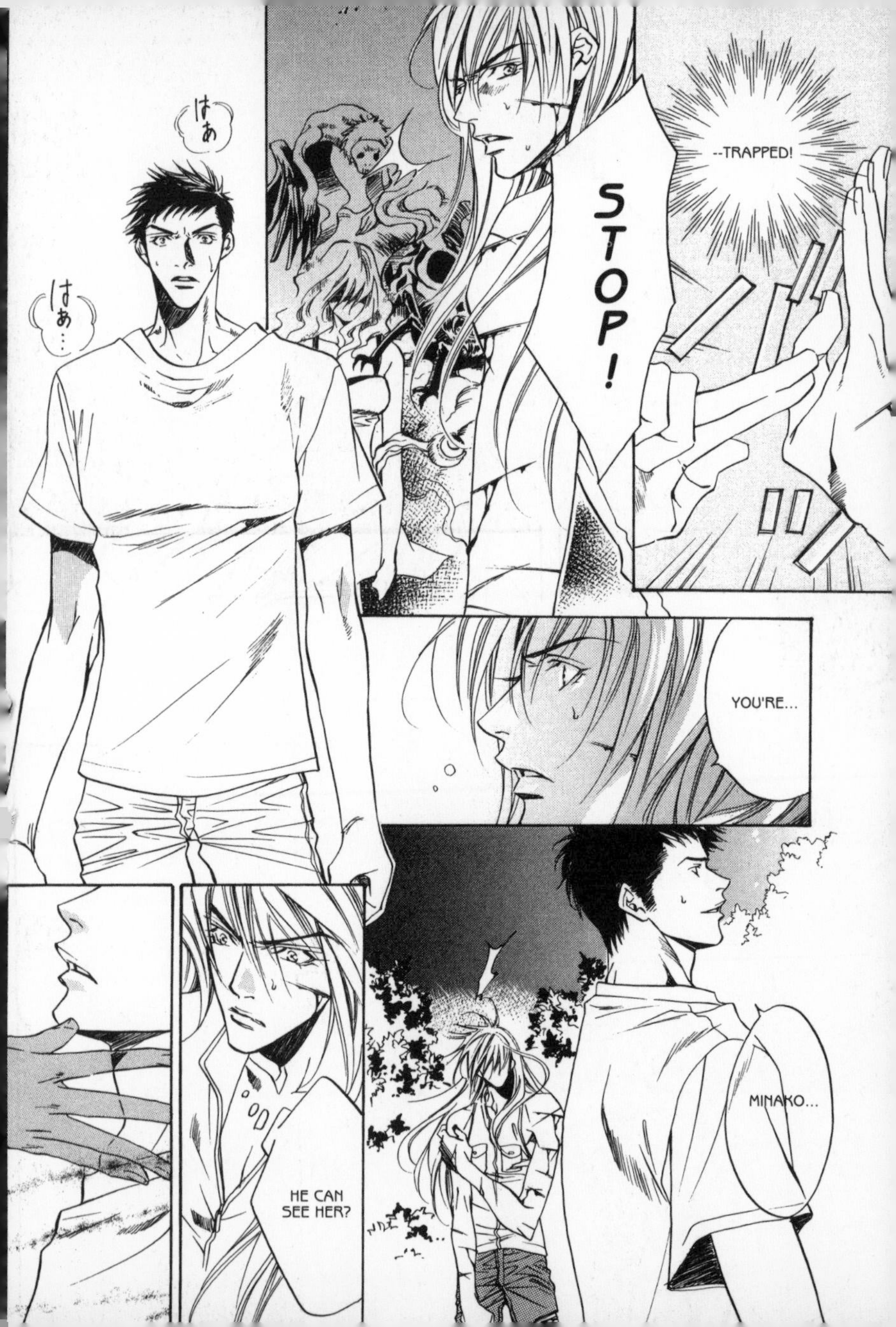
--TRAPPED!
STOP!
はぁ
はぁ…
YOU'RE...
MINAKO...
HE CAN SEE HER?

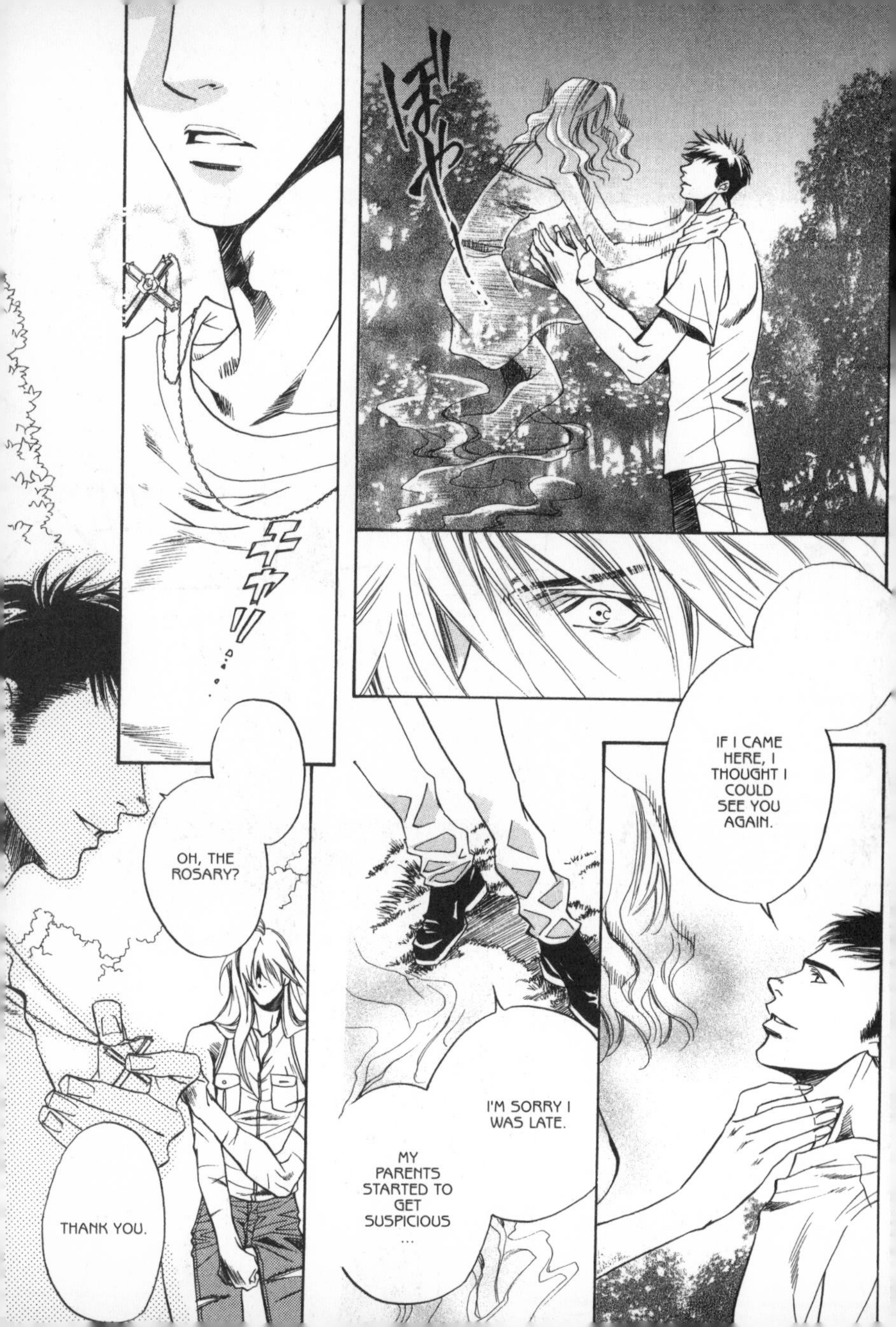
チャリッ
IF I CAME HERE, I THOUGHT I COULD SEE YOU AGAIN.
I'M SORRY I WAS LATE.
MY PARENTS STARTED TO GET SUSPICIOUS …
OH, THE ROSARY?
THANK YOU.

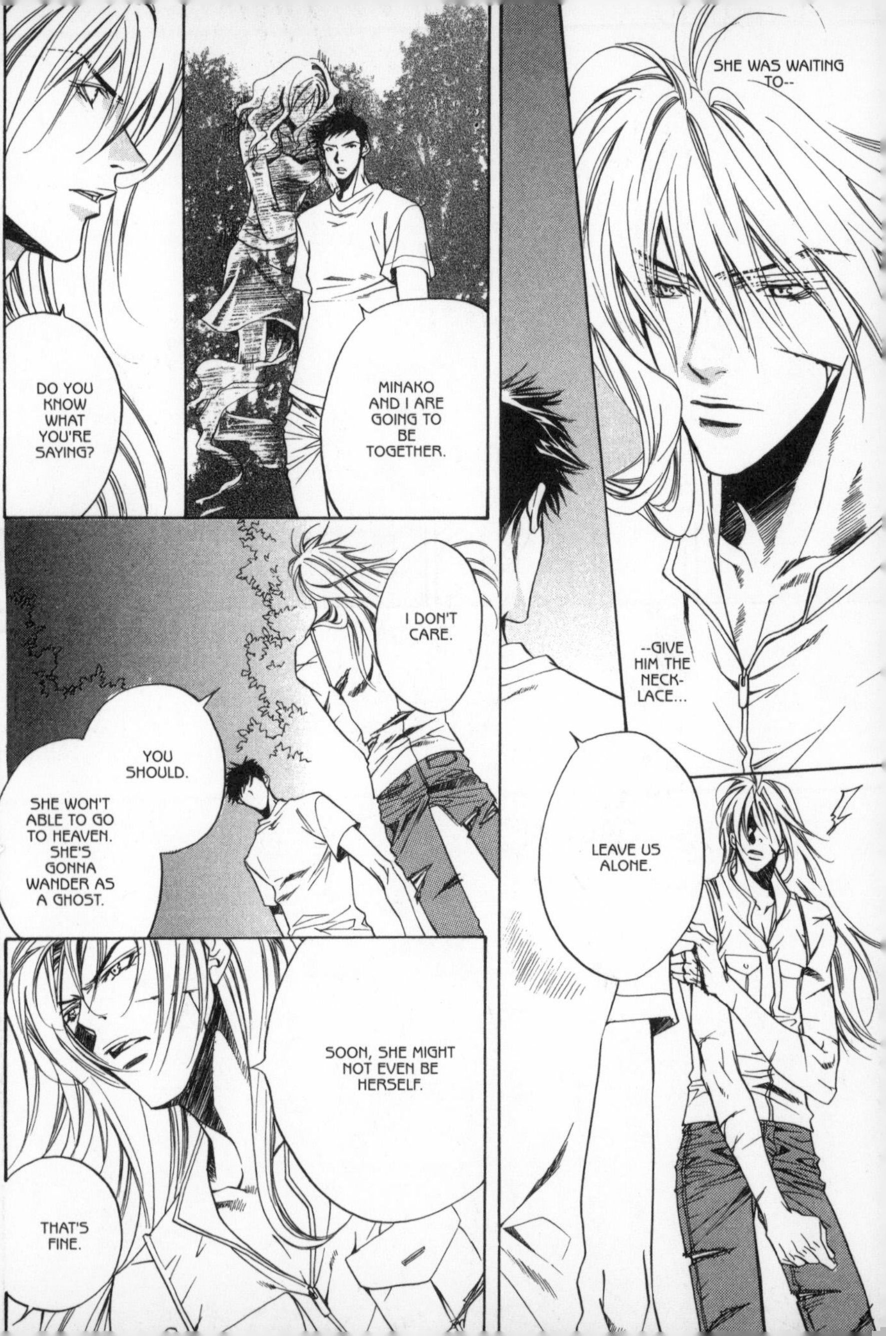
SHE WAS WAITING TO--
--GIVE HIM THE NECK-LACE...
LEAVE US ALONE.
MINAKO AND I ARE GOING TO BE TOGETHER.
DO YOU KNOW WHAT YOU'RE SAYING?
I DON'T CARE.
YOU SHOULD.
SHE WON'T ABLE TO GO TO HEAVEN. SHE'S GONNA WANDER AS A GHOST.
SOON, SHE MIGHT NOT EVEN BE HERSELF.
THAT'S FINE.

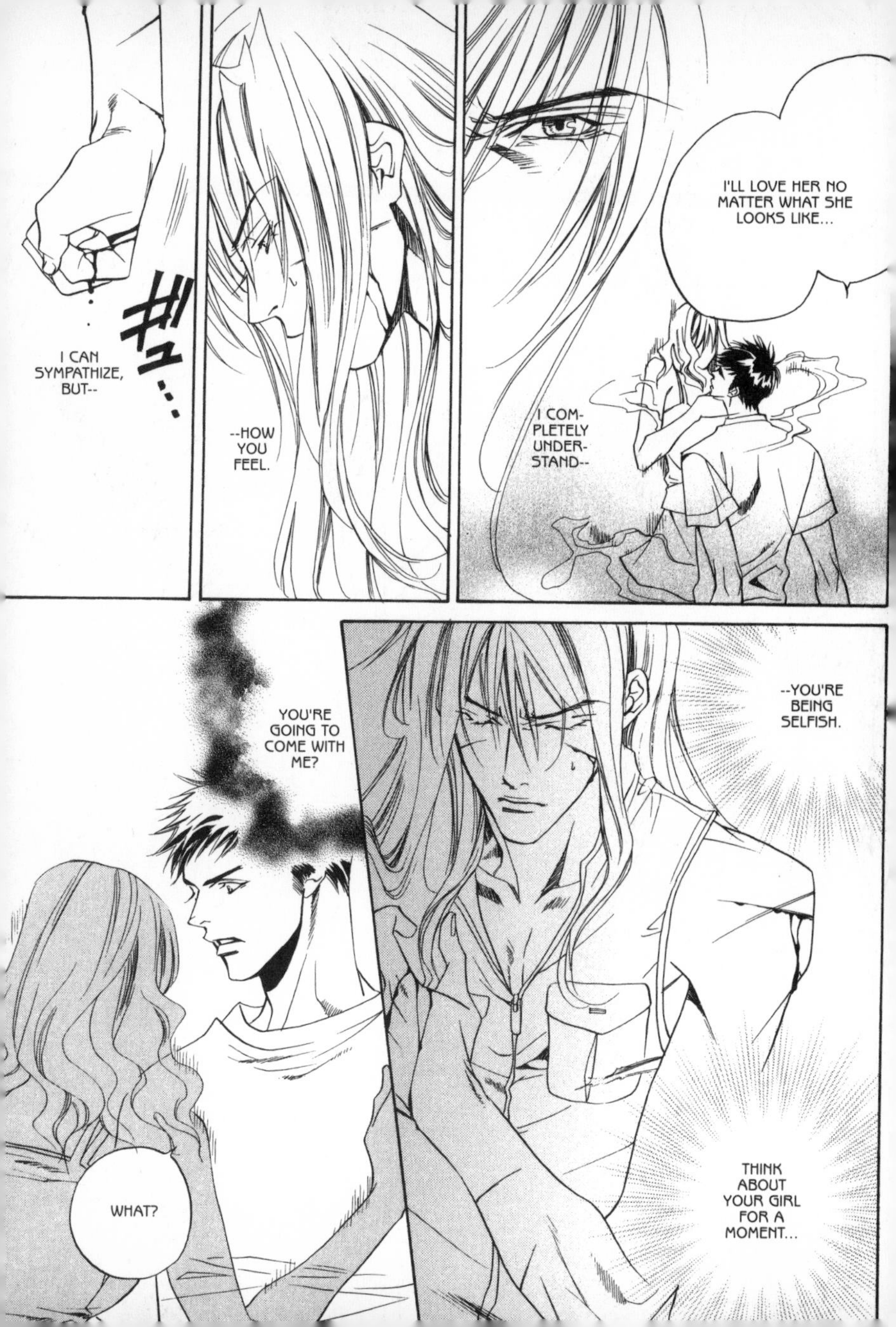
I'LL LOVE HER NO MATTER WHAT SHE LOOKS LIKE...
I COM-PLETELY UNDER-STAND--
--HOW YOU FEEL.
ギュ...
I CAN SYMPATHIZE, BUT--
--YOU'RE BEING SELFISH.
THINK ABOUT YOUR GIRL FOR A MOMENT...
YOU'RE GOING TO COME WITH ME?
WHAT?

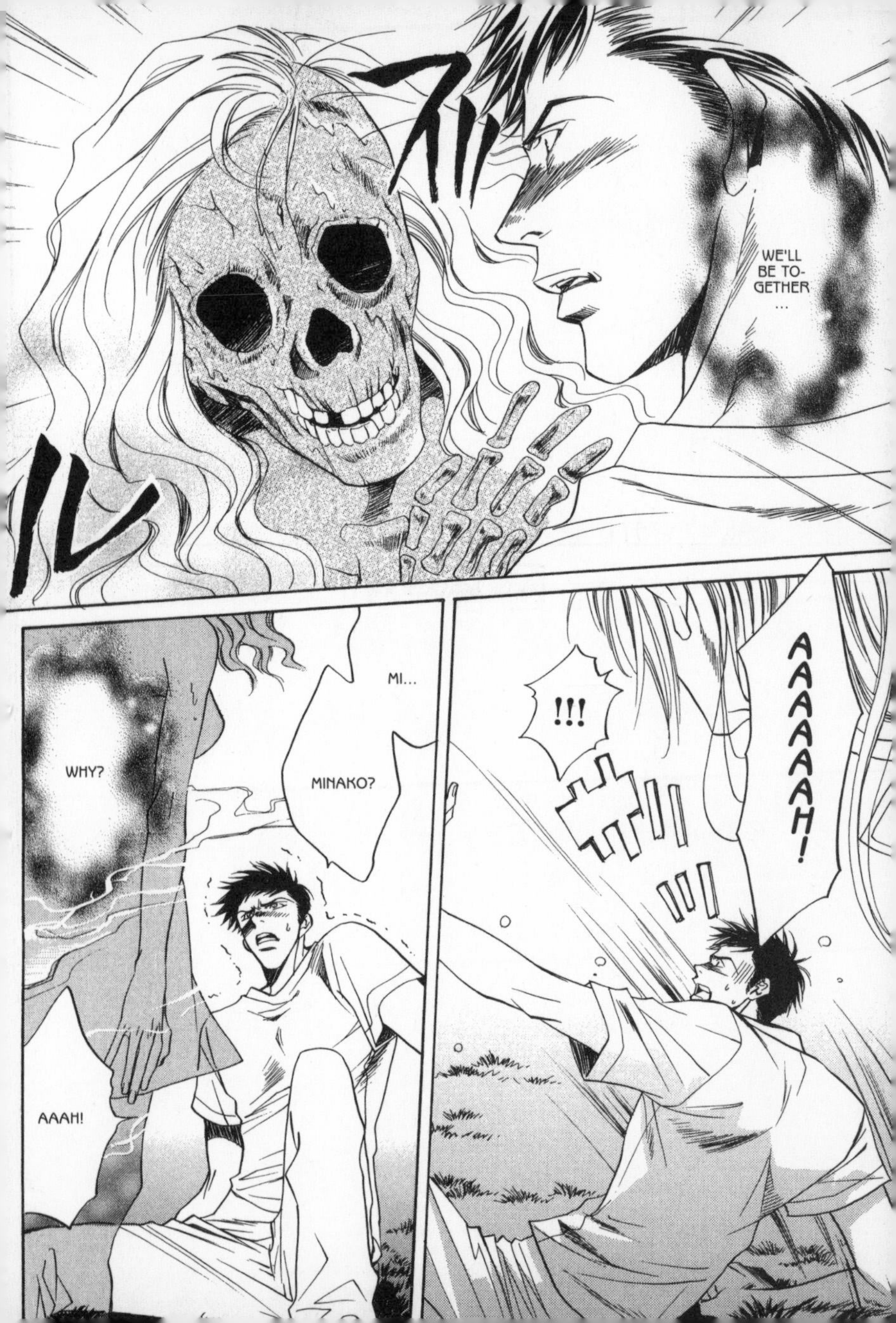

スル
WE'LL BE TO-GETHER ...
!!!
AAAAAAAH!
MI...
MINAKO?
WHY?
AAAH!

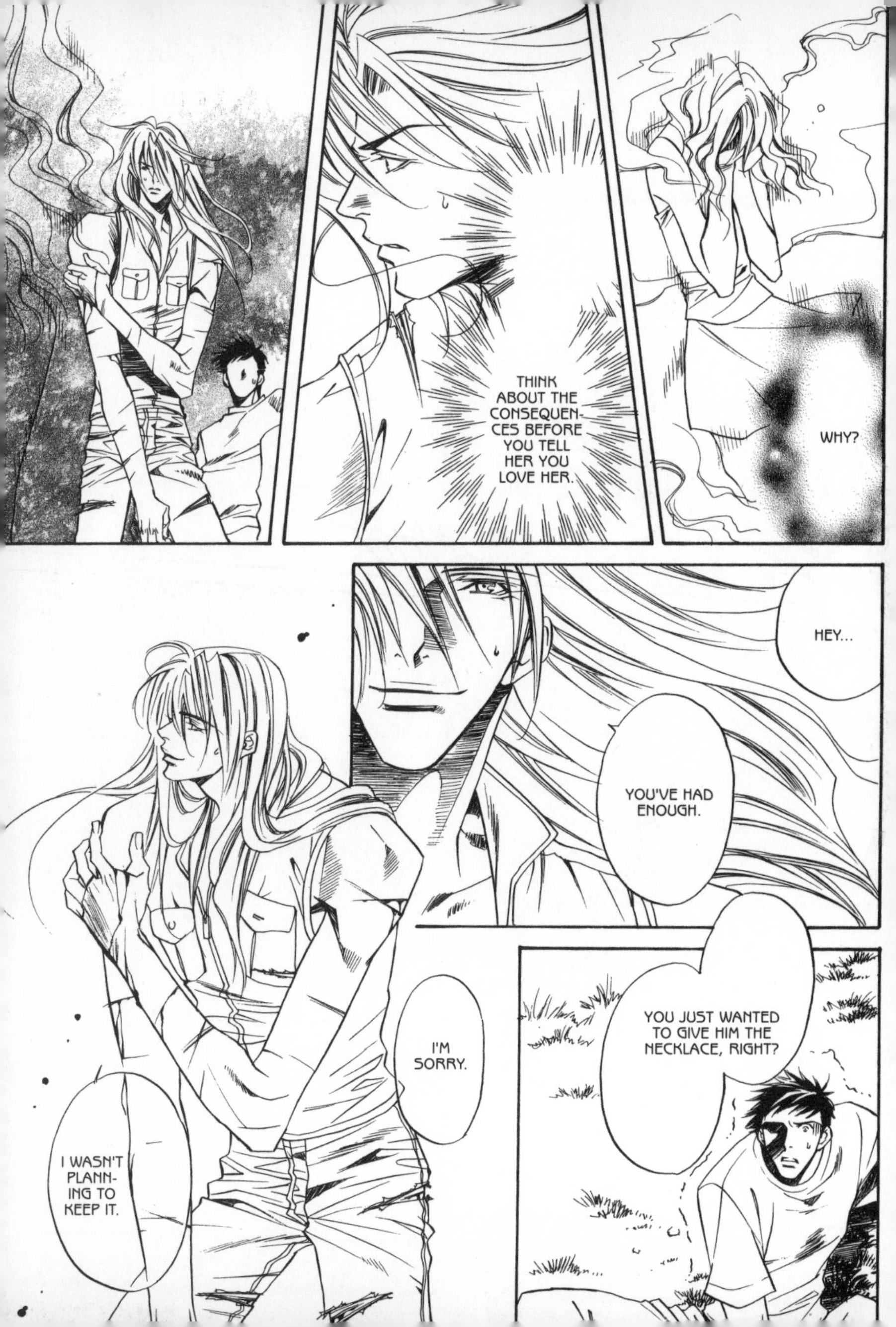
WHY?
THINK ABOUT THE CONSEQUENCES BEFORE YOU TELL HER YOU LOVE HER.
HEY...
YOU'VE HAD ENOUGH.
YOU JUST WANTED TO GIVE HIM THE NECKLACE, RIGHT?
I'M SORRY.
I WASN'T PLANNING TO KEEP IT.

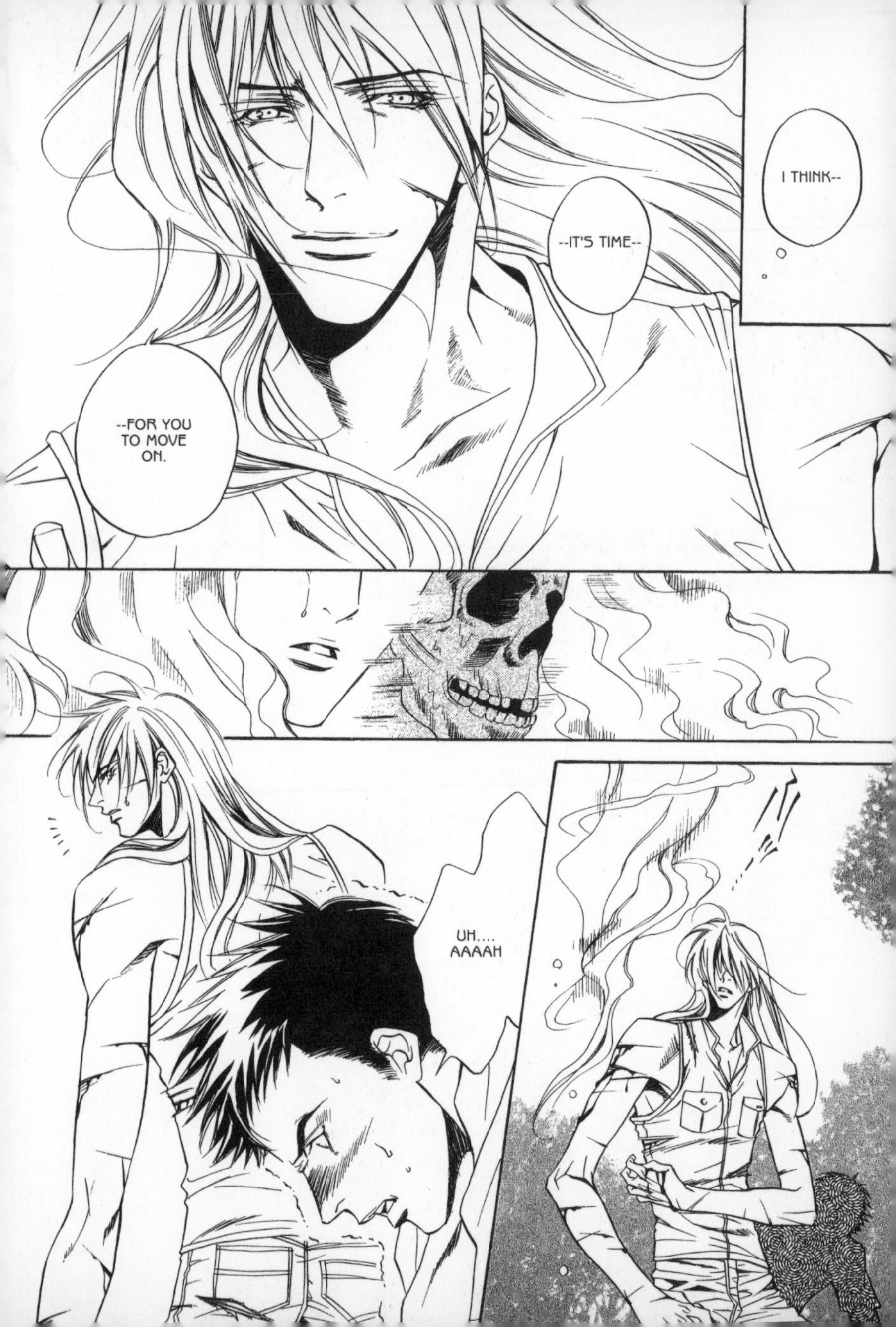
I THINK--
--IT'S TIME--
--FOR YOU TO MOVE ON.
UH.... AAAAH

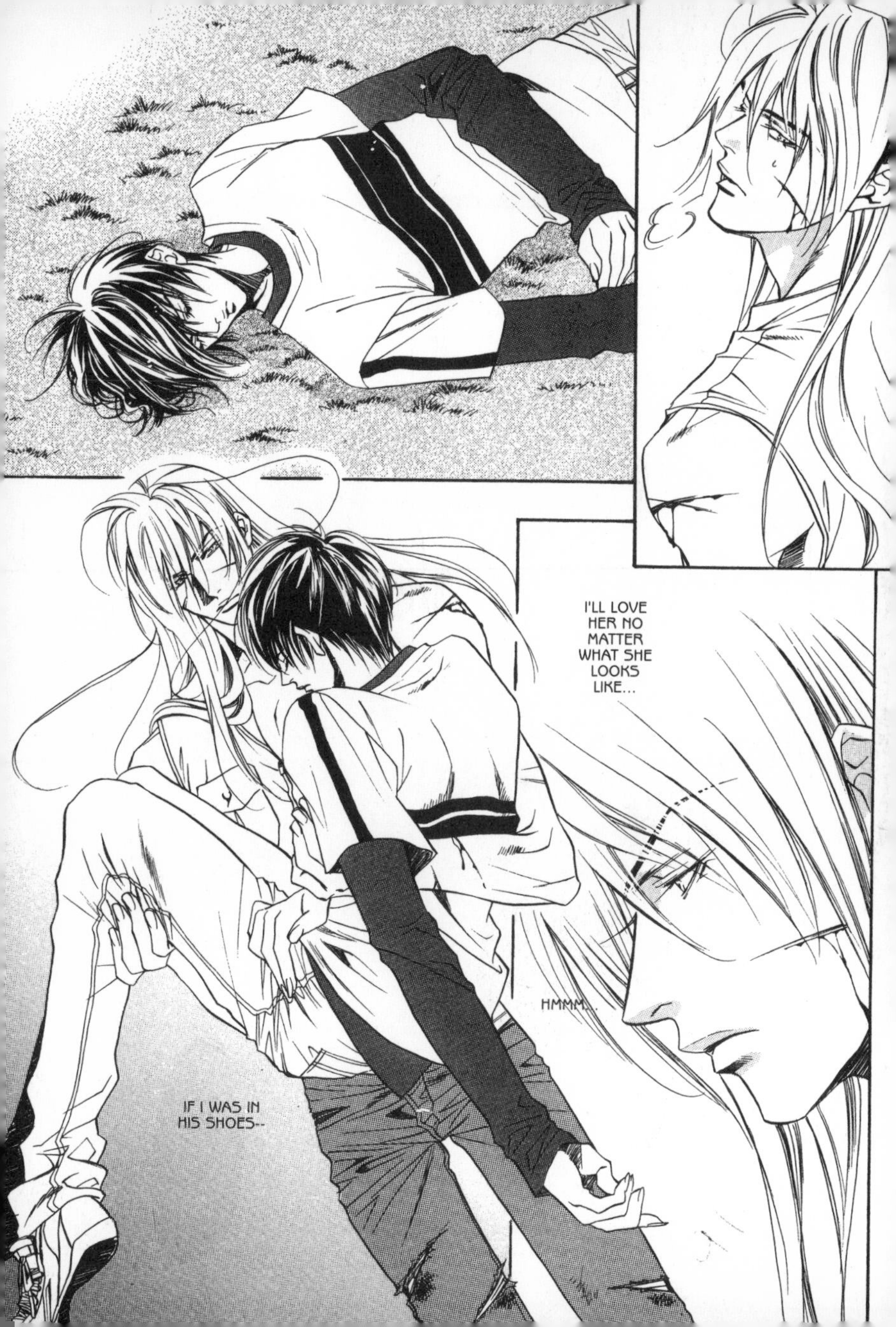
I'LL LOVE HER NO MATTER WHAT SHE LOOKS LIKE...
HMMM...
IF I WAS IN HIS SHOES--

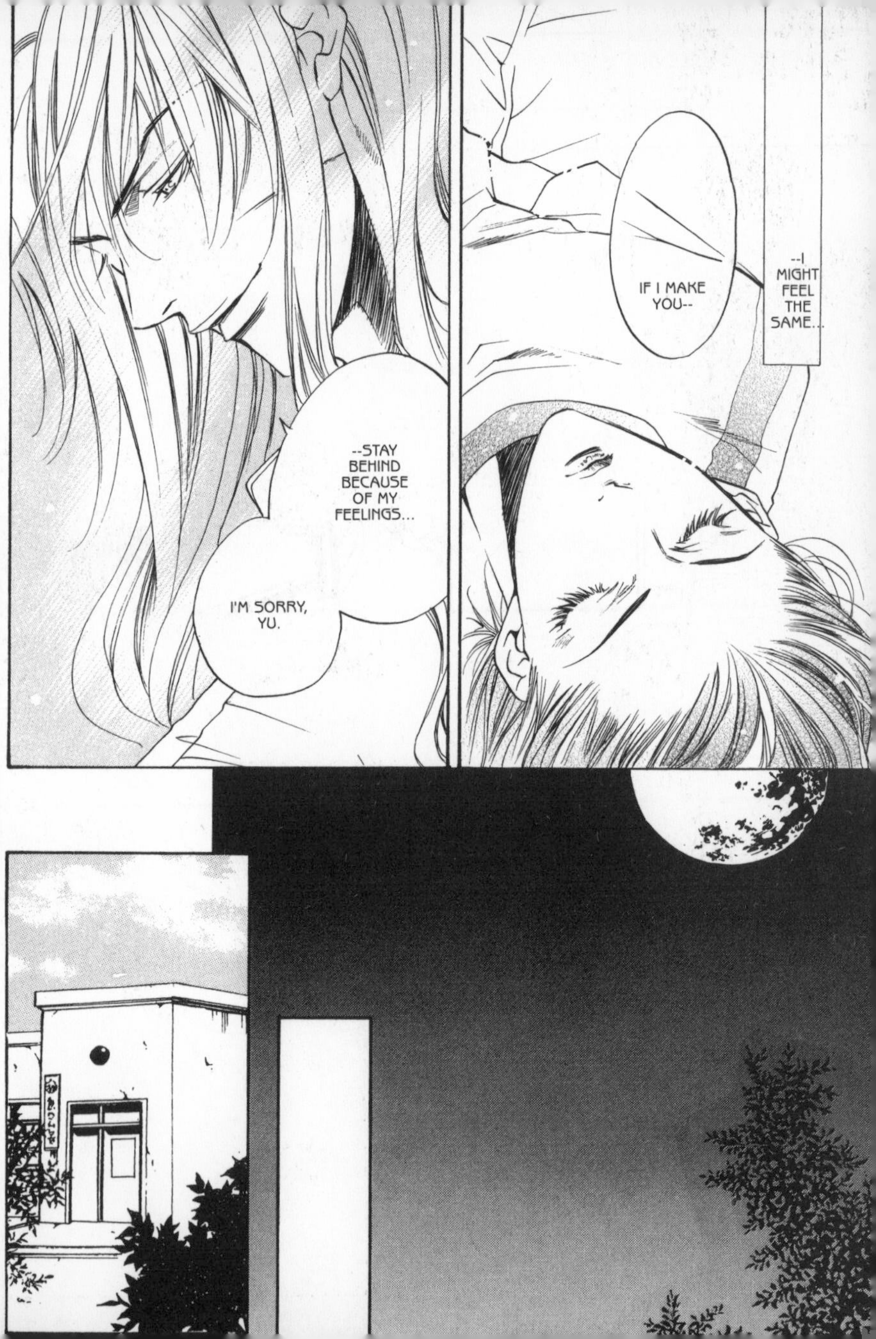
--I MIGHT FEEL THE SAME...
IF I MAKE YOU--
--STAY BEHIND BECAUSE OF MY FEELINGS...
I'M SORRY, YU.

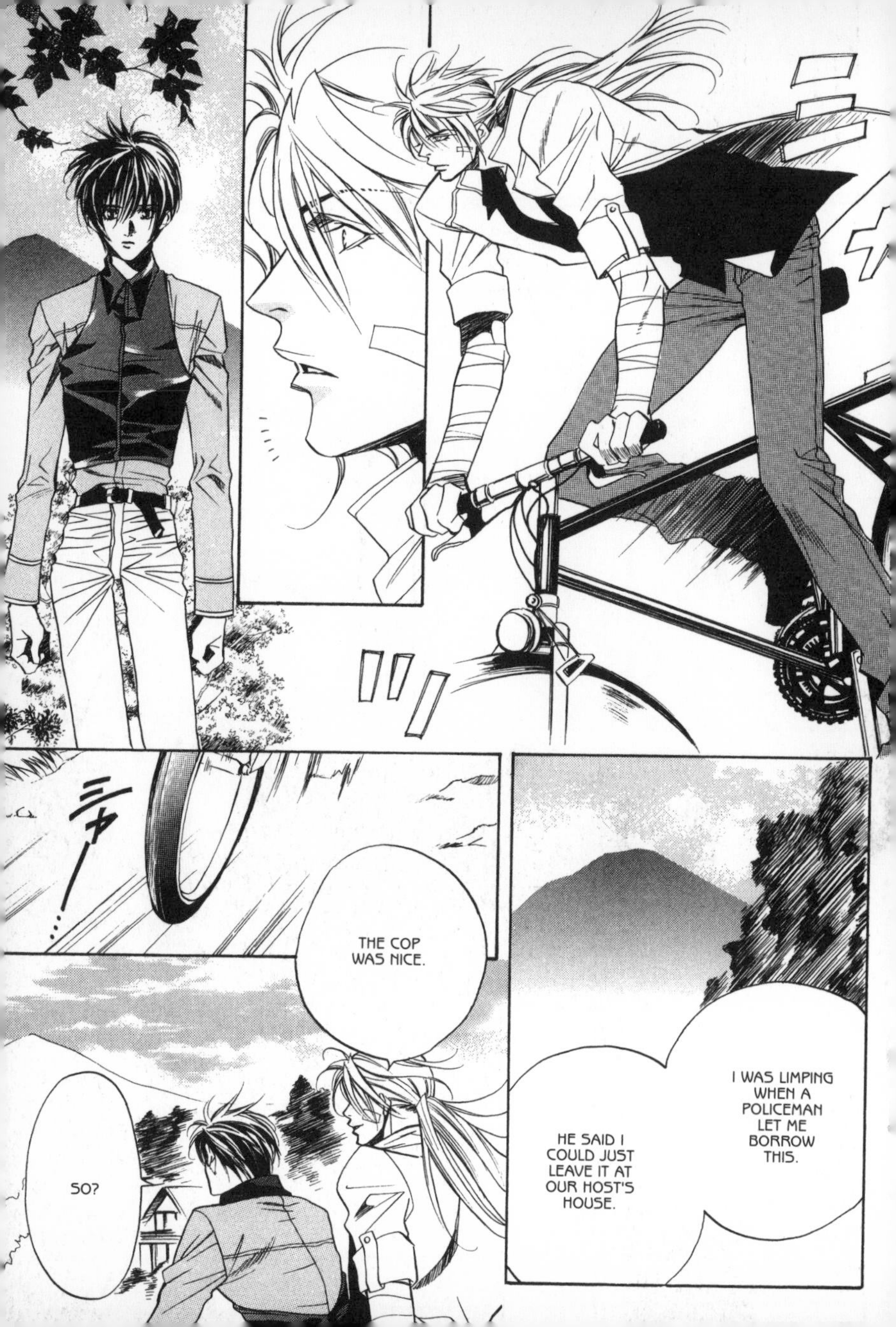
I WAS LIMPING WHEN A POLICEMAN LET ME BORROW THIS.
HE SAID I COULD JUST LEAVE IT AT OUR HOST'S HOUSE.
THE COP WAS NICE.
SO?

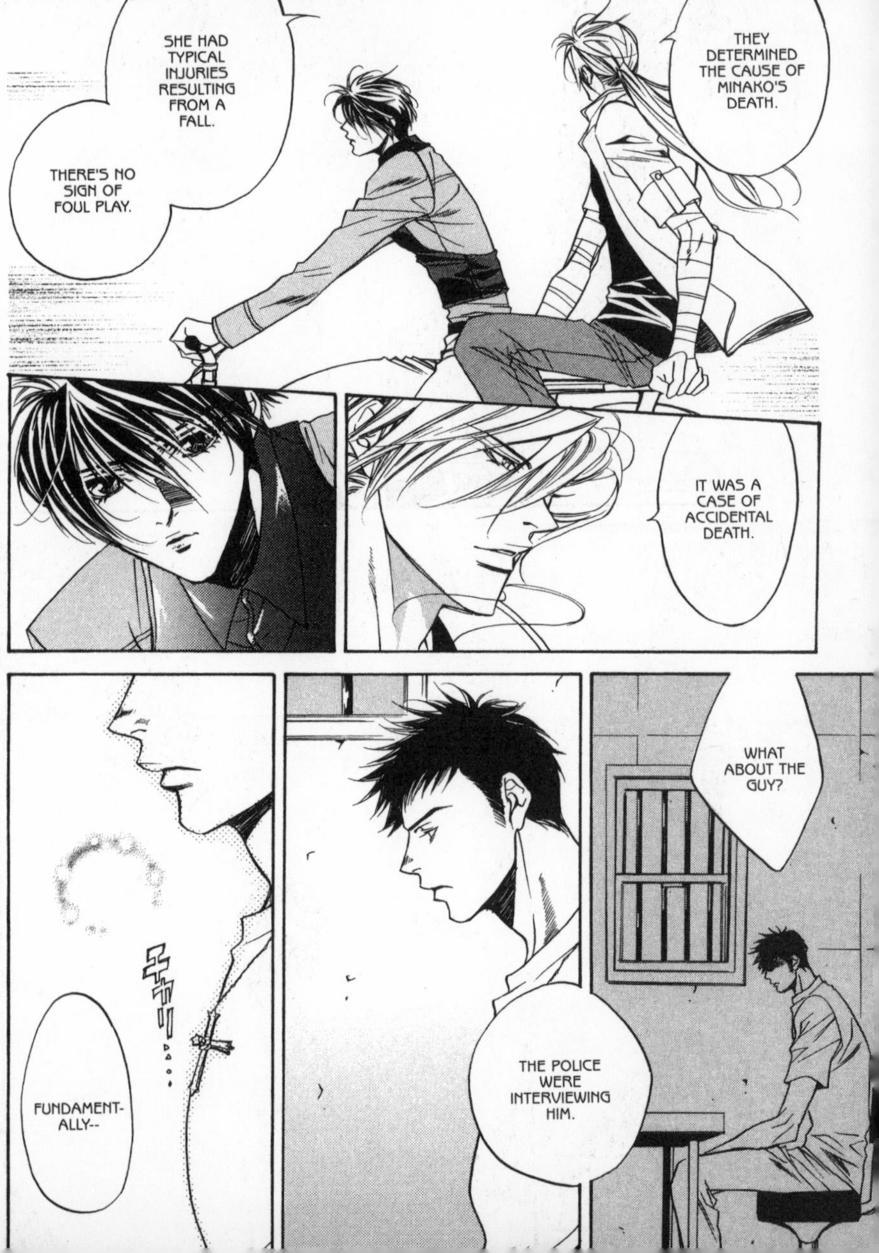
THEY DETERMINED THE CAUSE OF MINAKO'S DEATH.
SHE HAD TYPICAL INJURIES RESULTING FROM A FALL.
THERE'S NO SIGN OF FOUL PLAY.
IT WAS A CASE OF ACCIDENTAL DEATH.
WHAT ABOUT THE GUY?
THE POLICE WERE INTERVIEWING HIM.
FUNDAMENT-ALLY--

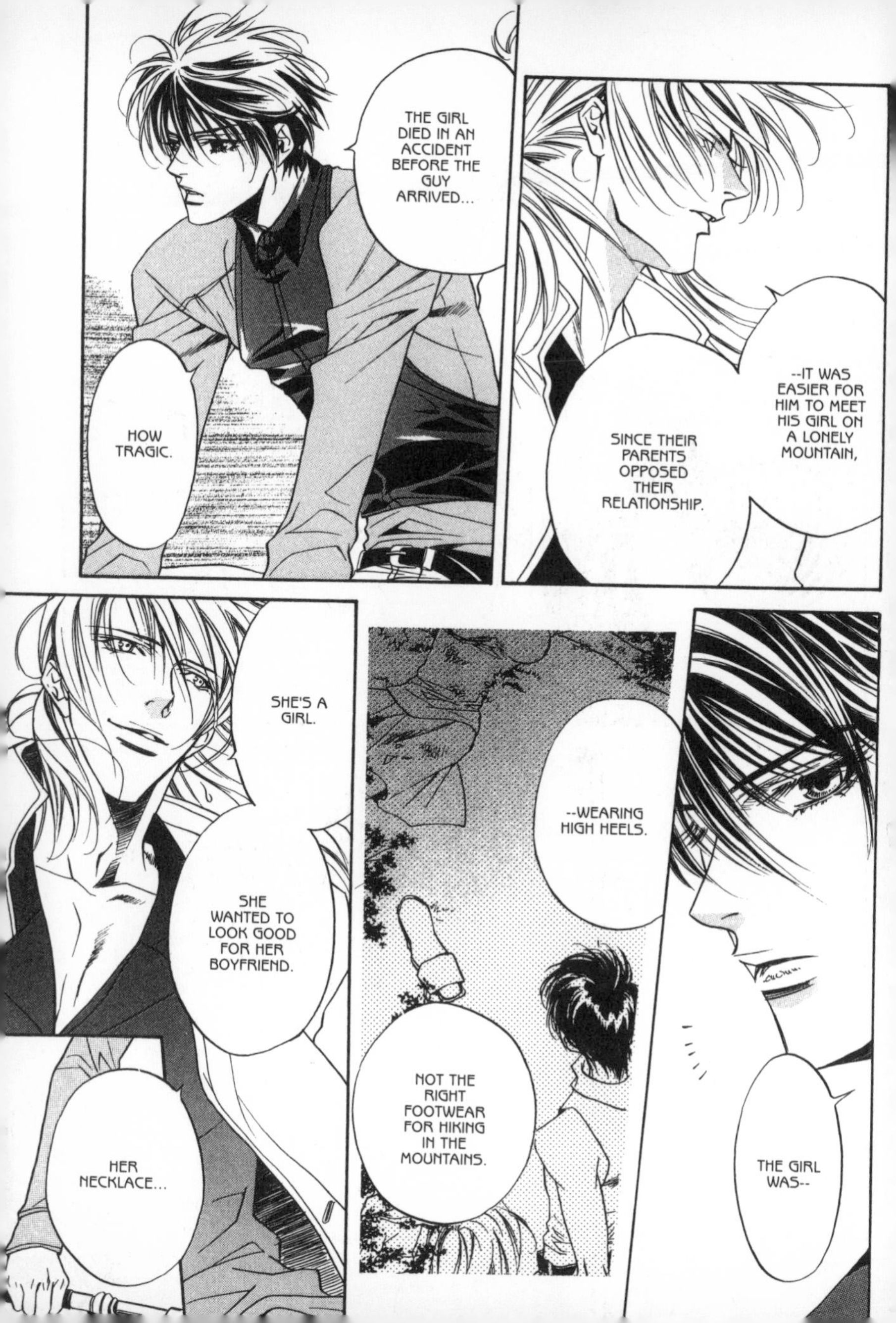
--IT WAS EASIER FOR HIM TO MEET HIS GIRL ON A LONELY MOUNTAIN,
SINCE THEIR PARENTS OPPOSED THEIR RELATIONSHIP.
THE GIRL DIED IN AN ACCIDENT BEFORE THE GUY ARRIVED...
HOW TRAGIC.
THE GIRL WAS--
--WEARING HIGH HEELS.
NOT THE RIGHT FOOTWEAR FOR HIKING IN THE MOUNTAINS.
SHE'S A GIRL.
SHE WANTED TO LOOK GOOD FOR HER BOYFRIEND.
HER NECKLACE...

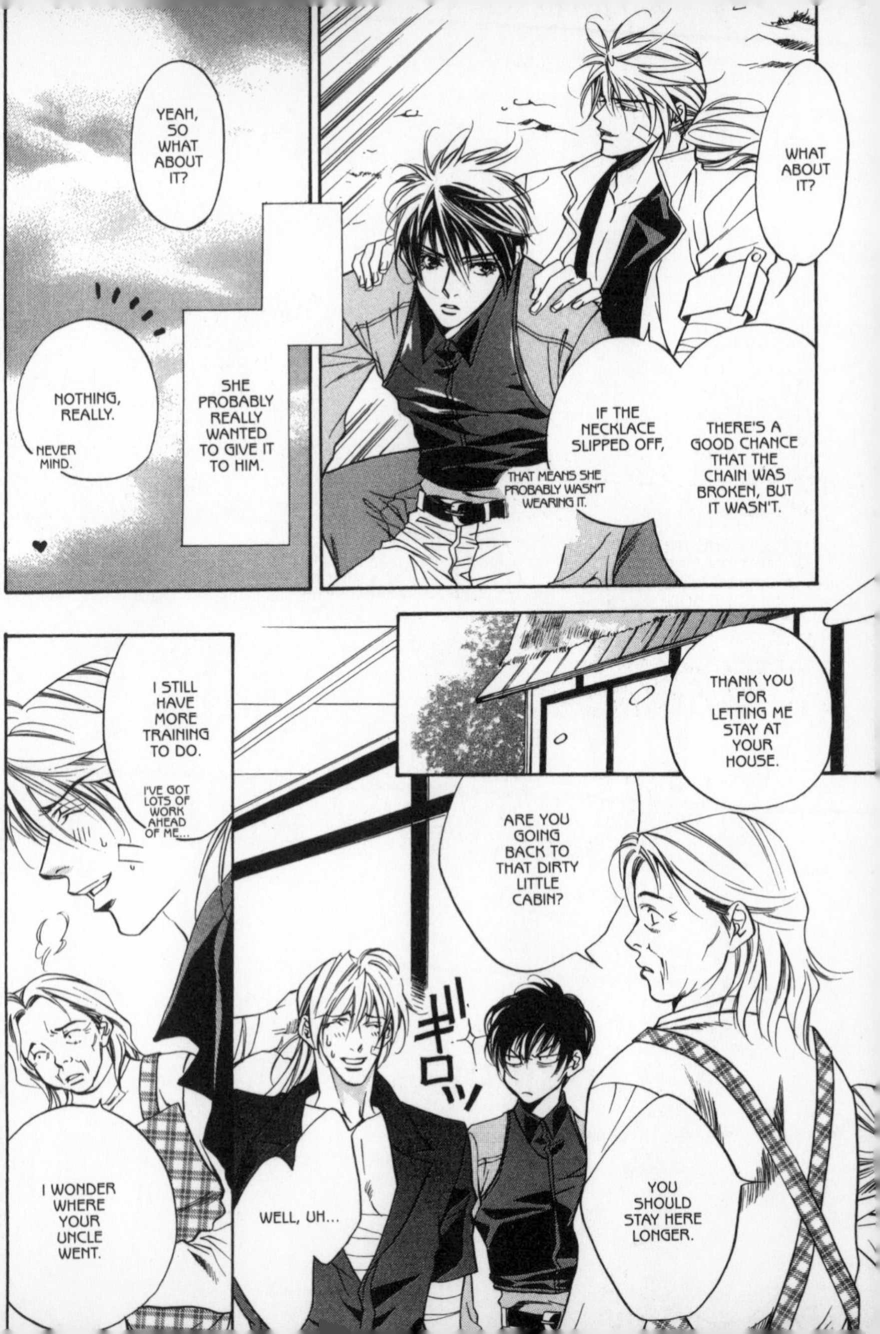
WHAT ABOUT IT?
THERE'S A GOOD CHANCE THAT THE CHAIN WAS BROKEN, BUT IT WASN'T.
IF THE NECKLACE SLIPPED OFF,
THAT MEANS SHE PROBABLY WASN'T WEARING IT.
YEAH, SO WHAT ABOUT IT?
SHE PROBABLY REALLY WANTED TO GIVE IT TO HIM.
NOTHING, REALLY.
NEVER MIND.
THANK YOU FOR LETTING ME STAY AT YOUR HOUSE.
ARE YOU GOING BACK TO THAT DIRTY LITTLE CABIN?
I STILL HAVE MORE TRAINING TO DO.
I'VE GOT LOTS OF WORK AHEAD OF ME...
ギロッ
YOU SHOULD STAY HERE LONGER.
WELL, UH...
I WONDER WHERE YOUR UNCLE WENT.

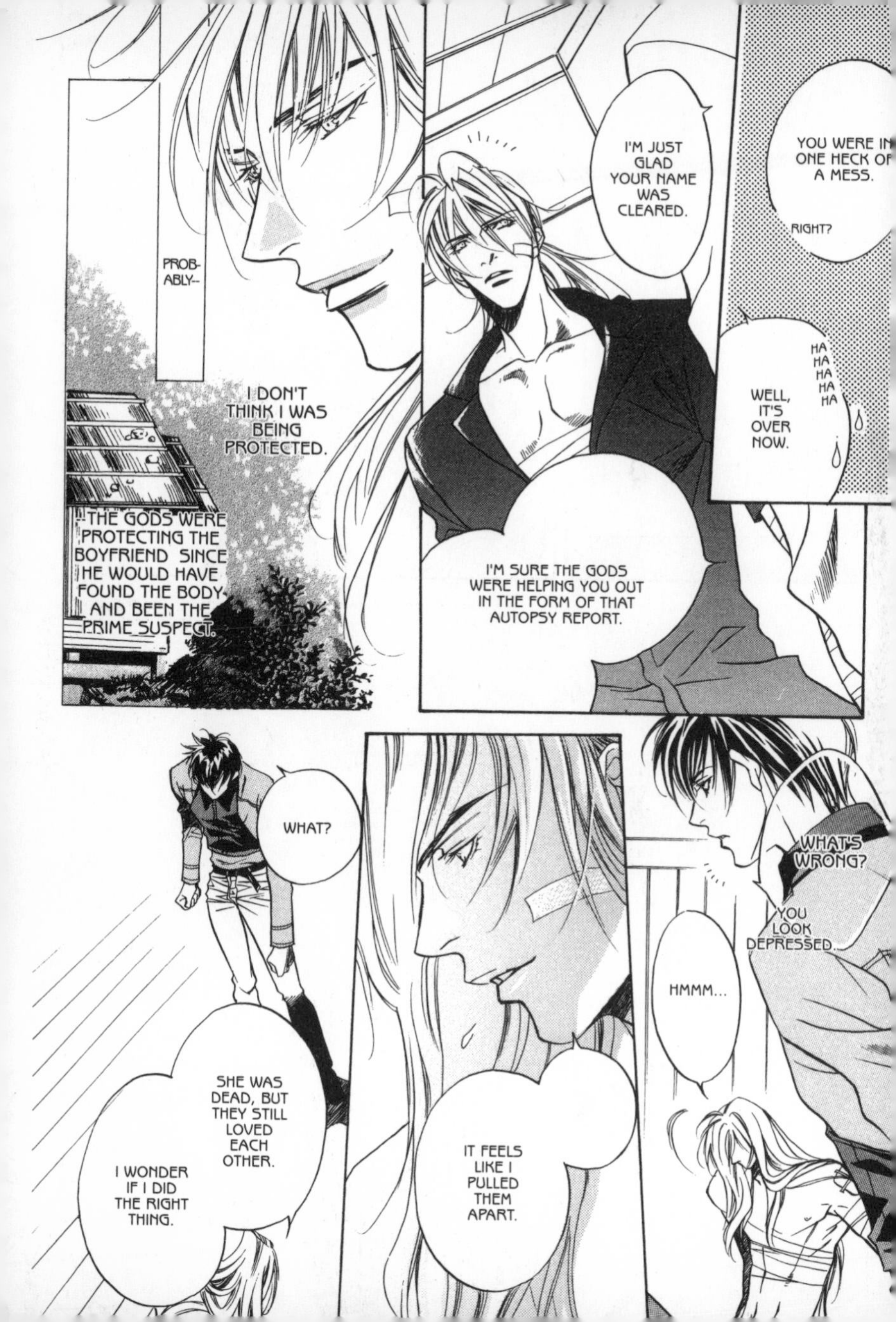

YOU WERE IN ONE HECK OF A MESS.
RIGHT?
HA HA HA HA HA
WELL, IT'S OVER NOW.
I'M JUST GLAD YOUR NAME WAS CLEARED.
I'M SURE THE GODS WERE HELPING YOU OUT IN THE FORM OF THAT AUTOPSY REPORT.
PROBABLY--
I DON'T THINK I WAS BEING PROTECTED.
--THE GODS WERE PROTECTING THE BOYFRIEND SINCE HE WOULD HAVE FOUND THE BODY AND BEEN THE PRIME SUSPECT.
WHAT'S WRONG?
YOU LOOK DEPRESSED...
HMMM...
IT FEELS LIKE I PULLED THEM APART.
WHAT?
SHE WAS DEAD, BUT THEY STILL LOVED EACH OTHER.
I WONDER IF I DID THE RIGHT THING.

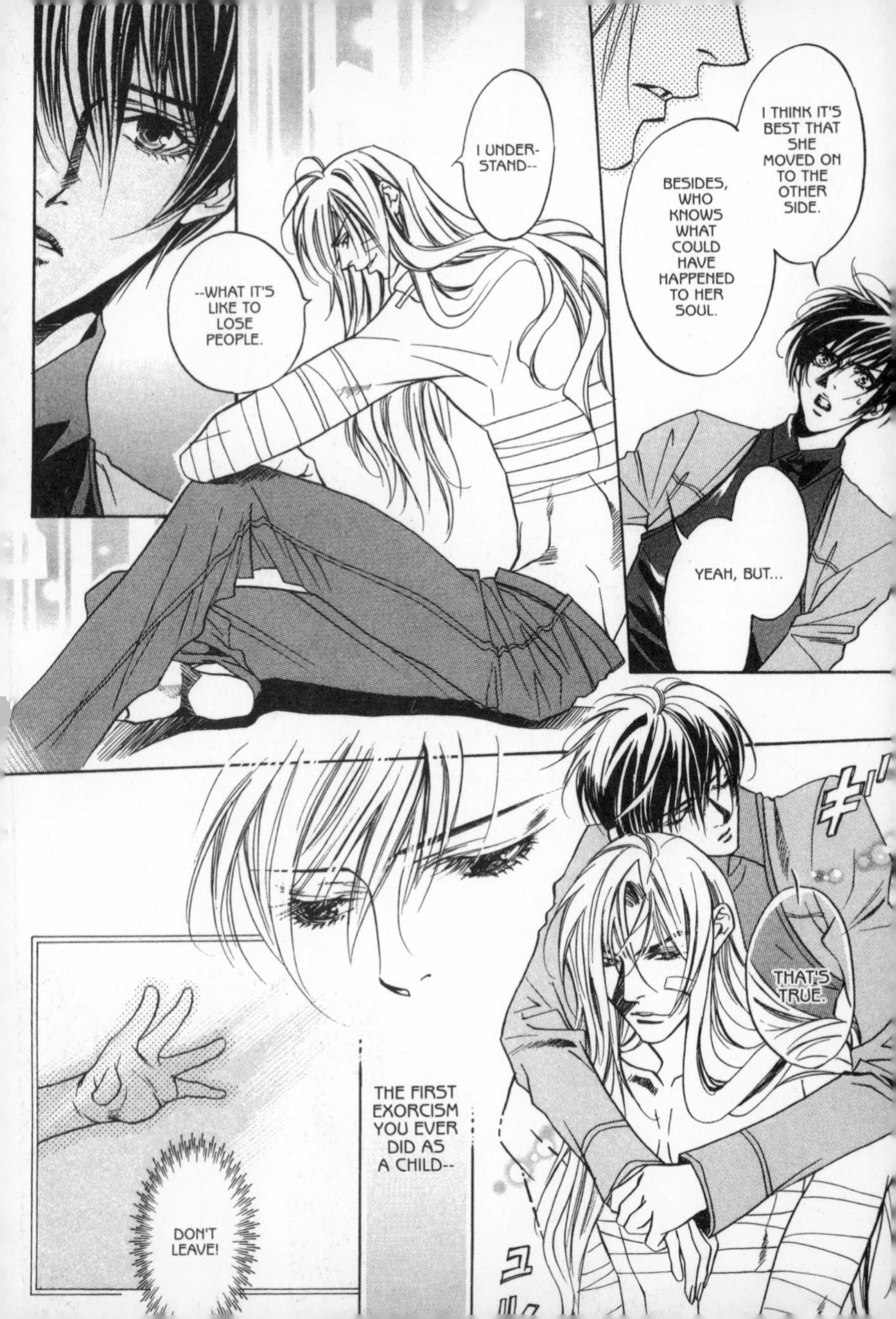
I THINK IT'S BEST THAT SHE MOVED ON TO THE OTHER SIDE.
BESIDES, WHO KNOWS WHAT COULD HAVE HAPPENED TO HER SOUL.
YEAH, BUT...
I UNDER-STAND--
--WHAT IT'S LIKE TO LOSE PEOPLE.
THAT'S TRUE.
THE FIRST EXORCISM YOU EVER DID AS A CHILD--
DON'T LEAVE!

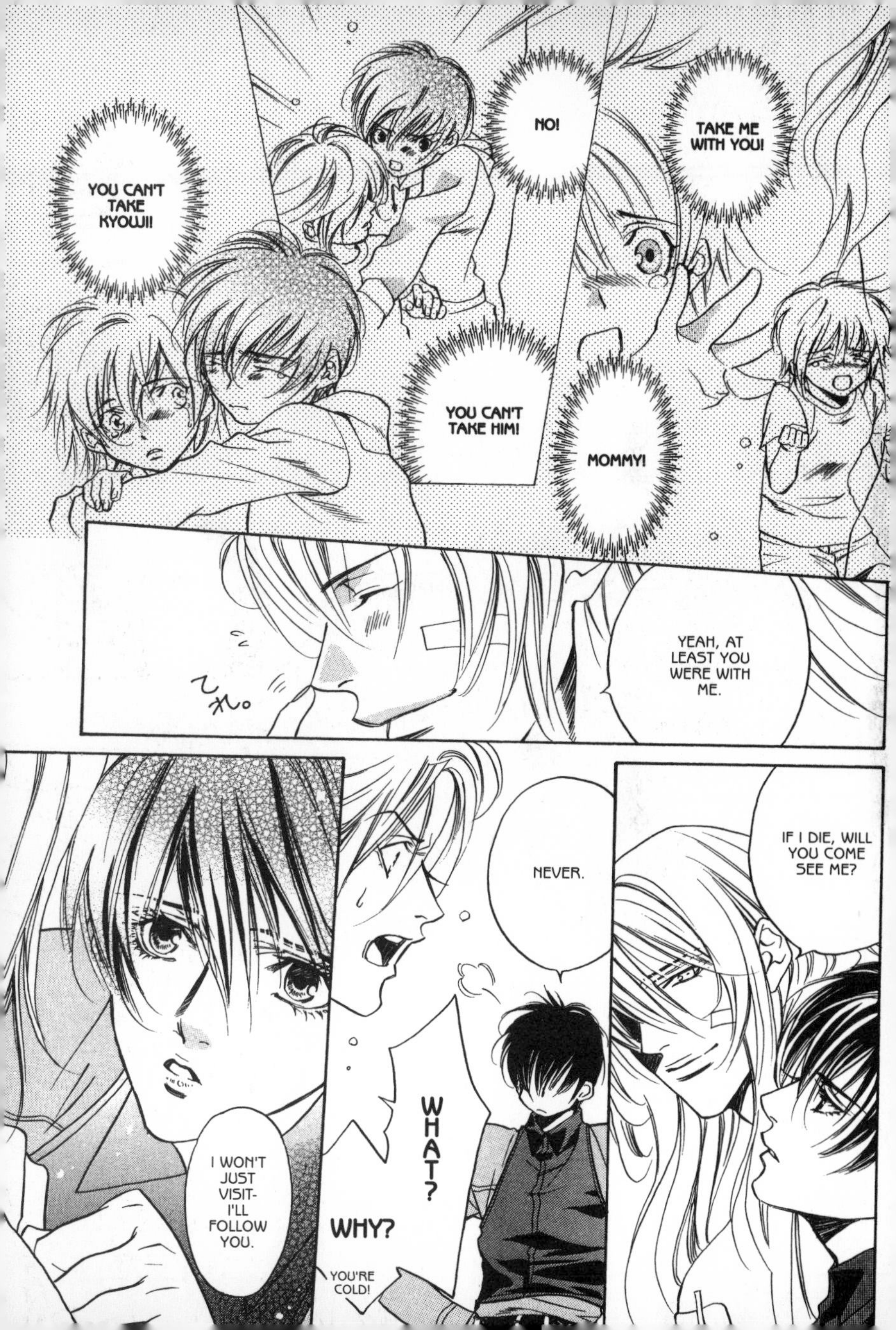
TAKE ME WITH YOU!
NO!
MOMMY!
YOU CAN'T TAKE HIM!
YOU CAN'T TAKE KYOUJI!
YEAH, AT LEAST YOU WERE WITH ME.
IF I DIE, WILL YOU COME SEE ME?
NEVER.
WHAT?
WHY?
YOU'RE COLD!
I WON'T JUST VISIT- I'LL FOLLOW YOU.

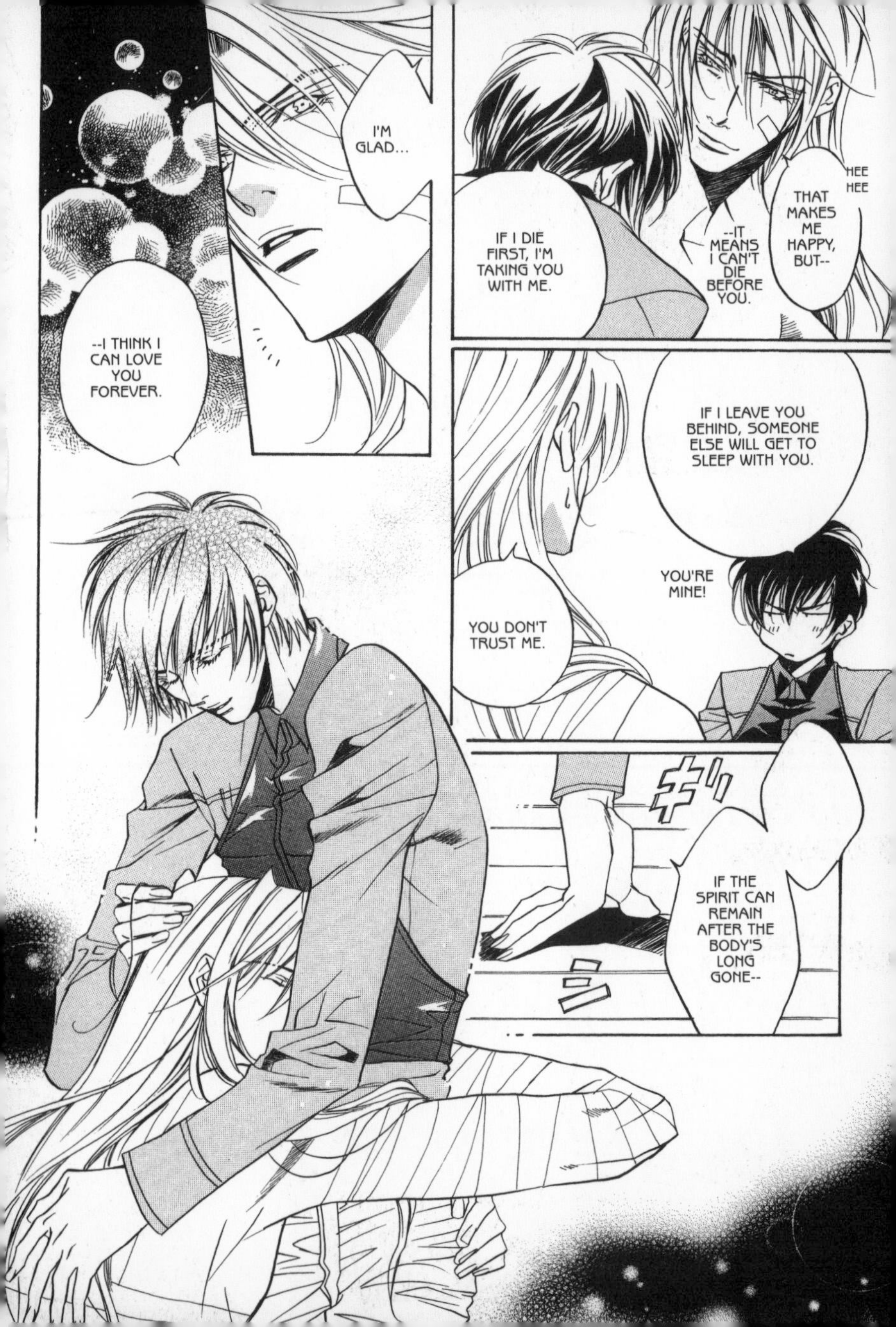
HEE HEE
THAT MAKES ME HAPPY, BUT--
--IT MEANS I CAN'T DIE BEFORE YOU.
IF I DIE FIRST, I'M TAKING YOU WITH ME.
IF I LEAVE YOU BEHIND, SOMEONE ELSE WILL GET TO SLEEP WITH YOU.
YOU'RE MINE!
YOU DON'T TRUST ME.
IF THE SPIRIT CAN REMAIN AFTER THE BODY'S LONG GONE--
I'M GLAD...
--I THINK I CAN LOVE YOU FOREVER.

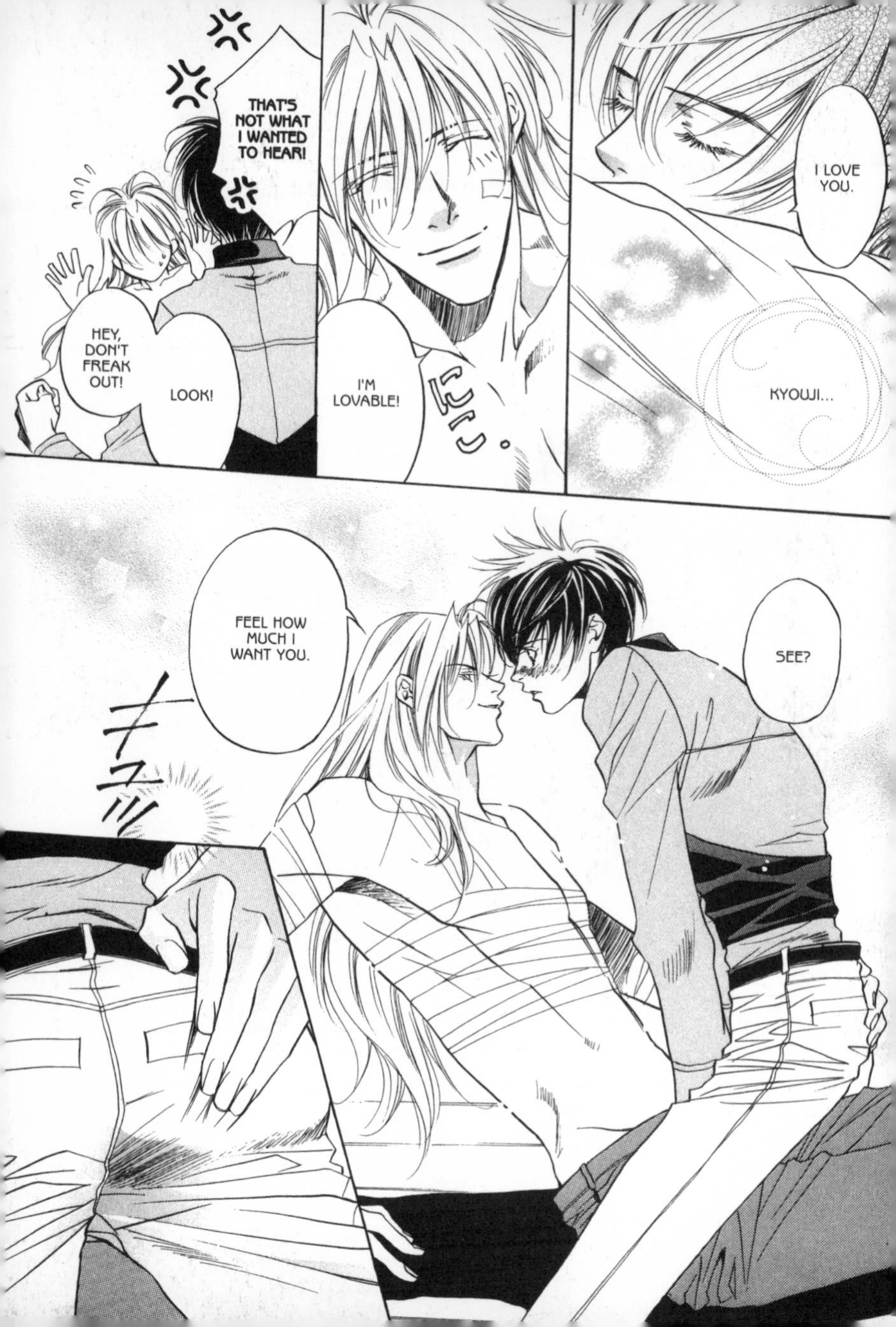
KYOUJI...
I LOVE YOU.
I'M LOVABLE!
にこ
THAT'S NOT WHAT I WANTED TO HEAR!
LOOK!
HEY, DON'T FREAK OUT!
SEE?
FEEL HOW MUCH I WANT YOU.

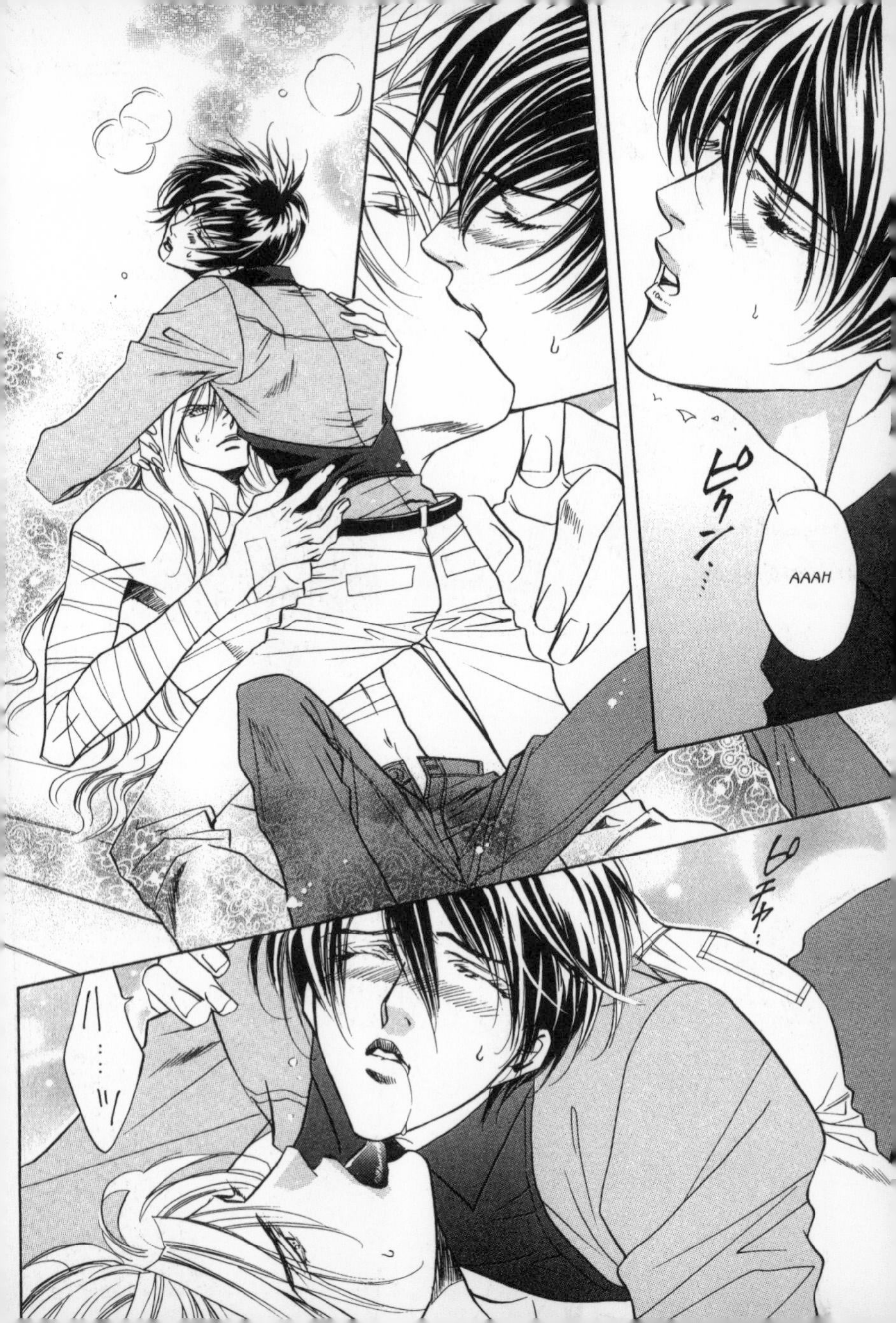

ピクン…
AAAH
ピチャ…
ハ…ッ

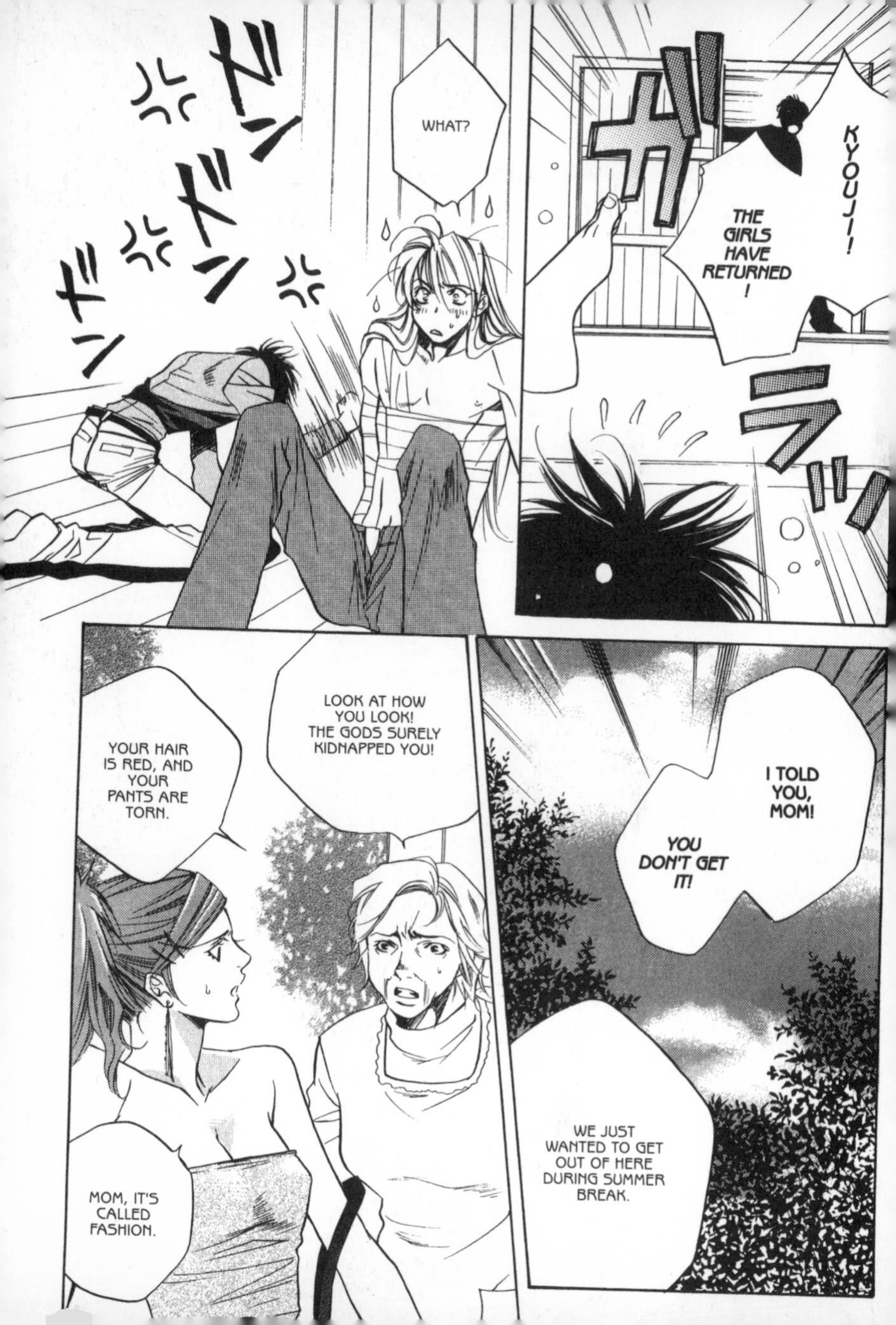

KYOUJI!
THE GIRLS HAVE RETURNED!
ガッ
ラッ
WHAT?
ドン
ドン
ドン
I TOLD YOU, MOM!
YOU DON'T GET IT!
WE JUST WANTED TO GET OUT OF HERE DURING SUMMER BREAK.
LOOK AT HOW YOU LOOK! THE GODS SURELY KIDNAPPED YOU!
YOUR HAIR IS RED, AND YOUR PANTS ARE TORN.
MOM, IT'S CALLED FASHION.

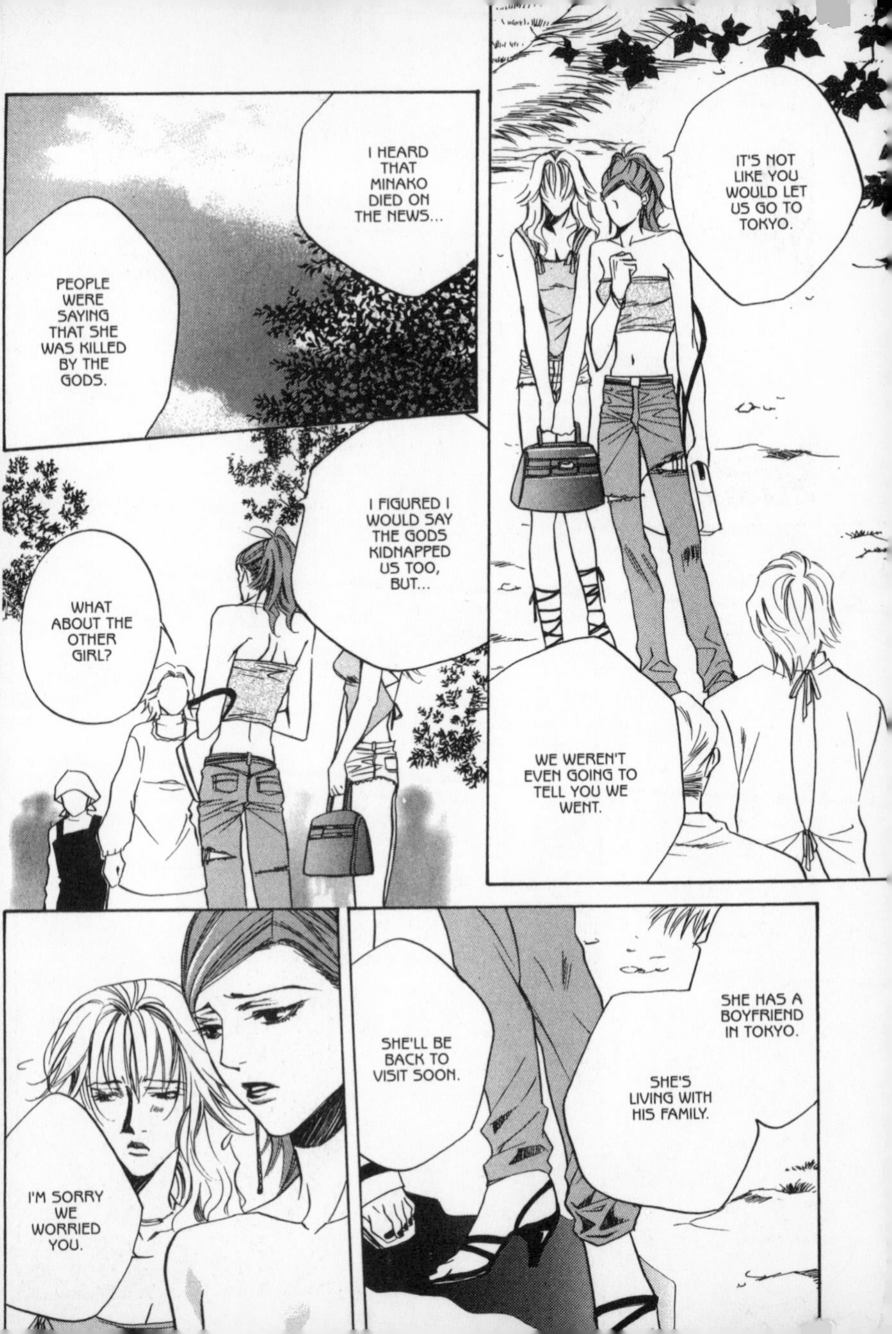
IT'S NOT LIKE YOU WOULD LET US GO TO TOKYO.
WE WEREN'T EVEN GOING TO TELL YOU WE WENT.
I HEARD THAT MINAKO DIED ON THE NEWS...
PEOPLE WERE SAYING THAT SHE WAS KILLED BY THE GODS.
I FIGURED I WOULD SAY THE GODS KIDNAPPED US TOO, BUT...
WHAT ABOUT THE OTHER GIRL?
SHE HAS A BOYFRIEND IN TOKYO.
SHE'S LIVING WITH HIS FAMILY.
SHE'LL BE BACK TO VISIT SOON.
I'M SORRY WE WORRIED YOU.

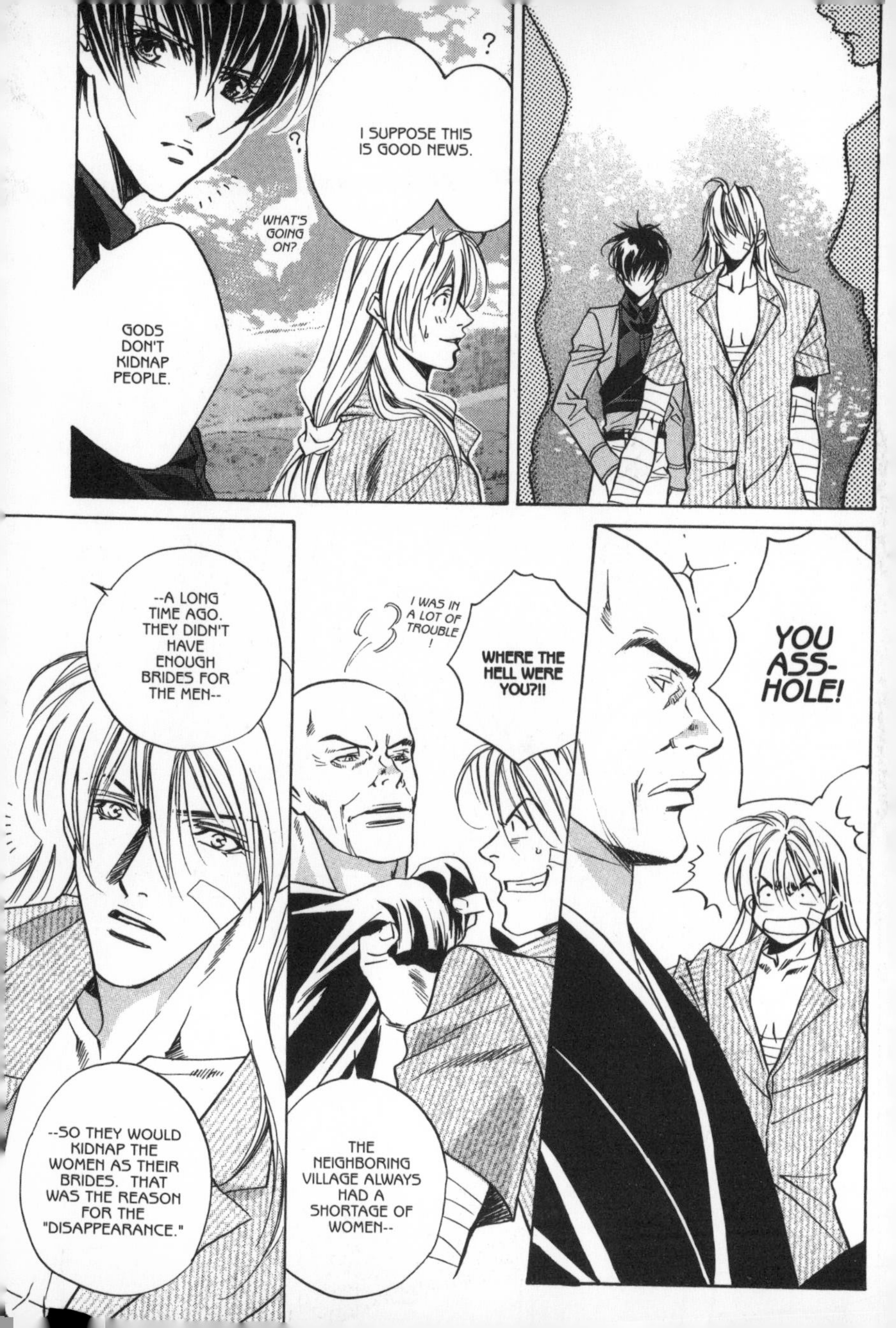

I SUPPOSE THIS IS GOOD NEWS.
WHAT'S GOING ON?
GODS DON'T KIDNAP PEOPLE.
YOU ASS-HOLE!
WHERE THE HELL WERE YOU?!!
I WAS IN A LOT OF TROUBLE!
THE NEIGHBORING VILLAGE ALWAYS HAD A SHORTAGE OF WOMEN--
--A LONG TIME AGO. THEY DIDN'T HAVE ENOUGH BRIDES FOR THE MEN--
--SO THEY WOULD KIDNAP THE WOMEN AS THEIR BRIDES. THAT WAS THE REASON FOR THE "DISAPPEARANCE."

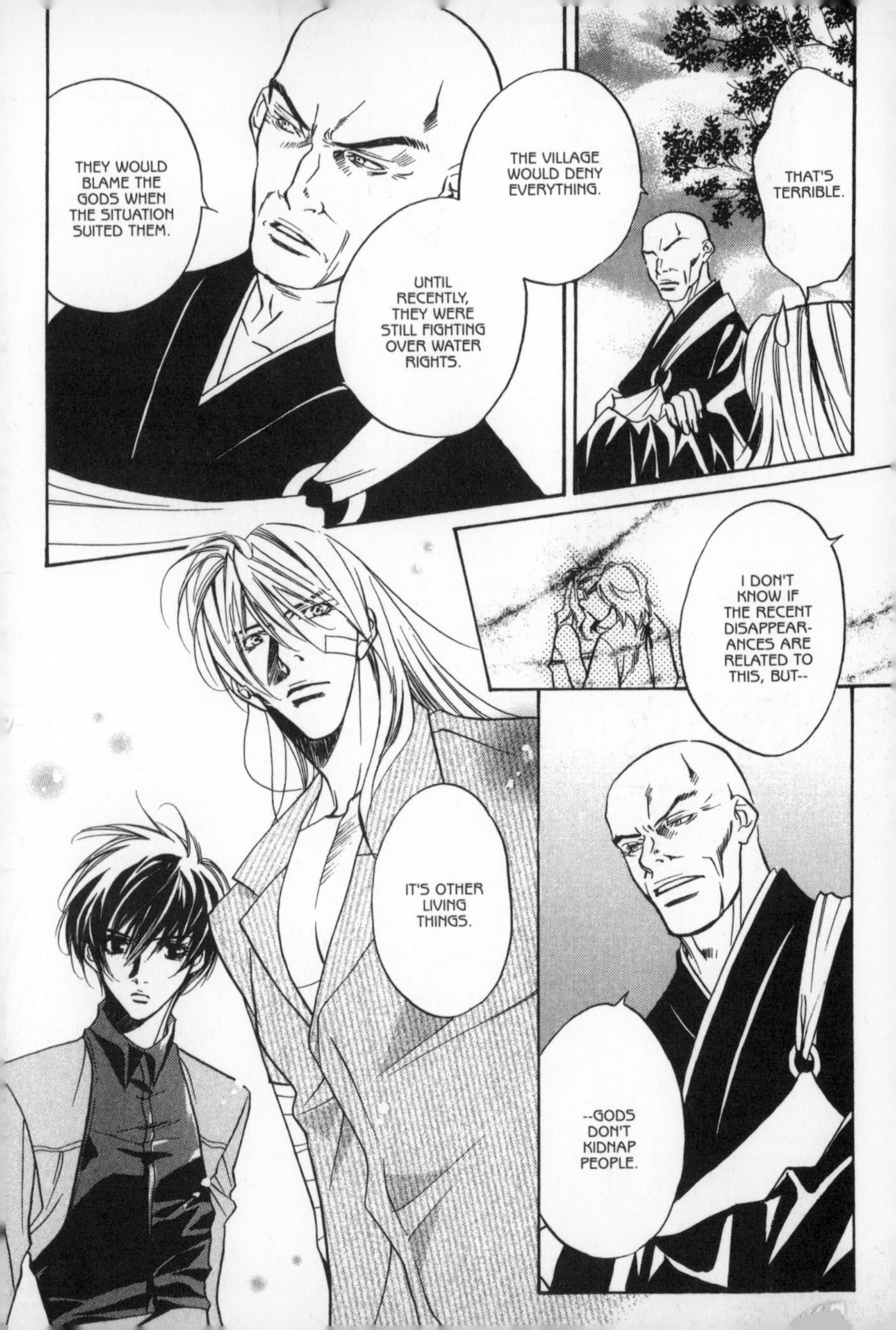
THAT'S TERRIBLE.
THE VILLAGE WOULD DENY EVERYTHING.
UNTIL RECENTLY, THEY WERE STILL FIGHTING OVER WATER RIGHTS.
THEY WOULD BLAME THE GODS WHEN THE SITUATION SUITED THEM.
I DON'T KNOW IF THE RECENT DISAPPEAR-ANCES ARE RELATED TO THIS, BUT--
--GODS DON'T KIDNAP PEOPLE.
IT'S OTHER LIVING THINGS.

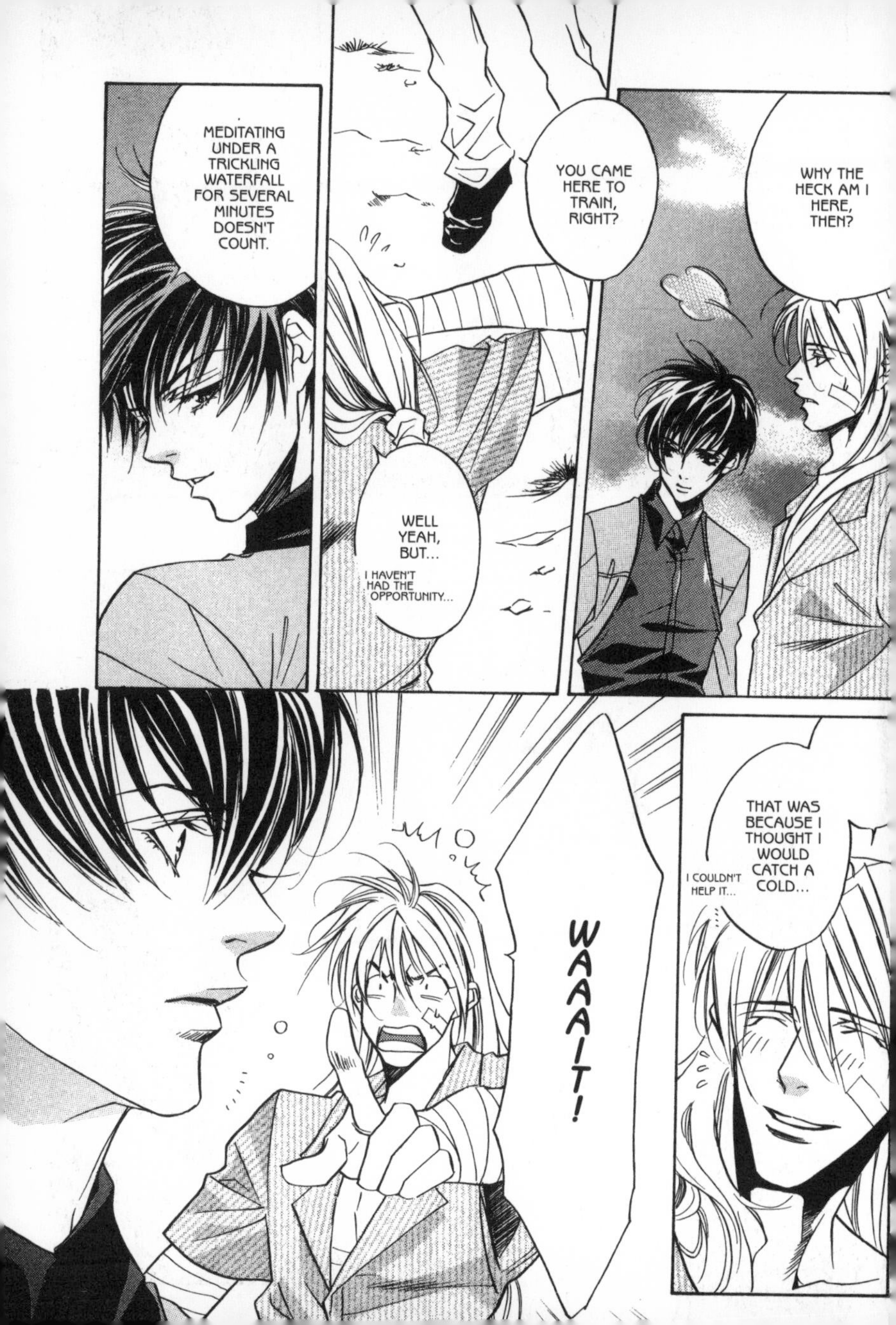
WHY THE HECK AM I HERE, THEN?
YOU CAME HERE TO TRAIN, RIGHT?
WELL YEAH, BUT...
I HAVEN'T HAD THE OPPORTUNITY...
MEDITATING UNDER A TRICKLING WATERFALL FOR SEVERAL MINUTES DOESN'T COUNT.
THAT WAS BECAUSE I THOUGHT I WOULD CATCH A COLD...
I COULDN'T HELP IT...
WAAAIT!

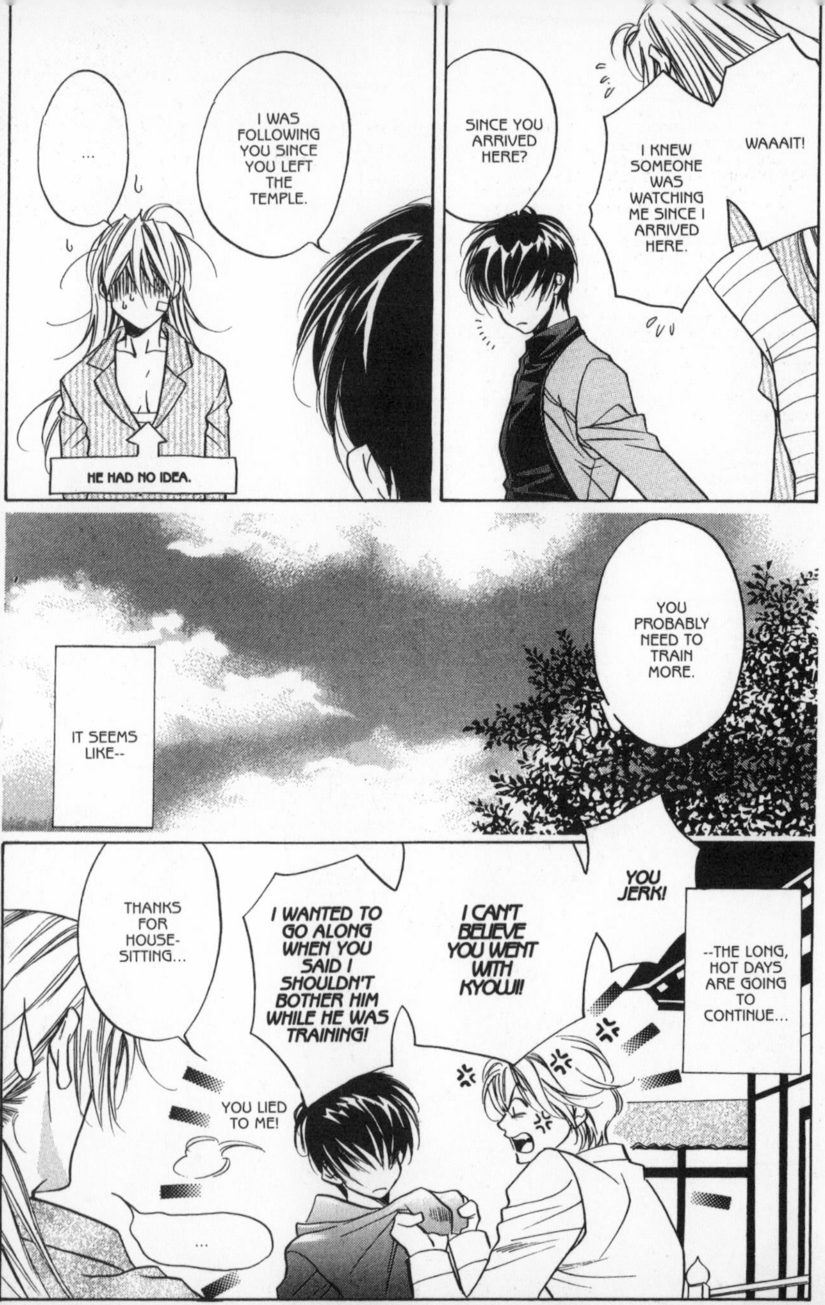
WAAAIT!
I KNEW SOMEONE WAS WATCHING ME SINCE I ARRIVED HERE.
SINCE YOU ARRIVED HERE?
I WAS FOLLOWING YOU SINCE YOU LEFT THE TEMPLE.
...
HE HAD NO IDEA.
YOU PROBABLY NEED TO TRAIN MORE.
IT SEEMS LIKE--
--THE LONG, HOT DAYS ARE GOING TO CONTINUE...
YOU JERK!
I CAN'T BELIEVE YOU WENT WITH KYOUJI!
I WANTED TO GO ALONG WHEN YOU SAID I SHOULDN'T BOTHER HIM WHILE HE WAS TRAINING!
THANKS FOR HOUSE-SITTING...
YOU LIED TO ME!
...

I CAN'T STOP WANTING YOU / END

⇨ COMMENT

コメント

IT'S BEEN A YEAR SINCE THE LAST VOLUME WAS RELEASED. "I CAN'T STOP LOVING YOU 2" HAS FINALLY BEEN PUBLISHED! IT SEEMS LIKE ALL THE EDITING AND CORRECTIONS I DID FOR VOLUME 1 WAS LIKE A DREAM... I CAN'T COMPLAIN. I TRIED REALLY HARD, BUT LIFE JUST DOES NOT GO THE WAY YOU WANT IT TO. I WAS THINKING OF VARIOUS DIFFERENT VERSIONS OF THE TITLE FOR THE FINAL EPISODE, BUT... OH WELL.

I'D LIKE TO SUPPORT ALL MY FANS AND EVERYONE THAT SENT ME FAN MAIL. I CAN'T THANK YOU ENOUGH! IT'S TOO BAD THAT I COULDN'T TALK MORE ABOUT KYOUJI'S SITUATION, OR WHY KAORU WAS IN HONG KONG, ETC ... I'M SORRY.

THE CHARACTERS WERE REALLY MY FAVORITE, AND SOMEWHAT TYPICAL OF THE TOP/BOTTOM RELATIONSHIP THAT'S STANDARD IN BOY'S LOVE STORIES. THE TOP IS A HOT SEXY GUY, AND THE BOTTOM IS A STRONG, HORNY (WELL, THEY'RE BOYS AFTER ALL) PERSON. IT WASN'T JUST ABOUT ROMANCE, BUT ALSO ABOUT CARING FOR EACH OTHER. RECENTLY, THERE HAVE BEEN MORE STORIES OF THE BOTTOM PURSING THE TOP... HEH HEH HEH. THAT'S WHAT I LIKE TO SEE! I REALLY WANTED TO MAKE THEM A SUPER HAPPY COUPLE, BUT I'M SURE THEY'RE RUNNING AROUND AND HAVING FUN SOMEWHERE. I HOPE THE STORY REMAINS A FOND MEMORY FOR MY READERS. THANK YOU SO MUCH FOR YOUR SUPPORT.

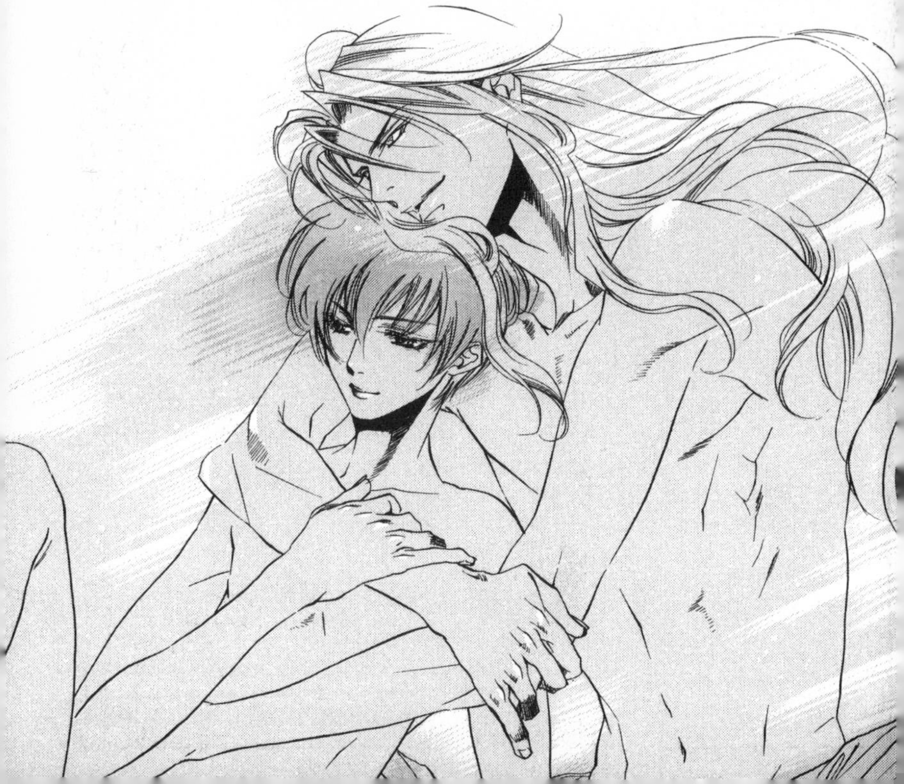

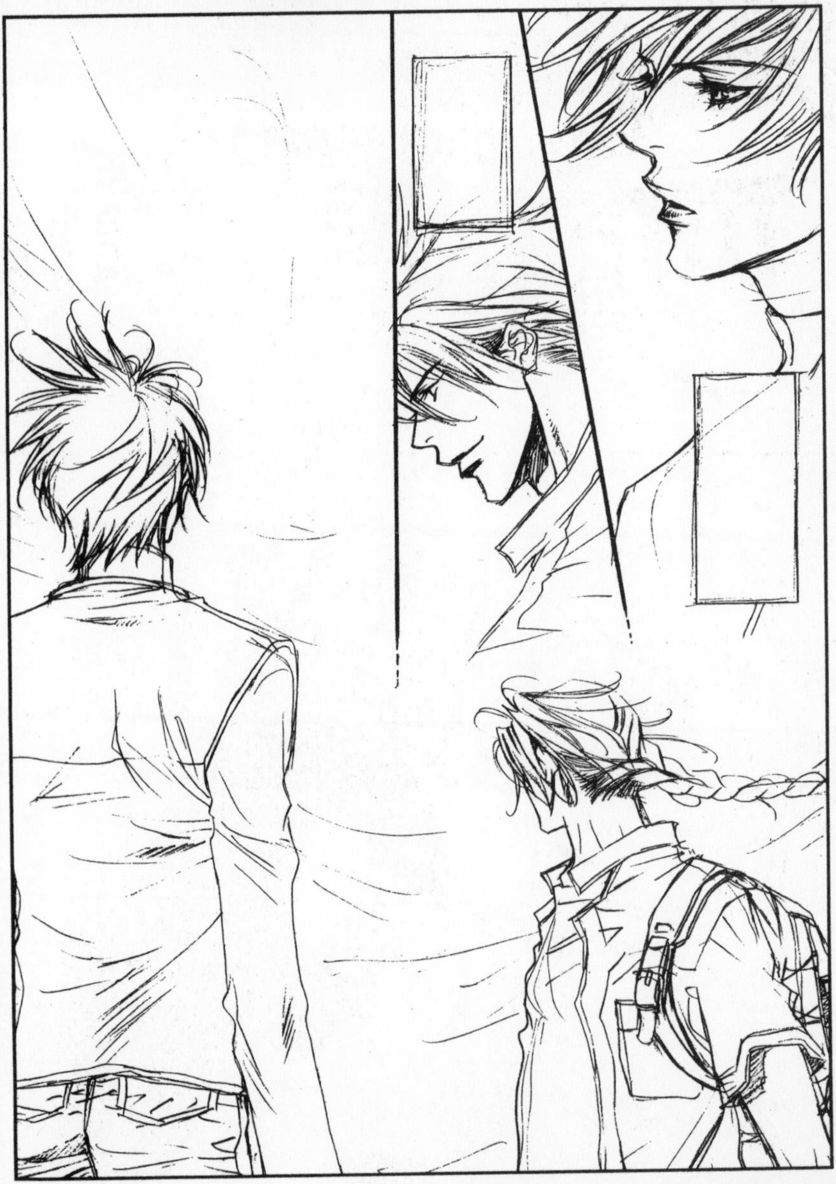

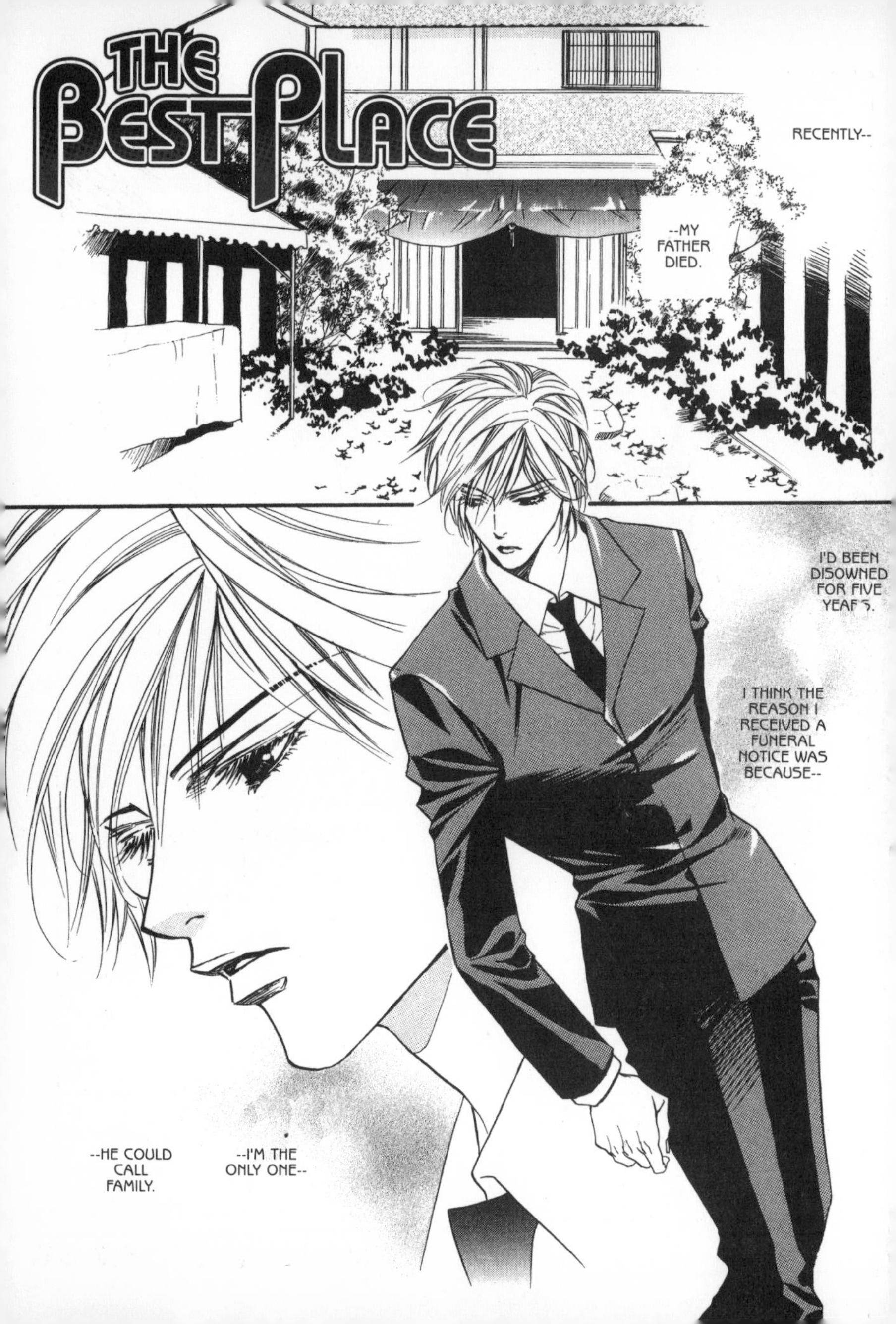
THE BEST PLACE
RECENTLY--
--MY FATHER DIED.
I'D BEEN DISOWNED FOR FIVE YEARS.
I THINK THE REASON I RECEIVED A FUNERAL NOTICE WAS BECAUSE--
--I'M THE ONLY ONE--
--HE COULD CALL FAMILY.

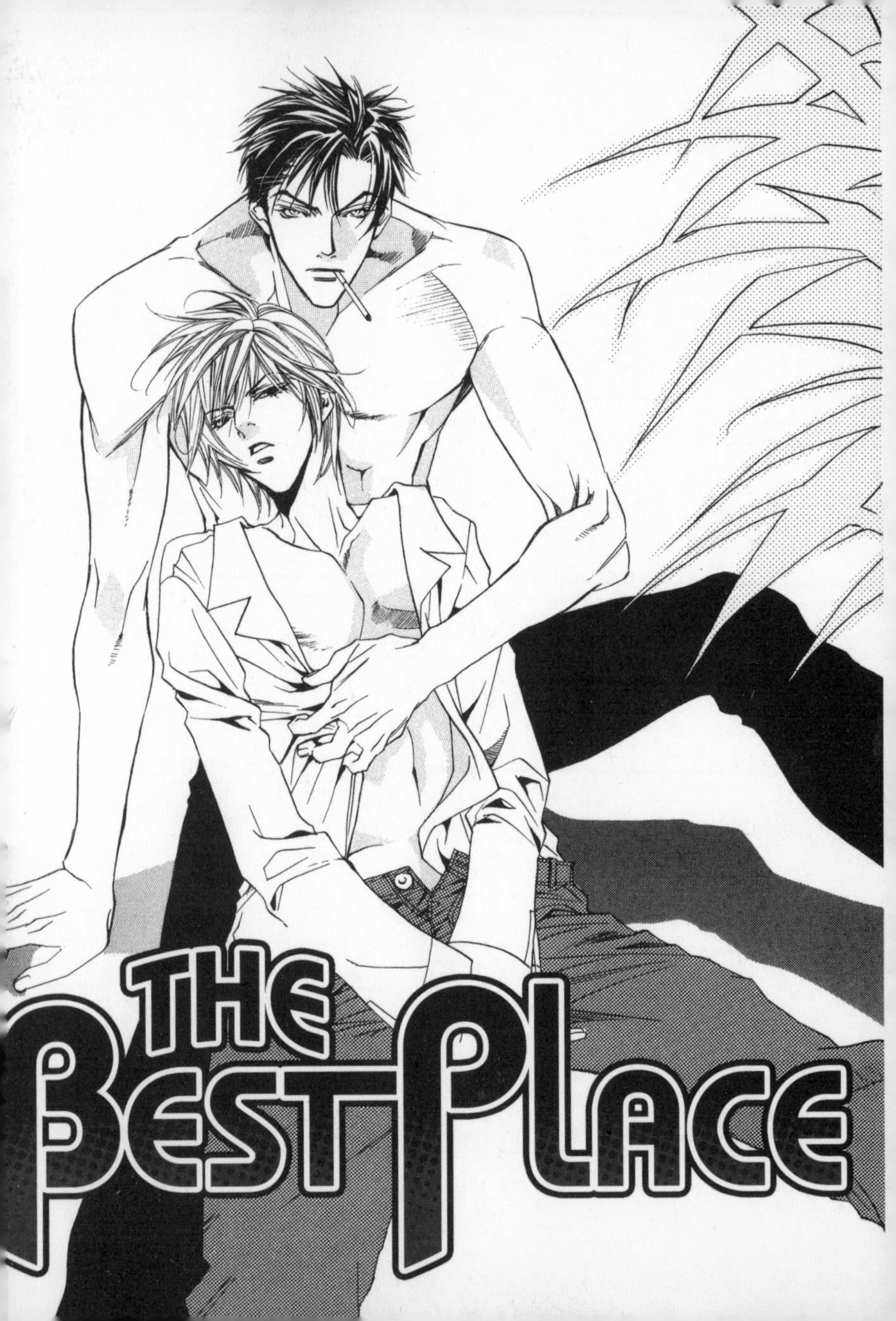
THE
BEST PLACE

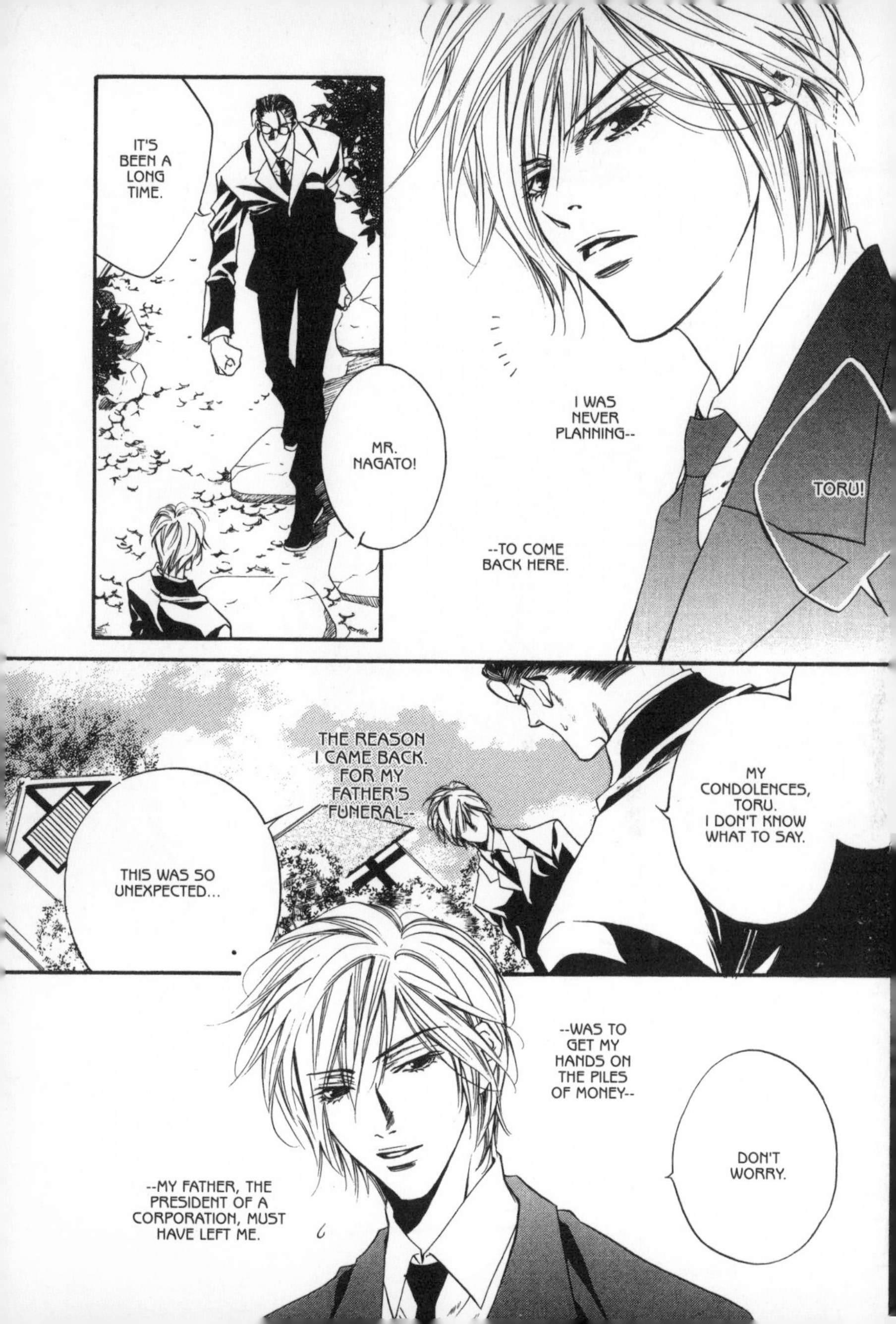
TORU!
I WAS NEVER PLANNING--
--TO COME BACK HERE.
MR. NAGATO!
IT'S BEEN A LONG TIME.
MY CONDOLENCES, TORU. I DON'T KNOW WHAT TO SAY.
THE REASON I CAME BACK. FOR MY FATHER'S FUNERAL--
THIS WAS SO UNEXPECTED...
DON'T WORRY.
--WAS TO GET MY HANDS ON THE PILES OF MONEY--
--MY FATHER, THE PRESIDENT OF A CORPORATION, MUST HAVE LEFT ME.

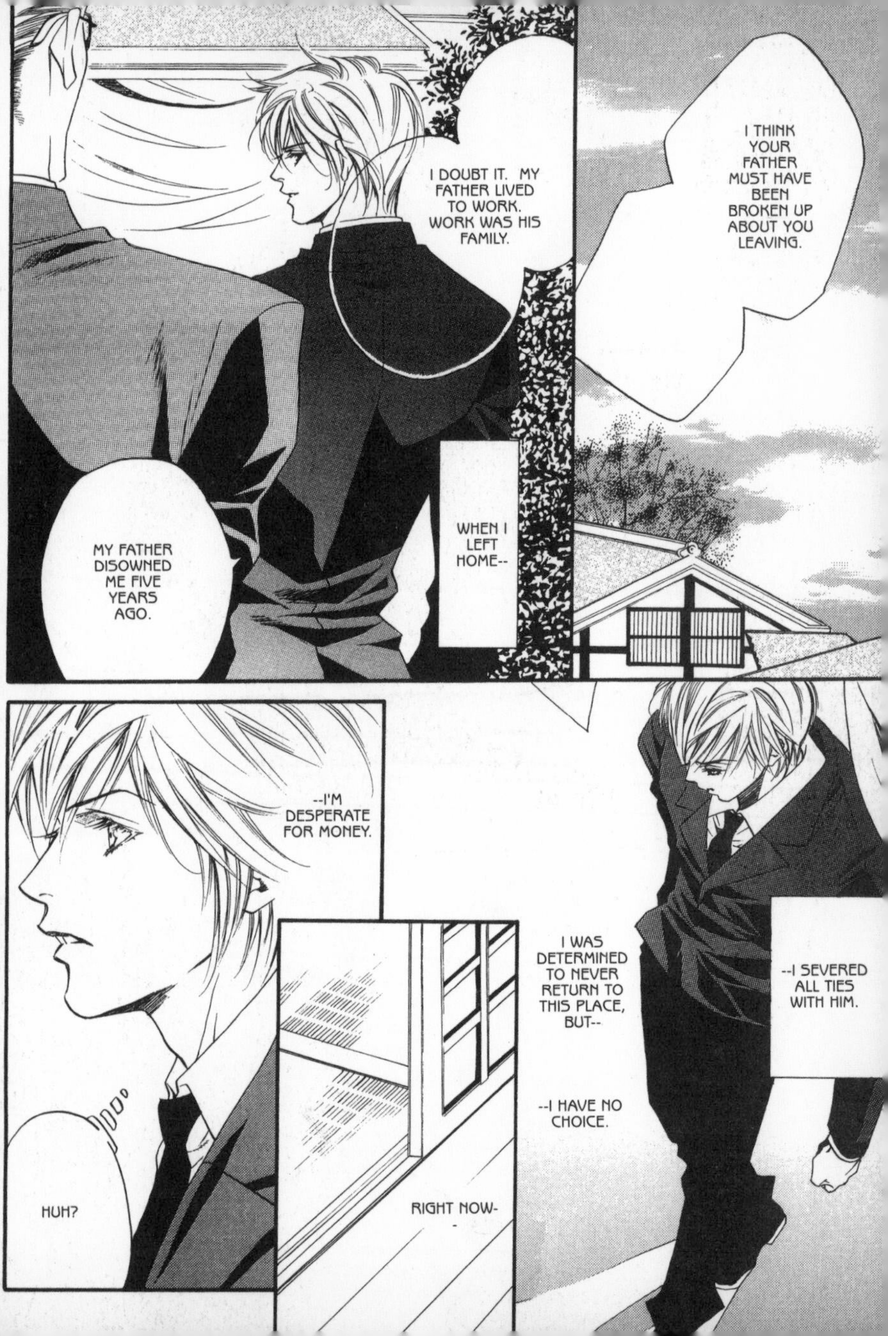
I THINK YOUR FATHER MUST HAVE BEEN BROKEN UP ABOUT YOU LEAVING.
I DOUBT IT. MY FATHER LIVED TO WORK. WORK WAS HIS FAMILY.
WHEN I LEFT HOME--
MY FATHER DISOWNED ME FIVE YEARS AGO.
--I SEVERED ALL TIES WITH HIM.
I WAS DETERMINED TO NEVER RETURN TO THIS PLACE, BUT--
--I HAVE NO CHOICE.
RIGHT NOW--
--I'M DESPERATE FOR MONEY.
HUH?

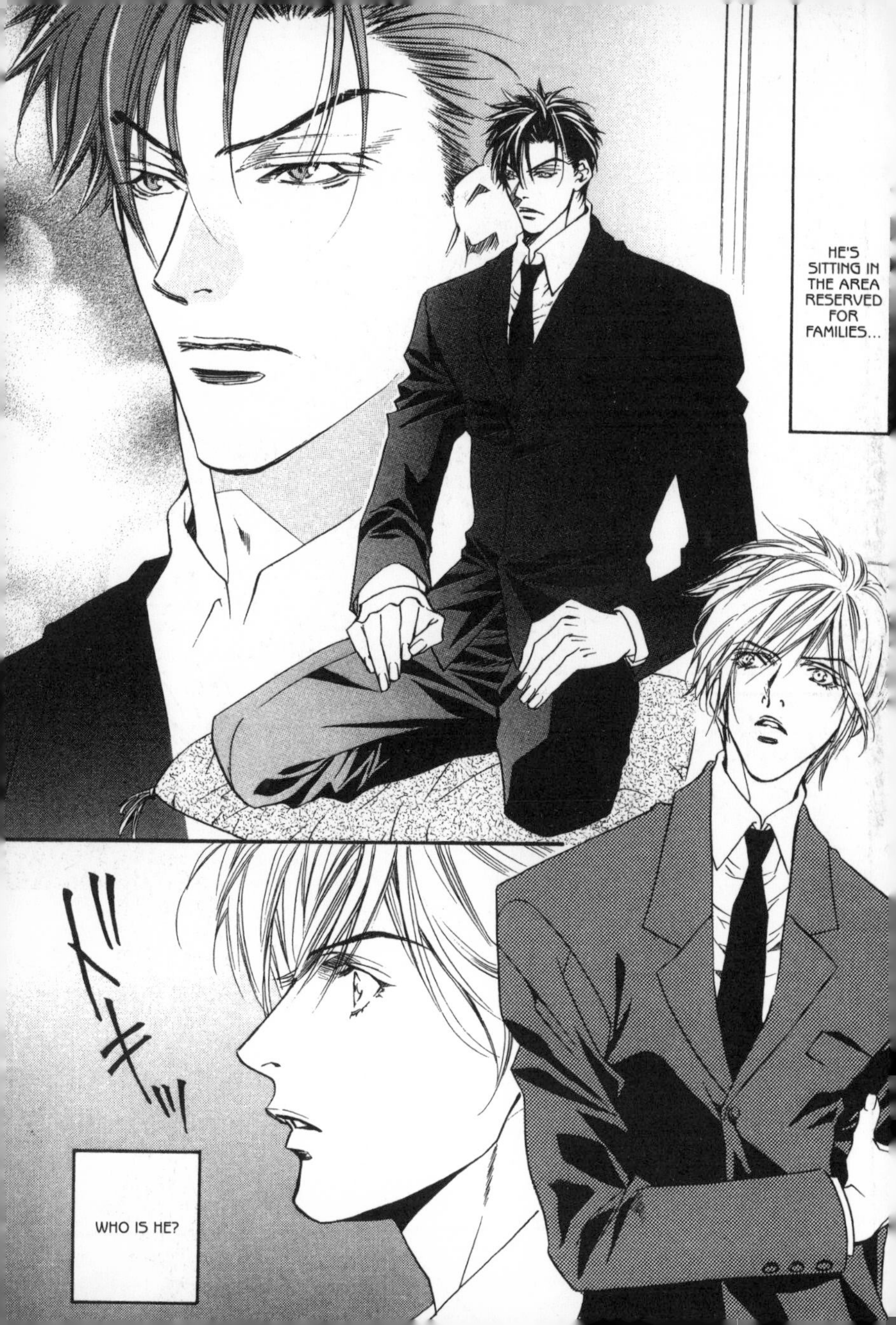
HE'S SITTING IN THE AREA RESERVED FOR FAMILIES...
WHO IS HE?

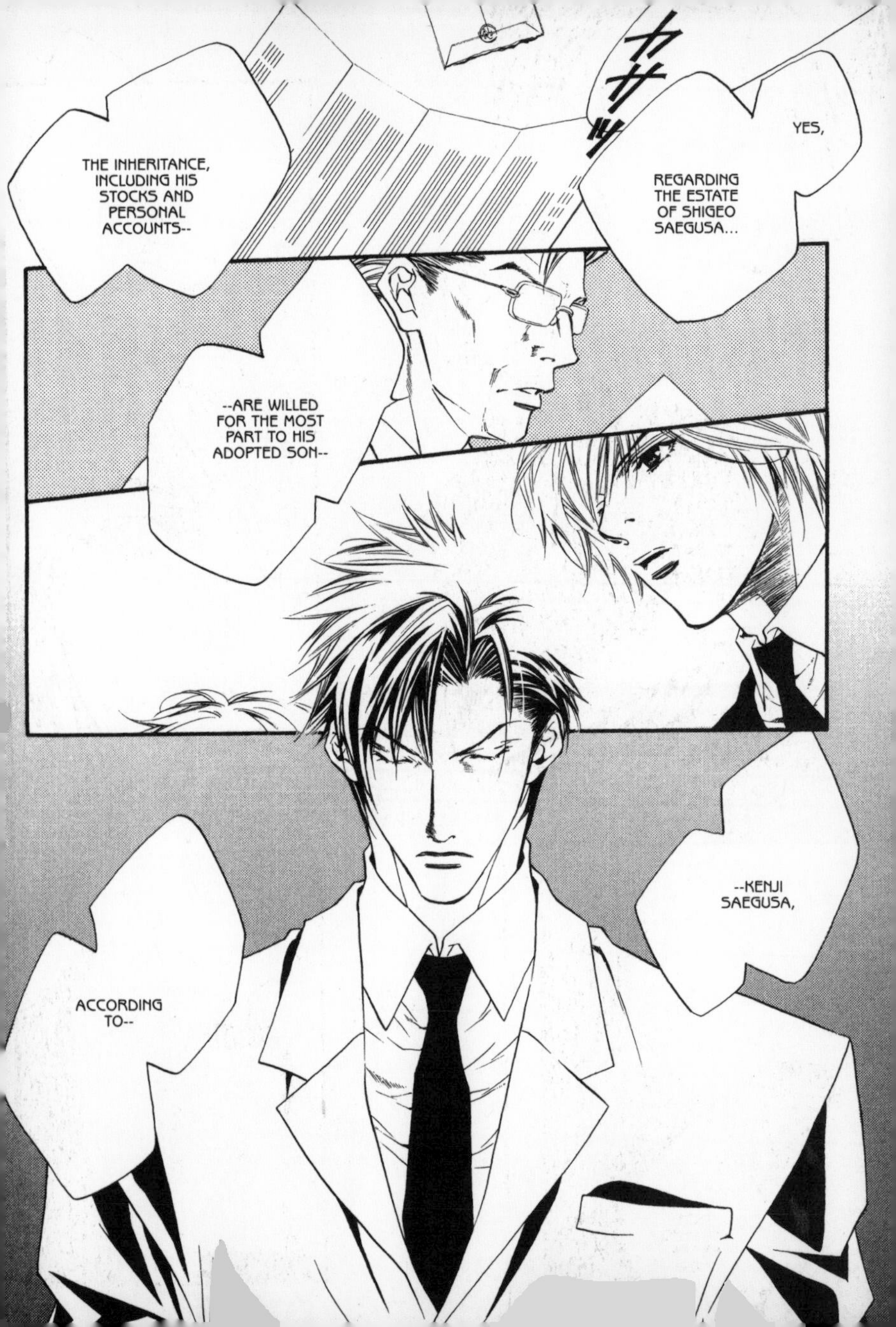

YES,
REGARDING THE ESTATE OF SHIGEO SAEGUSA...
カサッ
THE INHERITANCE, INCLUDING HIS STOCKS AND PERSONAL ACCOUNTS--
--ARE WILLED FOR THE MOST PART TO HIS ADOPTED SON--
--KENJI SAEGUSA,
ACCORDING TO--

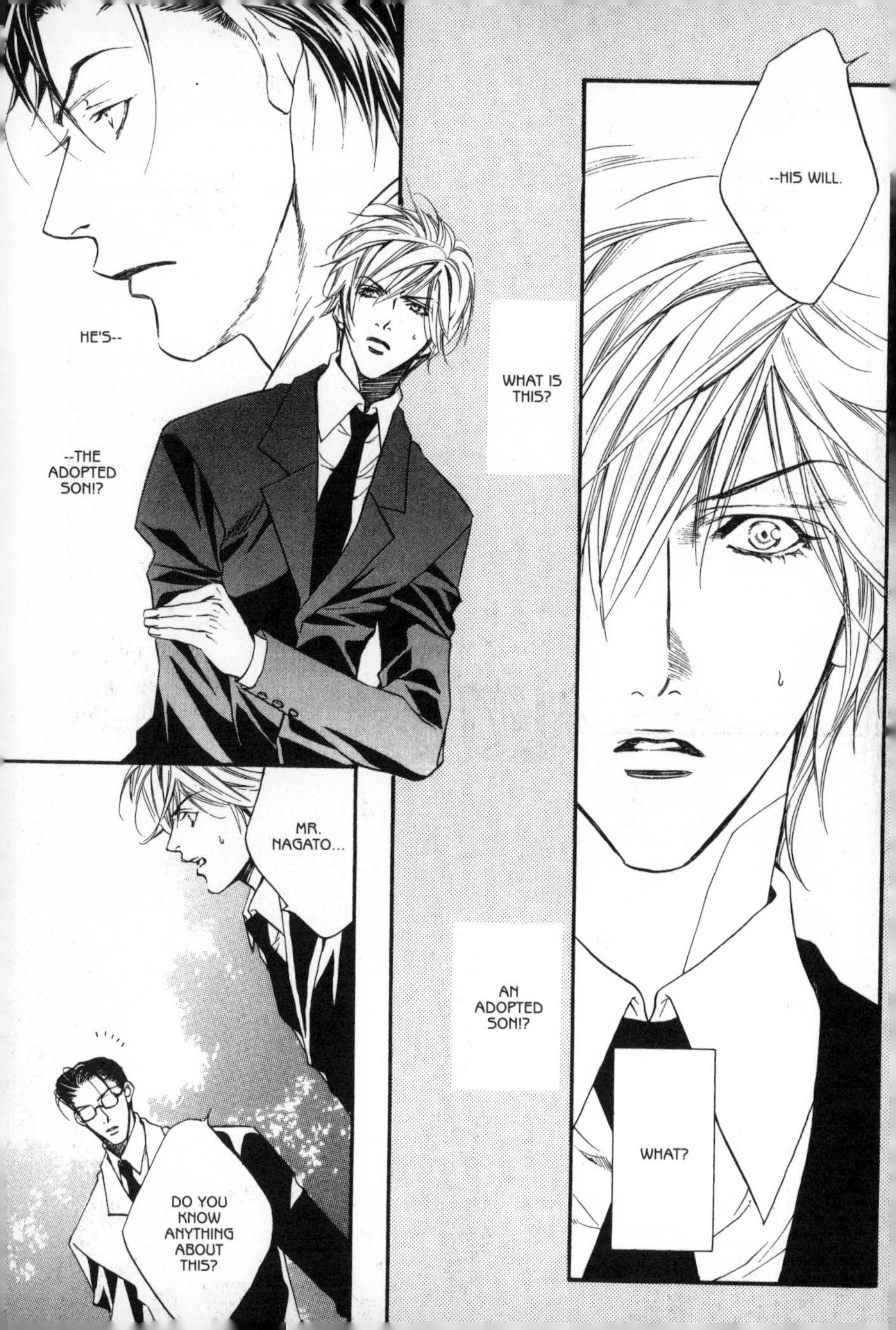
--HIS WILL.
WHAT IS THIS?
AN ADOPTED SON!?
WHAT?
HE'S--
--THE ADOPTED SON!?
MR. NAGATO...
DO YOU KNOW ANYTHING ABOUT THIS?

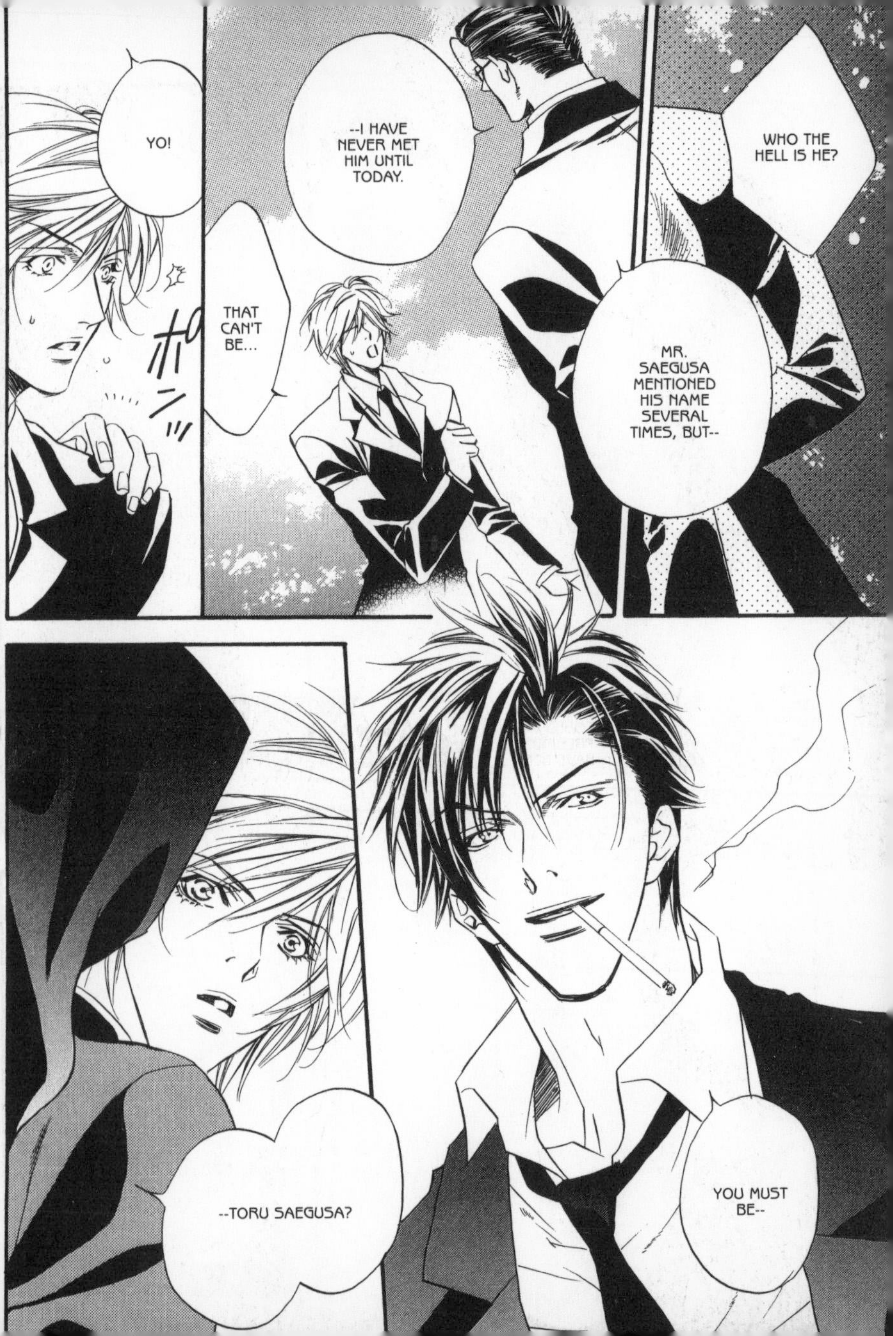
WHO THE HELL IS HE?
MR. SAEGUSA MENTIONED HIS NAME SEVERAL TIMES, BUT--
--I HAVE NEVER MET HIM UNTIL TODAY.
THAT CAN'T BE...
YO!
YOU MUST BE--
--TORU SAEGUSA?

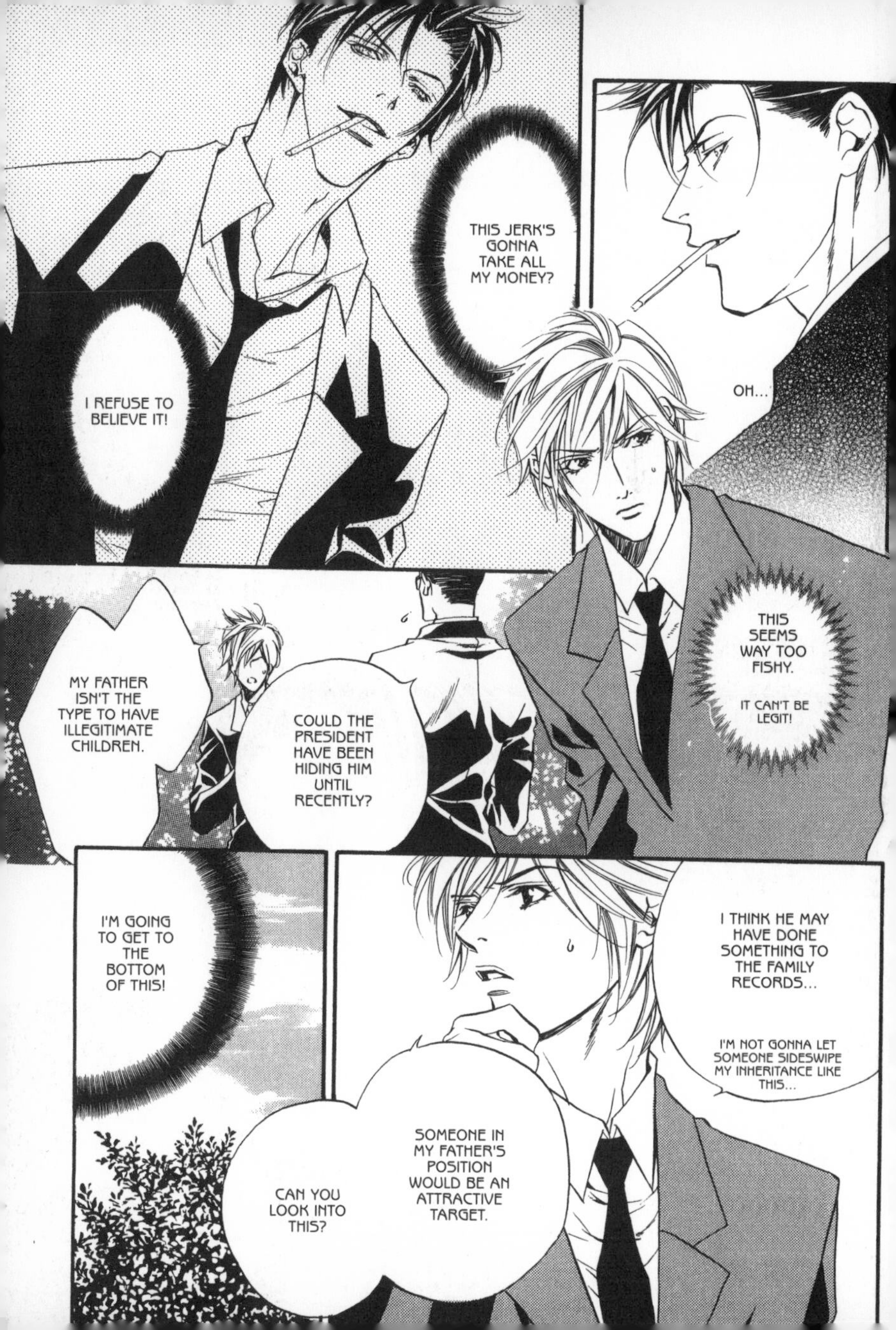
OH...
THIS JERK'S GONNA TAKE ALL MY MONEY?
I REFUSE TO BELIEVE IT!
THIS SEEMS WAY TOO FISHY.
IT CAN'T BE LEGIT!
COULD THE PRESIDENT HAVE BEEN HIDING HIM UNTIL RECENTLY?
MY FATHER ISN'T THE TYPE TO HAVE ILLEGITIMATE CHILDREN.
I THINK HE MAY HAVE DONE SOMETHING TO THE FAMILY RECORDS...
I'M NOT GONNA LET SOMEONE SIDESWIPE MY INHERITANCE LIKE THIS...
SOMEONE IN MY FATHER'S POSITION WOULD BE AN ATTRACTIVE TARGET.
CAN YOU LOOK INTO THIS?
I'M GOING TO GET TO THE BOTTOM OF THIS!

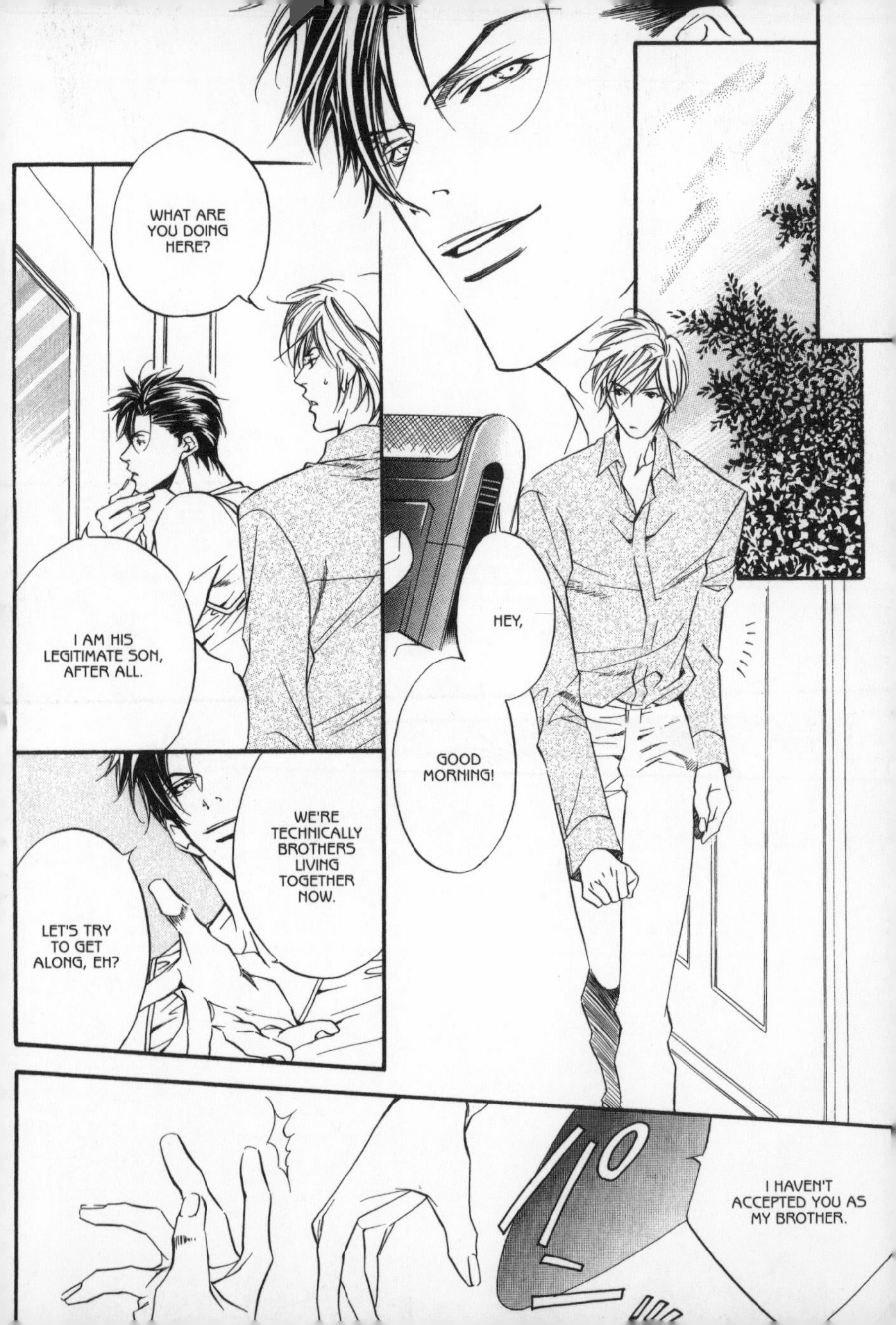
HEY,
GOOD MORNING!
WHAT ARE YOU DOING HERE?
I AM HIS LEGITIMATE SON, AFTER ALL.
WE'RE TECHNICALLY BROTHERS LIVING TOGETHER NOW.
LET'S TRY TO GET ALONG, EH?
I HAVEN'T ACCEPTED YOU AS MY BROTHER.

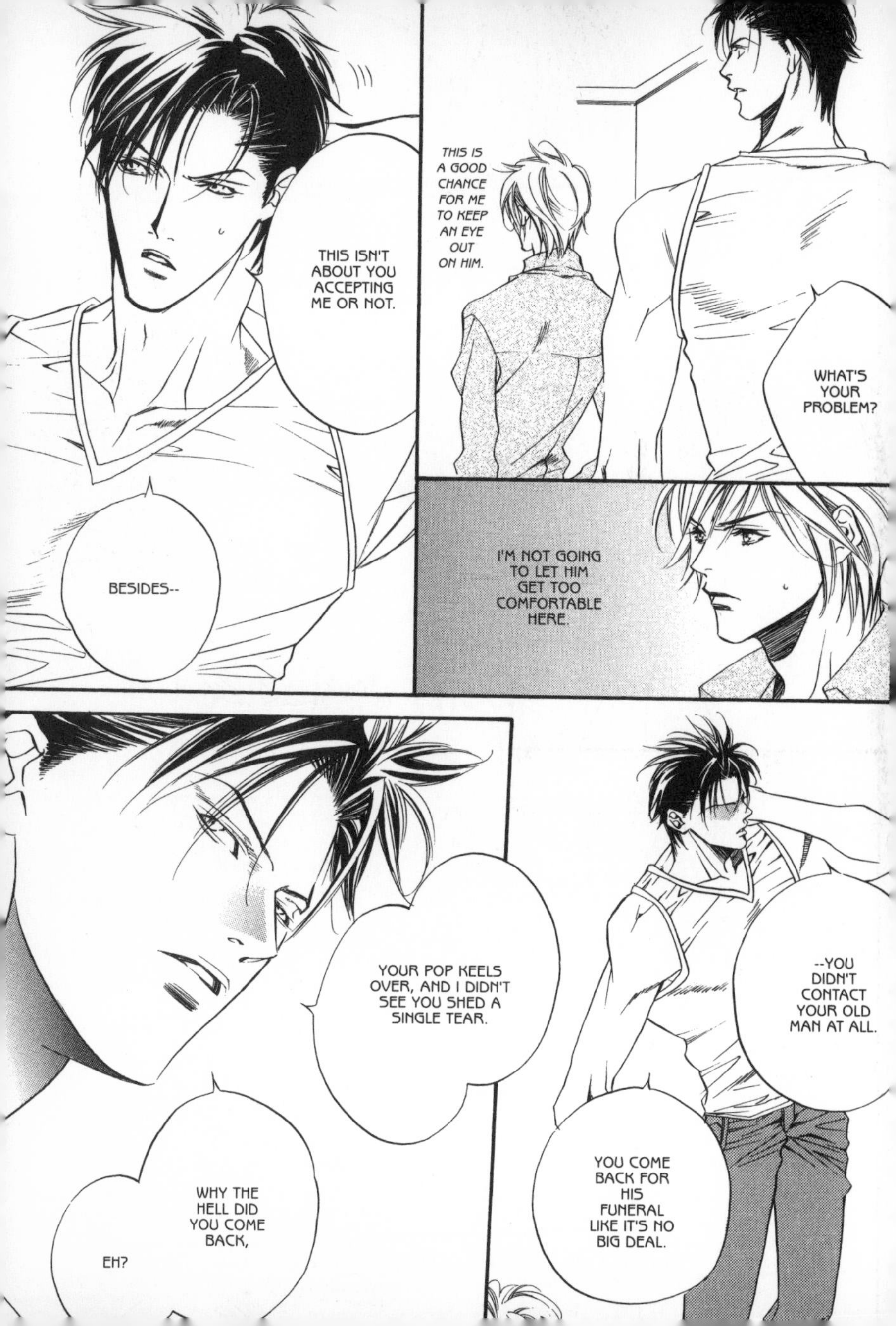
WHAT'S YOUR PROBLEM?
THIS IS A GOOD CHANCE FOR ME TO KEEP AN EYE OUT ON HIM.
I'M NOT GOING TO LET HIM GET TOO COMFORTABLE HERE.
THIS ISN'T ABOUT YOU ACCEPTING ME OR NOT.
BESIDES--
--YOU DIDN'T CONTACT YOUR OLD MAN AT ALL.
YOU COME BACK FOR HIS FUNERAL LIKE IT'S NO BIG DEAL.
YOUR POP KEELS OVER, AND I DIDN'T SEE YOU SHED A SINGLE TEAR.
WHY THE HELL DID YOU COME BACK,
EH?

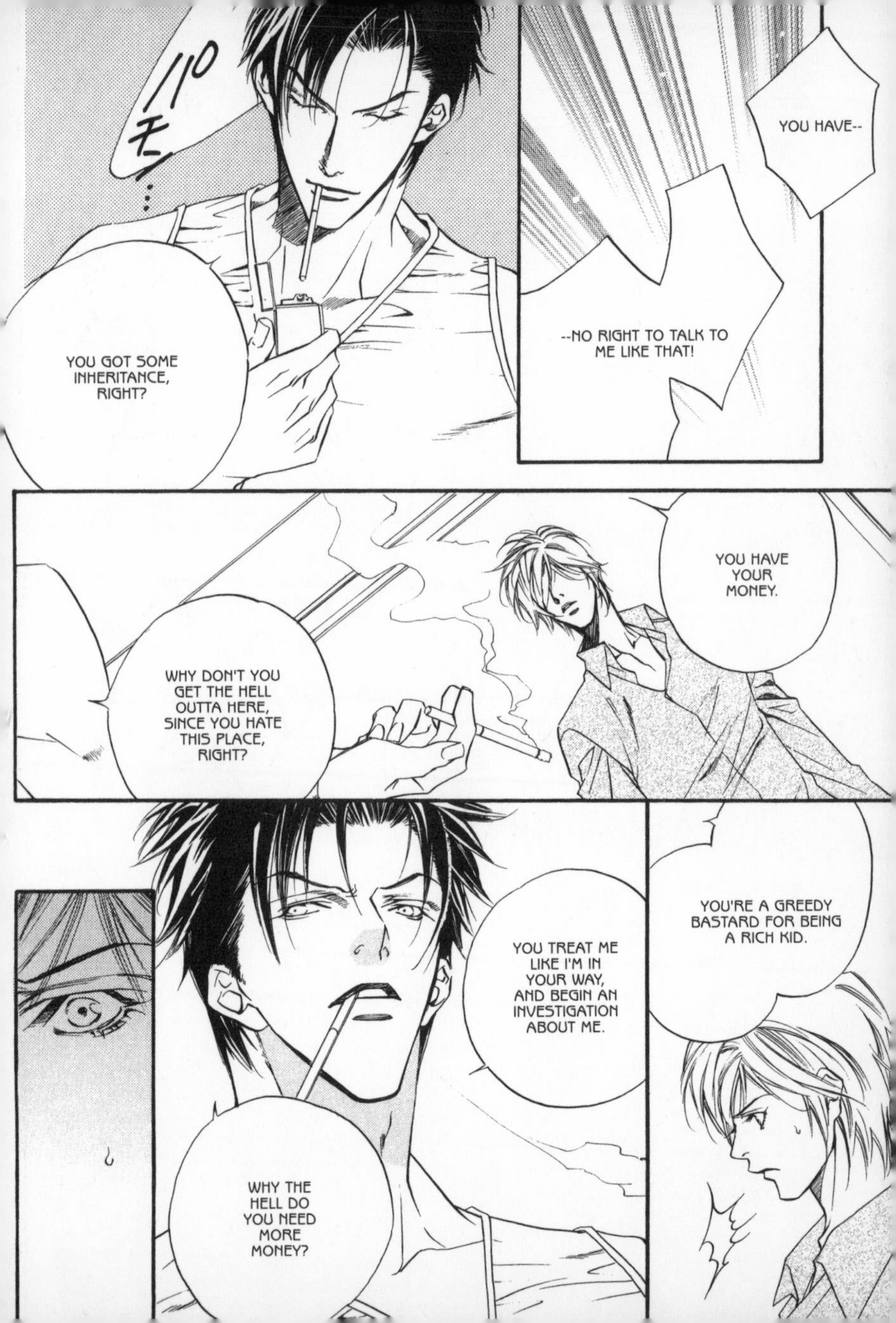
YOU HAVE--
--NO RIGHT TO TALK TO ME LIKE THAT!
YOU GOT SOME INHERITANCE, RIGHT?
YOU HAVE YOUR MONEY.
WHY DON'T YOU GET THE HELL OUTTA HERE, SINCE YOU HATE THIS PLACE, RIGHT?
YOU'RE A GREEDY BASTARD FOR BEING A RICH KID.
YOU TREAT ME LIKE I'M IN YOUR WAY, AND BEGIN AN INVESTIGATION ABOUT ME.
WHY THE HELL DO YOU NEED MORE MONEY?

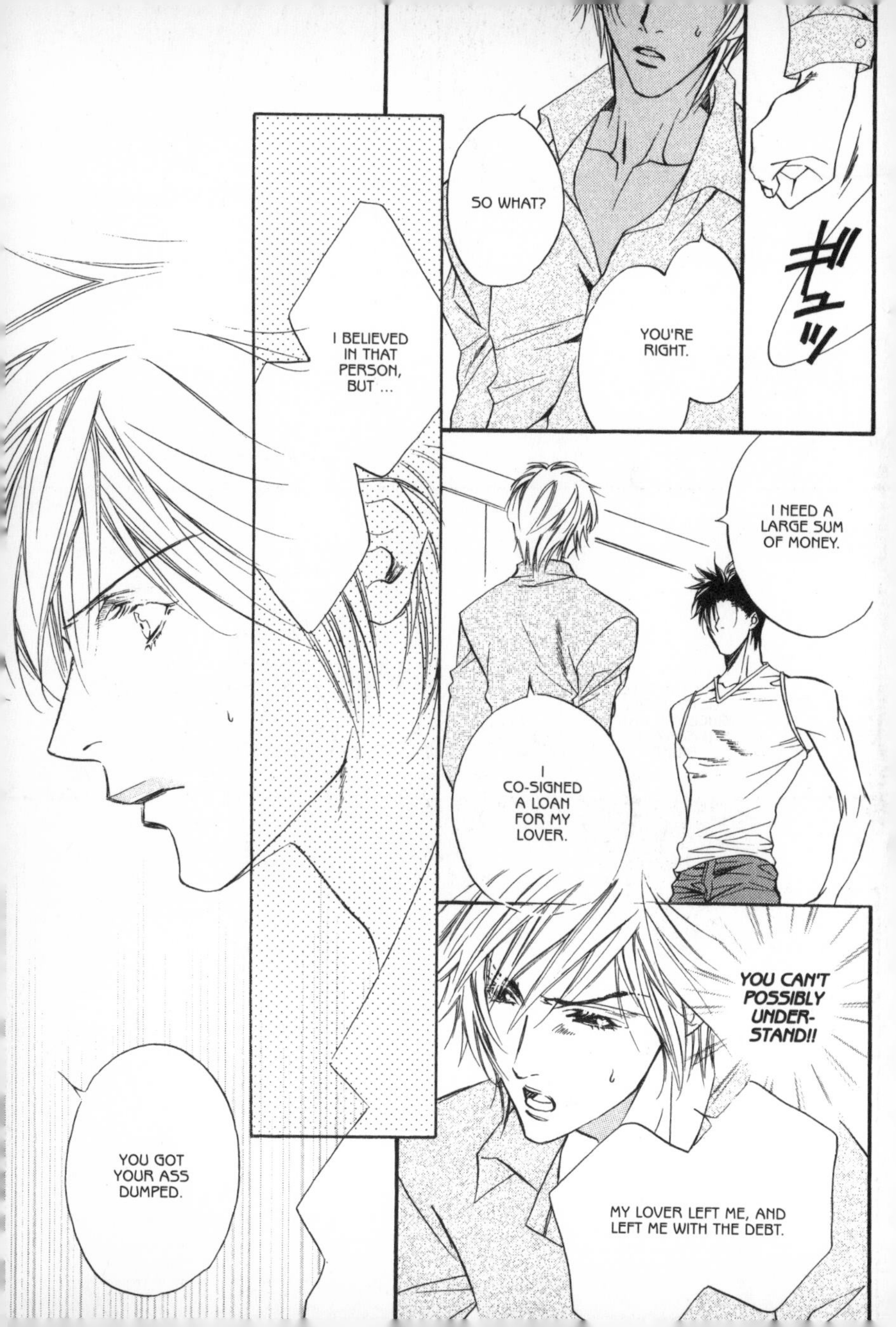

ギュッ
SO WHAT?
YOU'RE RIGHT.
I NEED A LARGE SUM OF MONEY.
I CO-SIGNED A LOAN FOR MY LOVER.
I BELIEVED IN THAT PERSON, BUT ...
YOU CAN'T POSSIBLY UNDER-STAND!!
MY LOVER LEFT ME, AND LEFT ME WITH THE DEBT.
YOU GOT YOUR ASS DUMPED.

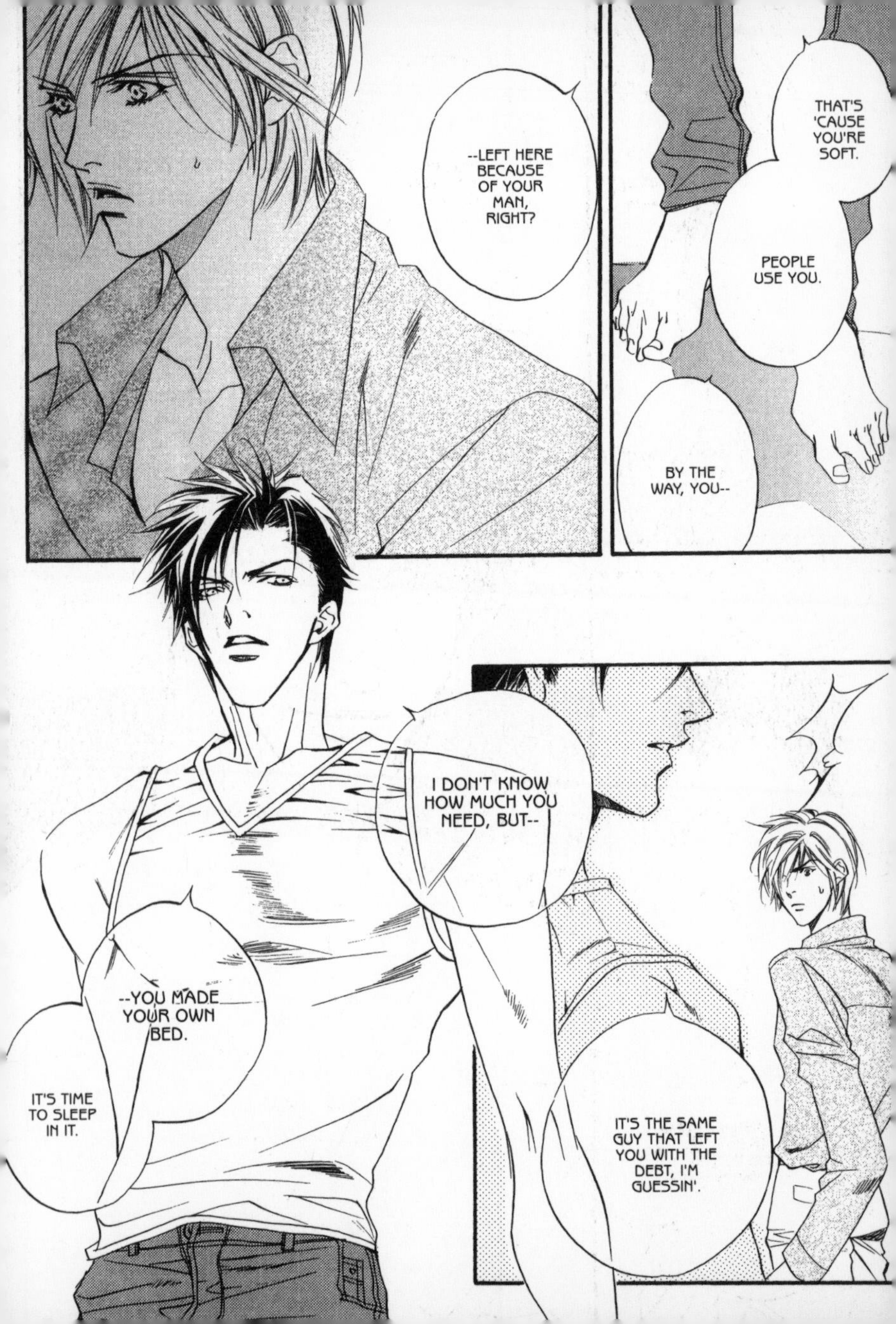
THAT'S 'CAUSE YOU'RE SOFT.
PEOPLE USE YOU.
BY THE WAY, YOU--
--LEFT HERE BECAUSE OF YOUR MAN, RIGHT?
IT'S THE SAME GUY THAT LEFT YOU WITH THE DEBT, I'M GUESSIN'.
I DON'T KNOW HOW MUCH YOU NEED, BUT--
--YOU MADE YOUR OWN BED.
IT'S TIME TO SLEEP IN IT.

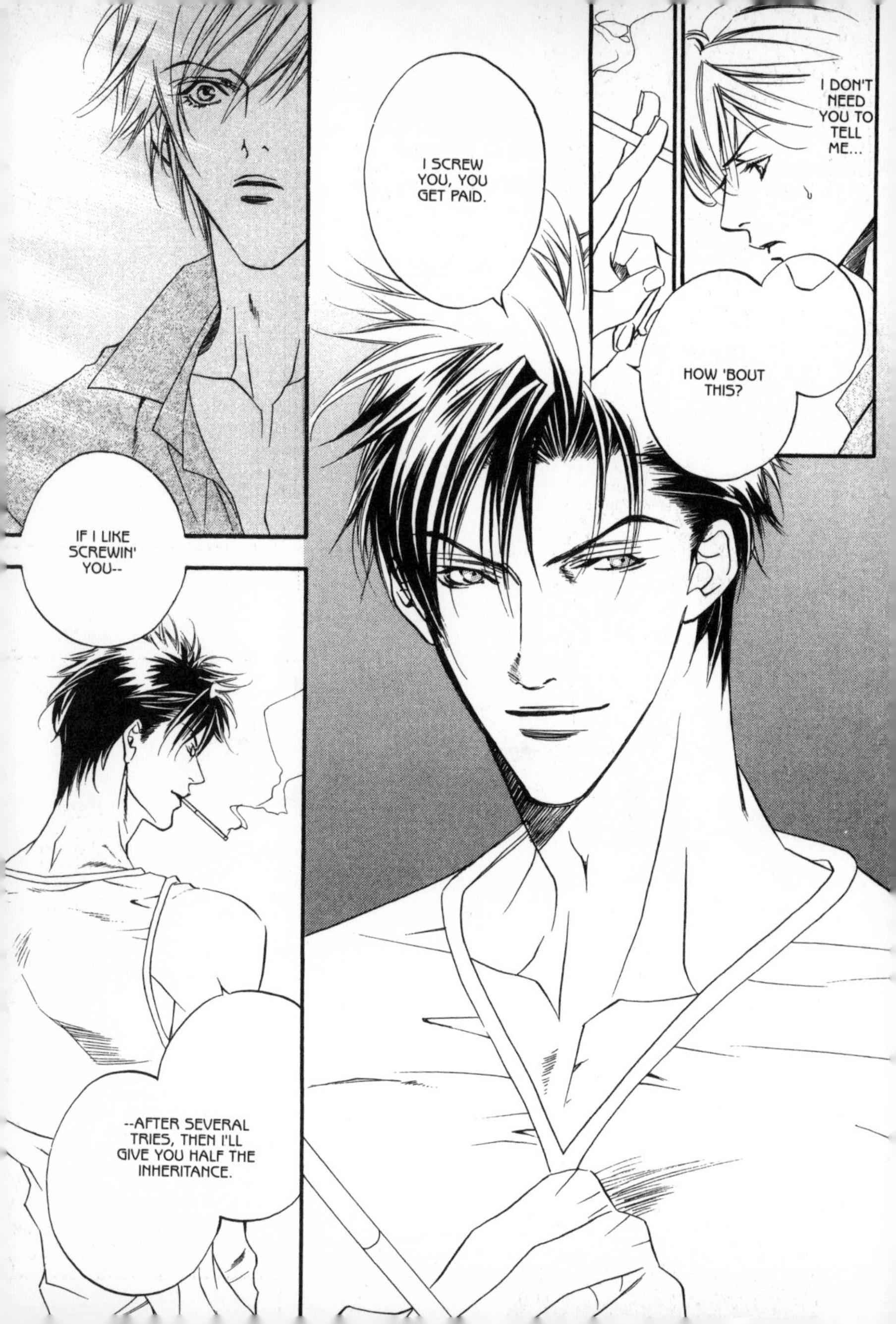
I SCREW YOU, YOU GET PAID.
I DON'T NEED YOU TO TELL ME...
HOW 'BOUT THIS?
IF I LIKE SCREWIN' YOU--
--AFTER SEVERAL TRIES, THEN I'LL GIVE YOU HALF THE INHERITANCE.

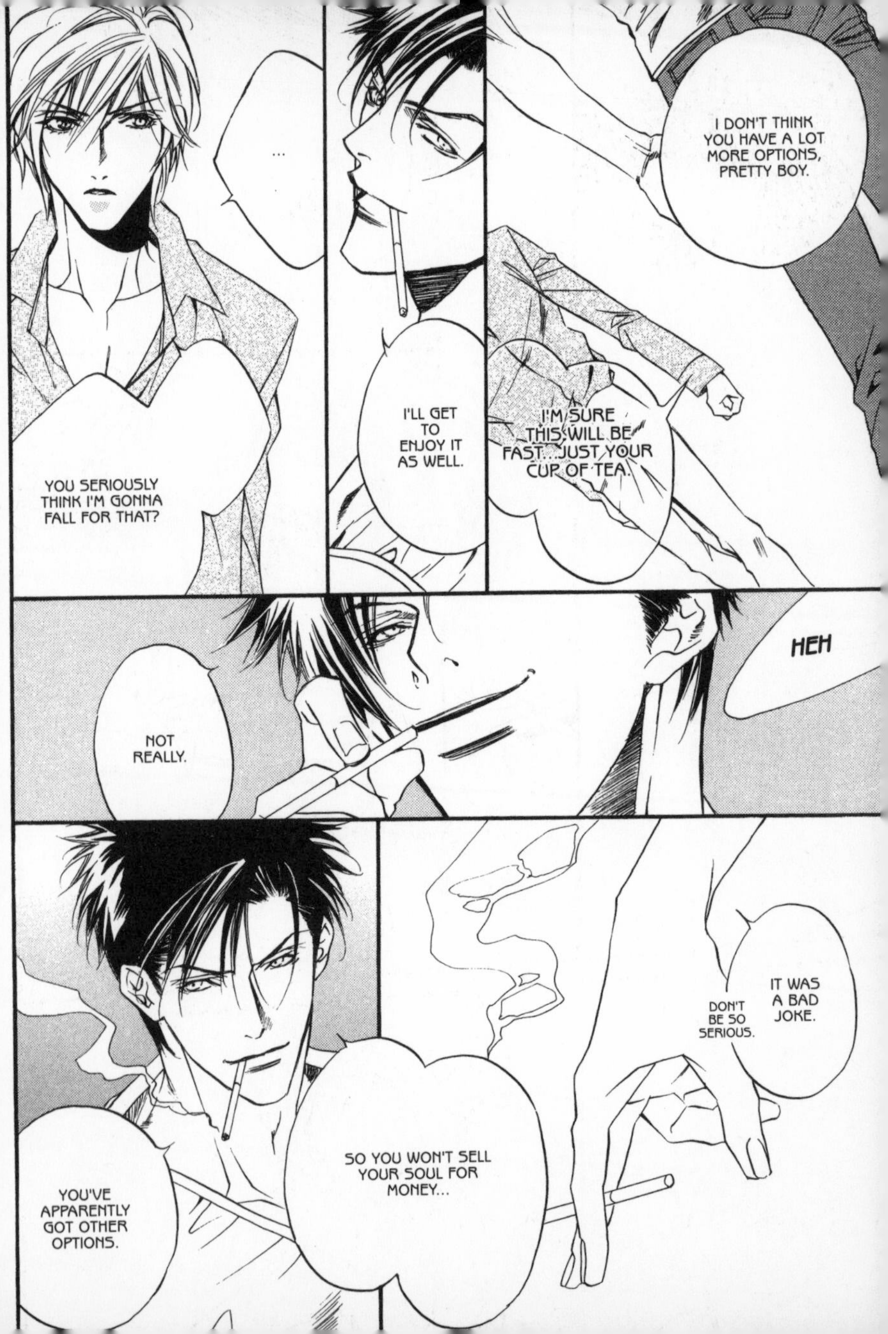
I DON'T THINK YOU HAVE A LOT MORE OPTIONS, PRETTY BOY.
I'M SURE THIS WILL BE FAST...JUST YOUR CUP OF TEA.
I'LL GET TO ENJOY IT AS WELL.
...
YOU SERIOUSLY THINK I'M GONNA FALL FOR THAT?
HEH
NOT REALLY.
IT WAS A BAD JOKE.
DON'T BE SO SERIOUS.
SO YOU WON'T SELL YOUR SOUL FOR MONEY...
YOU'VE APPARENTLY GOT OTHER OPTIONS.

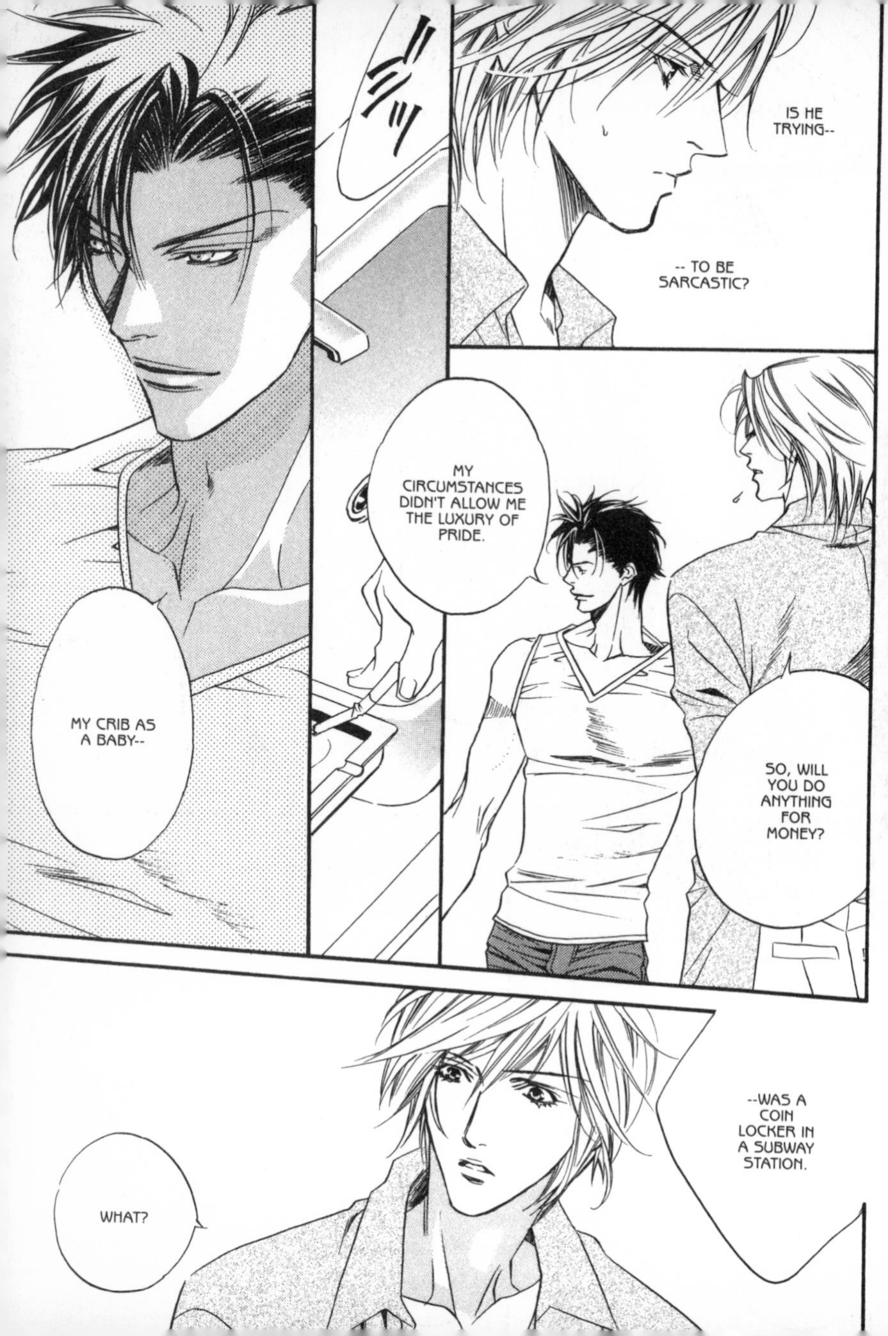
IS HE TRYING--
-- TO BE SARCASTIC?
SO, WILL YOU DO ANYTHING FOR MONEY?
MY CIRCUMSTANCES DIDN'T ALLOW ME THE LUXURY OF PRIDE.
MY CRIB AS A BABY--
--WAS A COIN LOCKER IN A SUBWAY STATION.
WHAT?

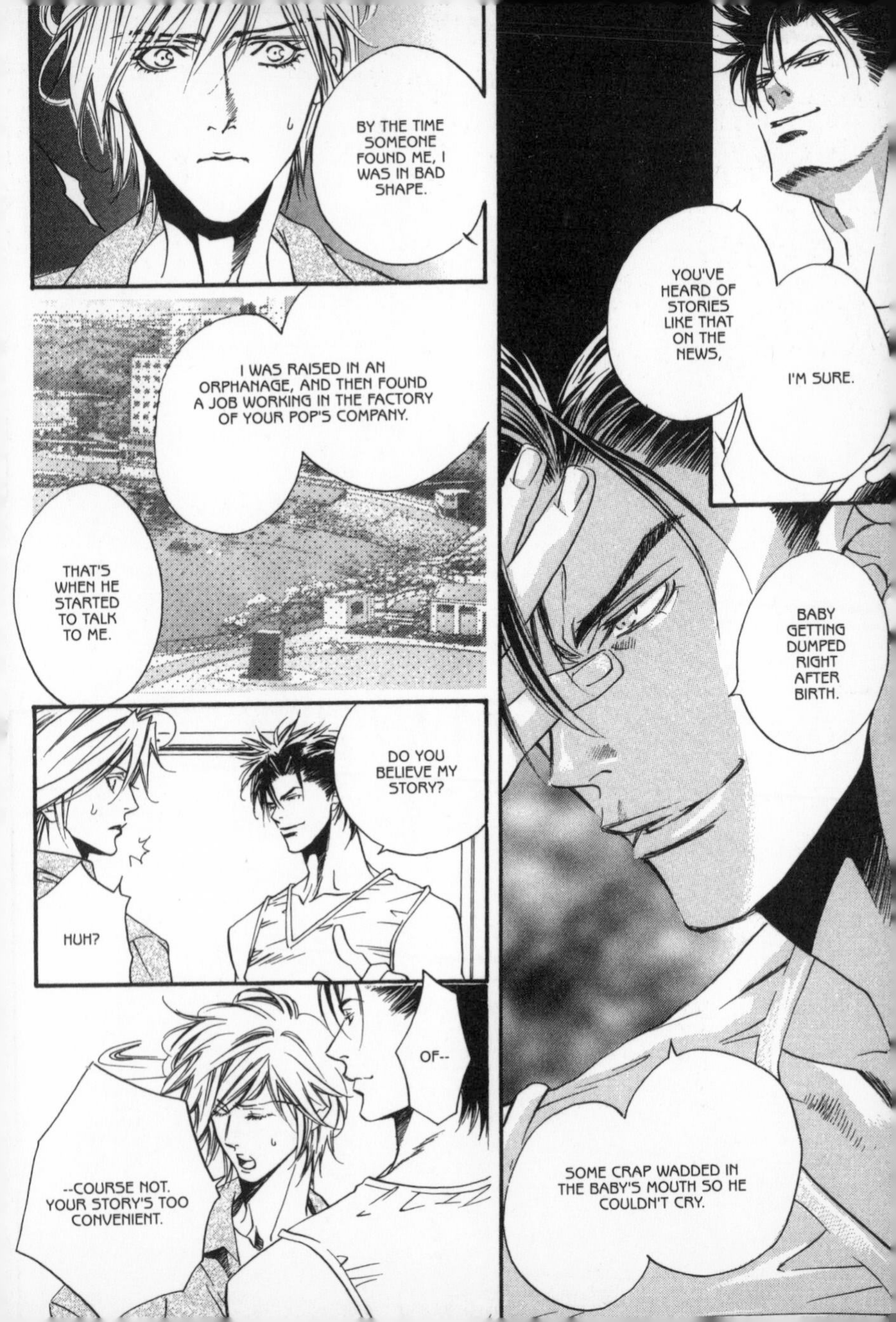
YOU'VE HEARD OF STORIES LIKE THAT ON THE NEWS,
I'M SURE.
BABY GETTING DUMPED RIGHT AFTER BIRTH.
SOME CRAP WADDED IN THE BABY'S MOUTH SO HE COULDN'T CRY.
BY THE TIME SOMEONE FOUND ME, I WAS IN BAD SHAPE.
I WAS RAISED IN AN ORPHANAGE, AND THEN FOUND A JOB WORKING IN THE FACTORY OF YOUR POP'S COMPANY.
THAT'S WHEN HE STARTED TO TALK TO ME.
DO YOU BELIEVE MY STORY?
HUH?
OF--
--COURSE NOT. YOUR STORY'S TOO CONVENIENT.

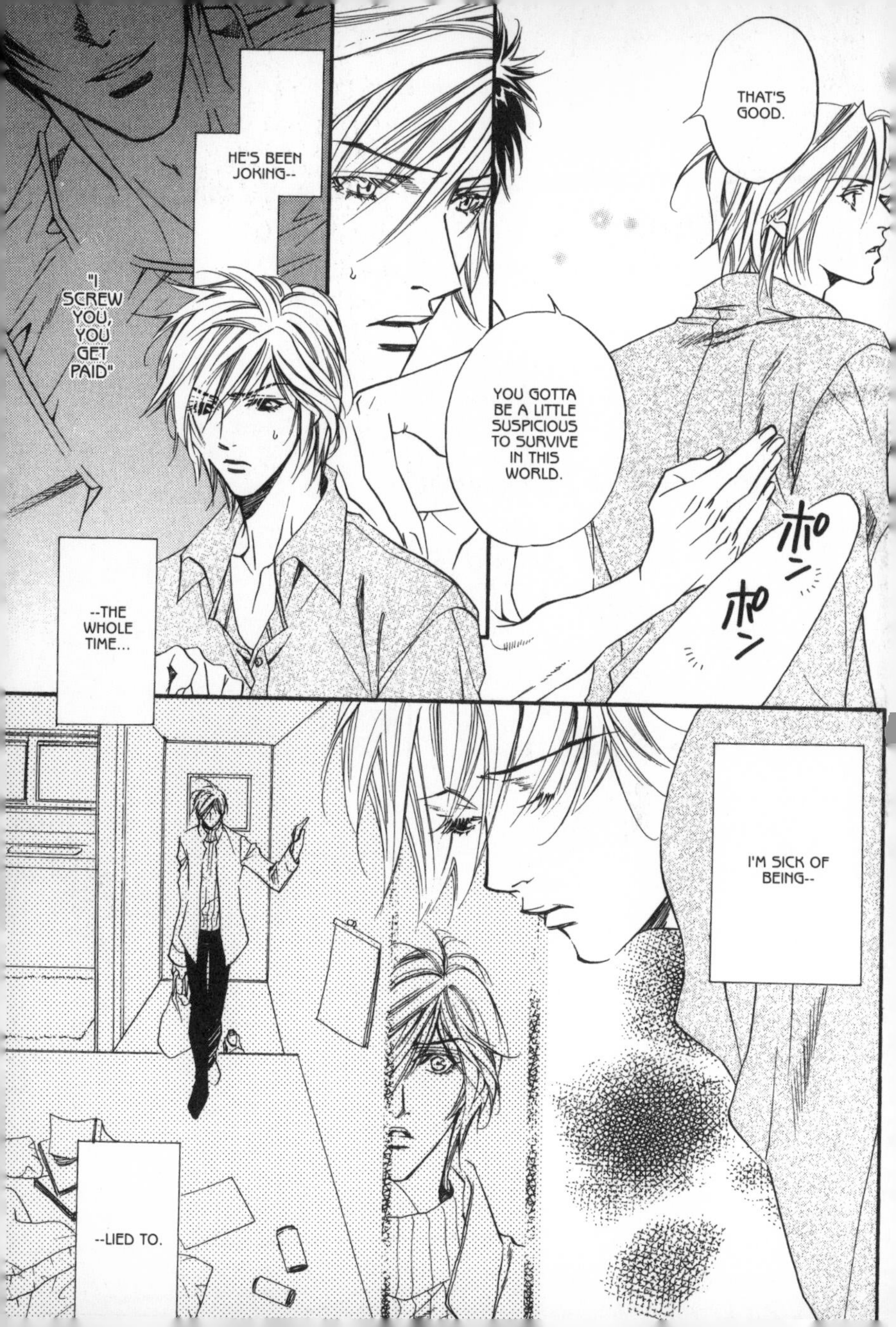
THAT'S GOOD.
YOU GOTTA BE A LITTLE SUSPICIOUS TO SURVIVE IN THIS WORLD.
ポン
ポン
HE'S BEEN JOKING--
"I SCREW YOU, YOU GET PAID"
--THE WHOLE TIME...
I'M SICK OF BEING--
--LIED TO.

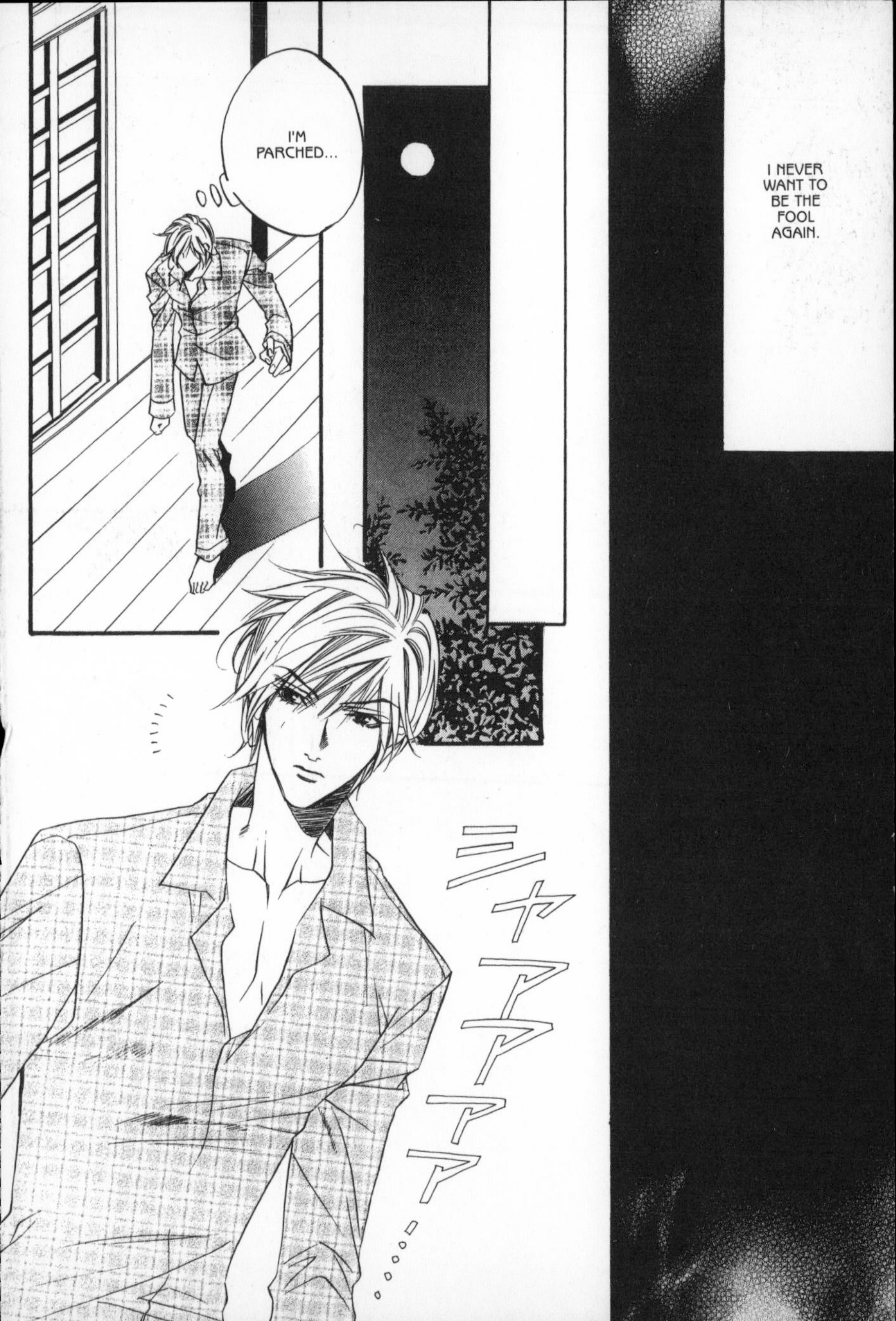
I NEVER WANT TO BE THE FOOL AGAIN.
I'M PARCHED...
シャアアア...

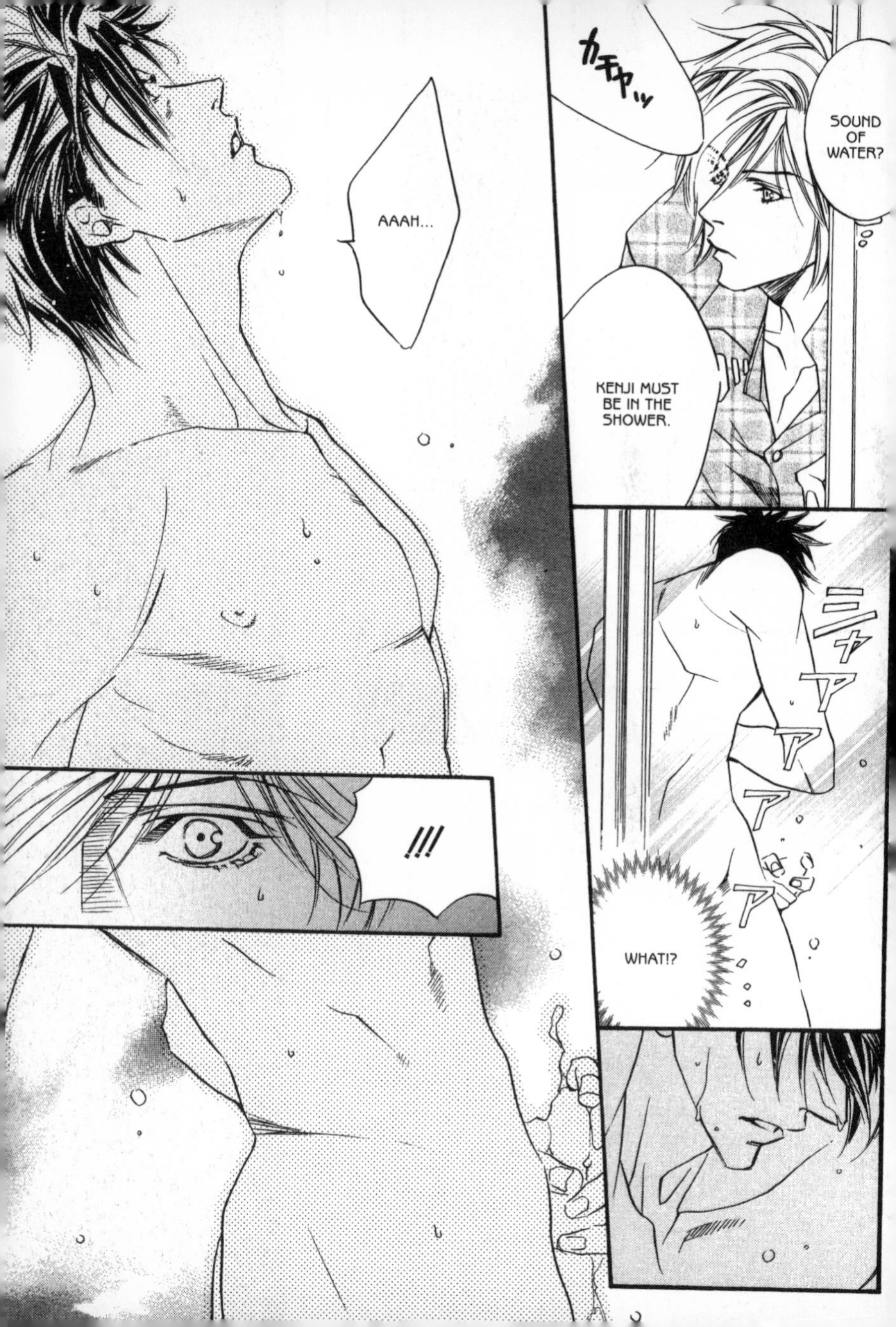

カチャッ
SOUND OF WATER?
KENJI MUST BE IN THE SHOWER.
WHAT!?
AAAH...
!!!

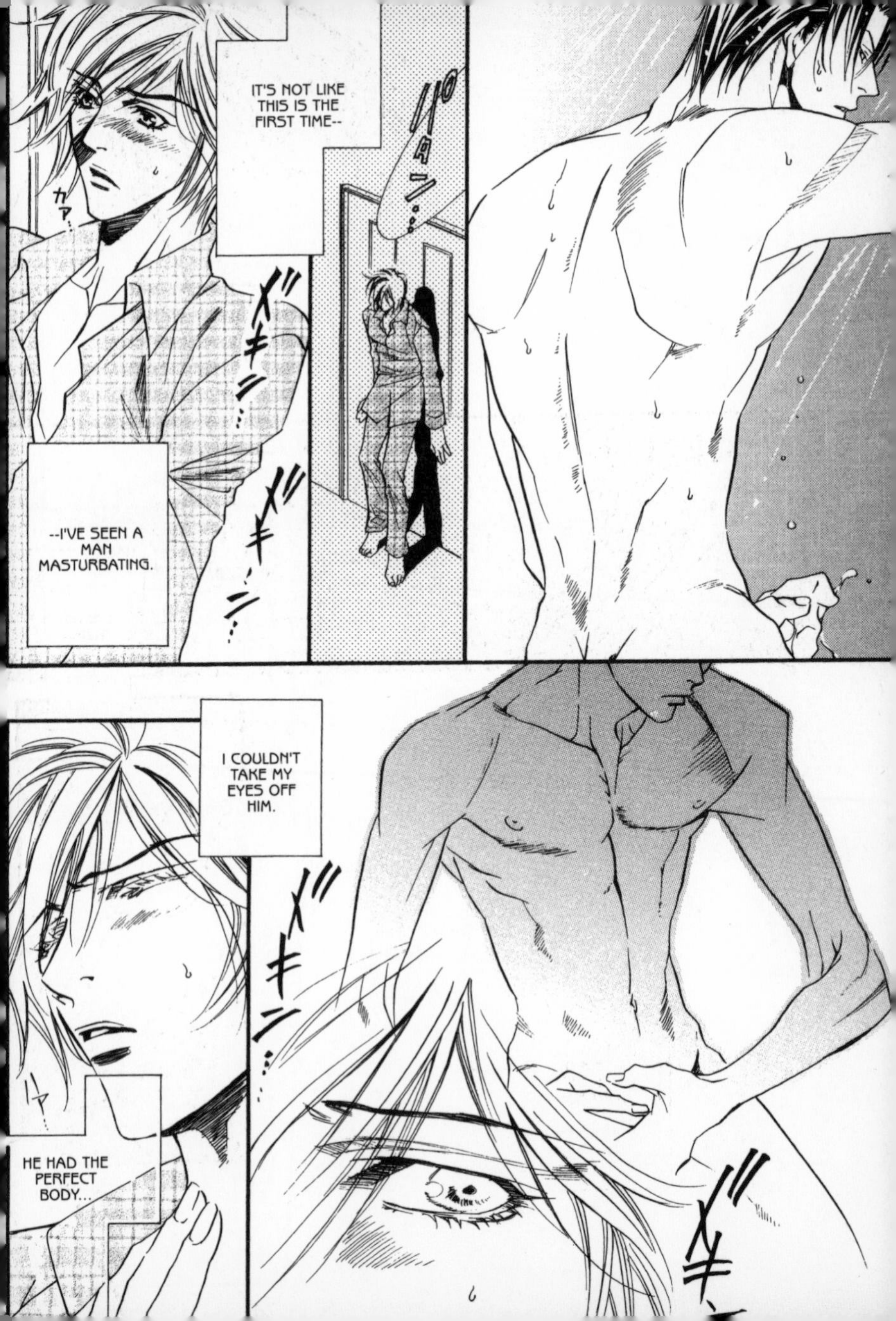

パタン...
IT'S NOT LIKE THIS IS THE FIRST TIME--
カァ...
ドキン...
ドキン...
--I'VE SEEN A MAN MASTURBATING.
I COULDN'T TAKE MY EYES OFF HIM.
ドキン...
HE HAD THE PERFECT BODY...

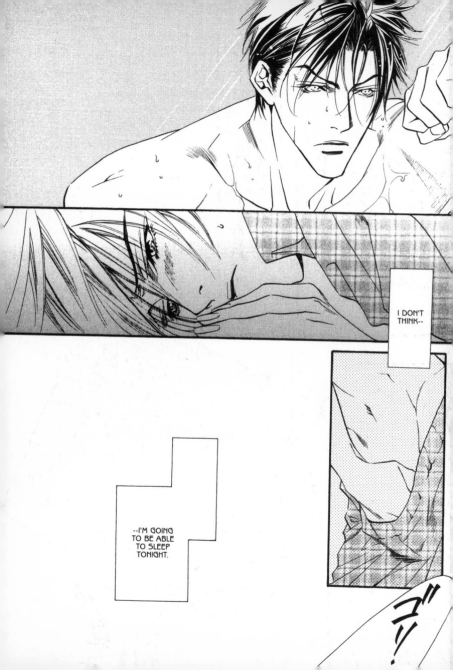

I DON'T
THINK--

--I'M GOING
TO BE ABLE
TO SLEEP
TONIGHT.

ゴリ！

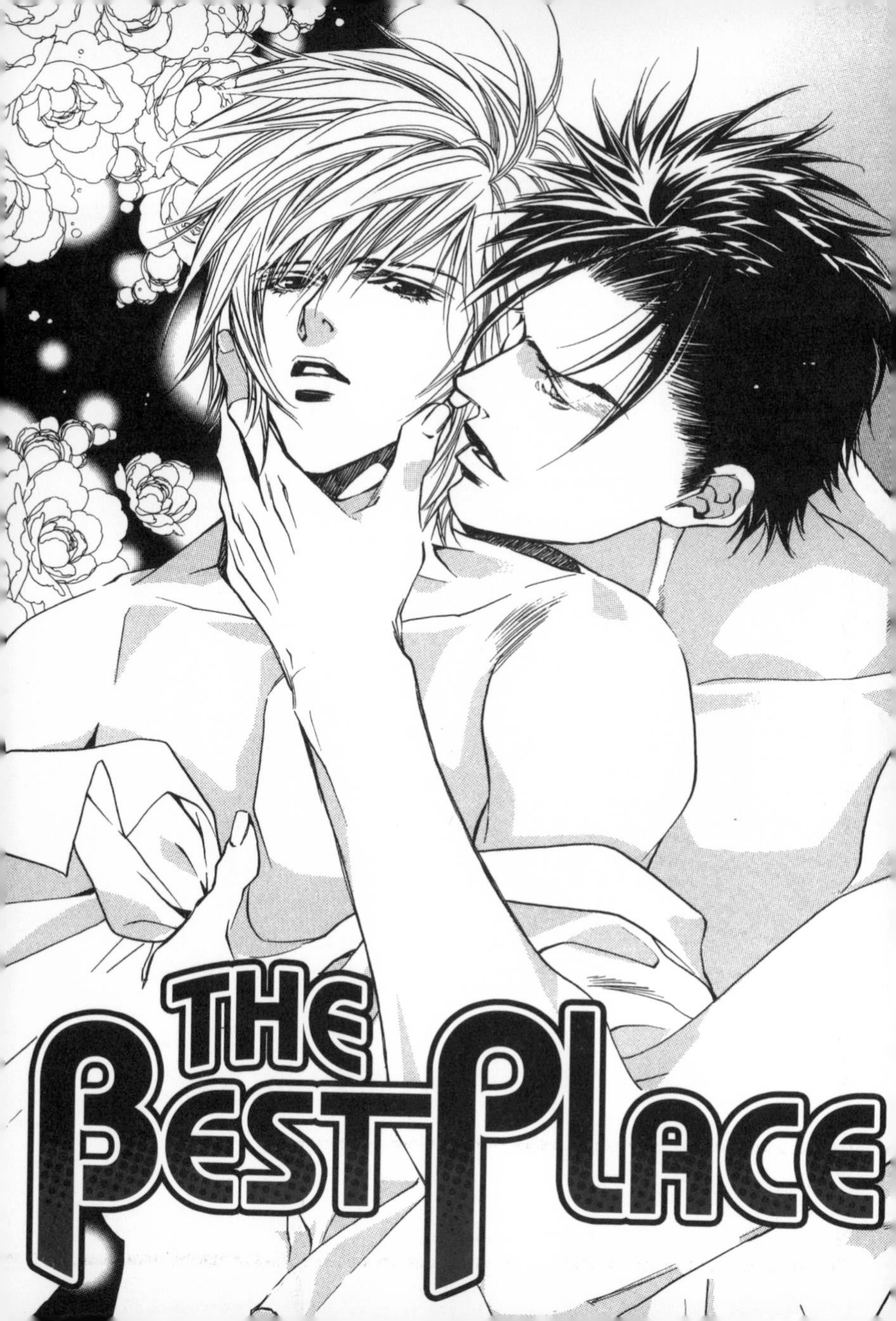
THE BEST PLACE

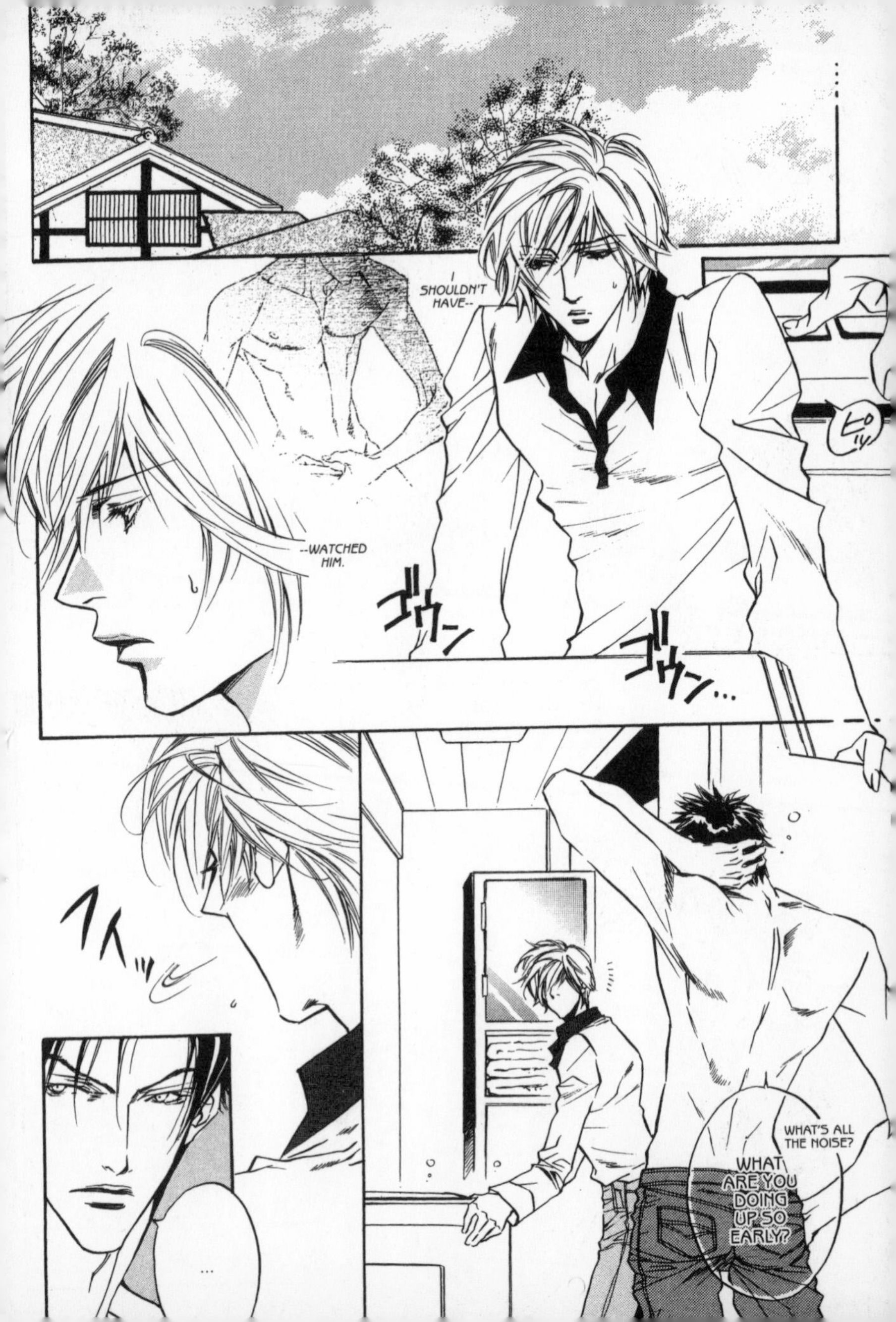

I SHOULDN'T HAVE--
--WATCHED HIM.
ゴウーン
ゴウーン…
…
WHAT'S ALL THE NOISE?
WHAT ARE YOU DOING UP SO EARLY?

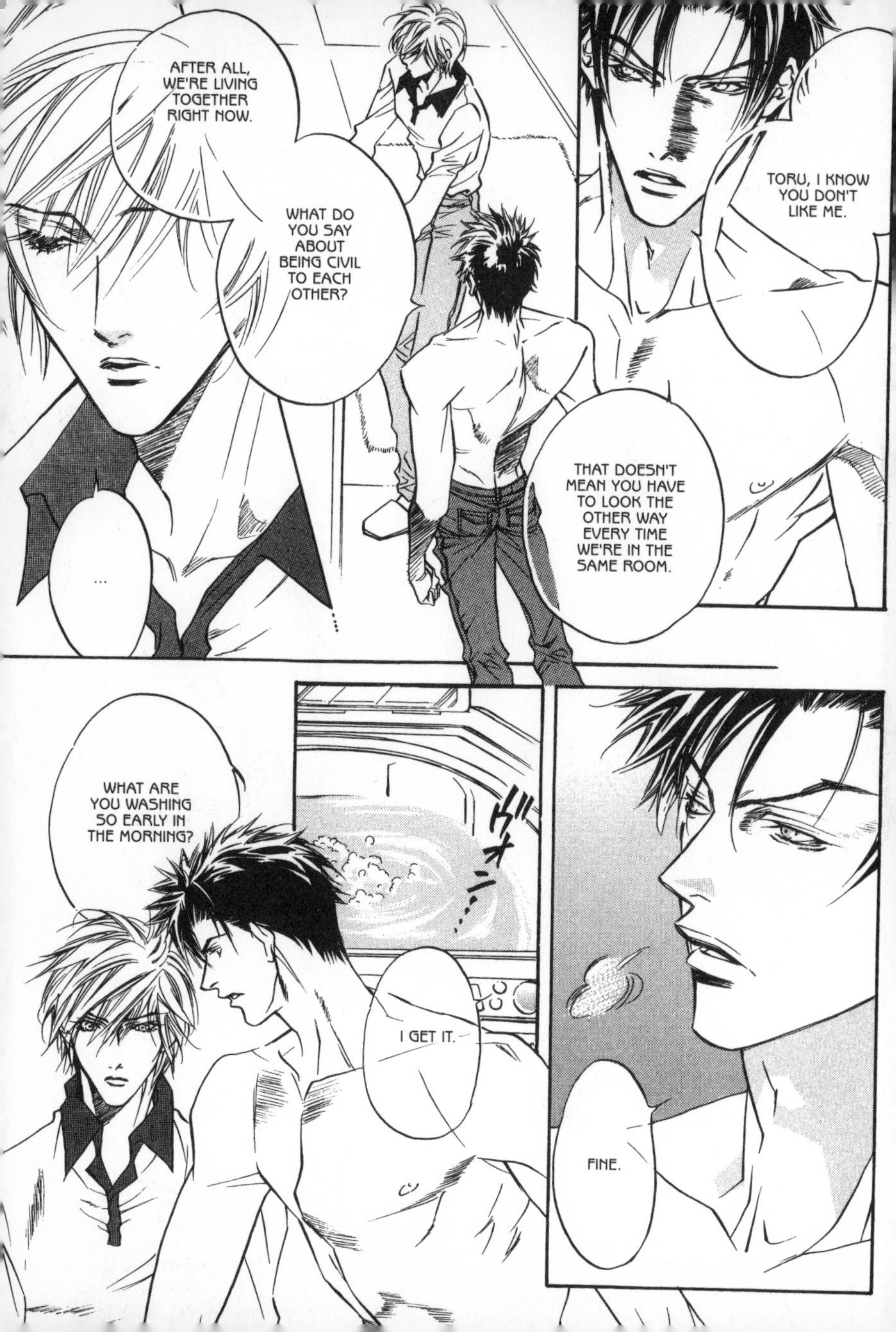
TORU, I KNOW YOU DON'T LIKE ME.
THAT DOESN'T MEAN YOU HAVE TO LOOK THE OTHER WAY EVERY TIME WE'RE IN THE SAME ROOM.
AFTER ALL, WE'RE LIVING TOGETHER RIGHT NOW.
WHAT DO YOU SAY ABOUT BEING CIVIL TO EACH OTHER?
...
FINE.
I GET IT.
WHAT ARE YOU WASHING SO EARLY IN THE MORNING?

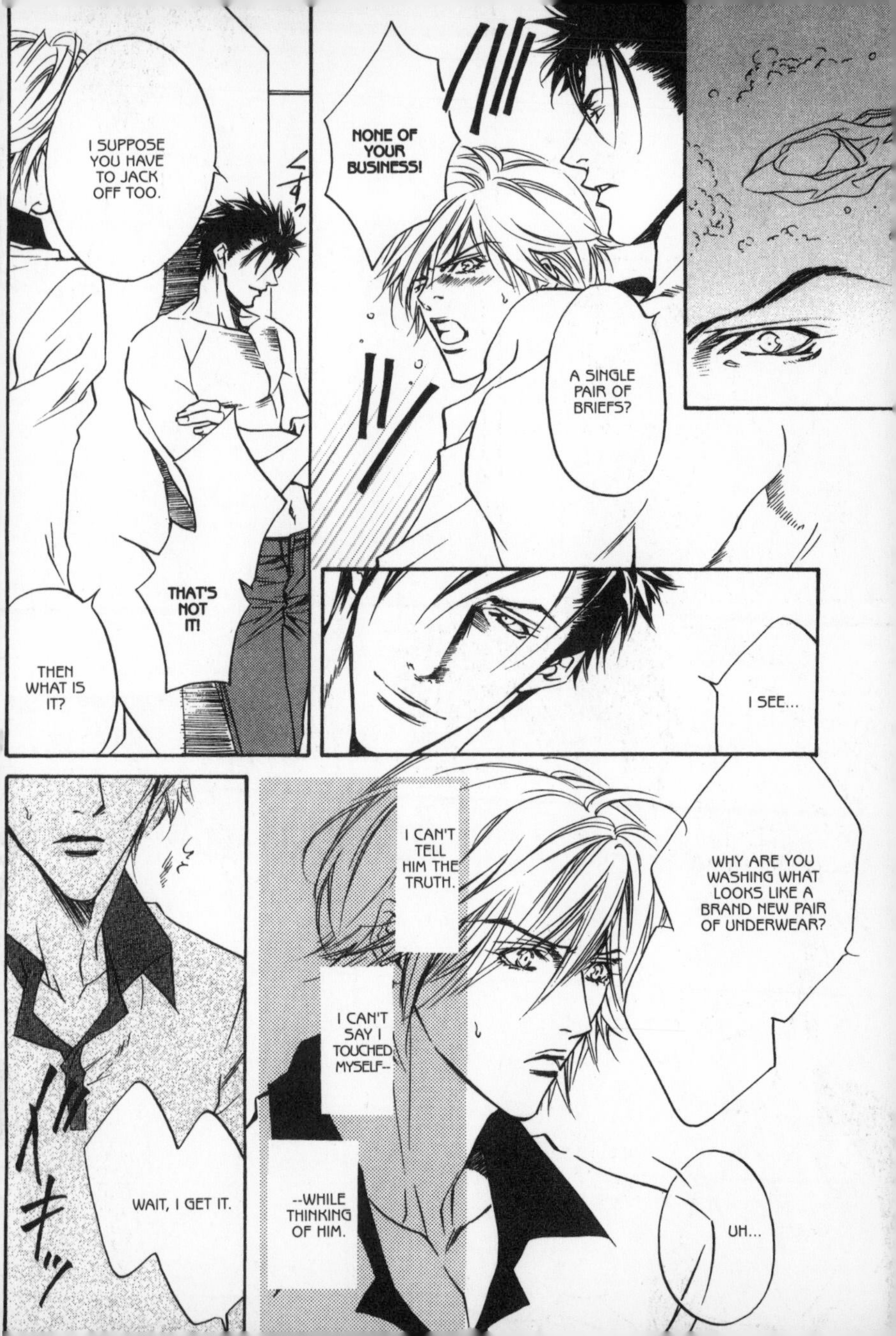
A SINGLE PAIR OF BRIEFS?
NONE OF YOUR BUSINESS!
I SEE...
I SUPPOSE YOU HAVE TO JACK OFF TOO.
THAT'S NOT IT!
THEN WHAT IS IT?
WHY ARE YOU WASHING WHAT LOOKS LIKE A BRAND NEW PAIR OF UNDERWEAR?
UH...
I CAN'T TELL HIM THE TRUTH.
I CAN'T SAY I TOUCHED MYSELF--
--WHILE THINKING OF HIM.
WAIT, I GET IT.

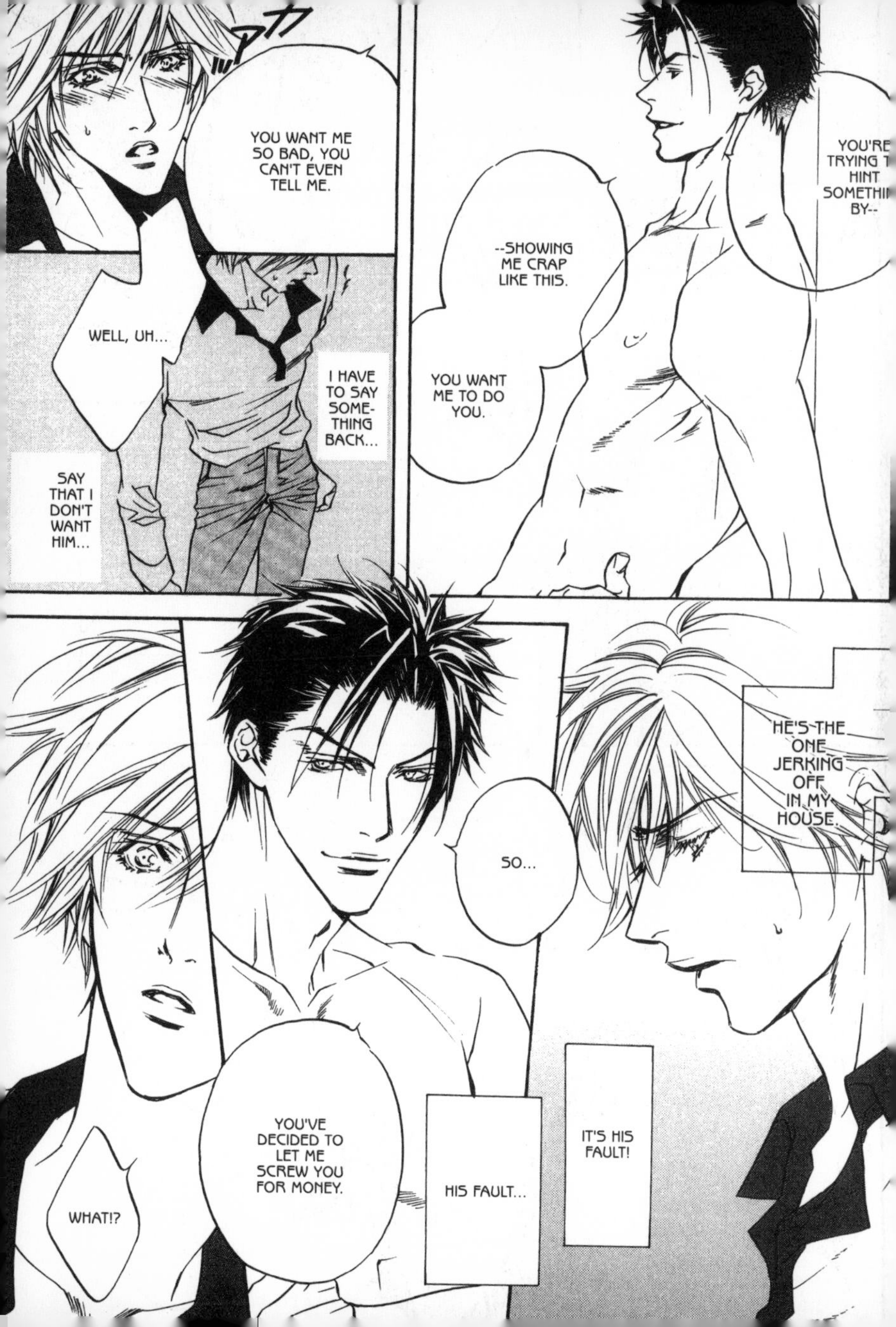

YOU'RE TRYING T HINT SOMETHI BY--
--SHOWING ME CRAP LIKE THIS.
YOU WANT ME TO DO YOU.
YOU WANT ME SO BAD, YOU CAN'T EVEN TELL ME.
I HAVE TO SAY SOME-THING BACK...
WELL, UH...
SAY THAT I DON'T WANT HIM...
HE'S THE ONE JERKING OFF IN MY HOUSE.
IT'S HIS FAULT!
HIS FAULT...
SO...
YOU'VE DECIDED TO LET ME SCREW YOU FOR MONEY.
WHAT!?

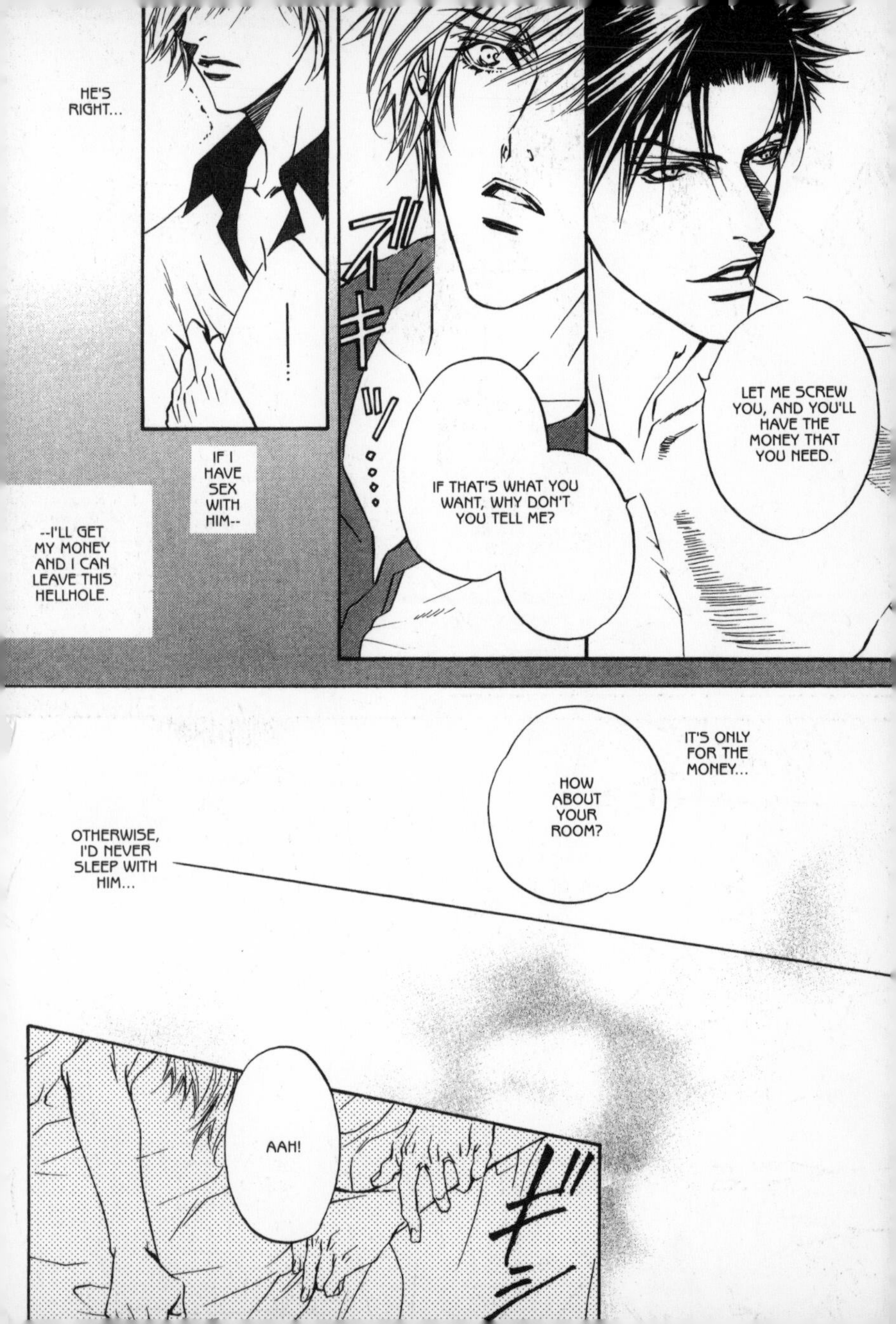
LET ME SCREW YOU, AND YOU'LL HAVE THE MONEY THAT YOU NEED.
IF THAT'S WHAT YOU WANT, WHY DON'T YOU TELL ME?
HE'S RIGHT...
IF I HAVE SEX WITH HIM--
--I'LL GET MY MONEY AND I CAN LEAVE THIS HELLHOLE.
IT'S ONLY FOR THE MONEY...
HOW ABOUT YOUR ROOM?
OTHERWISE, I'D NEVER SLEEP WITH HIM...
AAH!

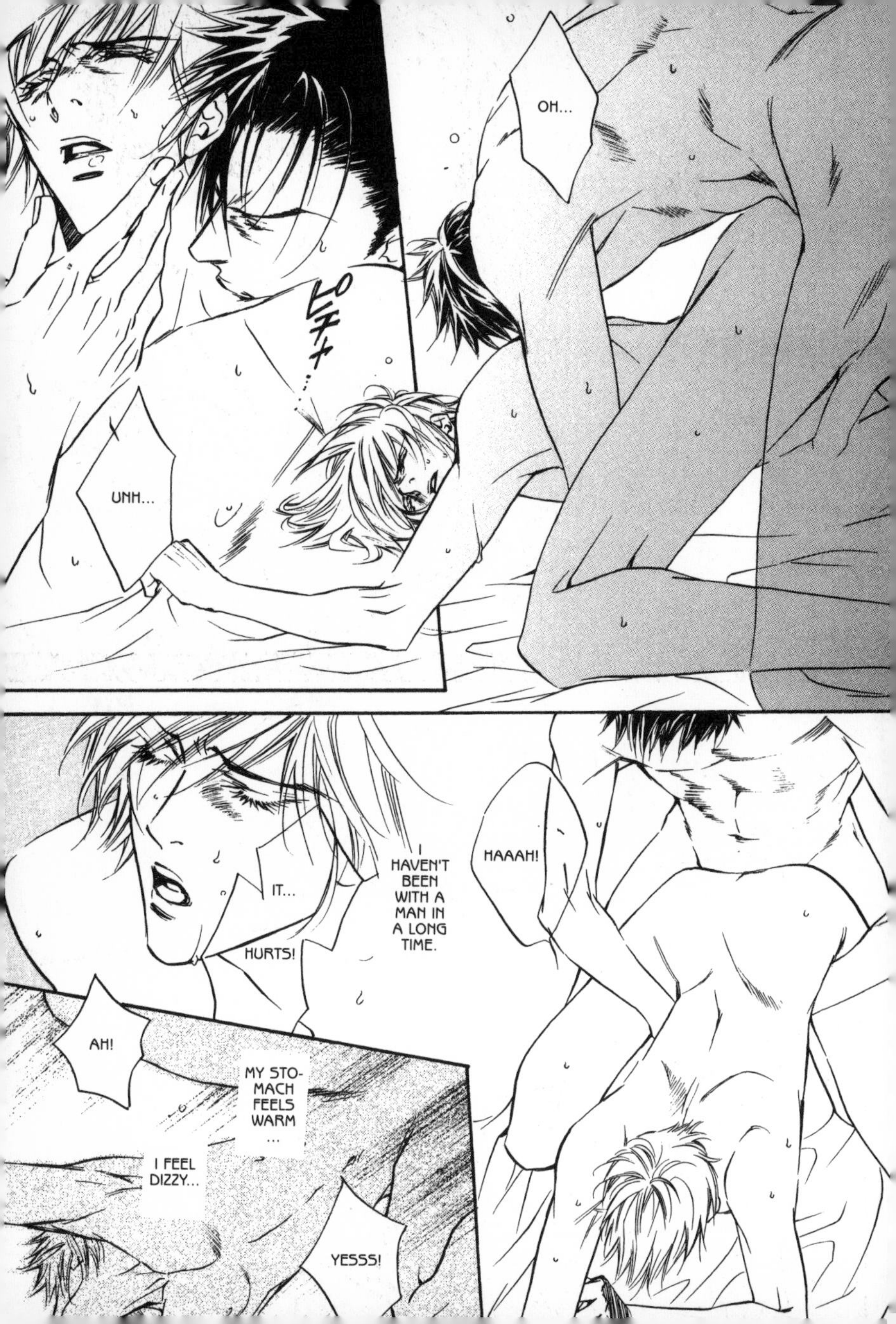
OH...
UNH...
HAAAH!
I HAVEN'T BEEN WITH A MAN IN A LONG TIME.
IT...
HURTS!
AH!
MY STO-MACH FEELS WARM ...
I FEEL DIZZY...
YESSS!

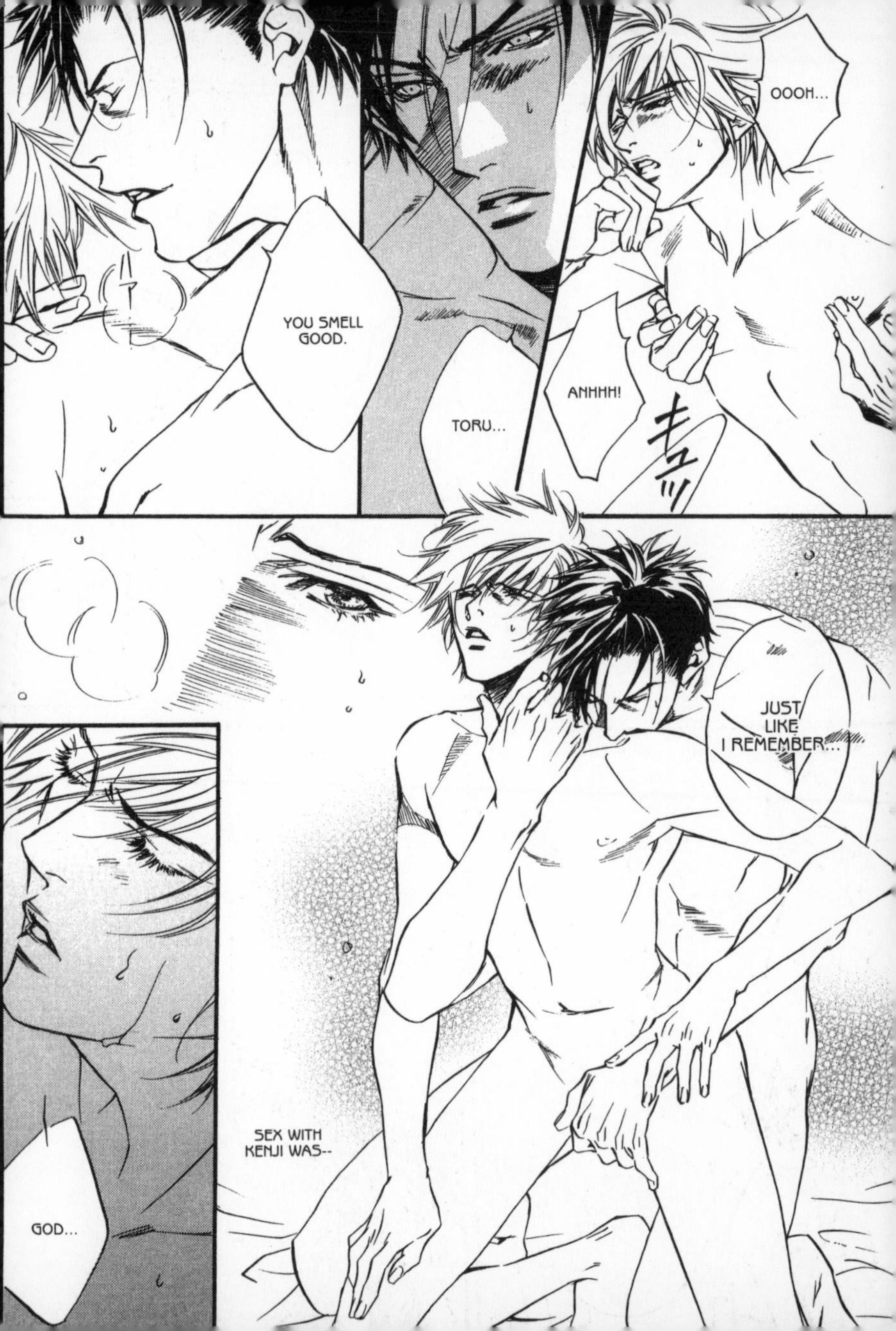

OOOH...
ANHHH!
キュッ
TORU...
YOU SMELL GOOD.
JUST LIKE I REMEMBER...
SEX WITH KENJI WAS--
GOD...

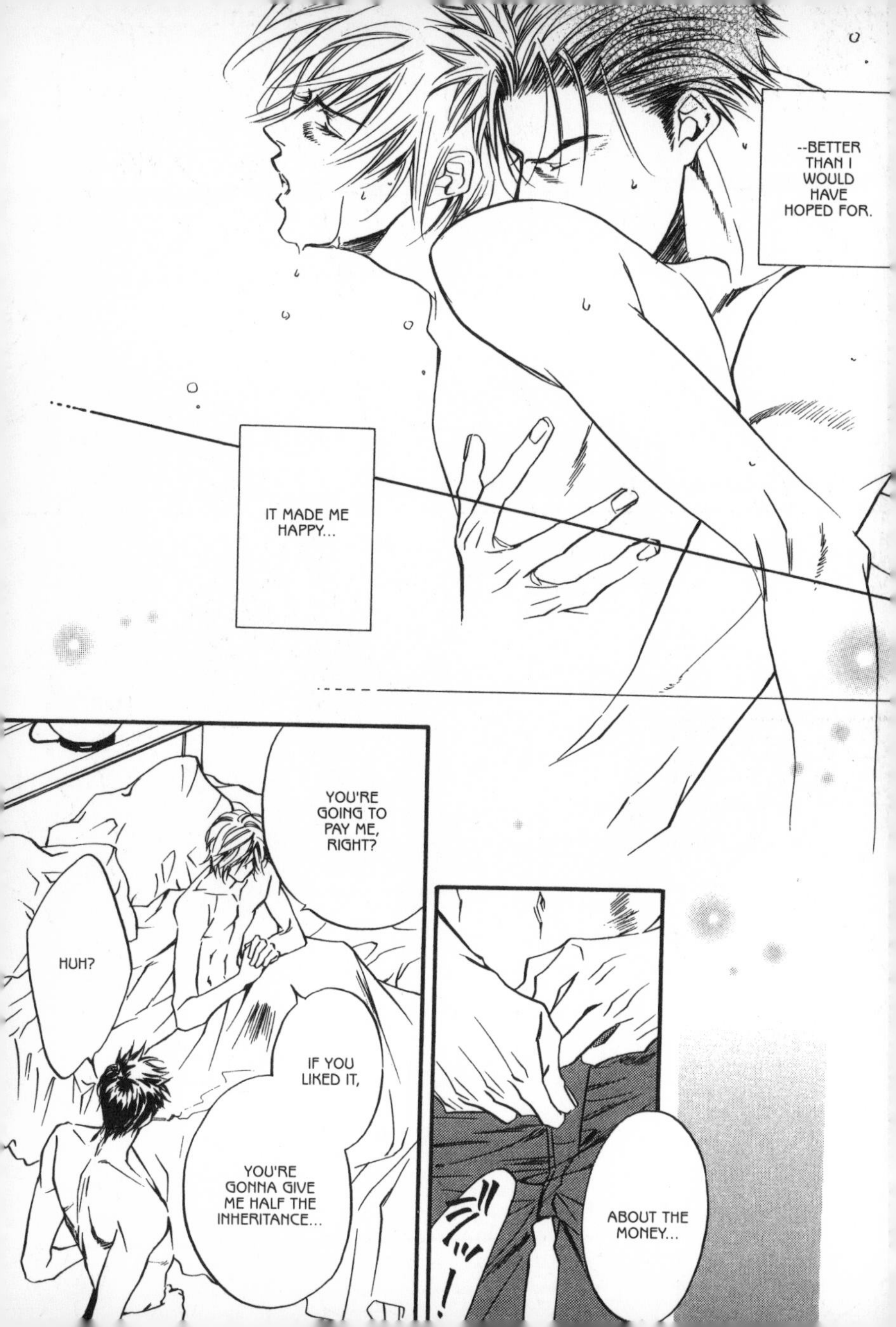
--BETTER THAN I WOULD HAVE HOPED FOR.
IT MADE ME HAPPY...
ABOUT THE MONEY...
YOU'RE GOING TO PAY ME, RIGHT?
HUH?
IF YOU LIKED IT,
YOU'RE GONNA GIVE ME HALF THE INHERITANCE...

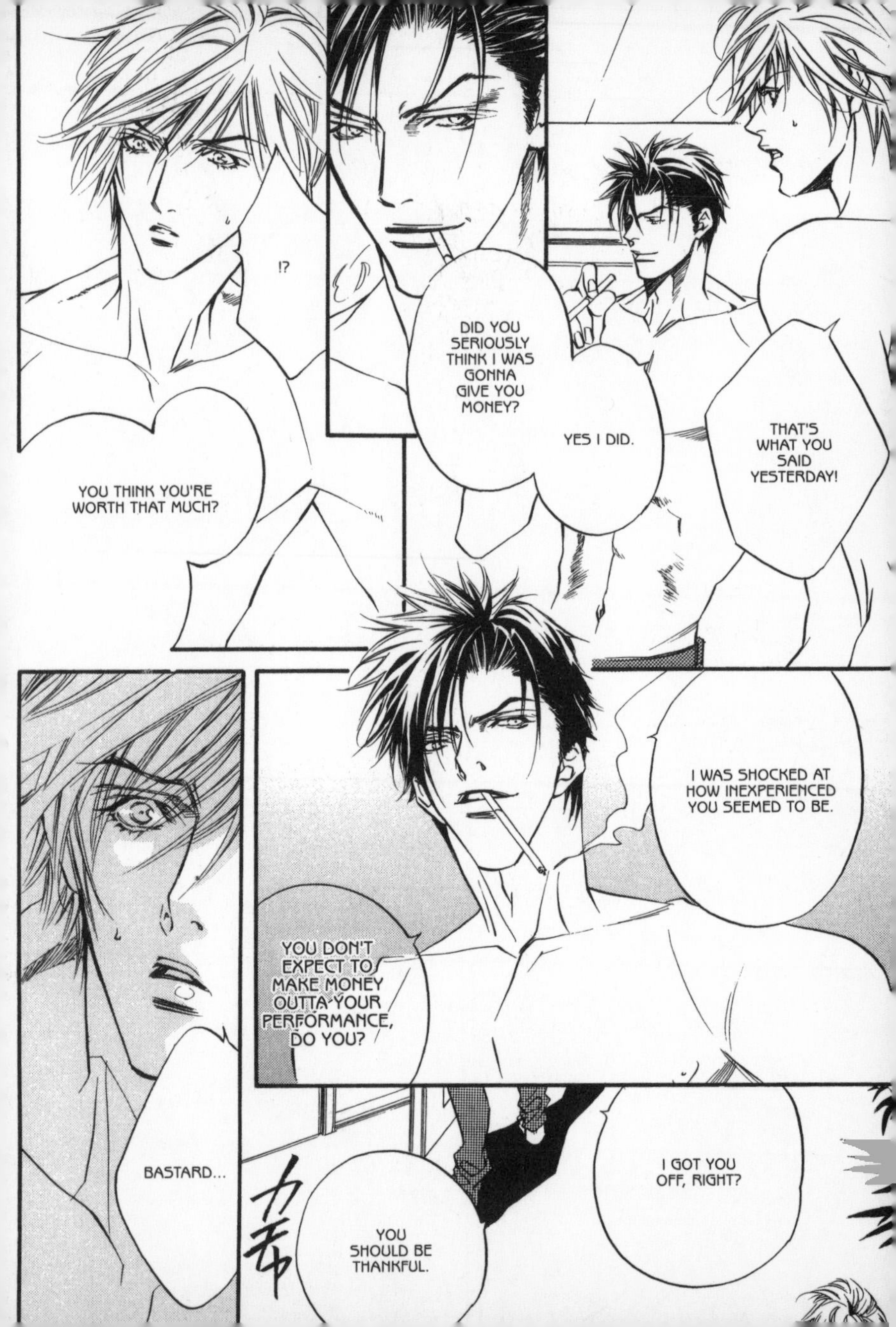
THAT'S WHAT YOU SAID YESTERDAY!
YES I DID.
DID YOU SERIOUSLY THINK I WAS GONNA GIVE YOU MONEY?
!?
YOU THINK YOU'RE WORTH THAT MUCH?
I WAS SHOCKED AT HOW INEXPERIENCED YOU SEEMED TO BE.
YOU DON'T EXPECT TO MAKE MONEY OUTTA YOUR PERFORMANCE, DO YOU?
I GOT YOU OFF, RIGHT?
YOU SHOULD BE THANKFUL.
BASTARD...

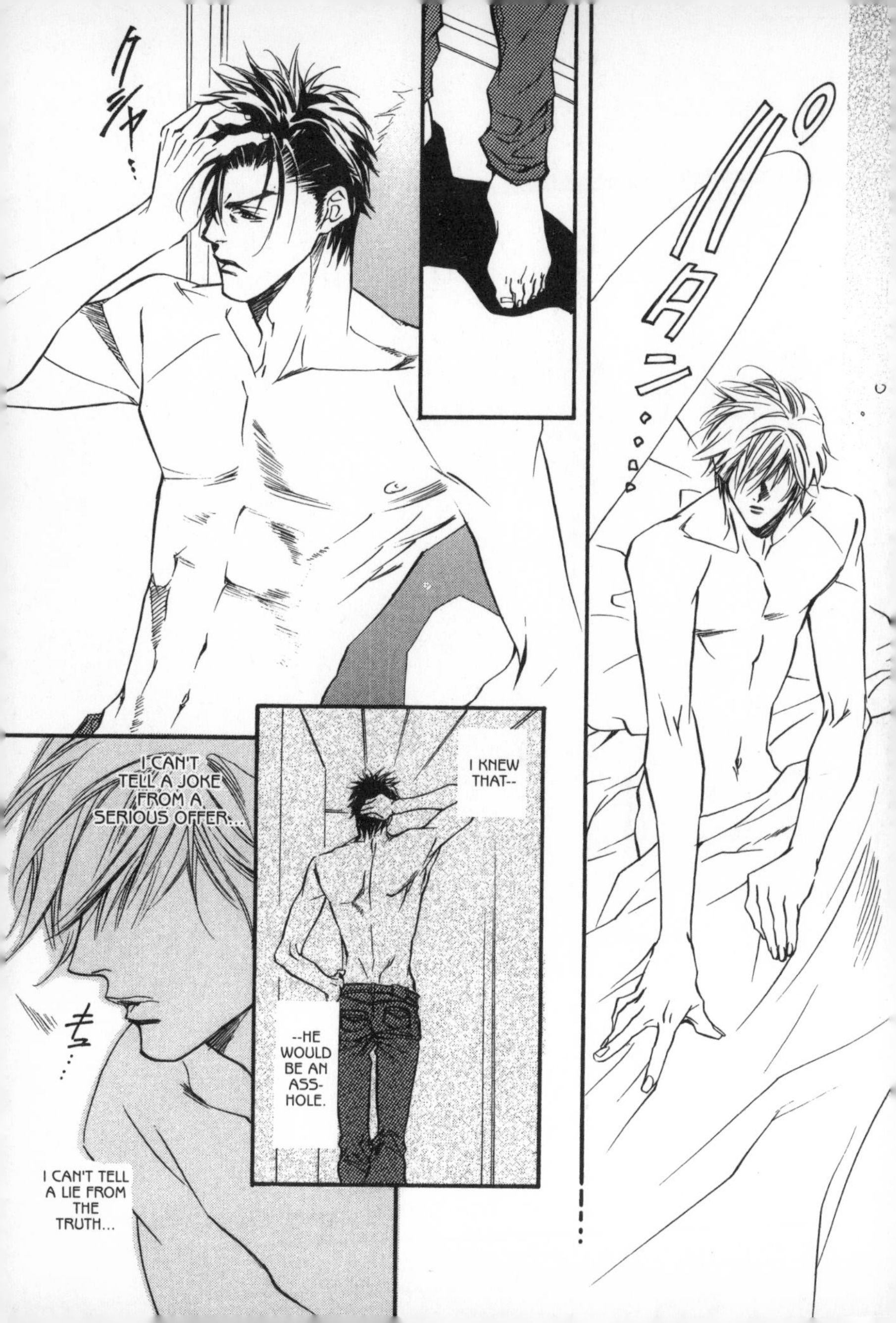
パタン…
クシャ…
I KNEW THAT--
--HE WOULD BE AN ASS-HOLE.
I CAN'T TELL A JOKE FROM A SERIOUS OFFER...
I CAN'T TELL A LIE FROM THE TRUTH...

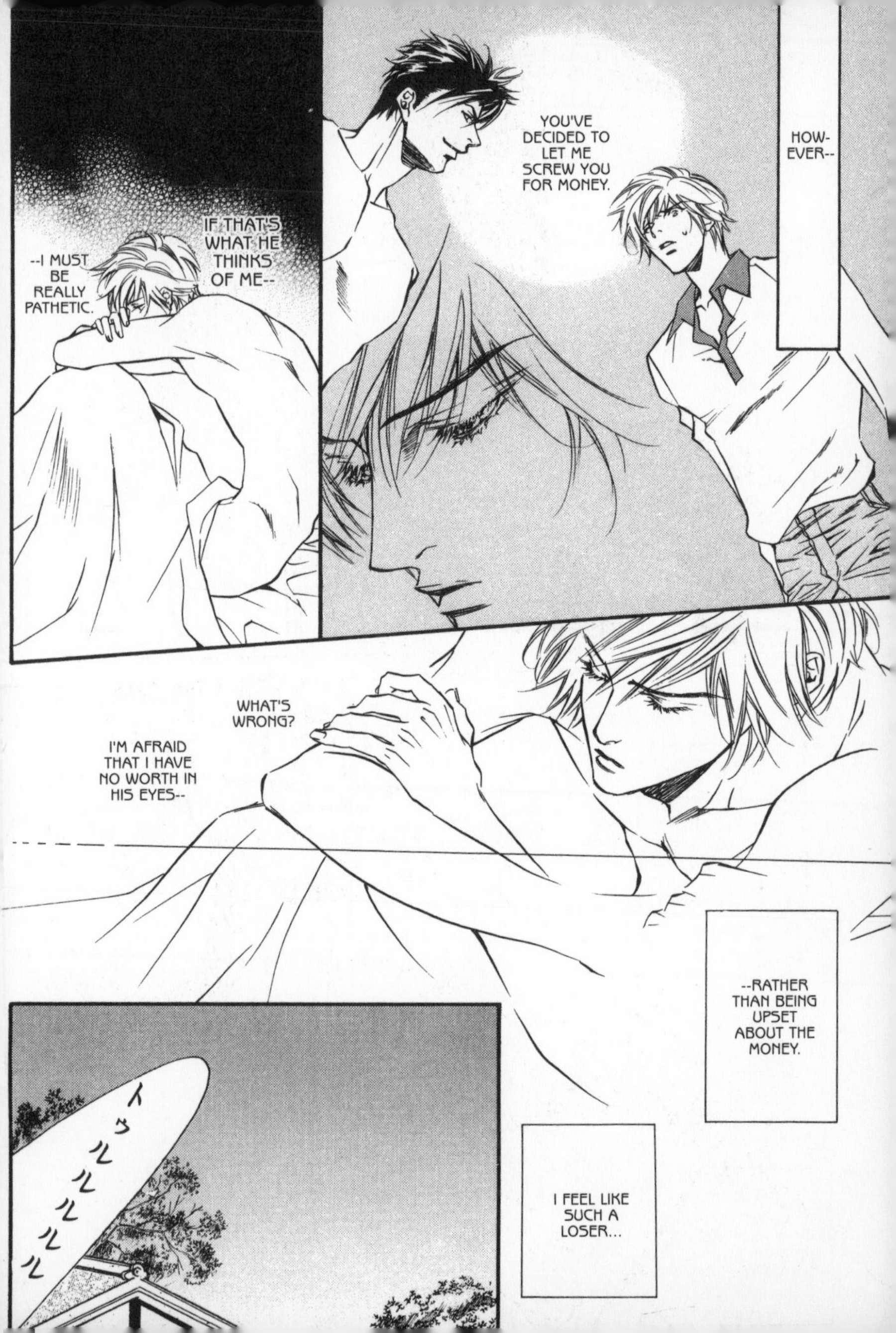

HOW-EVER--
YOU'VE DECIDED TO LET ME SCREW YOU FOR MONEY.
IF THAT'S WHAT HE THINKS OF ME--
--I MUST BE REALLY PATHETIC.
WHAT'S WRONG?
I'M AFRAID THAT I HAVE NO WORTH IN HIS EYES--
--RATHER THAN BEING UPSET ABOUT THE MONEY.
I FEEL LIKE SUCH A LOSER...
トゥルルルルルル

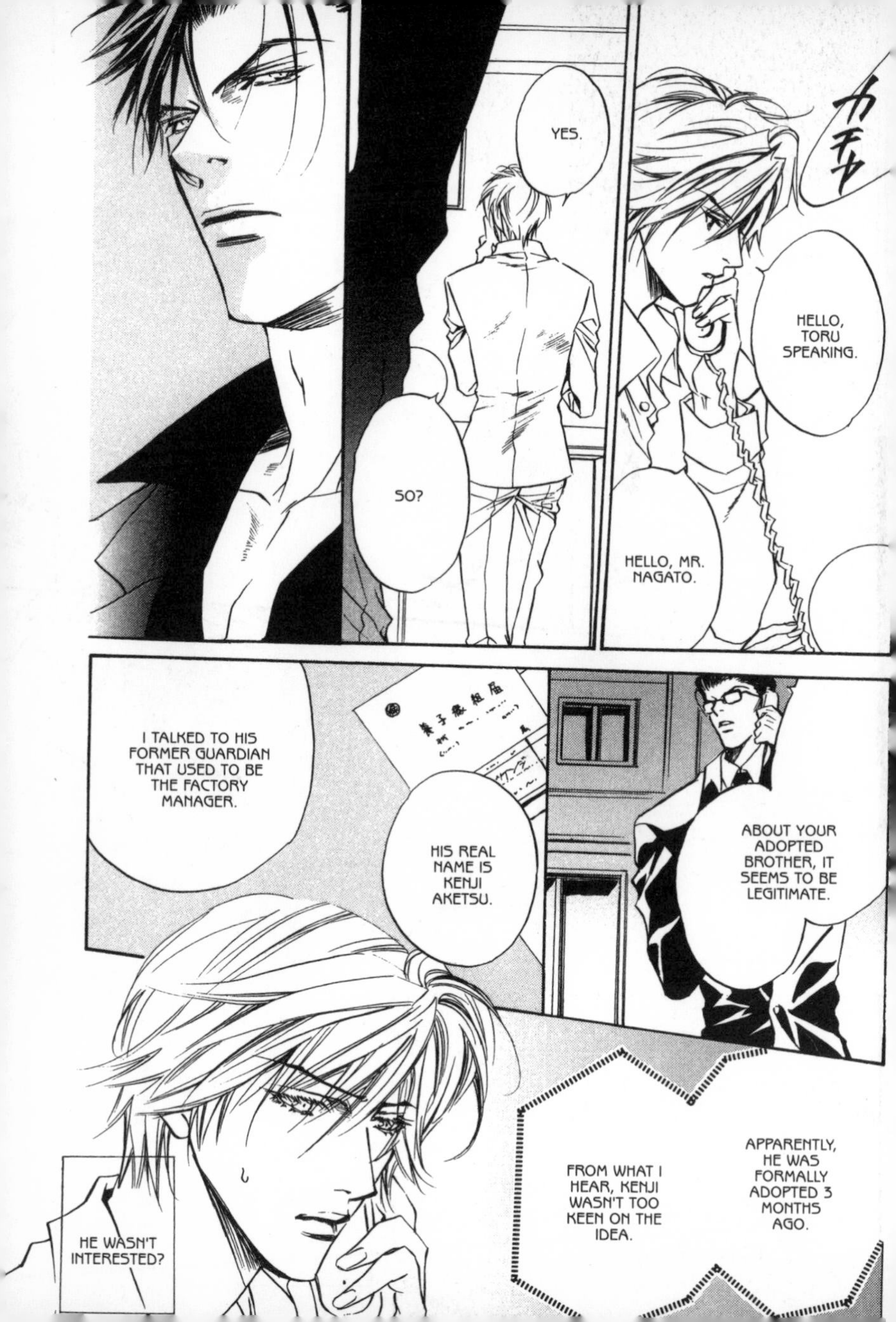
カチャ
HELLO, TORU SPEAKING.
HELLO, MR. NAGATO.
YES.
SO?
ABOUT YOUR ADOPTED BROTHER, IT SEEMS TO BE LEGITIMATE.
HIS REAL NAME IS KENJI AKETSU.
I TALKED TO HIS FORMER GUARDIAN THAT USED TO BE THE FACTORY MANAGER.
APPARENTLY, HE WAS FORMALLY ADOPTED 3 MONTHS AGO.
FROM WHAT I HEAR, KENJI WASN'T TOO KEEN ON THE IDEA.
HE WASN'T INTERESTED?

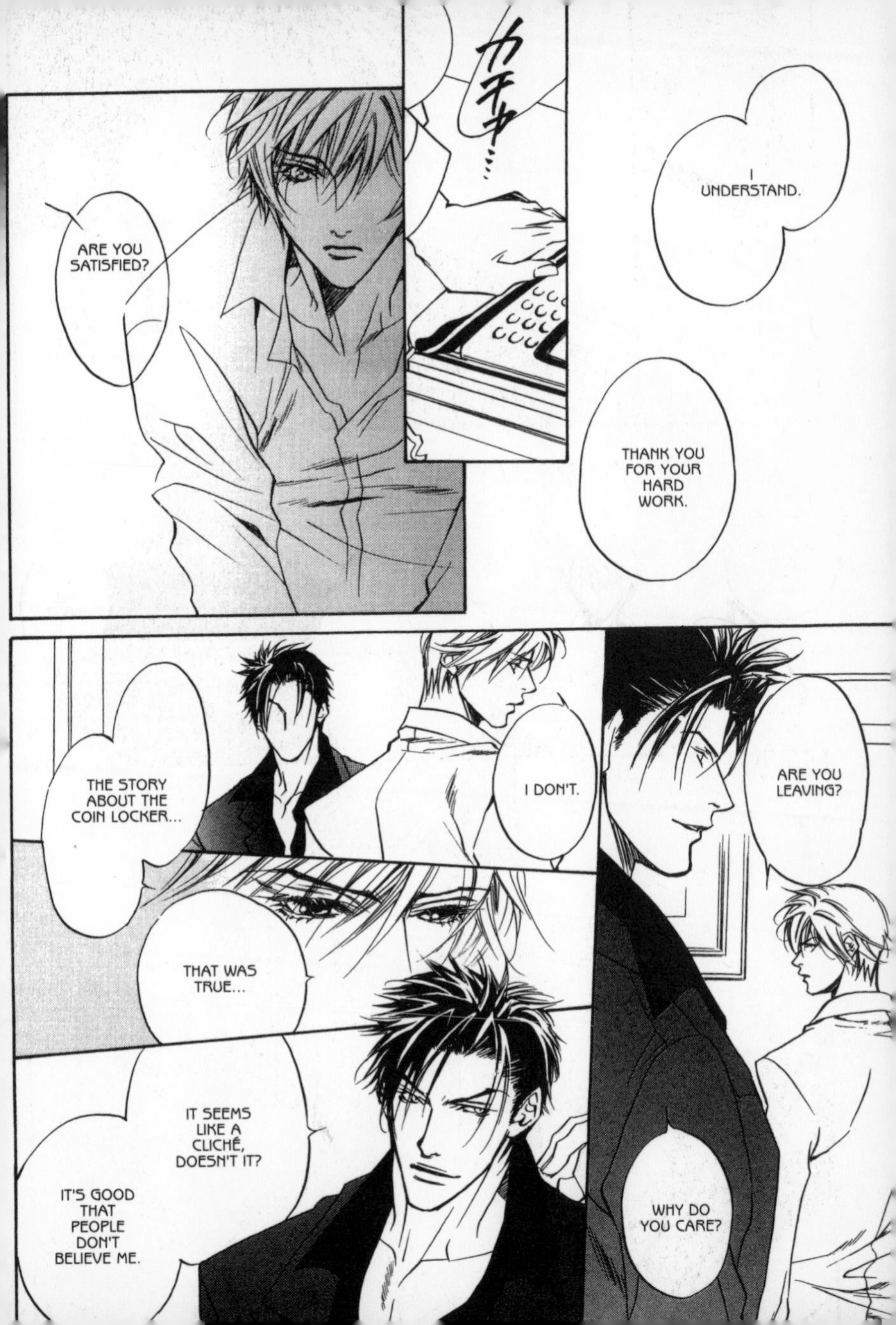
I UNDERSTAND.
THANK YOU FOR YOUR HARD WORK.
カチャ…
ARE YOU SATISFIED?
ARE YOU LEAVING?
WHY DO YOU CARE?
I DON'T.
THE STORY ABOUT THE COIN LOCKER...
THAT WAS TRUE...
IT SEEMS LIKE A CLICHÉ, DOESN'T IT?
IT'S GOOD THAT PEOPLE DON'T BELIEVE ME.

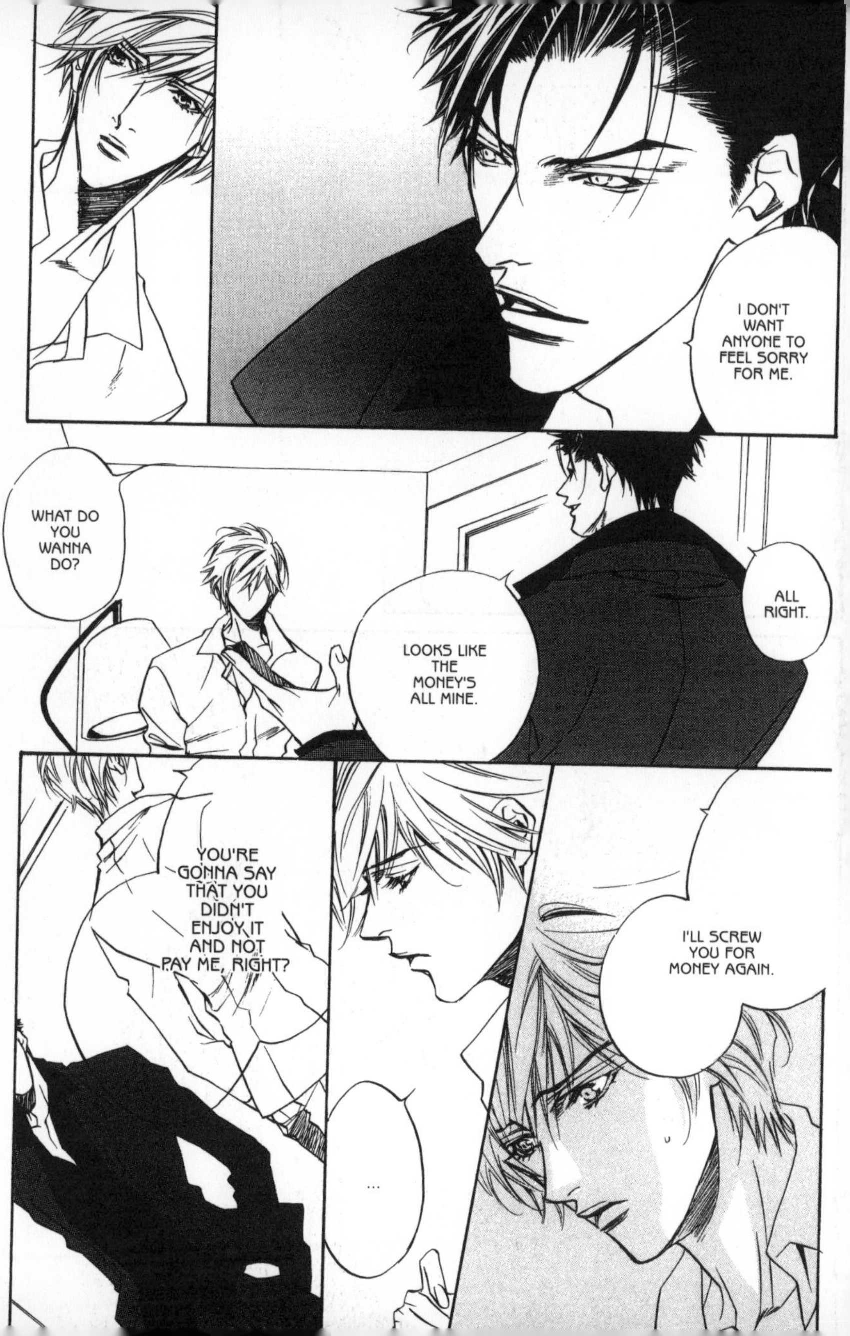
I DON'T WANT ANYONE TO FEEL SORRY FOR ME.
ALL RIGHT.
LOOKS LIKE THE MONEY'S ALL MINE.
WHAT DO YOU WANNA DO?
I'LL SCREW YOU FOR MONEY AGAIN.
...
YOU'RE GONNA SAY THAT YOU DIDN'T ENJOY IT AND NOT PAY ME, RIGHT?

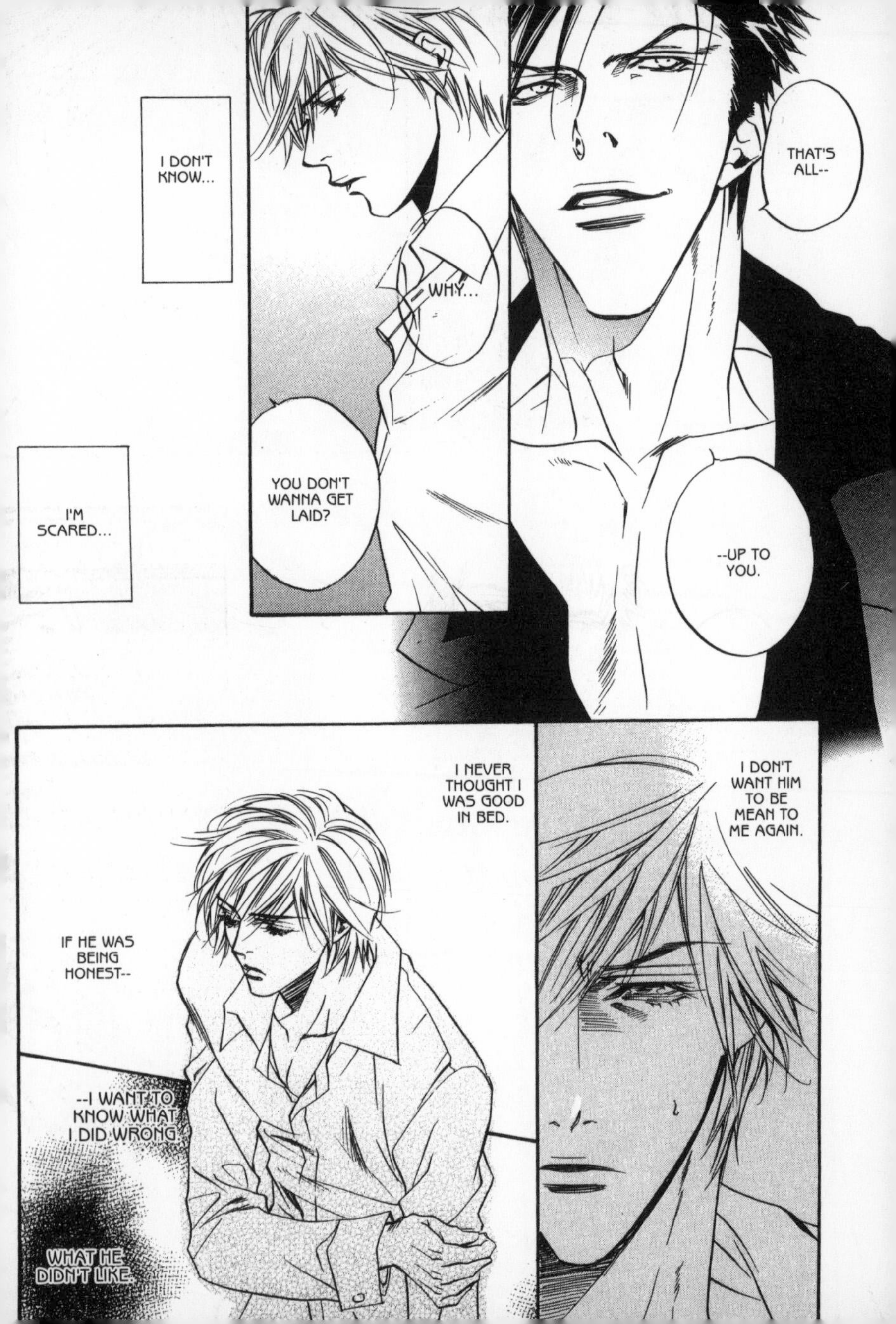
THAT'S ALL--
--UP TO YOU.
WHY...
YOU DON'T WANNA GET LAID?
I DON'T KNOW...
I'M SCARED...
I DON'T WANT HIM TO BE MEAN TO ME AGAIN.
I NEVER THOUGHT I WAS GOOD IN BED.
IF HE WAS BEING HONEST--
--I WANT TO KNOW WHAT I DID WRONG
WHAT HE DIDN'T LIKE.

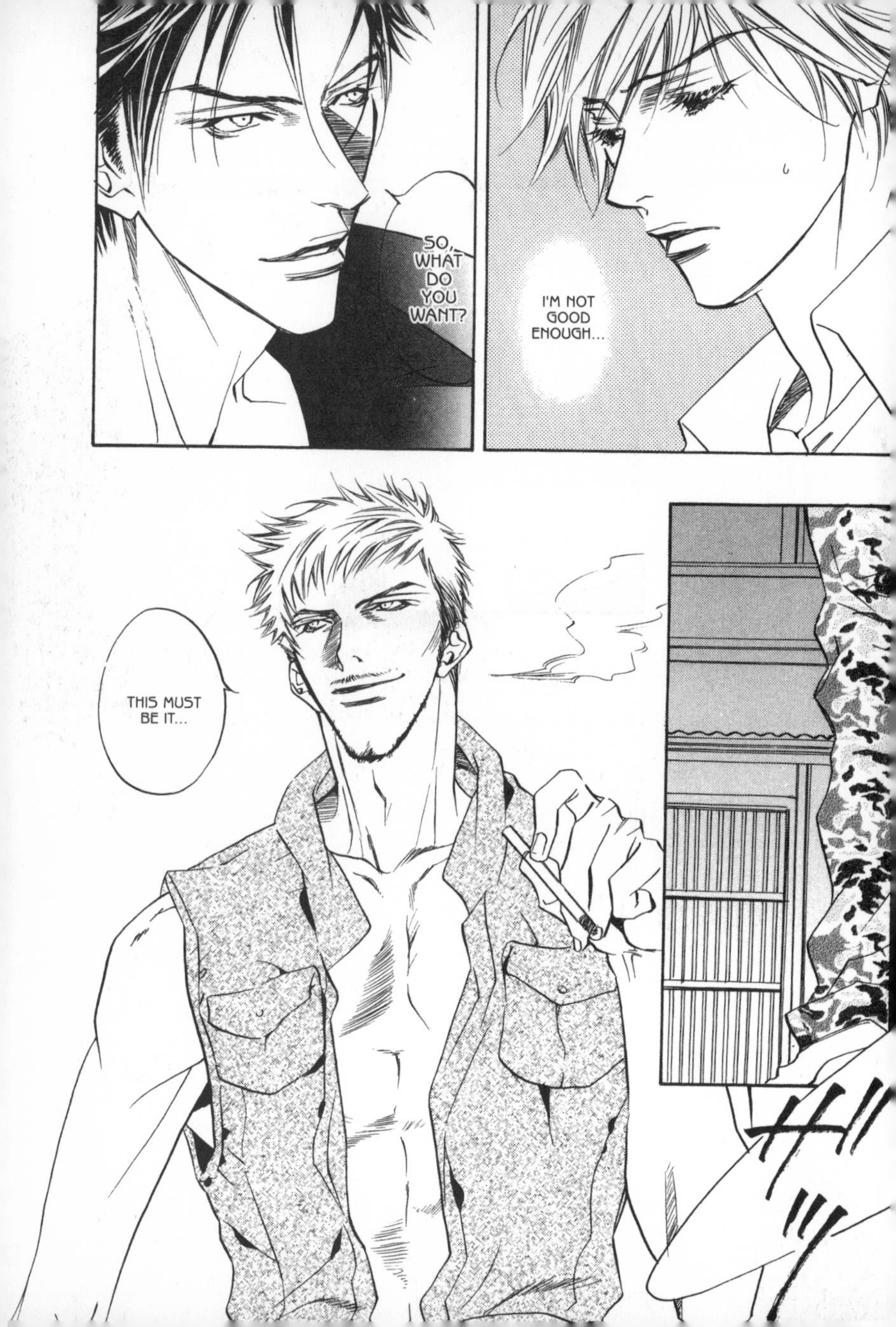
I'M NOT GOOD ENOUGH...
SO, WHAT DO YOU WANT?
THIS MUST BE IT...

THE BEST PLACE

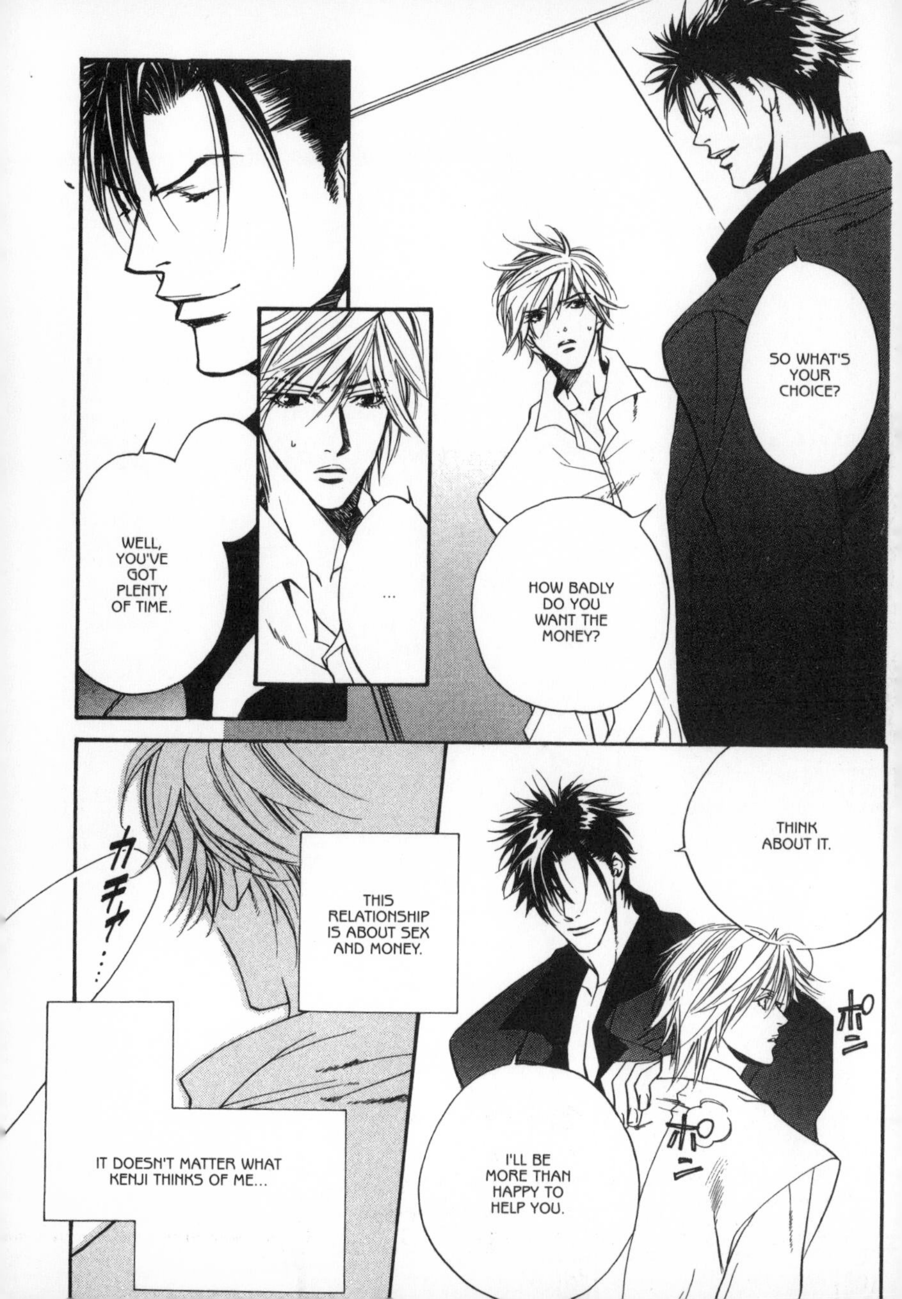
SO WHAT'S YOUR CHOICE?
HOW BADLY DO YOU WANT THE MONEY?
...
WELL, YOU'VE GOT PLENTY OF TIME.
THINK ABOUT IT.
ポン
ポン
I'LL BE MORE THAN HAPPY TO HELP YOU.
THIS RELATIONSHIP IS ABOUT SEX AND MONEY.
カチャ…
IT DOESN'T MATTER WHAT KENJI THINKS OF ME...

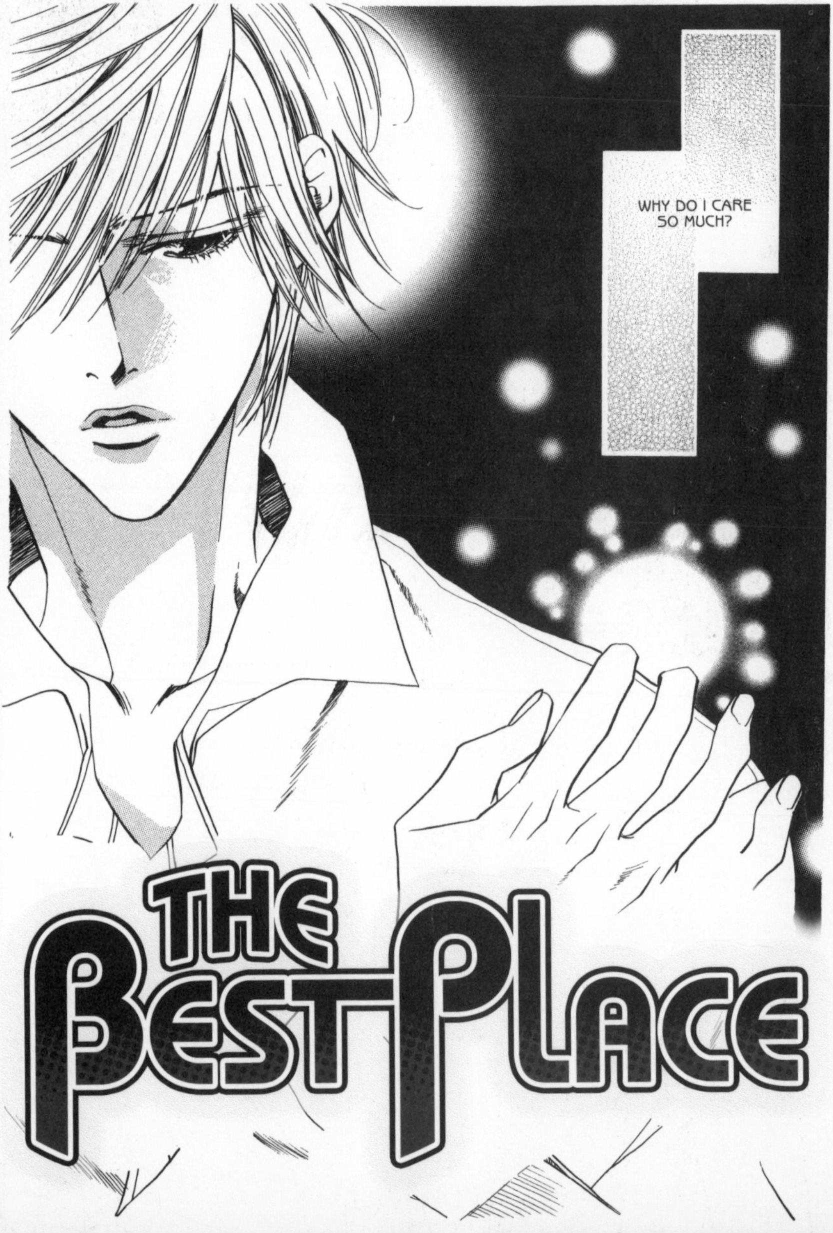
WHY DO I CARE SO MUCH?
THE BEST PLACE

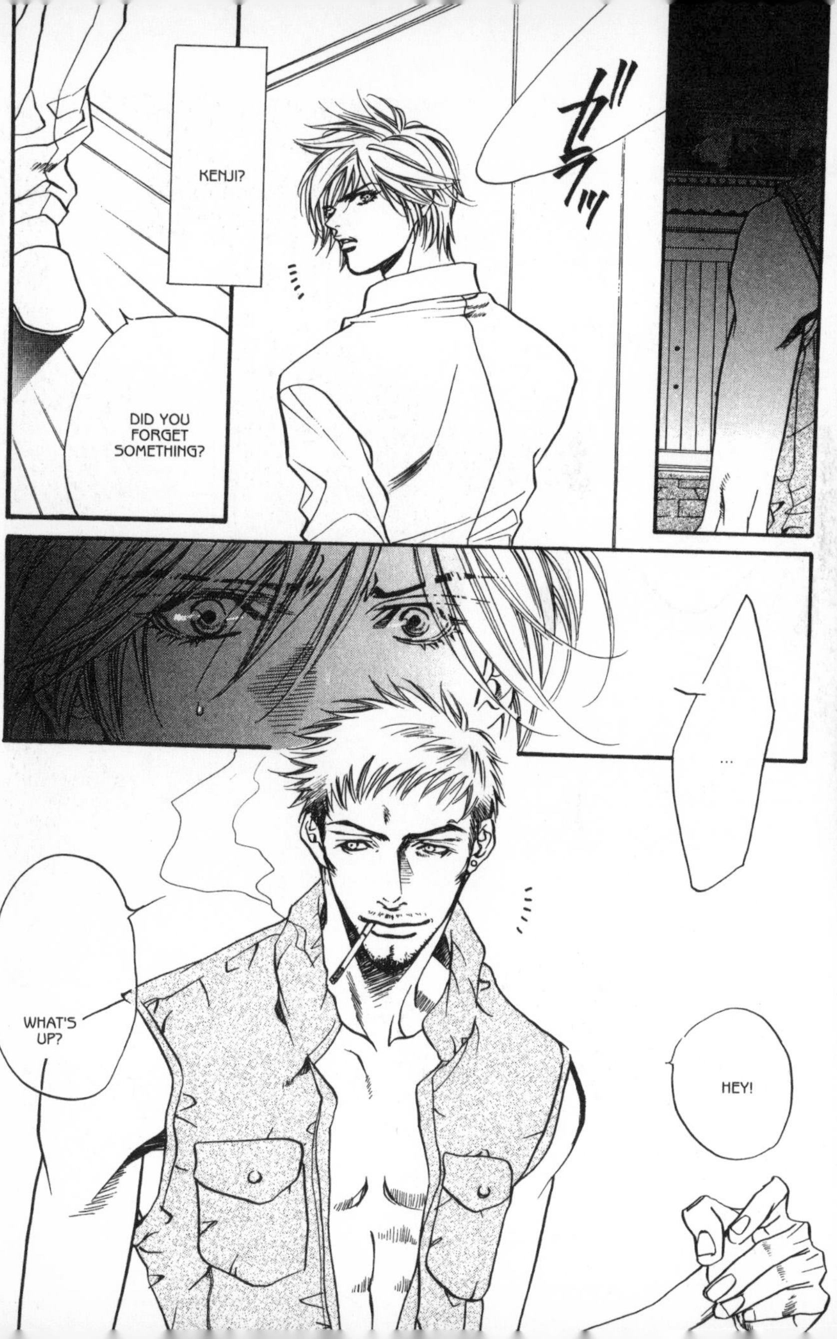
ガラッ
KENJI?
DID YOU FORGET SOMETHING?
...
HEY!
WHAT'S UP?

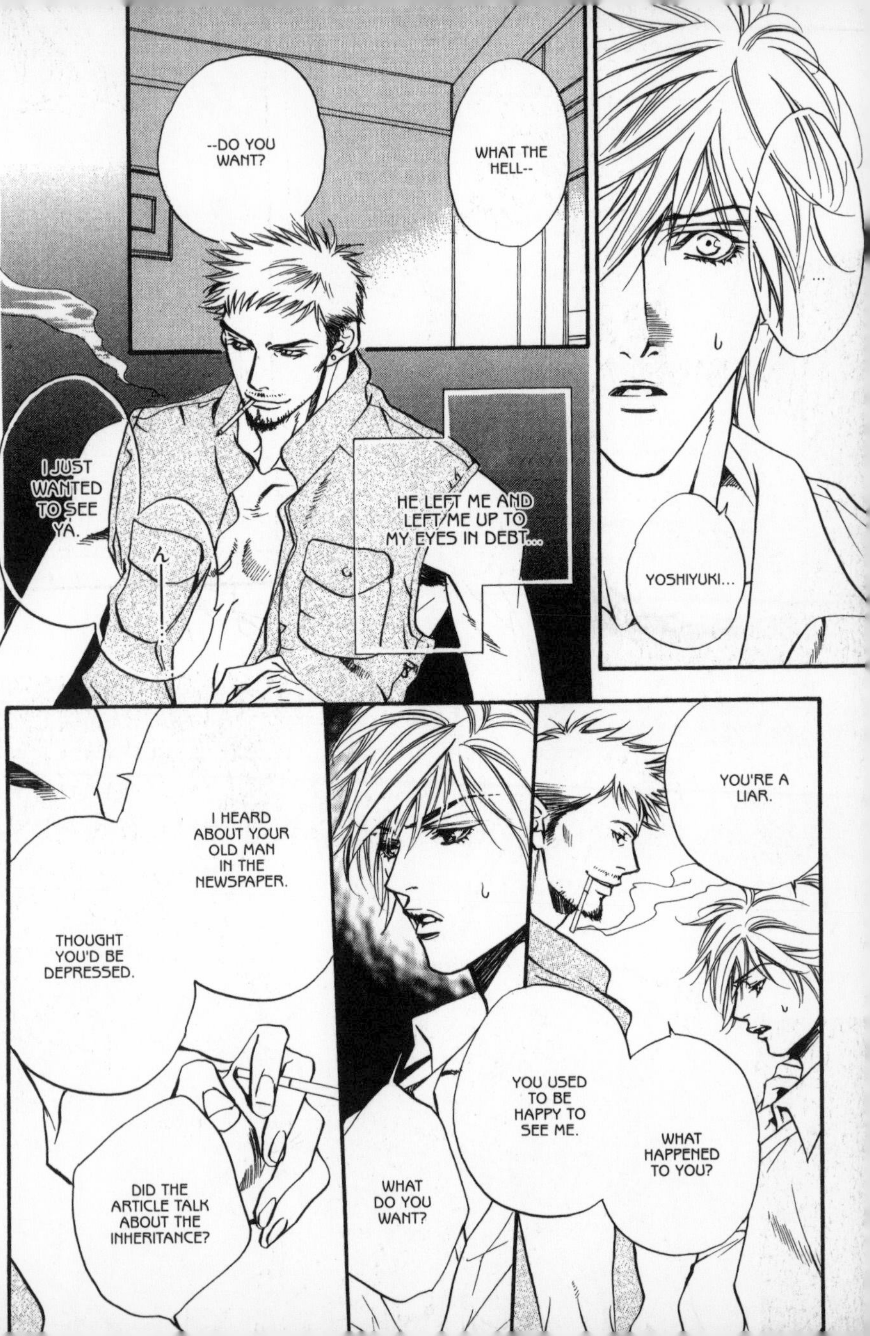
...
YOSHIYUKI...
WHAT THE HELL--
--DO YOU WANT?
HE LEFT ME AND LEFT ME UP TO MY EYES IN DEBT...
I JUST WANTED TO SEE YA.
YOU'RE A LIAR.
WHAT HAPPENED TO YOU?
YOU USED TO BE HAPPY TO SEE ME.
WHAT DO YOU WANT?
I HEARD ABOUT YOUR OLD MAN IN THE NEWSPAPER.
THOUGHT YOU'D BE DEPRESSED.
DID THE ARTICLE TALK ABOUT THE INHERITANCE?

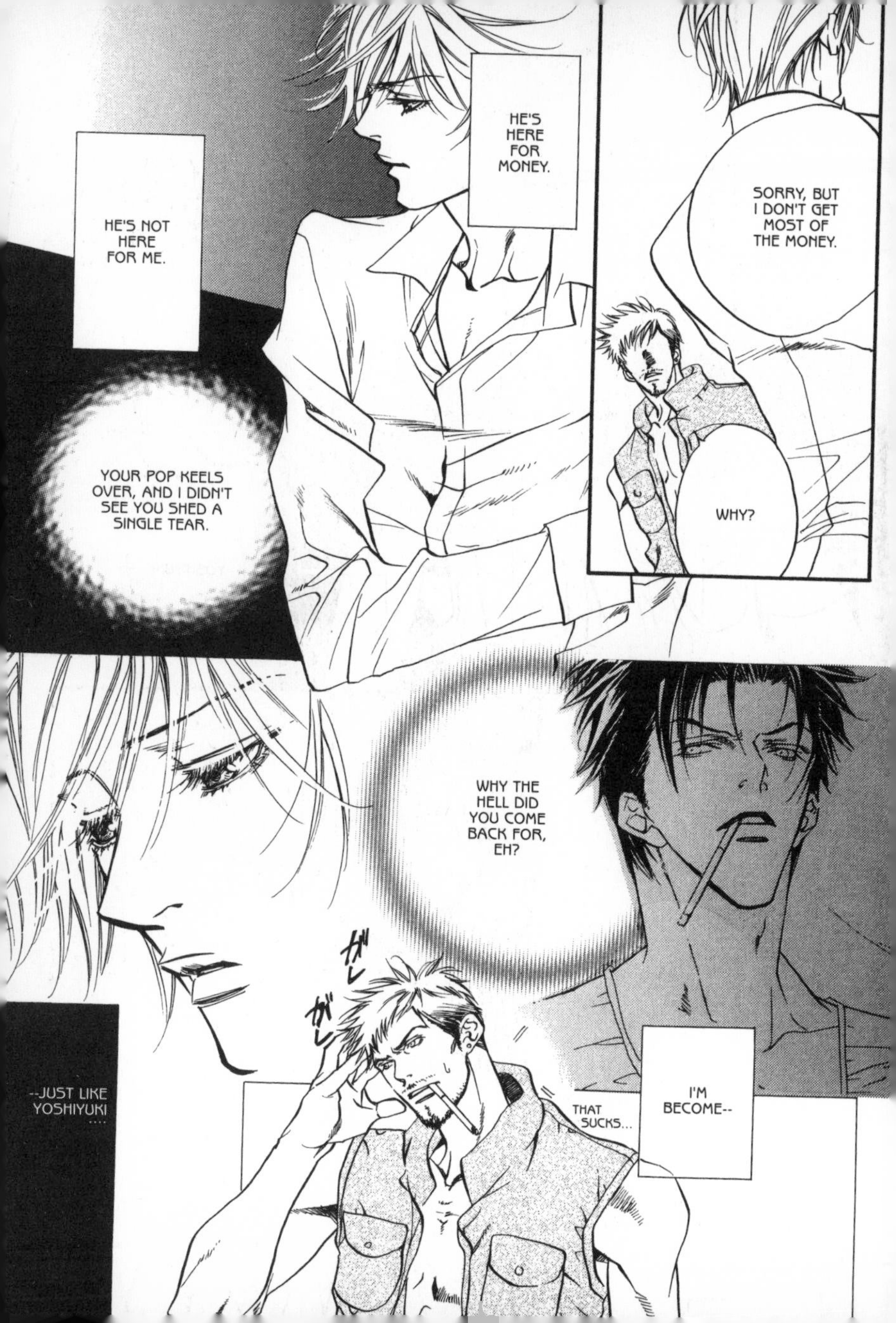

SORRY, BUT I DON'T GET MOST OF THE MONEY.
WHY?
HE'S HERE FOR MONEY.
HE'S NOT HERE FOR ME.
YOUR POP KEELS OVER, AND I DIDN'T SEE YOU SHED A SINGLE TEAR.
WHY THE HELL DID YOU COME BACK FOR, EH?
I'M BECOME--
THAT SUCKS...
がし
がし
--JUST LIKE YOSHIYUKI ....

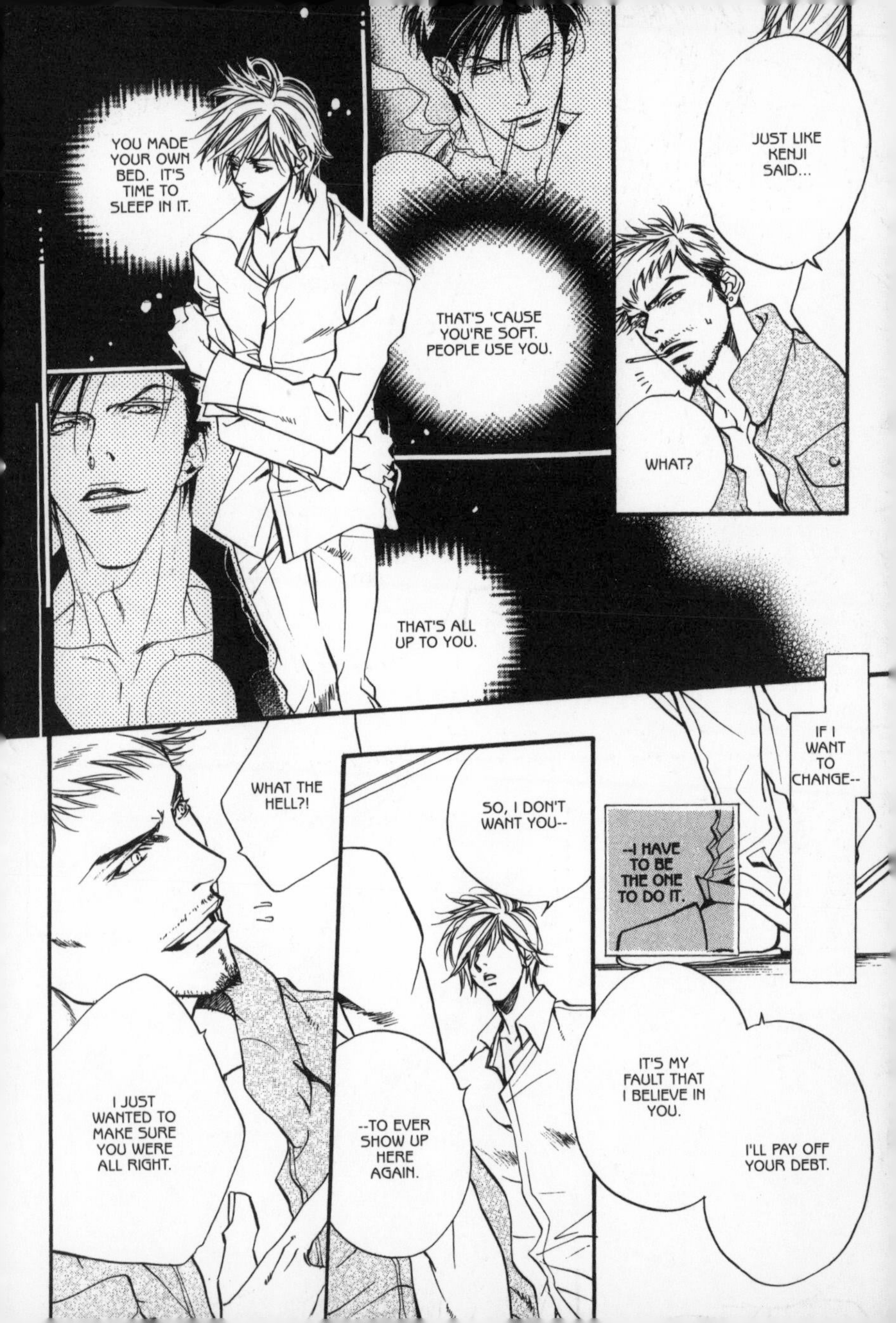
JUST LIKE KENJI SAID...
WHAT?
YOU MADE YOUR OWN BED. IT'S TIME TO SLEEP IN IT.
THAT'S 'CAUSE YOU'RE SOFT. PEOPLE USE YOU.
THAT'S ALL UP TO YOU.
IF I WANT TO CHANGE--
--I HAVE TO BE THE ONE TO DO IT.
IT'S MY FAULT THAT I BELIEVE IN YOU.
I'LL PAY OFF YOUR DEBT.
SO, I DON'T WANT YOU--
--TO EVER SHOW UP HERE AGAIN.
WHAT THE HELL?!
I JUST WANTED TO MAKE SURE YOU WERE ALL RIGHT.

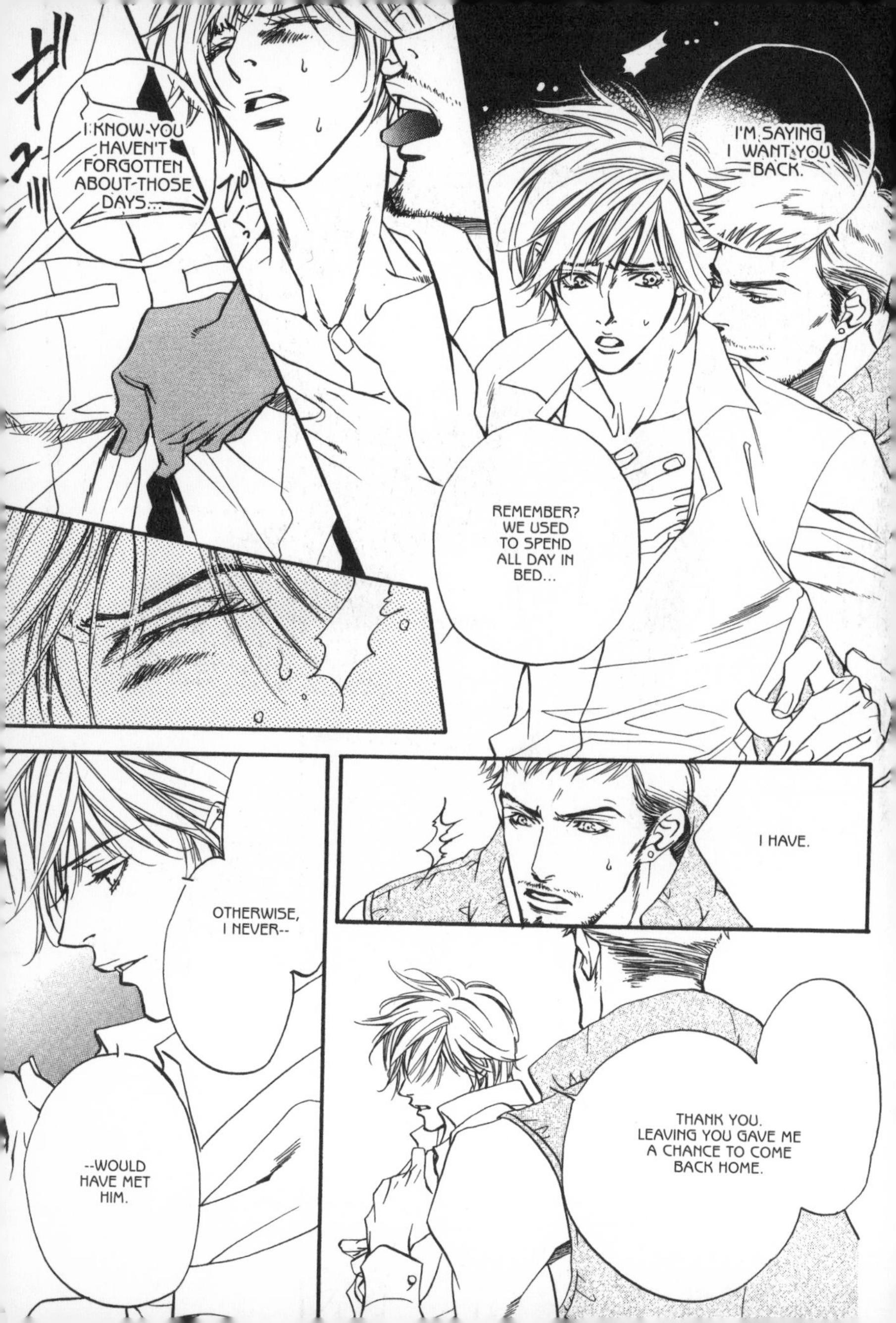
I'M SAYING I WANT YOU BACK.
I KNOW YOU HAVEN'T FORGOTTEN ABOUT THOSE DAYS...
REMEMBER? WE USED TO SPEND ALL DAY IN BED...
I HAVE.
THANK YOU. LEAVING YOU GAVE ME A CHANCE TO COME BACK HOME.
OTHERWISE, I NEVER--
--WOULD HAVE MET HIM.

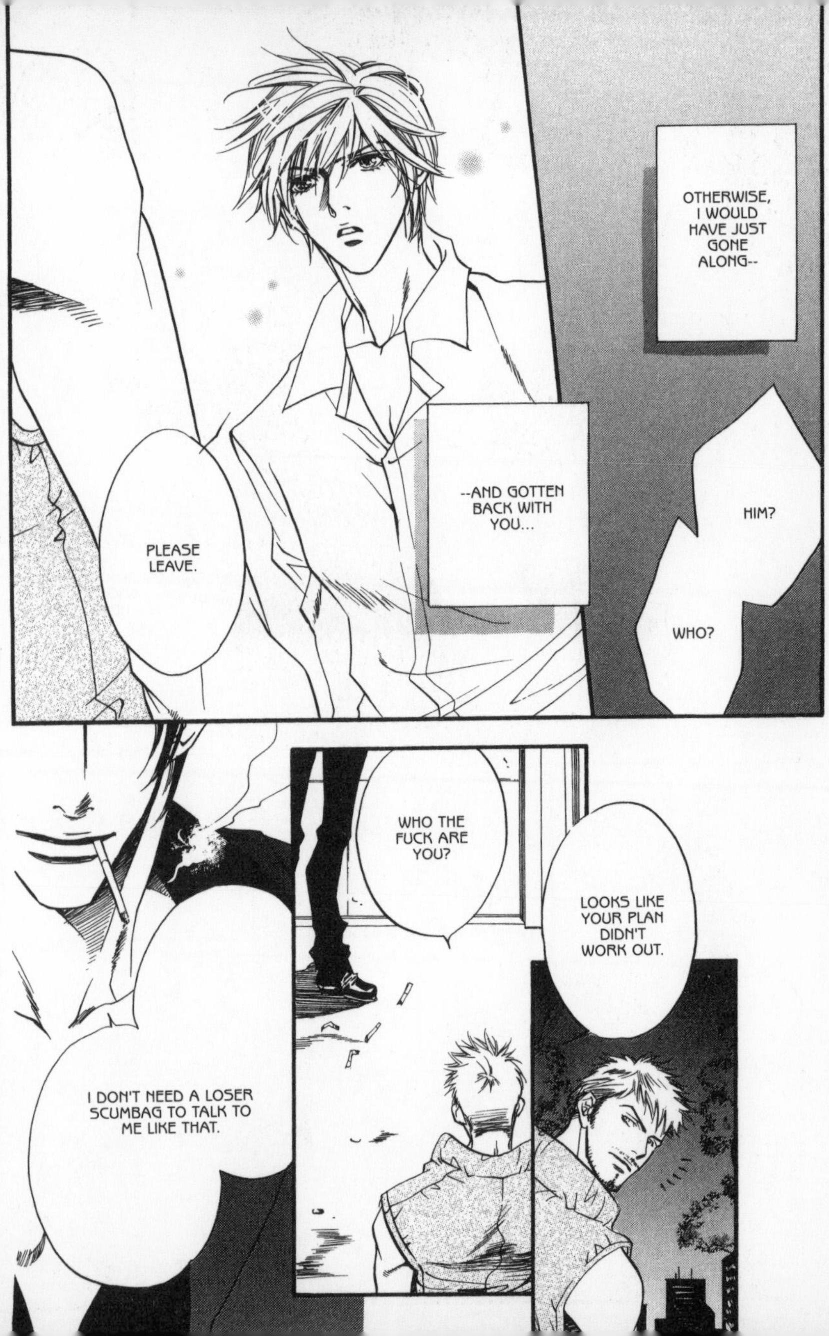
OTHERWISE, I WOULD HAVE JUST GONE ALONG--
--AND GOTTEN BACK WITH YOU...
HIM?
WHO?
PLEASE LEAVE.
LOOKS LIKE YOUR PLAN DIDN'T WORK OUT.
WHO THE FUCK ARE YOU?
I DON'T NEED A LOSER SCUMBAG TO TALK TO ME LIKE THAT.

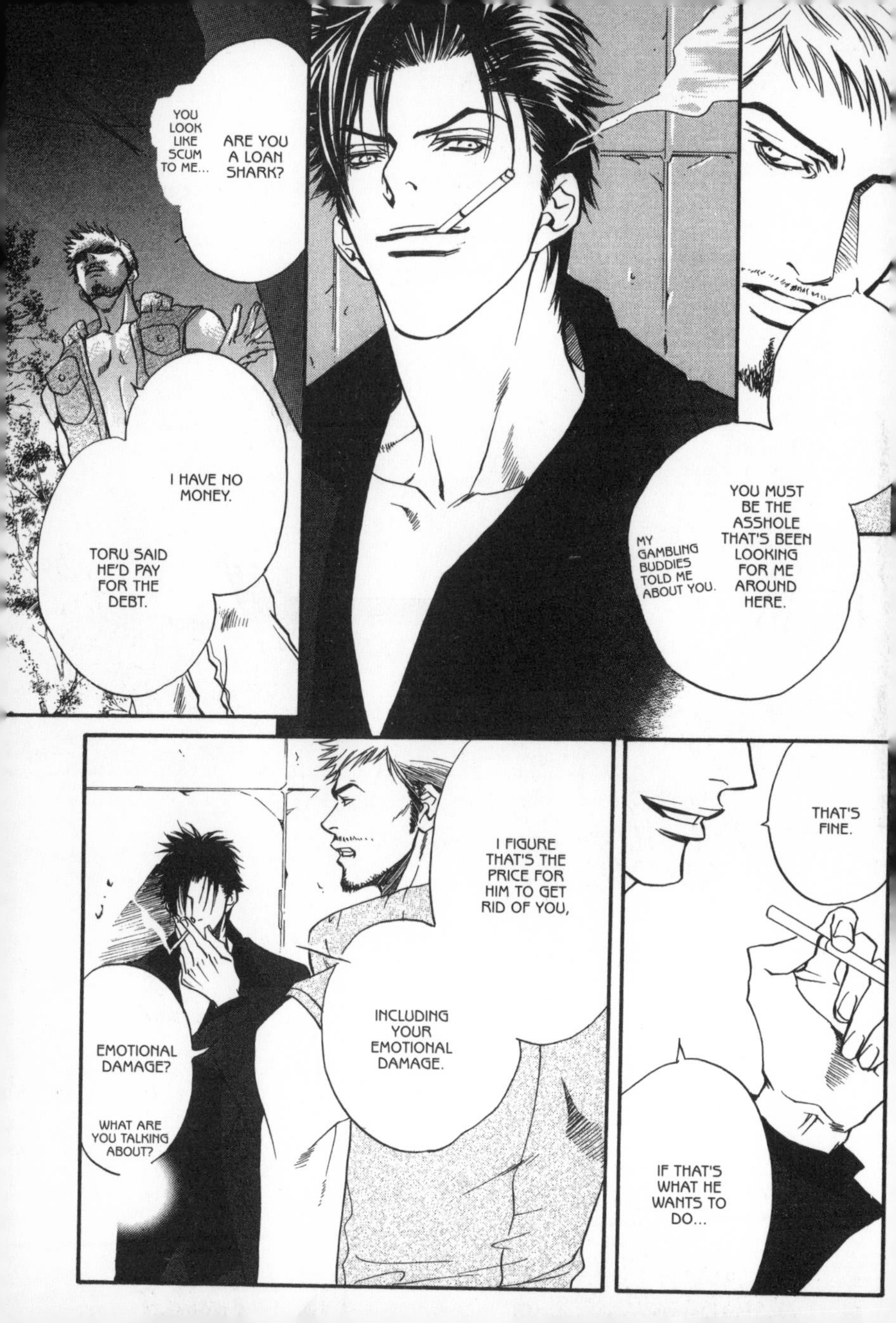
YOU MUST BE THE ASSHOLE THAT'S BEEN LOOKING FOR ME AROUND HERE.
MY GAMBLING BUDDIES TOLD ME ABOUT YOU.
ARE YOU A LOAN SHARK?
YOU LOOK LIKE SCUM TO ME...
I HAVE NO MONEY.
TORU SAID HE'D PAY FOR THE DEBT.
THAT'S FINE.
IF THAT'S WHAT HE WANTS TO DO...
I FIGURE THAT'S THE PRICE FOR HIM TO GET RID OF YOU,
INCLUDING YOUR EMOTIONAL DAMAGE.
EMOTIONAL DAMAGE?
WHAT ARE YOU TALKING ABOUT?

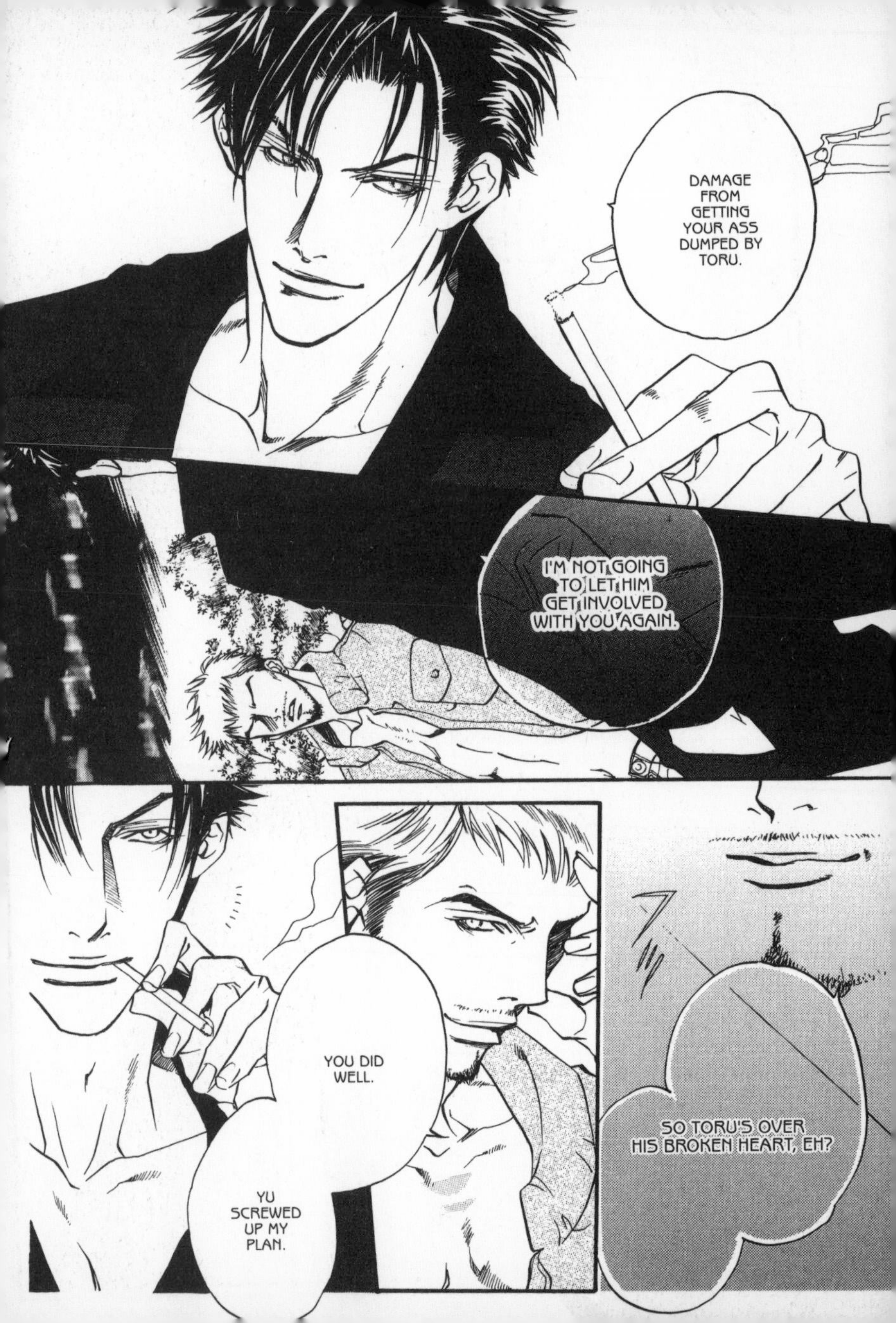
DAMAGE FROM GETTING YOUR ASS DUMPED BY TORU.
I'M NOT GOING TO LET HIM GET INVOLVED WITH YOU AGAIN.
SO TORU'S OVER HIS BROKEN HEART, EH?
YOU DID WELL.
YU SCREWED UP MY PLAN.

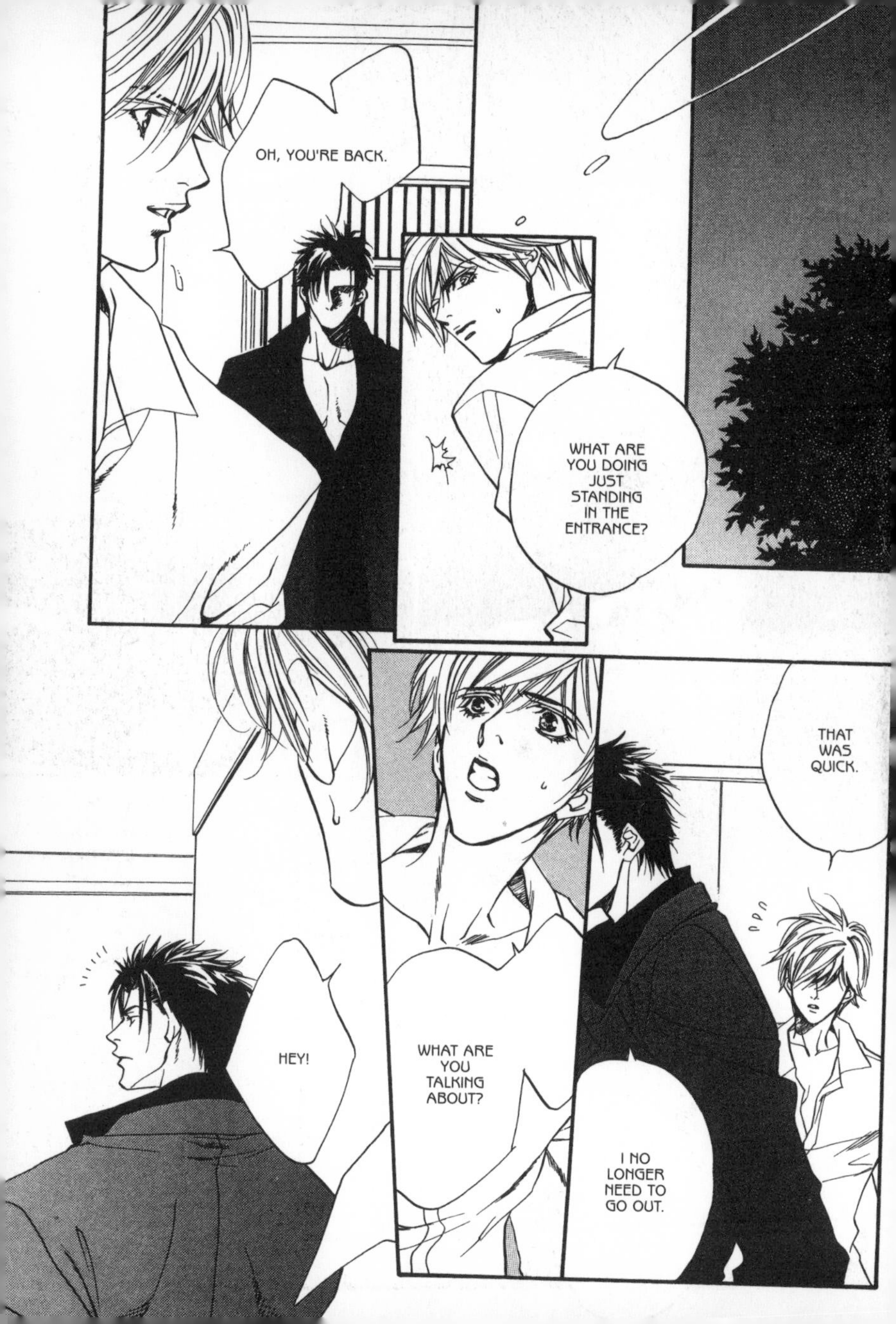
OH, YOU'RE BACK.
WHAT ARE YOU DOING JUST STANDING IN THE ENTRANCE?
THAT WAS QUICK.
I NO LONGER NEED TO GO OUT.
WHAT ARE YOU TALKING ABOUT?
HEY!

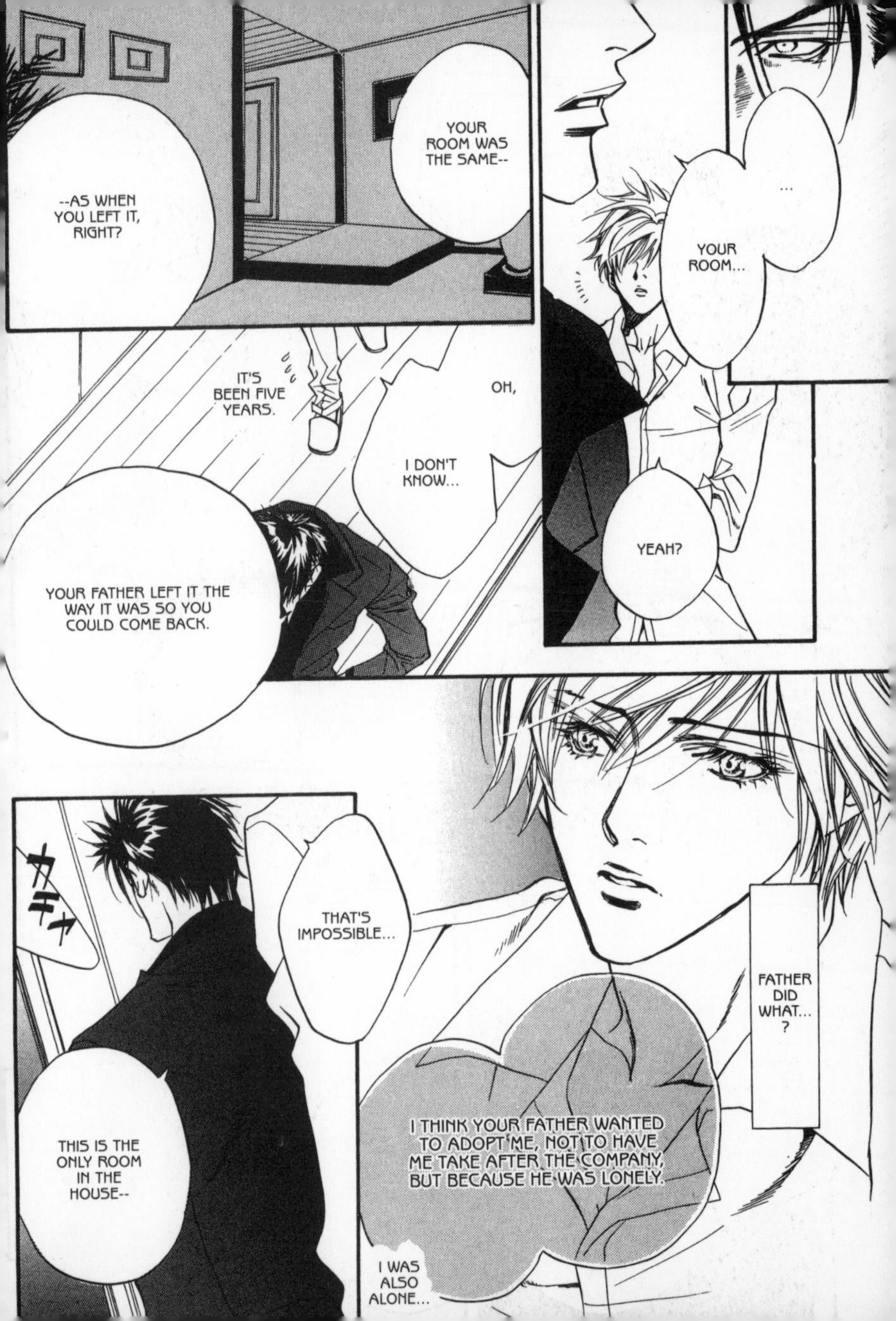
...
YOUR ROOM...
YOUR ROOM WAS THE SAME--
--AS WHEN YOU LEFT IT, RIGHT?
YEAH?
OH,
I DON'T KNOW...
IT'S BEEN FIVE YEARS.
YOUR FATHER LEFT IT THE WAY IT WAS SO YOU COULD COME BACK.
FATHER DID WHAT...?
THAT'S IMPOSSIBLE...
I THINK YOUR FATHER WANTED TO ADOPT ME, NOT TO HAVE ME TAKE AFTER THE COMPANY, BUT BECAUSE HE WAS LONELY.
I WAS ALSO ALONE...
カチャ
THIS IS THE ONLY ROOM IN THE HOUSE--

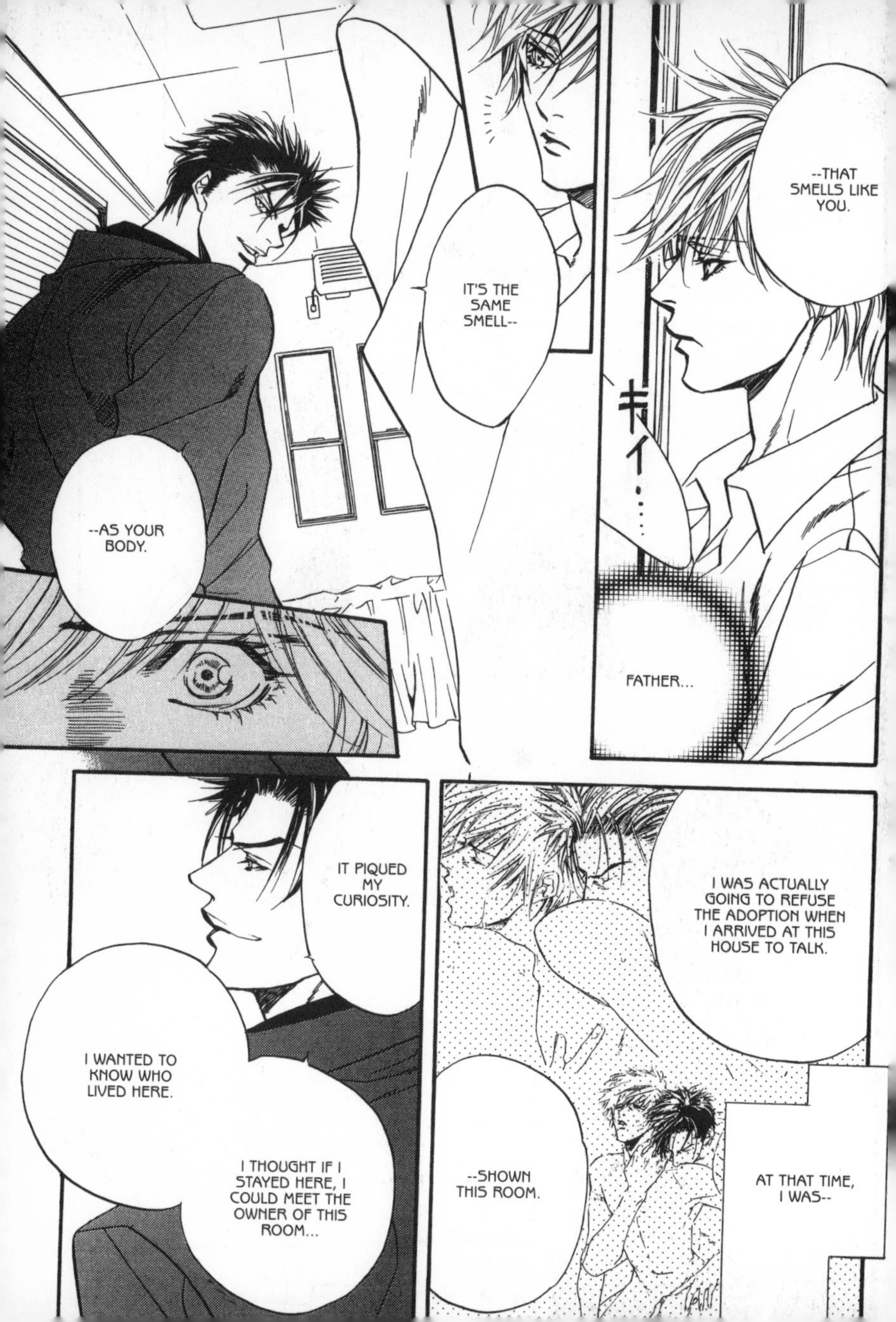
--THAT SMELLS LIKE YOU.
キィ…
FATHER...
IT'S THE SAME SMELL--
--AS YOUR BODY.
I WAS ACTUALLY GOING TO REFUSE THE ADOPTION WHEN I ARRIVED AT THIS HOUSE TO TALK.
AT THAT TIME, I WAS--
--SHOWN THIS ROOM.
IT PIQUED MY CURIOSITY.
I WANTED TO KNOW WHO LIVED HERE.
I THOUGHT IF I STAYED HERE, I COULD MEET THE OWNER OF THIS ROOM...

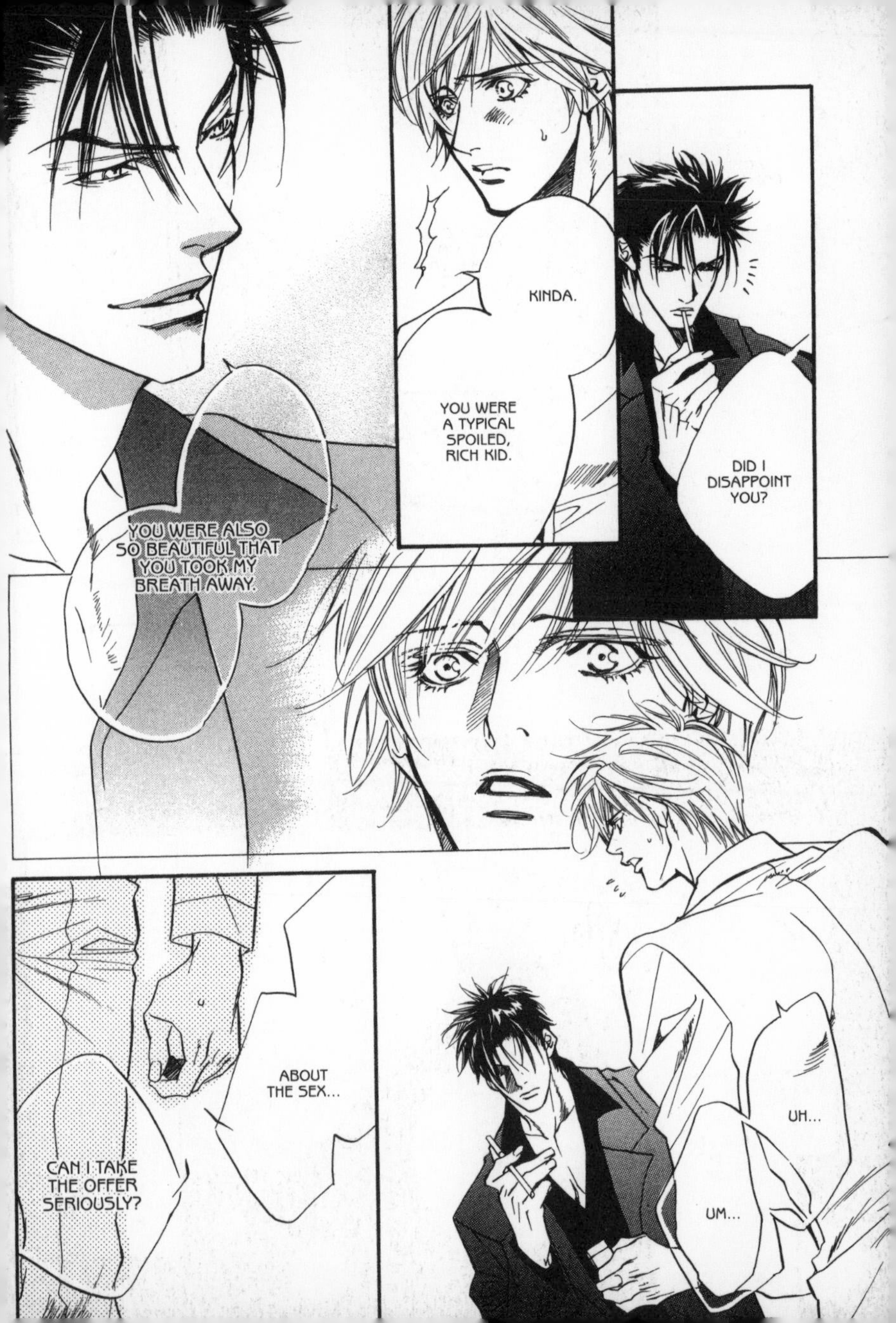
DID I DISAPPOINT YOU?
KINDA.
YOU WERE A TYPICAL SPOILED, RICH KID.
YOU WERE ALSO SO BEAUTIFUL THAT YOU TOOK MY BREATH AWAY.
UH...
UM...
ABOUT THE SEX...
CAN I TAKE THE OFFER SERIOUSLY?

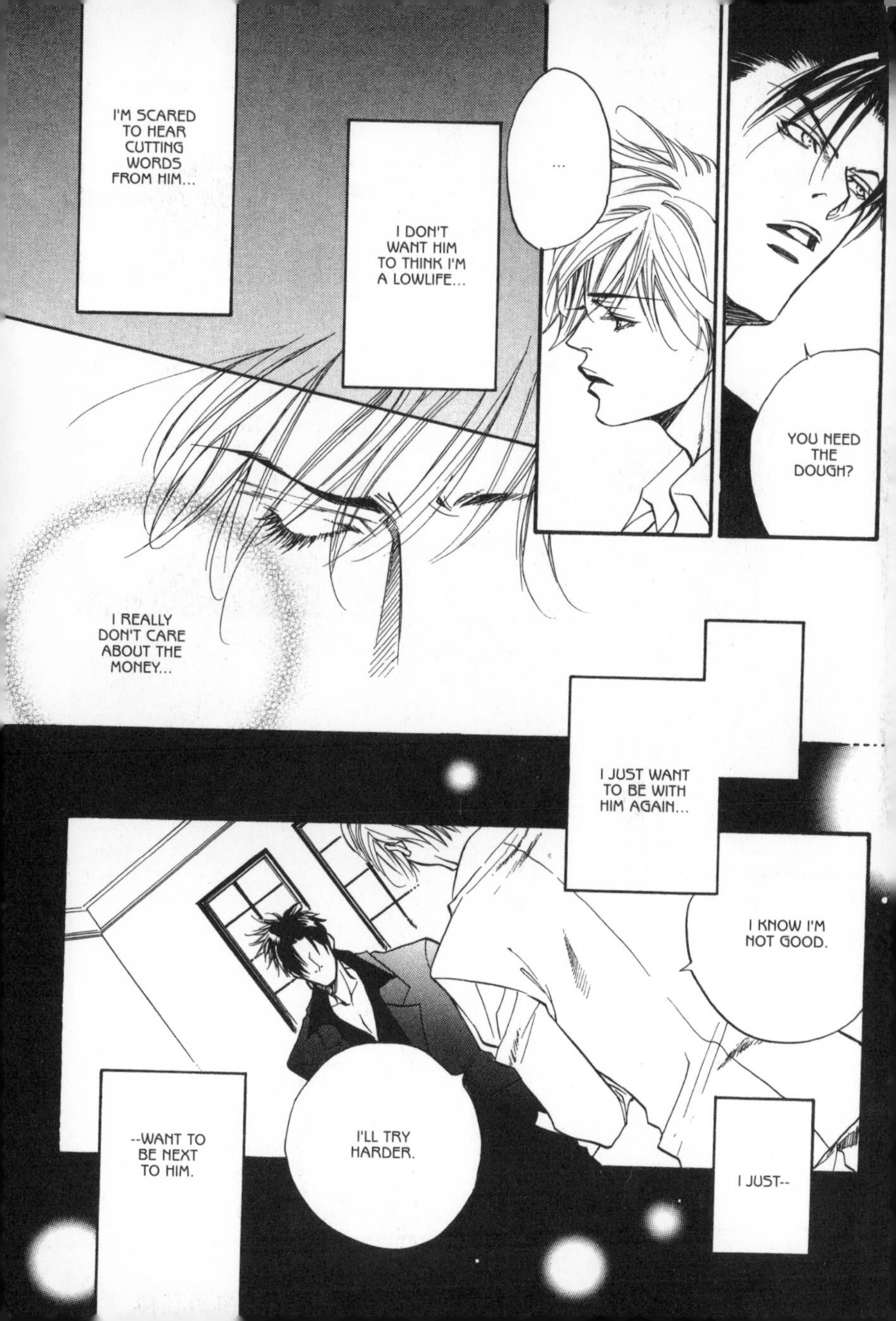
YOU NEED THE DOUGH?
...
I DON'T WANT HIM TO THINK I'M A LOWLIFE...
I'M SCARED TO HEAR CUTTING WORDS FROM HIM...
I REALLY DON'T CARE ABOUT THE MONEY...
I JUST WANT TO BE WITH HIM AGAIN...
I KNOW I'M NOT GOOD.
I'LL TRY HARDER.
I JUST--
--WANT TO BE NEXT TO HIM.

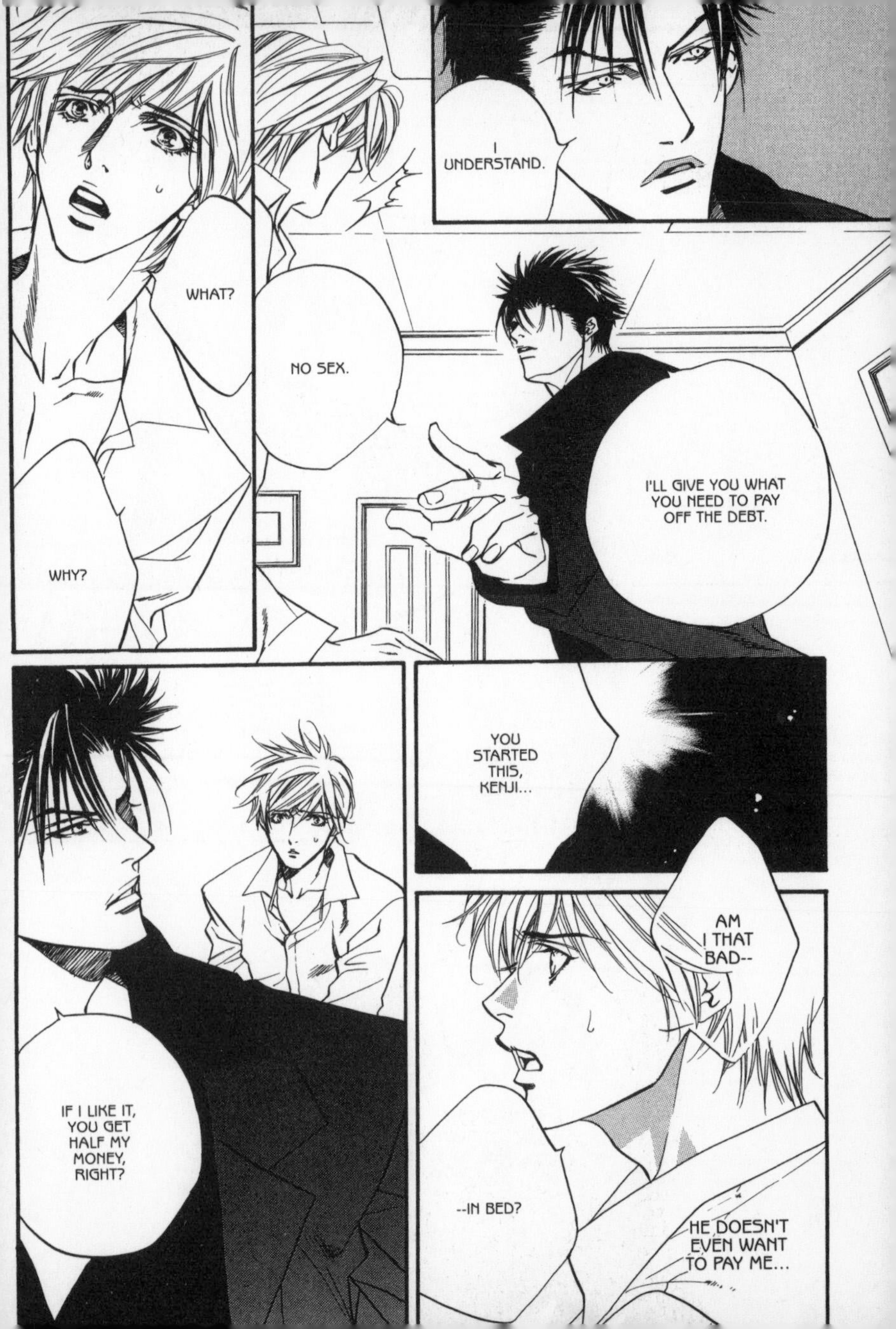
I UNDERSTAND.
I'LL GIVE YOU WHAT YOU NEED TO PAY OFF THE DEBT.
NO SEX.
WHAT?
WHY?
YOU STARTED THIS, KENJI...
IF I LIKE IT, YOU GET HALF MY MONEY, RIGHT?
AM I THAT BAD--
--IN BED?
HE DOESN'T EVEN WANT TO PAY ME...

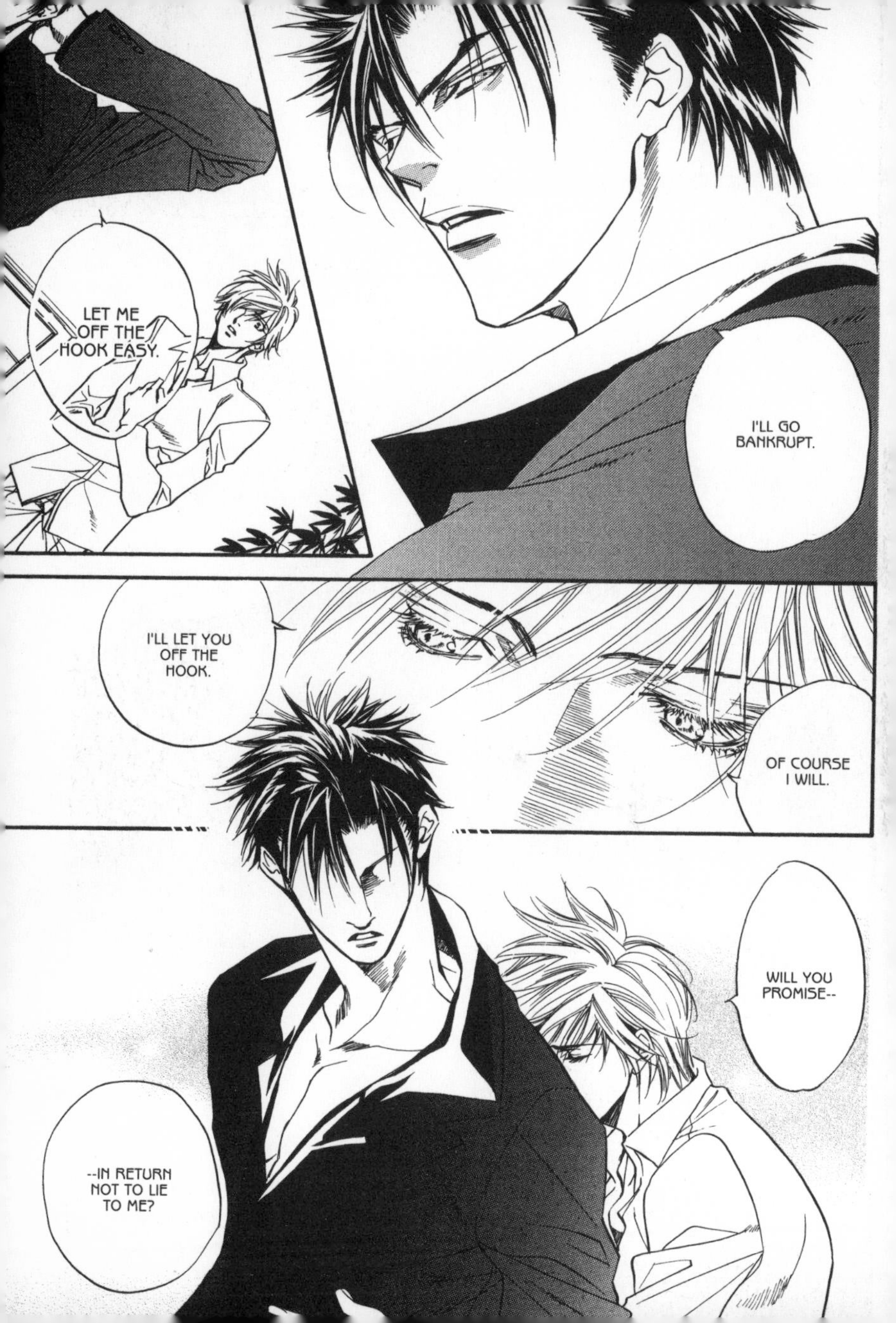
I'LL GO BANKRUPT.
LET ME OFF THE HOOK EASY.
OF COURSE I WILL.
I'LL LET YOU OFF THE HOOK.
WILL YOU PROMISE--
--IN RETURN NOT TO LIE TO ME?

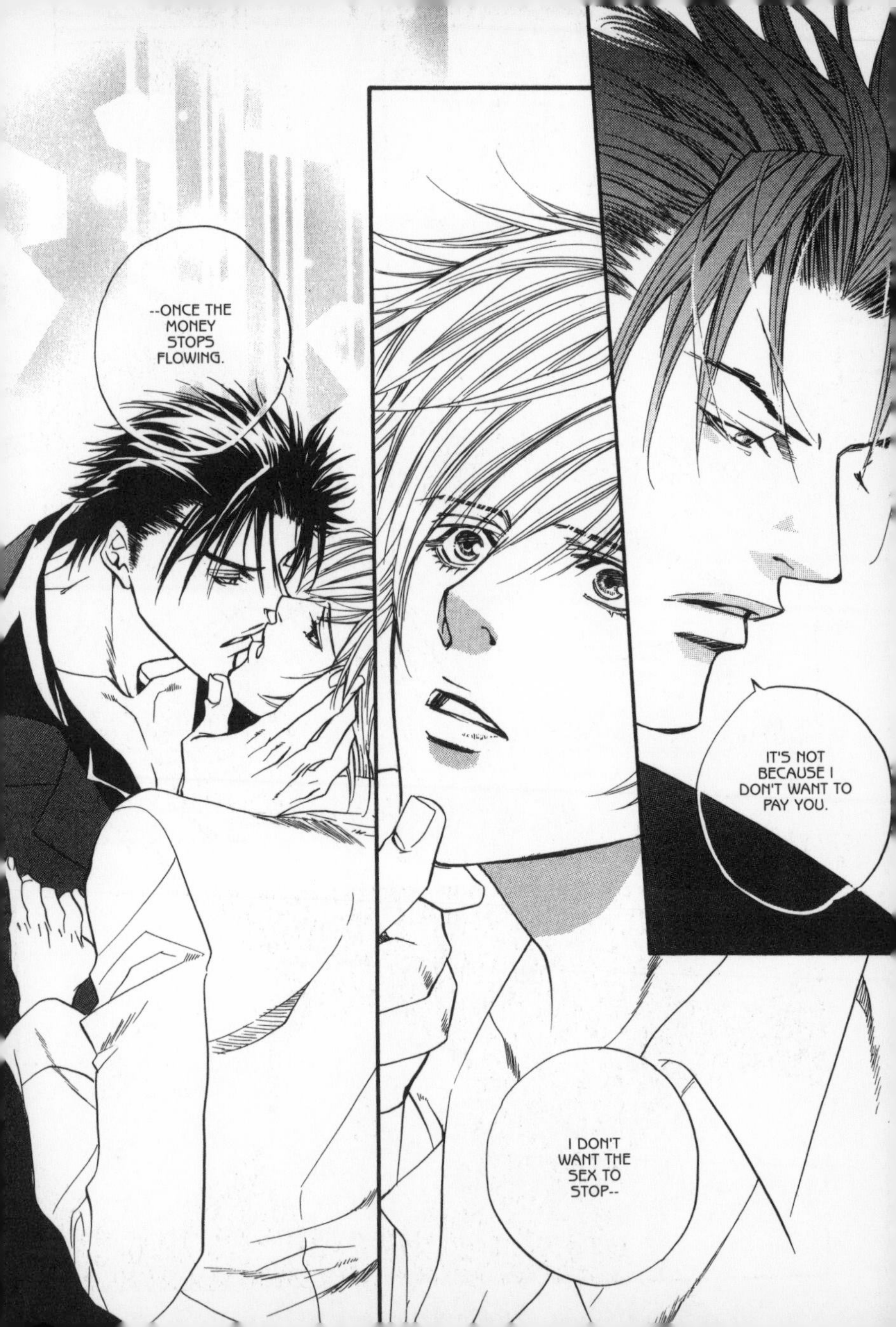
IT'S NOT BECAUSE I DON'T WANT TO PAY YOU.
I DON'T WANT THE SEX TO STOP--
--ONCE THE MONEY STOPS FLOWING.

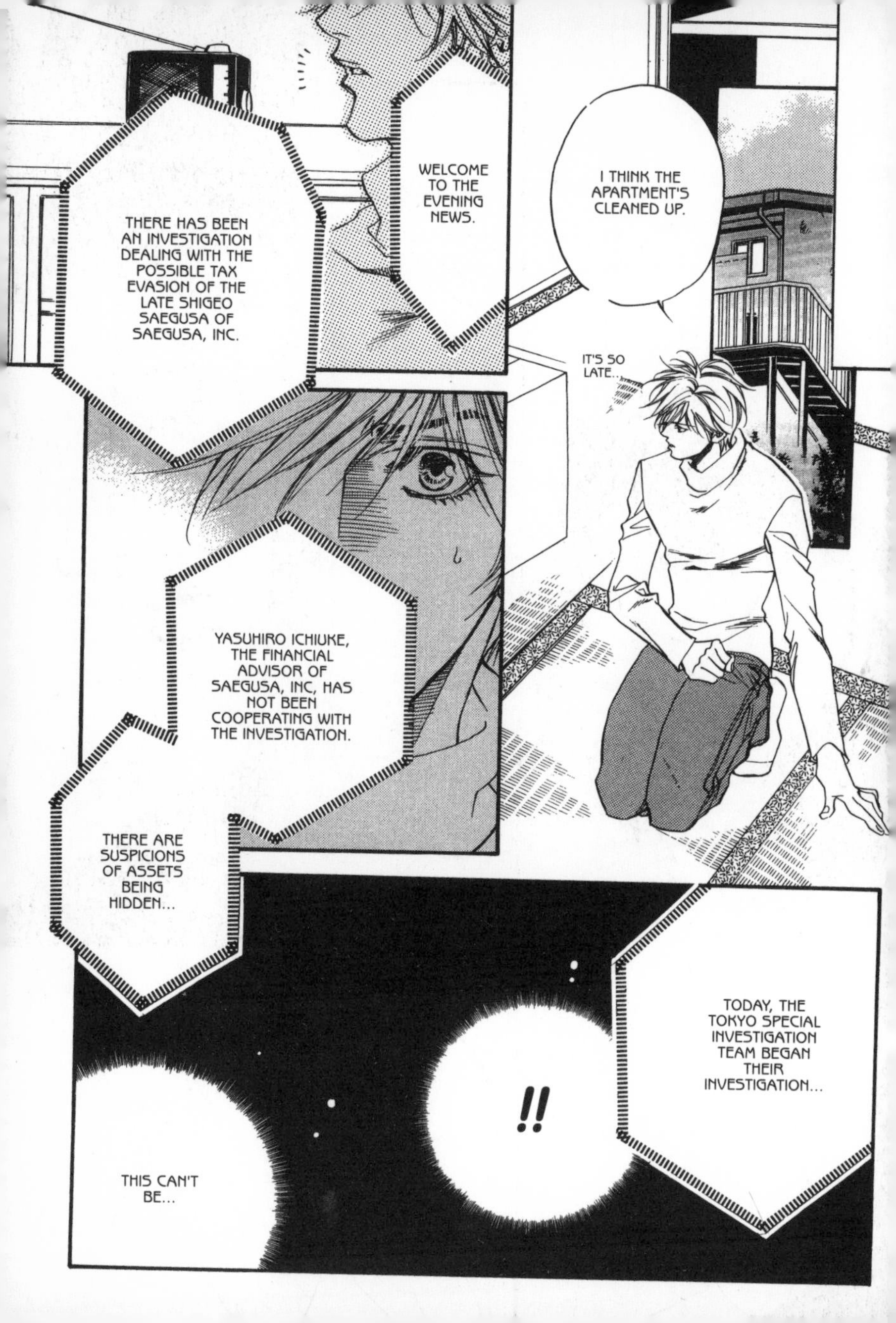
I THINK THE APARTMENT'S CLEANED UP.
IT'S SO LATE...
WELCOME TO THE EVENING NEWS.
THERE HAS BEEN AN INVESTIGATION DEALING WITH THE POSSIBLE TAX EVASION OF THE LATE SHIGEO SAEGUSA OF SAEGUSA, INC.
YASUHIRO ICHIUKE, THE FINANCIAL ADVISOR OF SAEGUSA, INC, HAS NOT BEEN COOPERATING WITH THE INVESTIGATION.
THERE ARE SUSPICIONS OF ASSETS BEING HIDDEN...
TODAY, THE TOKYO SPECIAL INVESTIGATION TEAM BEGAN THEIR INVESTIGATION...
!!
THIS CAN'T BE...

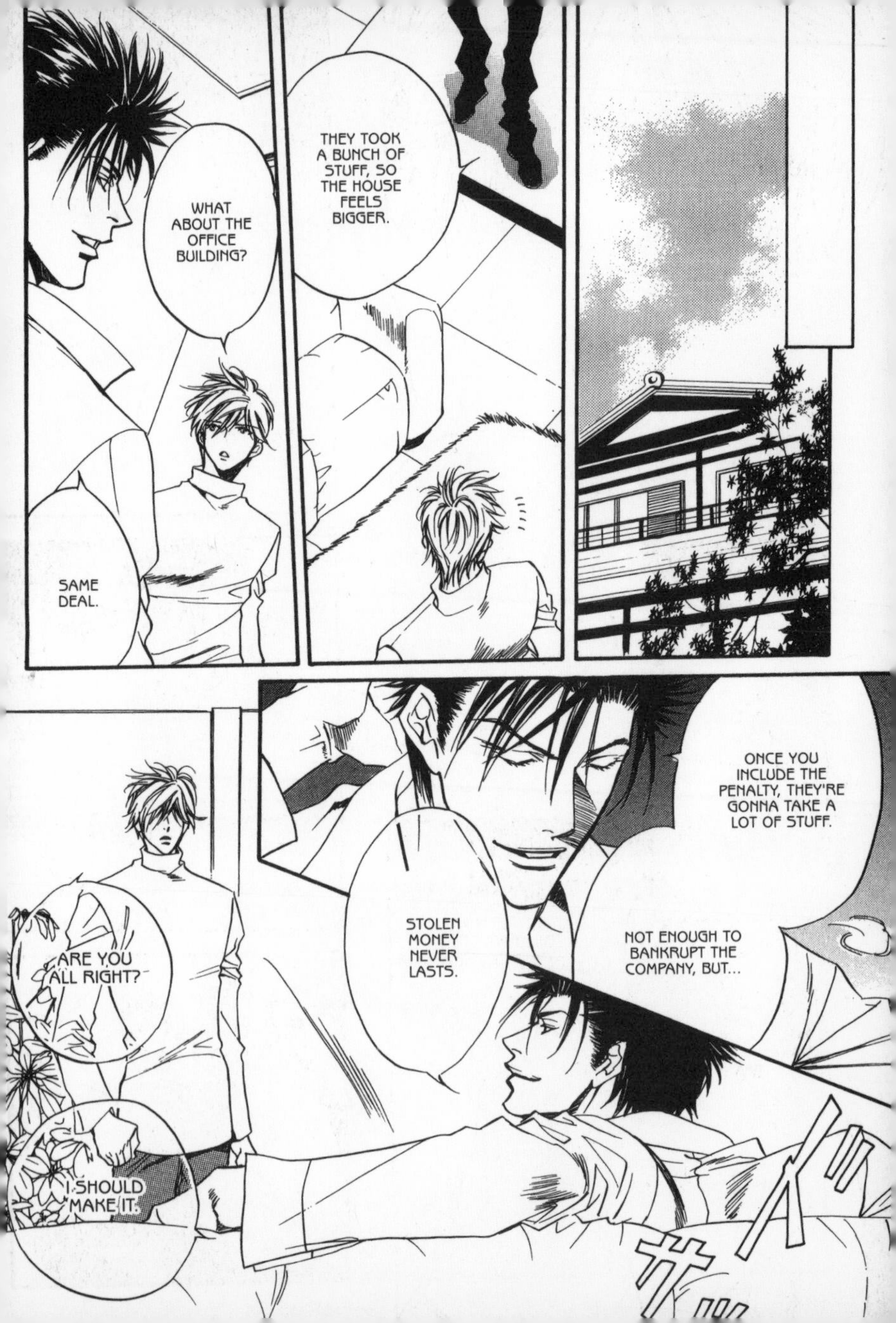
THEY TOOK A BUNCH OF STUFF, SO THE HOUSE FEELS BIGGER.
WHAT ABOUT THE OFFICE BUILDING?
SAME DEAL.
ONCE YOU INCLUDE THE PENALTY, THEY'RE GONNA TAKE A LOT OF STUFF.
NOT ENOUGH TO BANKRUPT THE COMPANY, BUT...
STOLEN MONEY NEVER LASTS.
ARE YOU ALL RIGHT?
I SHOULD MAKE IT.

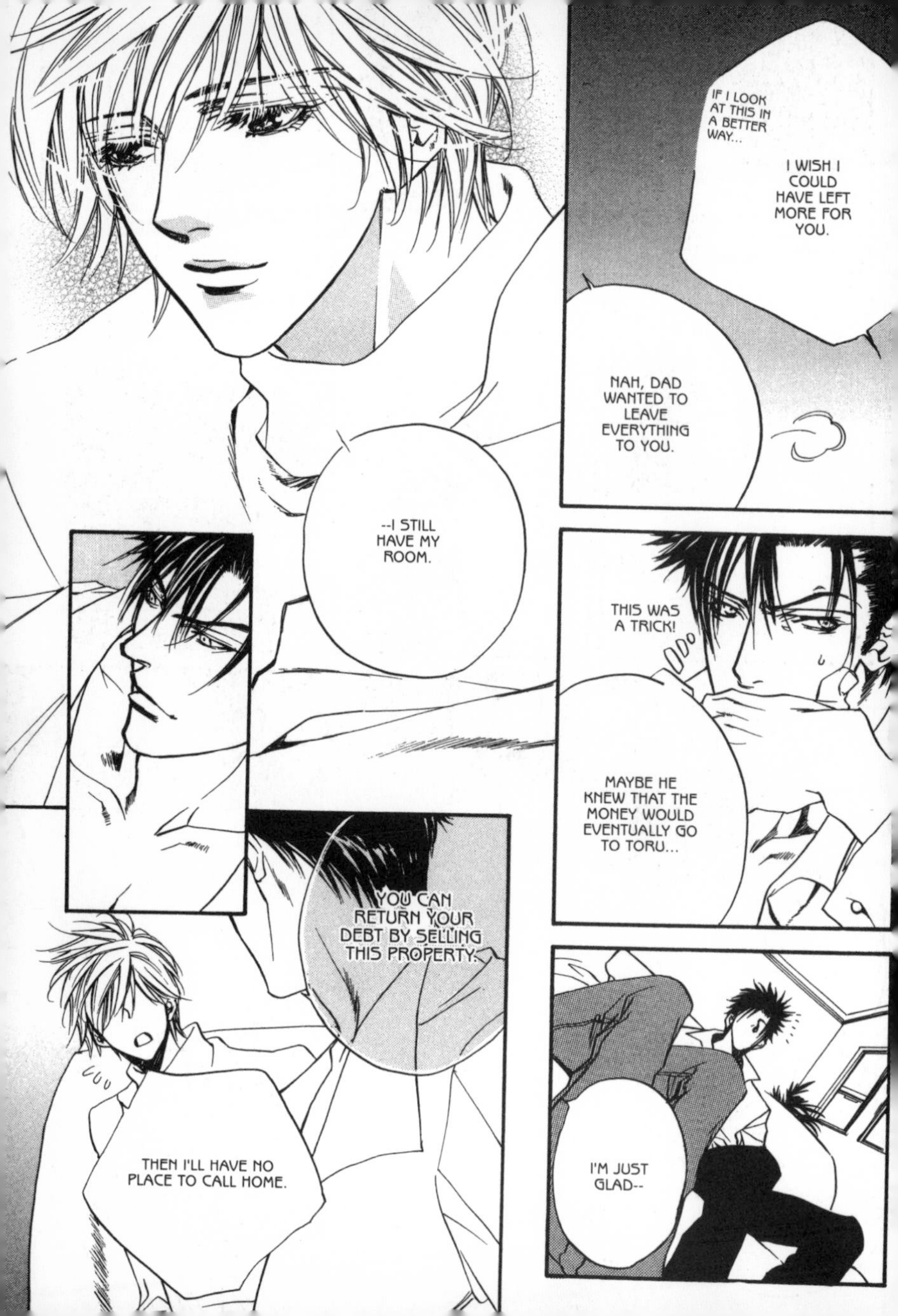

IF I LOOK AT THIS IN A BETTER WAY...
I WISH I COULD HAVE LEFT MORE FOR YOU.
NAH, DAD WANTED TO LEAVE EVERYTHING TO YOU.
--I STILL HAVE MY ROOM.
THIS WAS A TRICK!
MAYBE HE KNEW THAT THE MONEY WOULD EVENTUALLY GO TO TORU...
I'M JUST GLAD--
YOU CAN RETURN YOUR DEBT BY SELLING THIS PROPERTY.
THEN I'LL HAVE NO PLACE TO CALL HOME.

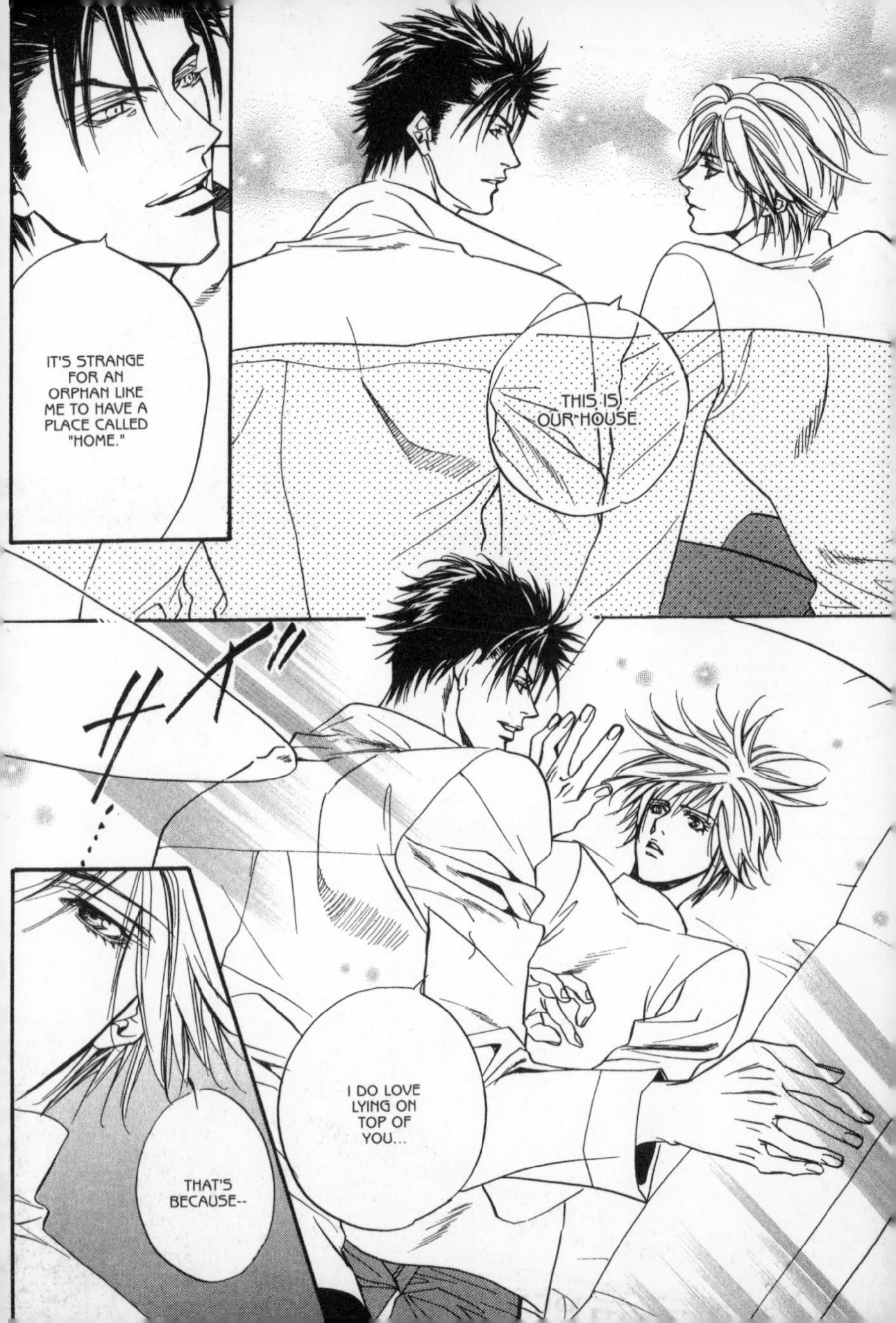
THIS IS OUR HOUSE
IT'S STRANGE FOR AN ORPHAN LIKE ME TO HAVE A PLACE CALLED "HOME."
I DO LOVE LYING ON TOP OF YOU...
...
THAT'S BECAUSE--

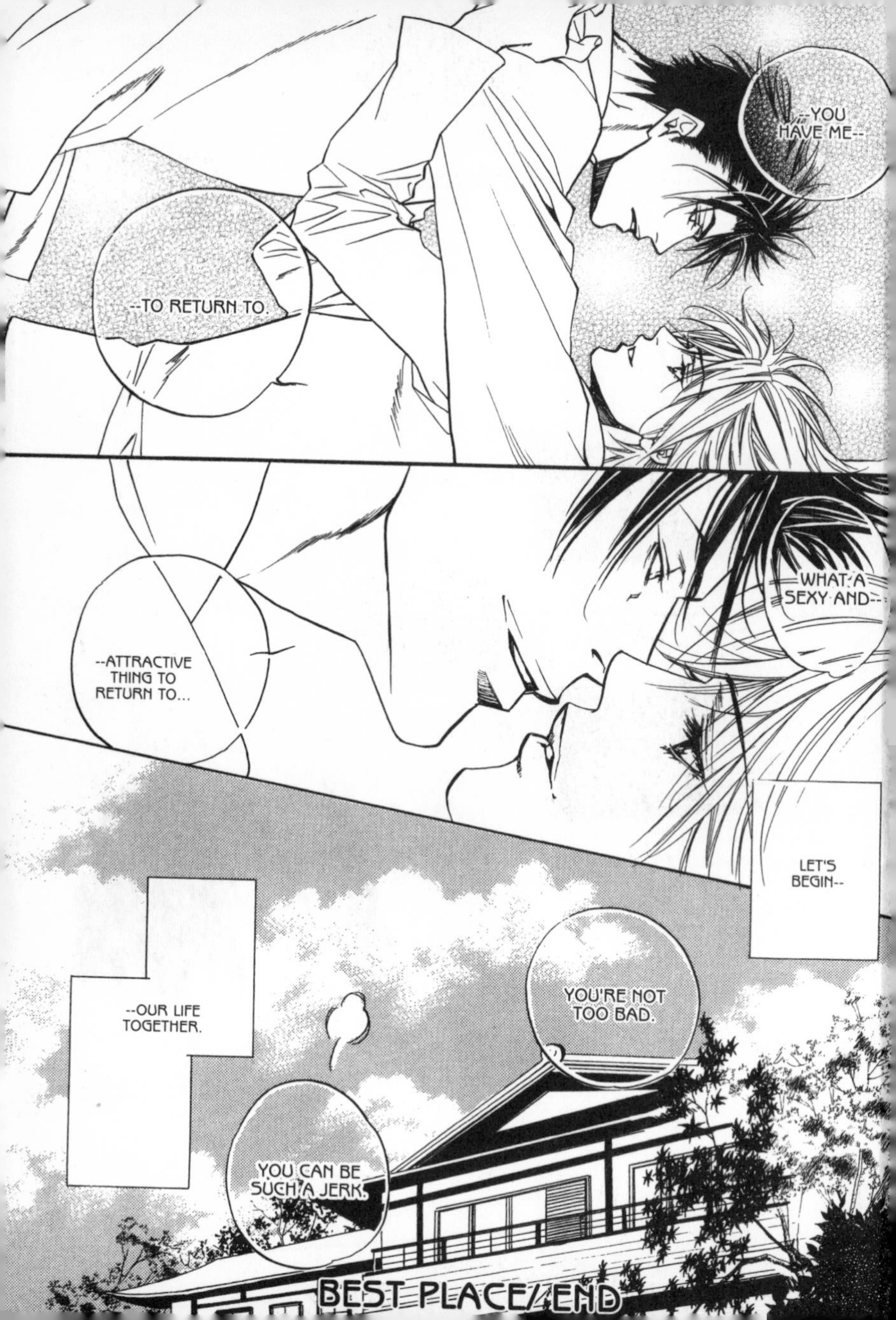
--YOU HAVE ME--
--TO RETURN TO.
WHAT A SEXY AND--
--ATTRACTIVE THING TO RETURN TO...
LET'S BEGIN--
--OUR LIFE TOGETHER.
YOU'RE NOT TOO BAD.
YOU CAN BE SUCH A JERK.
BEST PLACE/END

あとがき

STSCRIPT

OUT "BEST PLACE," THERE'S A LOT OF BACK-STORY REGARDING
, PROJECT. IT'S QUICKLY BECOME ONE OF MY FAVORITES. I
NTED TO RE-DO IT WHEN IT WAS PUBLISHED, BUT TO NO
AIL... IT'S BEEN PRESENTED HERE WITHOUT ANY REVISION OR
RRECTIONS. ACTUALLY, I DID CORRECT A SMALL SECTION.
ERE ARE MANY PLACES WITHIN THE STORY WHERE IT WAS
RAWN DIRECTLY, WITHOUT ANY ROUGH DRAFTS. AT ONE
OINT, AN EDITOR HAD ASSUMED I WAS A WARM, FUZZY,
YPE, SO I CREATED THIS STORY TO MAKE A POINT. THE
TORY WAS A BIT MATURE FOR B-BOY, BUT IT'S TOO LATE
IOW...

T WAS ALSO SUPPOSED TO END IN TWO EPISODES, BUT IT TOOK LONGER... I RECEIVED FAN MAIL FOR THIS STORY, I WAS ALSO WRITING ESSAYS WHEN THE STORY WAS PUBLISHED, SO I ALSO RECEIVED FAN MAIL THERE AS WELL. THERE WERE LOTS OF HEARTFELT LETTERS, AND THIS STORY IS FILLED WITH GOOD MEMORIES. I'M GOING TO KEEP WORKING HARD, SO PLEASE CHEER ME ON!

THANKS, AND I'LL SEE YOU AGAIN...

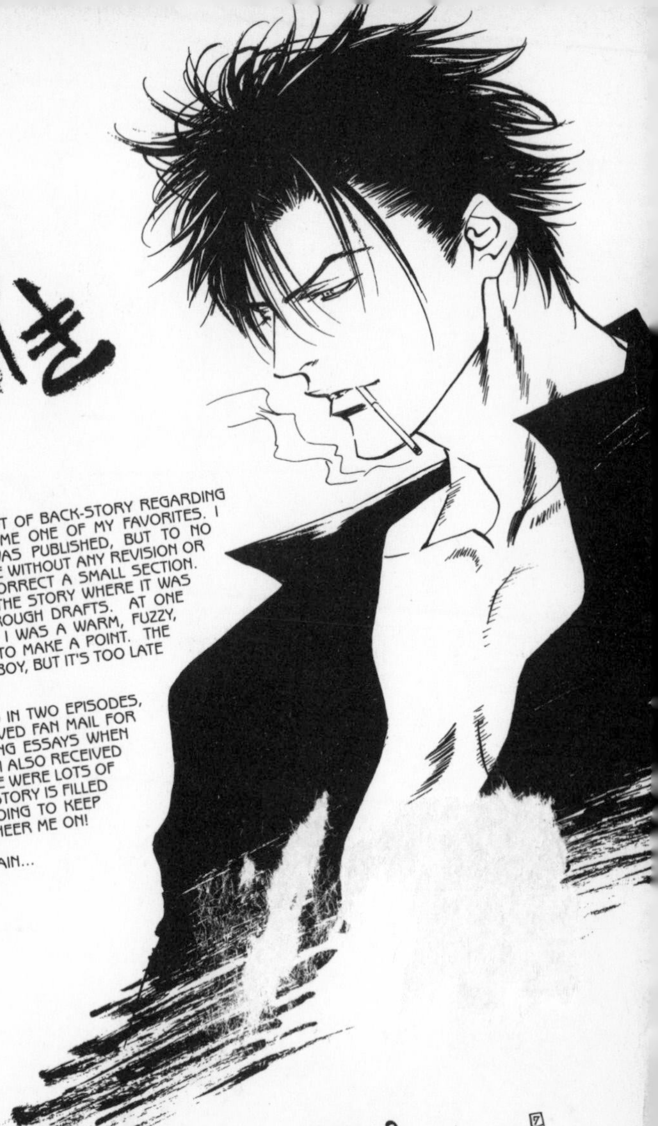

Row Takakura.